WORK IN TUMULTUOUS TIMES

Work in Tumultuous Times

Critical Perspectives

Edited by

VIVIAN SHALLA

AND

WALLACE CLEMENT

McGill-Queen's University Press
Montreal & Kingston • London • Ithaca

© McGill–Queen's University Press 2007
ISBN 978-0-7735-3140-6 (cloth)
ISBN 978-0-7735-3141-3 (paper)

Legal deposit second quarter 2007
Bibliothèque nationale du Québec

Printed in Canada on acid-free paper.

This book has been published with the help of a grant from the
Canadian Federation for the Humanities and Social Sciences,
through the Aid to Scholarly Publications Programme, using
funds provided by the Social Sciences and Humanities Research
Council of Canada.

McGill-Queen's University Press acknowledges the support of
the Canada Council for the Arts for our publishing program. We
also acknowledge the financial support of the Government of
Canada through the Book Publishing Industry Development
Program (BPIDP) for our publishing activities.

Portions of chapter 12, previously published in *Citizenship Studies*
6, no. 4 (2002): 395–414, are reprinted by permission of Taylor
& Francis, www.tandf.co.uk/journals.

Library and Archives Canada Cataloguing in Publication

Work in tumultuous times : Critical perspectives / edited by
Vivian Shalla and Wallace Clement.

Includes bibliographical references and index.

ISBN 978-0-7735-3140-6 (cloth)
ISBN 978-0-7735-3141-3 (paper)

1. Labor–Canada. 2. Job security–Canada. 3. Discrimination
in employment–Canada. I. Shalla, Vivian. II. Clement, Wallace

HD8106.5.W668 2006   331.0971   C2006-903641-1

Typeset by Jay Tee Graphics Ltd. in New Baskerville 10/12

To the memory of

Bruce McFarlane

scholar, colleague, mentor, and friend

Contents

Tables and Figures

TABLES

FIGURES

Acknowledgments

We acknowledge our contributors for the time and care they took in the preparation of their chapters, sometimes with tight deadlines looming. Every author in this volume has played a key role in deepening our understanding of the transformation of work in tumultuous times. We also wish to express our profound gratitude to Philip Cercone at McGill-Queen's University Press for his wholehearted support for this collection. We are equally appreciative of the outstanding work of the staff at McGill-Queen's University Press, who moved us along in the project (with special thanks to Joan McGilvray, Ligy Alakkattussery, Joanne Pisano, and Brenda Prince). We extend our sincerest thanks to Judith Turnbull for her patient and meticulous copyediting of the text and for her keen interest in the book. We acknowledge the financial support from the Canadian Federation for the Humanities and Social Sciences through its Aid to Scholarly Publications Programme. We are grateful for the supportive comments made by two anonymous reviewers on an earlier draft of this book. We dedicate this book to the memory of Bruce McFarlane, who did so much to advance Canadian intellectual life, especially in the field of the sociology of work and the professions.

Contributors

HUGH ARMSTRONG is a professor in the School of Social Work and in the Institute of Political Economy at Carleton University. He has published articles on privatization in health care, the reorganization of work, and state workers. With Pat Armstrong, he has written widely on women and work and on health care. Their books include *Theorizing Women's Work* (1990), *The Double Ghetto: Canadian Women and Their Segregated Work* (third edition, 1994), *Wasting Away: The Undermining of Canadian Health Care* (second edition, 2003), and *Universal Health Care: What the United States Can Learn from the Canadian Experience* (1998). They have also co-authored several articles and reports, including a paper on health human resources for the Romanow Commission on the Future of Health Care in Canada. Hugh Armstrong served on the Board of Directors of the Ottawa Community Care Access Centre from 1999 until 2002 and now serves on the Board of Directors of the Council on Aging of Ottawa.

PAT ARMSTRONG has co-written or edited numerous books on health care. Her more recent works include *Caring For/Caring About: Women, Home Care, and Unpaid Caregiving* (2004), *Exposing Privatization: Women and Health Care Reform in Canada* (2002), *Unhealthy Times* (2001), *Heal Thyself: Managing Health Care Reform* (2000), and *Wasting Away: The Undermining of Canadian Health Care* (second edition, 2003). She has also published on a wide variety of issues related to women's work and to social policy, and has qualified as an expert on women's work and pay equity in a dozen cases brought before tribunals and courts. She has served as chair of the Department of Sociology at York University and director of the School of Canadian Studies at Carleton University. Currently, she is a partner in the National Network on Environments and Women's Health and chairs a working group on health reform that crosses the Centres of Excellence for Women's Health. She holds a Canadian Health Services Research Foundation (CHSRF)/ Canadian Institutes of Health Research (CIHR) chair in health services with a focus on gender.

WALLACE CLEMENT is a chancellor's professor of sociology and political economy at Carleton University. He co-authored (with John Myles) *Relations of Ruling: Class and Gender in Postindustrial Societies* (1994) and edited *The New Canadian Political Economy* (with Glen Williams, 1989), *Understanding Canada* (1997), and *Changing Canada: Political Economy as Transformation* (with Leah Vosko, 2003).

JUNE CORMAN is chair of sociology and director of labour studies at Brock University. She is concluding a Social Sciences and Humanities Research Council of Canada (SSHRC)–funded project on rural schoolteachers in the twentieth century and has started new projects on hydro workers in St Catharines and on farm families in Saskatchewan. She is the co-author (with Meg Luxton) of *Getting By in Hard Times: Gendered Labour at Home and on the Job* (2001).

GILLIAN CREESE is a professor in the Department of Sociology at the University of British Columbia. Her most recent book is *Contracting Masculinity: Gender, Class, and Race in a White-Collar Union, 1944–1994* (1999). She is currently researching the experiences of women and men who migrated from countries in Sub-Saharan Africa to the Lower Mainland. She is working on a book manuscript entitled "African/ Canadian Border Crossings: Migration, Exclusion and Belonging."

ALICE DE WOLFF is a researcher and activist who has worked for many years with women's groups, unions, and community organizations. She has written about precarious employment, the transformation of administrative support work, training, and the tensions between paid work and social reproduction. She was the community director of the SSHRC-funded Community-University Research Alliance on Contingent Work.

ANN DUFFY is a professor of sociology at Brock University. She has also been cross-appointed to the Labour Studies Program and teaches in the Women's Studies Program and in the Master's in Social Justice and Equity Studies Program. Her publications have focused, in general terms, on the interplay between family life and work. In particular, she has examined the ways in which a particular form of non-standard employment – part-time work – functions to ease the family-work conflict while at the same time creating and sustaining traditional gender inequalities. In her forthcoming book (in collaboration with Susan Wilson and Nancy Mandell), she examines the experiences of mid-life women, particularly as they pertain to issues of employment, intimate relationships, and health concerns.

ANDY KING is the national health, safety, and environment coordinator and department leader for the United Steelworkers. He has worked extensively in the field of occupational health, both as a lawyer and as a labour representative. He is also a sessional instructor, teaching courses on occupational health and safety at McMaster University.

KATE LAXER is a doctoral candidate in sociology at York University. Her thesis research is on the restructuring of support services in health care in Canada.

BELINDA LEACH holds a university research chair in rural gender studies at the University of Guelph and teaches in the Department of Sociology and Anthropology. She is the co-author of *Contingent Work, Disrupted Lives: Labour and Community in the New Rural Economy* (2002) and co-editor of *Culture, Economy, Power: Anthropology as Critique, Anthropology as Praxis* (2002). She has published in the areas of economic restructuring; formal, informal, and domestic work; and gender.

WAYNE LEWCHUK is a professor of labour studies and economics at McMaster University. He has written on the history of technology in the automobile industry and on recent trends in work organization. His current work focuses on the relationship between work organization and health.

DAVID W. LIVINGSTONE is Canada research chair in lifelong learning and work at the University of Toronto, head of the Centre for the Study of Education and Work, Department of Sociology and Equity Studies at the Ontario Institute for Studies in Education, University of Toronto, and director of the ssHRC-funded national research network on the Changing Nature of Work and Lifelong Learning (www.wall. oise.utoronto.ca). His recent publications include *The Education-Jobs Gap: Underemployment or Economic Democracy* (second edition, 2004) and

Hidden Knowledge: Organized Labour in the Information Age (with Peter Sawchuk, 2004).

MEG LUXTON is a professor of women's studies and social science at York University, where she is the director of the Graduate Program in Women's Studies and of the Centre for Feminist Research. She writes about women's paid and unpaid work, feminist theory, and the Canadian women's movement. Her most recent publications include *Getting By in Hard Times: Gendered Labour at Home and on the Job* (with June Corman, 2001) and *Social Reproduction: Feminist Political Economy Challenges Neo-Liberalism* (co-edited with Kate Bezanson, 2006).

NORENE PUPO is an associate professor in the Department of Sociology and the director of the Centre for Research on Work and Society at York University. She has researched and published in the areas of women and work, part-time employment, women and social policy, and work and economic restructuring. She is principal investigator of a SSHRC-funded Research Alliance, Restructuring Work and Labour in the New Economy, and is editor of an electronic journal, *Just Labour.*

ANTONIE SCHOLTZ is a doctoral student in the Department of Sociology and Equity Studies at the Ontario Institute for Studies in Education, University of Toronto.

VIVIAN SHALLA is an associate professor of sociology at the University of Guelph and was previously a senior policy researcher at the Library of Parliament in Ottawa. She is the editor of *Working in a Global Era* (2006) and has published articles on the changing nature of work in civil aviation and on working time in the service economy. She is currently working on a book manuscript entitled "Losing Ground in the Information Economy: The Transformation of Work in the Canadian Airline Industry."

JANET SILTANEN is a professor of sociology at Carleton University and was previously senior lecturer in sociology at the University of Edinburgh. Her publications include *Locating Gender* (1994), *Gender Inequality in the Labour Market* (1995), and articles in *Citizenship Studies; Work, Employment and Society; Royal Statistical Society Series A (Statistics and Society); International Journal of Sociology;* and the *International Journal of Social Research Methodology.* She is currently working on a book (with Andrea Doucet) entitled "Gender Relations in Canada – Intersectionality and Beyond."

LEAH F. VOSKO, Canada research chair in feminist political economy, is an associate professor of political science in the School of Social Sciences, Atkinson Faculty, York University. She is the author of *Temporary Work: The Gendered Rise of a Precarious Employment Relationship* (2000) and co-author of *Self-Employed Workers Organize: Law, Policy and Unions* (2005). She is also co-editor of *Changing Canada: Political Economy as Transformation* (2003) and *Challenging the Market: The Struggle to Regulate Work and Income* (2004) and editor of *Precarious Employment: Understanding Labour Market Insecurity in Canada* (2006). Currently, she is writing a book on gender and the transnational labour regulation of precarious employment and is overseeing a collaborative Gender and Work Database (GWD) project (www.genderwork.ca).

ROSEMARY WARSKETT is a professor in the Department of Law, Carleton University. Her current research interests centre on class, gender, and race relations within the paid labour force. She has written several articles on the Canadian labour movement and women in unions. She was a participant in the Restructuring Work and Labour in the New Economy project funded by a SSHRC grant awarded to the Centre for Research on Work and Society.

CHARLOTTE YATES is a professor of political science and the director of the Labour Studies Program at McMaster University. Her research falls into two broad areas: workers and labour markets in industry, with a particular focus on the automotive industry; and union renewal and diversity. Recent publications include "Challenging Misconceptions about Organizing Women into Unions" in *Gender, Work and Organization* (2006), *Trade Unions in Renewal* (co-edited with Peter Fairbrother, 2003), and numerous articles and chapters on workers, unions, and their communities, and the automotive industry.

WORK IN TUMULTUOUS TIMES

Theoretical Reflections on Work: A Quarter-Century of Critical Thinking

VIVIAN SHALLA

By far the most unwholesome work is the grinding of knife blades and forks, which, especially when done with a dry stone, entails certain early death. The unwholesomeness of this work lies in part in the bent posture, in which chest and stomach are cramped; but especially in the quantity of sharp-edged metal dust particles freed in the cutting, which fill the atmosphere, and are necessarily inhaled.   – Engels 1969 [1845], 229–30

The image of toiling in early industrial capitalism so painstakingly and vividly depicted by Friedrich Engels may seem alien to many who earn a decent living in the scores of workplaces that dot the landscape of post-industrial economies and who labour to care for their families in diverse household settings. However, for many others, this century-and-a-half-old snapshot is a frighteningly faithful reflection of their own experience of eking out a livelihood and trying to care for their families in late twentieth-century and early twenty-first-century capitalism. The advent of the Industrial Revolution and the shift to capitalism as the dominant mode of social and economic organization may seem far removed from the post-industrial globalized social and economic order. The palpable and fundamental discontinuities between these two moments of capitalist development serve to conceal important elements of continuity, despite very real and significant change, in the nature of work. Karl Marx (1967) revealed the centrality of work to people's lives during the tumult of early capitalism, and he provided a radical and critical analysis of capitalist work organizations and relations. The contributors to *Work in Tumultuous Times* continue the tradition of critically examining and analysing the changing nature, conditions, and relations of work in turbulent times. The focus in this volume is on work and its transformation during the past few decades, with particular attention to the world of work in Canada and comparatively.

BRAVERMAN AND BEYOND

The foundations of Marx's critical theory had relatively little impact on the study of work until the mid-1970s, when a revival of interest in changes in the nature and organization of work in advanced capitalist societies occurred. Harry Braverman's seminal treatise, *Labor and Monopoly Capital* (1974), which incorporated a restatement of Marx's conceptual categories and an application of these to major developments in work during the first seven decades of the twentieth century, played a pivotal role in provoking empirical research and setting off theoretical debates on work, spawning what came to be known as the labour process debate (Heron and Storey 1986b; Thompson 1989).

Braverman closely adhered to the central tenet of Marx's analysis by reinstating the imperative of capital accumulation as fundamental to the continuous transformation of the labour process and the degradation of work in capitalist societies. He recognized that employers had gained greater control over the labour process during the early stages of capitalism, but argued that with the onset and consolidation of monopoly capitalism they had embraced scientific management or Taylorism as the ultimate means to deskill, control, and cheapen labour. He also maintained that during the monopoly phase of capitalism there occurred a more deliberate substitution of research and development for technological tinkering, a phenomenon that both complemented and compounded Taylorism in the subsumption of labour to capital. Braverman also focused on how capital movements and the ever-extending areas of capitalist commodity production gave rise to new labour processes. This led him to examine the shift in the occupational structure from blue-collar to white-collar employment. Braverman revealed that workers in the new clerical and service occupations and industries were also being subjected to Taylorism and automation as employers sought to wrest the maximum surplus labour from their purchased commodity, labour power. Braverman's book, which received much praise but has also been subjected to deep criticism over the years, provided important insights into the changing nature of work in contemporary societies.

Notwithstanding the key role played by Braverman's treatise in reviving the critical study of work, social science theorists and researchers in other countries had also begun to question mainstream assumptions about work under advanced capitalism. In Canada, for example, James Rinehart's *The Tyranny of Work* (1975) presented a scathing analysis of the social relations of capitalism through an in-depth exploration of the alienation engendered by contemporary workplace and labour market structures and relations. In contrast to Braverman, Marx's concept of alienation – the stultification of human beings' ability to produce their own means of existence and to actualize the full flowering of creative capacity and human potentiality through labour – was more central to Rinehart's analysis. He nonetheless arrived at conclusions similar to Braverman's about the degradation of blue-collar and white-collar work throughout twentieth-century Canadian capitalist development. Rinehart's careful and detailed investigation of workers' attempts to combat alienation at work stood in sharp contrast to Braverman's deliberate eschewal of an examination of worker resistance and class struggle, a decision that was harshly criticized by scores of participants in the labour process debate as well as by many others who studied workers and their organizations.

Following a long period when critical studies of work were the exception rather than the rule, the mid- to late 1970s and the 1980s were marked by a blossoming of theoretical and theoretically informed empirical studies that profoundly questioned the dominant relations of work and steadfastly rejected the management-oriented concerns that guided the large majority of organizational and industrial relations studies (Burawoy 1979; Clement 1981; Cockburn 1983, 1985; Littler and Salaman 1982; Mackenzie 1977; Schwarz 1977; Stark 1980; Edwards 1979; Friedman 1977; Heron and Storey 1986a; Littler 1982; Noble 1977; Thompson and Bannon 1985; Wood 1982, 1989; Zimbalist 1979). While critical research on and the theorization of work were influenced by the Marxist perspective, those who investigated and reflected on work using this perspective did not mawkishly or slavishly adopt holus-bolus its assumptions and directions. Indeed, during an incredibly fertile period of analysis, critical studies of work succeeded in pushing debates about work in advanced industrialized nations in new directions, thereby ensuring a more nuanced, textured, and dynamic understanding of this life-sustaining dimension of social reality.

The research and theoretical considerations on work that began to flourish in the mid-1970s had not evolved in a vacuum. Material conditions prompted a more critical investigation and reconceptualization of what it meant to work in advanced capitalist societies. Although mainstream social sciences, and more particularly the work of Daniel Bell (1973), had proclaimed the advent of a post-industrial society built around more leisure time, less work time, and more knowledge work, it was becoming apparent that most people's lives remained highly defined and structured by work in one form or another. What is more, the workplaces and labour markets that structured and coloured people's lives had undergone important changes, especially in the postwar period. In addition, workplace conflict had dramatically increased in most Western countries beginning in the late 1960s, a situation that put into question the generally accepted notion that workplace conflict had been contained in the postwar period and that harmonious and consensual workplace relations were predominant. Tempestuous relations in the workplace in the 1960s and 1970s fuelled, and were fuelled by, social unrest in other spheres of society.

The critical approach to understanding work reflected, but also contributed to, the radicalization of the social sciences that had begun in the early 1970s. Although some social sciences were infused with radicalism more than others, the study of work stood at the centre of the leftward shift. This transformation in academe was spurred by a resurgence of Marxism and other radical paradigms that vigorously challenged the mainstream current dominant in the social sciences in the postwar period. In Canada, the rekindling of the Marxist tradition was deeply intertwined with a growing nationalism that saw a strong revival, but also a deep radicalization, of the Canadian political economy approach (Clement and Williams 1989; Clement 1997).

One of the most significant challenges to both mainstream and Marxist explanations of the transformation of work came from the second-wave feminist movement beginning in the mid-1970s. While Marxian-influenced studies countered mainstream accounts of work in industrial societies and reaffirmed the inherently class-based nature of work under capitalism, second-wave feminism challenged the adequacy of the critical framework because of its failure both to identify and to satisfactorily account for gender divisions and relations, as well as for women's subordination in society. Feminists from different philosophical standpoints argued that what mainstream and radical non-feminist discourses were presenting as universal and absolute knowledge of the world of work was really partial and skewed knowledge created from the experiences of a limited group of male actors.

In the late 1970s and throughout the 1980s, second-wave feminism provided the impetus for a number of theoretically grounded case studies of women workers. Many of these workplace studies expanded upon themes central to labour process theory (Cavendish 1982; Faulkner and Arnold 1985; Feminist Review 1986; Game an Pringle 1983; Gannagé 1986; Phillips and Taylor 1986; Pollert 1981; Reiter 1991; Steedman 1986; West 1982; Westwood 1984). They made important contributions to our understanding of how skill is constructed ideologically and politically and how gender relations shape strategies of control in the workplace. These studies also went beyond critical analyses of work by revealing how technological change is a social process that reflects, reproduces, and transforms not only class but also gender divisions and relations. Feminist scholarship helped shift the agenda of the study of work by recognizing that paid work in advanced capitalism is more likely to involve manipulating symbols or providing services than producing and handling tangible products. During the 1970s and 1980s, feminist-informed research and theorizing also challenged labour market segmentation theories (which were flourishing during this period) by analysing the processes that gave rise to, and entrenched, a gender division of labour that assigned women to low-paying jobs with little benefits or opportunities for upward mobility (Beechey 1977; Beechey and Perkins 1987; Bruegel 1979; Connelly 1978; Hartmann 1979; Kenrick 1981; Rubery 1978; Walby 1986; West 1982). Fundamental to feminist analyses of women's work, and perhaps the contribution that most challenged the gender-blindness of mainstream and progressive literature on work, was a focus on the interconnections between women's place in paid workplaces and labour markets, or the public sphere, on the one hand, and their role in shouldering the lion's share of unpaid work in the home, or the private sphere, on the other hand (Armstrong and Armstrong 1990; Barrett 1980; Eisenstein 1979; Jenson 1986; Lewis 1983; Luxton 1980; Sargent 1981). Through what was dubbed the domestic labour debate, Canadian scholars made an important contribution to the analysis of social reproduction, which refers to the processes whereby people's basic needs are met on a daily and generational basis (Fox 1980; Molyneux 1979).

These various developments, which pushed forward and refined our understanding and analysis of the changing organization and relations of work, were important for the sake of knowledge production itself. They were also crucial to providing workers and their families, the labour and women's movements, progressive policy and community groups, and scholars with the necessary knowledge to develop strategies for political struggles at the organizational and discursive levels to ameliorate the work experiences and life conditions of the large majority of the population pushed to the outskirts of power relationships that are integral to capitalist societies.

A second drift from radical studies of work, beginning in the late 1980s, helped to blunt the sharp edge of progressive critique and stifle the move towards greater equality at work. Many disciplines in the social sciences have been swept up in the postmodern paradigm that gained momentum in academe and popular culture at the same time as socialism was in decline and Western academic Marxism was in crisis and rapidly losing ground (for critiques, see Callinicos 1989; Eagleton 1991; Skeggs 1991; Thrift 1999). Since that time, postmodern theory has had a strong influence on the study of work and organizations.

The postmodernist agenda focuses on language and texts (which are seen as constitutive of social relations) and emphasizes discourse, deconstruction, and identities rather than an analysis of political economy, the material conditions of production, material inequalities, and structural divisions in society. Harkening back to pronouncements made by early post-industrial theorists of the 1960s and 1970s, postmodernists have championed the notion that we have entered a post-work society where consumption and consumption relations are more significant than production and production relations and, consequently, that work and class have been decentred in formations of identity and in political practice. Many have argued that collective and solidaristic values based on class no longer hold sway and, hence, that class conflict belongs in the dustbins of history (for examples, see Casey 1995; du Gay 1996; O'Doherty and Willmott 2001; for critiques, see Nelson and Smith 1999; Thompson and Ackroyd 1995). Such thinking has resulted in the elision of labour as a resistive subject and in the erasure of the capital-labour power relation, notwithstanding a significant body of scholarship that shows that work and employment relationships actively reproduce the structured antagonism inherent in the capital-labour dynamic, and that workers continue to be active agents in moulding this relationship. In addition, enquiry into the diminishing power and influence of the labour movement, which occurred in the context of the myriad challenges brought about by organizational and labour market restructuring, the neo-liberal state agenda, and globalization, has revealed that this class- and work-based collective organization has been redefining its contours, visions, and strategies – albeit oftentimes with difficulties and setbacks – to build solidarity, ensure renewal, and vigorously protect and promote the well-being and security of workers and their families and communities (Gindin and Stanford 2003; Leisink 1999; Mantsios and Sweeney 1998; Wood, Meiksins, and Yates 1998; Munck 2002; Murray 2004).

Postmodernism has also had a strong influence on feminist theorizing (Butler 1990; for critiques, see Fraser 1989; Skeggs 1997). However, while an important strand of feminism has shifted its lens to culture, identity, difference, and recognition, critical feminist researchers have continued to probe how work organizations, labour markets, the state, and the family/household – as well as their interconnections – reproduce and mitigate gender inequalities. Critical feminist scholarship has also played a significant role in pushing forward analyses of the dynamic interplay and intersection among race, ethnicity, gender, and class in the creation and refashioning of divisions, relations, inequalities, and ideologies that permeate the contemporary world of work (Bannerji 2000; Creese 1999; Das Gupta 1996; Gabriel 1999; Stasiulis and Bakan 2005).

The drift from critical approaches to the study of work has also been exacerbated by the managerial perspective that has been gaining ground in the academic realm with the growth in size and power of business and management schools and programs. Graduates of these schools and programs have played a key role in deepening the alliances, networks, and influences among producers, purveyors, and users of knowledge within academe and those within organizations in both private business and government. Management thinking has strongly influenced the literature on the transformation of the workplace. A key premise is that new paradigms, such as flexible specialization, lean production, and Japanization, have ensured a more harmonious and flexible workplace, where employees from various occupational groups and in different sectors of the economy are provided with opportunities to become multi-skilled and participate in managerial tasks, thereby blurring the previous hierarchical differences between management and workers and eradicating class-based divisions. Progressive researchers have dismantled this ever-spreading Pollyannish argument by revealing that, to a large extent, Taylorist-Fordist principles and relations, with their attendant assault on human creativity, dignity, and physical and emotional well-being, have continued to define post-industrial, post-Taylorist, post-Fordist workplaces (Amin 1994; Elger and Smith 1994; Russell 1999; Smith 1994; Thompson and Warhurst 1998; Warhurst et al. 2004; Wood 1989). Myriad studies have also pointed to the modification of employment structures and relations that has enhanced managerial flexibility. The flexible deployment of labour, which has eroded the postwar standard employment relationship and reconfigured the social division of labour, has led to increased precariousness and deeper levels of insecurity for scores of labour force participants (Broad 2000; Felstead and Jewson 1999; Marchington et al. 2005; O'Reilly and Fagan 1998; Peck 1996; Preston and Giles 1997; Vosko 2000; Zeytinoğlu 1999). Research consistently denotes that certain segments of the population, including women, visible minorities, immigrants, Aboriginals, and the less skilled, have been particularly vulnerable to these employment trends.

Non-critical theoretical and ontological directions that have been gaining hegemony in academe have provided an aura of legitimacy to the neo-liberal economic policies and practices that have been introduced by nation-states over the past few decades. These policies and practices, buttressed by powerful ideological discourses, have been underwriting the restructuring of capitalism on a global scale. The strong tides of globalization and economic restructuring at the broader macro-level have been reshaping processes of production and reproduction, labour market dynamics, relations and divisions in paid workplaces and households, and the interconnections between public and private spheres at international, national, and local levels. As local governments, nation-states, and institutions of global governance introduce and strengthen social and economic policies that exacerbate polarization, precariousness, inequality, and social exclusion, people's livelihoods are increasingly under attack (Bakker 1996; Boyd 1997; Broad and Antony 1999; Burke, Mooers, and Shields 2000). The rapid transformations in paid work and employment relationships, together with women's increasing labour force participation, the erosion of state provision of various services and programs, and the non-establishment of forever-promised services such as childcare, have made it difficult for many, especially women, to balance paid work with their household and community responsibilities. Scholars have pointed out that the crisis in social reproduction that has ensued has tended to be resolved through reconstituted private household/family and public market relationships (Bakan and Stasiulus 1997; Crompton 1999; Jenson and Sineau 2001; Luxton and Corman 2001; Mutari and Figart 2001; O'Connor, Shola Orloff, and Shaver 1999). These solutions are often tenuous and give rise to new relationships that can be deeply gendered and racialized.

Thus, at a time when work appears to be in a constant state of crisis and flux and when postwar structures, relations, and institutions that putatively provided workers and their families with a degree of predictability, stability, and security are increasingly unravelling, critical perspectives on work have lost much of the space to which they had laid claim during the mid- to late 1970s and throughout the 1980s.

Despite this significant shift, critical voices on work and its transformation have not been silenced during the past two decades. Indeed, many social scientists within academe, working alongside and parallel to activists in the labour movement, the women's movement, and other progressive organizations and movements, have continued to study what has been happening in the worlds of work under neoliberal economic restructuring and political/ideological transfigurations, not only to better understand the dramatic changes, but also to help transform these worlds of work so that they might provide the foundation for better labours and more fulfilling lives.

The contributors to *Work in Tumultuous Times* are representative of social scientists and activists in Canada who, through their research, analysis, and actions, have persisted in their endeavours to challenge mainstream approaches and understandings of work in post-industrial capitalism. By putting into question deeply entrenched orthodoxies about work, the authors offer a critical perspective that attempts to uncover and expose the structures, practices, and ideas that facilitate the perpetuation of relations of domination and subordination, inequality, oppression, alienation, and exploitation.

UNIFYING THEMES OF THE COLLECTION

The essays in this collection are committed to a critical analysis informed by the progressive political economy tradition, which has become firmly rooted in the social sciences in Canada over the past several decades. Central to this approach is an understanding of the importance of social structures and social relations and their inherently contradictory, permeable, crisis-ridden, and therefore mutable nature. In applying the progressive political economy tradition to the study of work, the authors in this collection seek to develop a more complete and adequate explanation for the complexities of work and its transformation in the post-industrial era by identifying, analysing, and critiquing the power structures and social relations of work as well as the larger political economy that envelops (while giving shape to and being constructed by) these structures and relations.

The political economy approach adopted by the contributors to this book is informed by a materialist view of the social world. A materialist understanding of the social world is premised on the notion that societies must organize themselves to ensure the survival of their populations and that, in order to achieve the always potentially tenuous task of economic survival, people enter into relatively stable relationships, which form the basis of complex institutions and organizations. A materialist approach thus assumes that human beings, through collective actions or human labour, are capable of altering the conditions under which they live and can actively produce and reproduce their life, all the while producing and reproducing social relations that organize practical activity. In discussing various dimensions of the transformation of work, the authors in this collection are preoccupied with revealing and dissecting the particular material structures and relations that have come to underlie, govern, and transform the lives of individuals in post-industrial societies. Many of the contributors infuse this realist ontology with a critical eye to probing the centrality of gendered and racialized structures and relations to provide a more complete portrayal and fuller understanding of the nature of, and divisions in, work under contemporary capitalism.

A telling sign of the state of work during the transition to the new millennium is the focus in all the contributions to this volume on the uncertainty, insecurity, and instability faced by workers and their families in paid workplaces, households, and labour markets. As the authors demonstrate, these difficult circumstances take on different shapes according to workers' gender, race, and age, and as a result of varying workplace and labour market experiences and varying locations in the public and private spheres. These experiences are very real and are embedded in social relations of production and reproduction that intersect with other power relations in society. What is brought to light by the measurably real insecurity, as well as by the more difficult to grasp feelings of personal jeopardy, is the problematic way contemporary post-industrial capitalist societies are organized to produce and reproduce the conditions of life. Through an examination of how the structures and relations of the public and private realms result in individuals and families facing increasing challenges in eking out livelihoods, the contributors also underscore how unequal power relation- ships stultify individuals' ability to fulfil their human potential.

In analysing contemporary structures and experiences of work, as well as the power relations intrinsic to the organization of a capitalist post-industrial society, the contributors note that workers in both paid and unpaid spheres are actively engaged in changing their worlds. The authors view work and its transformation in terms of structural processes that develop through the interplay of deep-seated internally contradictory forces. The different sites of work explored in this book are understood to be located within broader structures that are also inherently contradictory. While the weight of what often appear as immutable structures is evident throughout this book, the contributors focus on the conflictual nature of the social relations of production and reproduction and the fundamental process of change generated by human beings acting collectively to resist domination and create better worlds of work. Hence, the authors view the materially located means of power, oppression, alienation, exploitation, and inequality not only as being reproduced through the relations of production and reproduction of the post-industrial globalized social and economic order, but also as contestable and contested by workers in the private and public spheres. Because of their commitment to progressive change, the contributors propose alternatives to the contemporary worlds of work that have constrained potentiality and restricted emancipation.

OVERVIEW OF THE COLLECTION

In chapter 2, "Methodological Considerations: Thinking about Researching Work," Wallace Clement gives shape to the entire collection by underscoring the fundamental importance of methodology as the engine that drives scholarly research and enquiry. His central argument is that methodology (which should be understood to include both "big-M Methods" that focus on the logic of enquiry and "small-m methods" that refer to research techniques) serves to mediate between theories, which attempt to make sense of the world, and the specificity of accounts, which identify the relationships between actors and subjects located in time and space. Methodology thus strengthens scholars' ability to move between levels of abstraction. Clement examines several examples of research carried out by other scholars to illustrate the various ways in which methodology is used to frame issues pertaining to the transformation of work. He discusses, for example, how research questions that offer accounts of social practices and those that offer explanations have been useful to further our understanding of the increasing prevalence of precarious employment. He also recounts how John Porter (1987) reassessed his theoretical assumptions about the post-industrial world and the knowledge economy on the basis of Braverman's (1974) methodological critique of occupational classification schemes. In another example, Clement provides an overview of the essays in the collection *Good Jobs, Bad Jobs, No Jobs*, edited by Ann Duffy, Daniel Glenday, and Norene Pupo (1997), in order to reinforce the relevance of research questions in determining which issues are made problematic in studying work. Two examples of comparative analysis, one on union density and the other on welfare states, help bring to light the importance both of probing data to uncover the decisions and judgments that lie behind the evidence that researchers invoke to develop accounts of the world of work, and of recognizing that data never produce full answers or explanations but rather suggest further research questions. Clement concludes his exposition of the centrality of methodology in framing research with an examination of his own research projects. In a first example, he discusses the methodology of relational analysis, which he is currently developing as the basis for a comparative study in order to more fully understand and explain the social, cultural, political, and economic relationships associated with the transformation of post-industrial societies. This innovative methodology involves locating the relationships of class, gender, and generations within the triangulation of connections among households, labour markets, and welfare states, and analysing how they are transformed by post-industrialism, not singularly but in combination. In a second example of the importance of solid methodological direction, Clement focuses on case study research he has conducted, notably on the fisheries. He argues that the detail of case studies allows him to move beyond appearances and puzzles to reveal underlying power relationships in this sector. He demonstrates how methodology serves the dual purpose of translating theory into the concrete and mediating back from the empirical to modify the theory, fostering the development of explanations that are the essence of scholarly insights.

The changing structure and dynamics of the labour market have become an important concern over the past decade, and Leah F. Vosko, in chapter 3, "Gendered Labour Market Insecurities: Manifestations of Precarious Employment in Different Locations," provides a comparative analysis of the overlapping yet distinct nature of gendered precarious employment in Australia, Canada, and the United States. Through a detailed portrayal of the expressions of precarious employment in these three liberal industrialized countries, Vosko challenges the widely held assumption that the deleterious transformations in labour markets and employment patterns are characterized predominantly by deviations from the postwar standard employment relationship. Vosko argues that, by focusing on the dichotomization of standard and non-standard work, our analysis fails both to uncover and to account for the trend towards deterioration in the quality and character of full-time permanent employment that is taking shape in some countries. Mindful that labour markets and employment relationships are constructed through the deeply entrenched yet always permeable practices and institutions that constitute social formations, Vosko demonstrates how the gender-contract configurations of particular social formations underlie distinct manifestations of employment precariousness and shape labour market insecurities. She also weaves through her analysis an exploration of the social, political, and legal structures, institutions, and practices that lie behind differing manifestations of, and expansions in, precariousness. Not content with limiting her study to a description and understanding of varied and divergent manifestations of precarious employment, Vosko develops a typology of models from which to carve out possible approaches to limiting precariousness. She carefully maps the location occupied by Australia, Canada, and the United States on two intersecting continua – one of different mechanisms of labour and social protection, and the other of different configurations of the gender contract – and concludes with reflections on how a life-course approach to labour and social protection founded on a shared-work/valued-care gender-contract or universal caregiver model offers a pathway, in liberal industrialized countries, towards the curtailment of precarious employment and the mitigation of gendered labour market insecurities.

In chapter 4, "Employment Strain, Precarious Employment, and Temporary Employment Agencies," Wayne Lewchuk, Alice de Wolff, and Andy King continue the exploration of the transformation of labour markets, but their contribution focuses more explicitly on the adverse consequences of the growing incidence of temporary employment relationships for the health of Canadian workers. Their findings signal the importance of going beyond the labour process – the usual terrain of studies on occupational health and safety – to examine how labour market structures and dynamics wreak havoc with workers' ability to maintain their health, especially in light of a trend towards more flexible and precarious employment relationships. The authors develop an innovative analytical framework centred around the concept of employment strain, which refers to the cumulative effect of workers' uncertainty over access to work and lack of control over its terms and conditions, the effort exerted by workers to maintain employment, and the nature and extent of workers' workplace, social, and household support. Lewchuk, de Wolff, and King provide an authoritative portrayal of how precariousness is etched onto non-standard employment relationships, particularly temporary employment relationships, and they identify the characteristics of employment relationships that contribute to particular health outcomes. They conclude that employment through temporary agencies is especially precarious and exposes workers to the greatest employment strain. The authors provide evidence that women and ethnic minorities are at higher risk of experiencing adverse health effects in the labour market because they are more likely to be compelled to engage in different types of temporary employment. Lewchuk, de Wolff, and King's timely study serves as a canary-in-the-mines warning because it raises serious concerns about the restructuring of labour markets and the re-regulation of employment standards. The authors conclude their analysis on an optimistic note, offering strong evidence that temporary workers have been engaging increasingly in collective action to effect positive changes in their work and life conditions despite considerable barriers. They also raise hopes for better futures for temporary workers and highlight the persistence of societal solidaristic values when they point out that the labour movement and community groups are actively planning strategies on how to organize these groups of workers.

The contribution by David W. Livingstone and Antonie Scholtz, "Contradictions of Labour Processes and Workers' Use of Skills in Advanced Capitalist Economies," chapter 5, puts into question one of the fundamental premises of post-industrial theories, that advanced capitalist countries have moved towards a knowledge-based economy founded on rapidly developing and sophisticated workplace technologies that require more educated, highly skilled, and self-motivated workers who are committed to work-related lifelong learning. Such arguments, according to the authors, are particularly dangerous because they dominate current public discourse as well as government policy options, which rely heavily on educational and training solutions to rectify the putative skills shortage that is seen to be impeding Canada's successful transition to a knowledge-based economy. Livingstone and Scholtz dismantle the upgrading canard of post-industrial theories through an analysis of the skills requirements of jobs in Canada and of Canadian workers' skills and ongoing commitment to learning. They build their analysis around the concept of underemployment – which refers to the underutilization of the knowledge and skills that workers bring to the market – and argue that underemployment is more prevalent than underqualification, especially for those in working-class positions. This finding should come as no surprise, the authors conclude, given that for the last forty years the working population has embarked upon a path of continual learning, one that has gone beyond formal schooling and adult or further education to encompass informal training and non-taught informal learning. Livingstone and Scholtz's explanatory model relies on a relational class analysis that points to the contradiction inherent to capitalism – that is, that owners must hire workers with sufficient knowledge, capabilities, and autonomy to ensure the production of goods and services, yet, in order to reduce production costs and realize profits, they must constantly exploit these skills, downgrade the skills requirements of jobs, and fend off workers' demands for higher wages and benefits. For Livingstone and Scholtz, this contradiction, which has been shrouded in powerful class-based practices and discourses, is exacerbating the underemployment of many workers, while the learning achievements of workers and of disadvantaged groups more particularly are making the contradiction more apparent. After laying bare the power relations that sustain hegemonic understandings about the nature of contemporary labour processes, skills, and training, the authors propose progressive economic reforms to address the education-jobs gap, focusing on economic democracy as an empowering tool for workers.

In chapter 6, "Industrial Work in a Post-Industrial Age," Charlotte Yates and Belinda Leach question the assumption that manufacturing has lost the pivotal role it played in the postwar Canadian economy. They make a sustained case for the continuing importance of manufacturing in the post-industrial economy and hence for the need to revitalize the study of this key sector. They argue that manufacturing matters, not only because it still represents a major source of employment, but just as significantly because it remains fundamental to an understanding of current and future trends in work and in the lives and communities of working people. At the heart of their chapter is an exploration of the transformations that manufacturing work has undergone over the course of the past few decades. Yates and Leach probe the myriad factors that define and redefine Canada's manufacturing sector, paying particular attention to ownership trends, the changing size and location of enterprises, employment contracts, pay scales, benefits and working conditions, and union representation. They conclude that Canadian manufacturing is increasingly made up of low-wage, labour-intensive firms, a situation that does not bode well for many workers and their families or for communities and the broader Canadian economy. In extending their analysis of the changing nature and structure of manufacturing to examine the composition of the workforce, Yates and Leach observe that white men, who once were overwhelmingly dominant in what was considered the jewel of the postwar economy, have either abandoned or been pushed out of this type of employment to be replaced by an increasingly educated workforce made up of a growing number of women and racialized minorities, including immigrants. The authors conclude with deep consternation that this radical transformation of the manufacturing sector, which has resulted in a downward spiralling of the postwar gold standard of wages, working conditions, benefits, and collective bargaining innovation, has had a ripple effect throughout the labour market and the economy. Yates and Leach's analysis exposes weaknesses in the discourses on the knowledge economy, revealing instead that Canadian employers and governments have chosen a low-wage path to competitiveness in which workers fail to reap the rewards of working harder and obtaining a higher education. The authors are also highly critical of a model of development that relies on the exploitation of women and racialized groups to ensure growth and competitiveness. For Yates and Leach, the very strong support for unionization found among these groups of workers provides a glimmer of hope for improvements in wages and working conditions.

Gillian Creese's contribution, "Racializing Work/Reproducing White Privilege," chapter 7, is a trenchant reminder that race and gender have long been central dimensions of the Canadian labour market. Drawing on feminist post-colonial theories, she argues that, despite the eradication of legal barriers that once prevented women and some racialized groups from entering certain jobs and educational programs, and notwithstanding the transformation of ideologies about gender and race, racialization remains central to the organization of a gendered labour market. Creese couches her analysis of contemporary labour market trends and patterns of racialization in Canada's history of nation-building, which was premised on an "imagined" white/European nation. Using a broad range of evidence, she demonstrates that these problematic racialized divisions and inequities in the labour market have worsened during the past two decades in the context of an economic restructuring that has deepened polarization in the labour market. This chasm has been marked by increased precariousness and marginalization for workers, many of whom are women, Aboriginals, members of a visible minority, or immigrants of colour. Creese is emphatic that racialization in the labour market cannot be reduced to individual prejudices and attitudes of employers and workers; rather this complex and uneven process is embedded in broader social structures and power relations in which white (male) privilege shapes the terms in which "others" are incorporated into the social fabric. For the author, then, work remains a central site for the production and reproduction of racial inequality and white privilege in Canada. Creese argues that patterns of labour market racialization are unlikely to be altered easily. She supports her claim by pointing to the relative weakness of employment equity legislation, the lack of popular support for stronger equity-based policies, and employers' focus on the corporate bottom line and their interest in retaining access to a relatively cheap, yet highly skilled, workforce. Notwithstanding this discouraging reality, she expresses a steadfast belief that a redefinition of the "imagined" community is essential to challenging racialized patterns of inequality at work and in other facets of social life.

In chapter 8, "Shifting Temporalities: Economic Restructuring and the Politics of Working Time," Vivian Shalla focuses on the changing working-time realities faced by service workers in the post-industrial era, paying particular attention to the temporal flexibility strategies adopted by employers under global economic restructuring and exploring the potentialities for worker resistance to worsening temporal conditions. The author's analysis is couched in a political-economy-of-work approach that understands material experiences and human agency within broader economic and political structures and ideological discourses. Shalla provides an in-depth examination of the transformation of the working time of two groups of front-line service workers at Air Canada, customer sales and service agents and flight attendants. Using tools of comparative analysis, she adeptly illustrates how distinct historical moments in the ongoing political-economic restructuring of the Canadian airline industry have similar, yet different, impacts on the temporal employment conditions of separate groups of front-line workers within the same organization. In the first case study, Shalla examines Air Canada's attempt, in the mid-1980s, to increase its utilization of part-time customer sales and service agents in the wake of liberalization and deregulation in civil aviation. She unveils how this temporal strategy deepened labour casualization and entrenched a two-tier working-time employment norm despite significant gains registered for part-time workers following a strike against Air Canada. In the second case study, Shalla investigates the lengthening of flight attendants' working time in the mid-2000s, following Air Canada's brush with bankruptcy during an era of neo-liberal hegemony that coloured government air transportation policy as well as air carriers' policies and practices. She demonstrates how this temporal strategy maximized flight attendants' working time, leaving them with reduced social times outside paid work. Shalla convincingly argues that the working-time and income insufficiency experienced by customer sales and service agents and the working-time overload experienced by flight attendants are important dimensions of the broader post-industrial working-time regime that is generating a crisis in care. These transformations thus have profound implications for social reproduction. Shalla concludes by proposing ways to address the problematic nature for workers and their families of the flexibility-oriented, capitalist-driven, post-industrial temporal order. She argues for the need for progressive social policies that would provide workers with greater time sovereignty and would challenge the dominance of commodified time, gendered patterns of paid working time, the gendered boundary between family and paid work, and the devalorization of life nurturing and caring activities. Shalla offers more than a glimmer of hope by noting that the foundational seeds are now being sown to shift temporalities to create better times for workers and their families.

In chapter 9, "Social Reproduction and the Changing Dynamics of Unpaid Household and Caregiving Work," June Corman and Meg Luxton shift the focus away from the world of paid work to the world of unpaid work. Their exploration of the politics of domestic labour is a vivid reminder that one of the premises of feminist political economy is that daily and intergenerational reproduction, much of which is carried out by women in an unpaid capacity and mostly in the confines of the private sphere of the home, is part of the material base of society and is central to the operation of capitalist economies. Corman and Luxton argue that the neo-liberal current that has guided corporations and governments on a global scale over the past several decades has created a major crisis in social reproduction that has the potential to undermine the fabric of society. Central to their analysis is the claim that, in the current context, people's efforts to provide caregiving confront a contradiction. As the standards of living for most working people are being eroded and levels of insecurity increase dramatically because of the market- and profit-driven direction of economic restructuring, but also because of reductions in social services and benefits, many must spend more time on income-generating work, thereby leaving individuals and their families with a serious time deficit and fewer resources to ensure caregiving. Yet, as Corman and Luxton remind us, caregiving is basic to human life and must be provided. Through the presentation of two case studies, the authors bring to life the caregiving crisis for Canadian families. They construct a solid basis for analysing household and caring work by creatively weaving together three main themes: the changing political economy of income-generating work; prevailing gender and familial divisions of labour, ideologies, and power relations; and family demographics, the stage in the life course, and intergenerational relations. Corman and Luxton conclude with a call for the greater use of critical and progressive analyses to help usher in alternative forms of social organization that would respect and value unpaid household and caregiving work and would create conditions more likely to foster people's willingness and ability to help each other and provide more care.

Norene Pupo and Ann Duffy, in chapter 10, "Blurring the Distinction between Public and Private Spheres: The Commodification of Household Work – Gender, Class, Community, and Global Dimensions," illuminate the very real and difficult consequences, more particularly for working-class women, of the transformations in the nature and organization of domestic work. By focusing on the complex interconnections among Canadian households, the marketplace, and the community, Pupo and Duffy expose the extent to which the boundary between the public and private spheres is becoming ever more permeable and elastic. Their main argument is that, in the changing context of community that is manifested through disconnections from the extended family and the neighbourhood, and as a result of governments' adoption of neo-liberal social policies, which have shifted caring responsibilities back into the home, individual households are viewed as pillars with weakened local links and increasingly strong connections to the realm of the market and the corporate world. Using the concepts of commodification and decommodification to frame their analysis, the authors highlight how the commercialization of various aspects of family life, especially areas involving children, has had a contradictory effect on households. Access to a marketplace for household services has somewhat eased the burden of domestic responsibility and labour, especially for women, yet it has contributed to financial, social, and competitive pressures within the household that have been exacerbated by cutbacks to social programs and benefits. In their detailed and insightful examination, Pupo and Duffy view the transfer of household work across the public-private boundary as a highly complicated and multi-levelled process, and their analysis reveals the blatant but also more subtle ways in which commodification and decommodification deepen class differences among women, with the result that there is less free time and increasing stress and time pressures for working-class women. Pupo and Duffy's study underlines how the commodification of household labour in Canada is dependent on goods and services produced in Third World countries by low-wage, insecure workers, or by poor and often vulnerable foreign workers hired to serve as replacements for family-provided care. The authors conclude that the commodification of household labour in Canada can only be fully understood as firmly located in gender, class, and international inequalities. The authors reflect on how decommodification needs to be further explored as a possible basis for non-monetarized non-exchange-based social relations.

In chapter 11, "Doubtful Data: Why Paradigms Matter in Counting the Health-Care Labour Force," Pat Armstrong, Hugh Armstrong, and Kate Laxer are also concerned with issues pertaining to caring work. They argue that the medical model that dominates health care is problematic because it sets considerable boundaries for the collection of data pertaining to health-care work. In examining different sources and types of evidence that demonstrate how particular occupational categories determine who are counted as health-care workers, the authors question the prevailing approach that defines the health-care labour force as those who diagnose, treat, and cure as well as those who directly assist the medical core. Armstrong, Armstrong, and Laxer make a convincing case for using the social determinants of health approach to counting health-care providers. They map how this approach, which focuses on a range of factors within the economic, social, and physical environments that influence people's health, allows us to expand considerably the number of people who get counted as health-care providers. By identifying the limitations of, and dislodging, the medical model of data gathering, the alternative proposed by Armstrong, Armstrong, and Laxer ensures the inclusion of the tremendous amount of work, sometimes paid but most often unpaid, carried out by family members, friends, and community volunteers, the large majority of whom are women. For the authors, the inclusion of these unregulated health-care providers in the data serves to redress the conceptual and methodological omissions that have resulted in women's traditional health-care work being hidden and devalued. This chapter clearly demonstrates that paradigms matter tremendously because they have a strong bearing on policy decisions about the direction of health-care provision and hence about the structure and definition of health-care work. The authors warn that the current reforms in health care, which centre on cost reduction through the contracting out of care work and the shifting of health services into private households and communities, threaten our ability to track and account for the considerable contributions of health-care providers. Moreover, new methods of categorization used by data-collection agencies such as Statistics Canada increase the risk that health-care providers will not be included in statistics on care. Armstrong, Armstrong, and Laxer conclude that excising and concealing health-care providers reinforces the devaluation of women's work, undermines the working conditions of paid health-care workers, and conscripts many into unremunerated care.

In "Social Citizenship and the Transformation of Paid Work: Reflections on Possibilities for Progressive Change," chapter 12, Janet Siltanen challenges the widely held assumption that social policy developments in Canada during the postwar period can be equated with the realization of the social rights of citizenship. Through a thoughtful critique of the conceptualization and positioning of the social rights of citizenship in discussions about the rise and decline of equality-focused social policy, she argues that an in-depth rethinking about how we view changes that have occurred in the past is essential to how we envision, and therefore fight for, possibilities for progressive policy development in the future. Such an exercise, according to Siltanen, is fundamental to our avoiding the risk of allowing the neo-liberal meta-narrative to colonize conceptualizations of the present. At the heart of the chapter is a call for a carefully crafted formulation of social citizenship that contests neo-liberals' central claim that the social and the market are separate spheres of activity, with the constitution of the former being dependent on the level of development of the latter. The author maintains that expanding the claim for the significance and presence of the social by reconceptualizing the market itself as deeply embedded in the social arena would broaden the scope for envisioning equality. Siltanen illustrates her argument by probing two dimensions of the current transformation of work: the chronic problem of the working poor, which has been exacerbated by shifts in both the structure of employment and the quality of employment contracts; and the ways in which individuals negotiate changes in work profiles, an issue that has emerged with particular intensity in the new economy. The author provides insights into how, in both of these types of circumstances, the actions of the market involve social conditions and relations that bring many aspects of an individual's life, and many sets of social relationships, into play. For Siltanen, then, questioning the separation and priority of the market opens up possibilities for mobilizing social citizenship claims to challenge the injustice of inequalities resulting from transformations in paid work.

In the final chapter, "Remaking the Canadian Labour Movement: Transformed Work and Transformed Labour Strategies," Rosemary Warskett reflects on the impact of the transformation of work and employment on the nature and structure of the Canadian labour movement and on labour's response to the profound changes engendered by neo-liberal restructuring. In order to better contextualize the current state of organized labour, Warskett traces the pattern of steady decline in union density and membership, linking these losses to the erosion of the Keynesian postwar standard employment relationship and the rise in contingent and precarious forms of work in both the private and public sectors, as well as to the growth in the private service sector at the expense of the private industrial sector and the public service sector. The author casts a critical eye on the legalistic industrial relations model that took hold in the postwar period, arguing that the relatively successful unionization strategies in the private industrial sector and the public service sector have not been an ideal blueprint for union forays into the private service sector. In her analysis, Warskett focuses on the imbalance of power between employees and employers to help explain why workers in the growing private service sector have not been able to gain union certification and negotiate substantial improvements in their terms and conditions of employment. She also explores the ways in which the labour movement's organizing and servicing models have tended to be narrow and patriarchal, resulting in unions' inability and unwillingness to organize smaller workplaces, where women and racialized groups are more likely found, and producing a passive membership not inclined to question the bureaucratic and hierarchical structure of unions. She describes several innovative attempts to organize workers that have challenged some of the restrictive structures of unions and subverted the constraining discourses that have sustained these structures. In proposing an alternative model, Warskett teases out the important lessons from these more creative attempts at unionization and links them to recent concerted efforts to revitalize and renew the labour movement. For Warskett, rebuilding the labour movement in the current political and economic context, where workplaces and labour markets have morphed quite substantially, and in the face of a workforce that is no longer built on the industrial breadwinner/dependent housewife model, requires a genuine commitment to creating a culture of inclusion, social justice, and democracy, to putting in place structures that facilitate the development of collective worker capacity, and to connecting the workplace to broader social and political issues in the community.

Taken together, the chapters in this collection provide a powerful critique of the hegemonizing force of capitalism that enables it to harness labour power in its never-ending quest for profitable accumulation. The contributors quite adeptly expose the different ways in which this force has influenced the experience of work in both private and public spheres. They also develop strong analyses of how structures and relations of class, gender, and race intersect, overlap, and come into contradiction to mould workplaces, labour markets, and households. Just as importantly, the authors emphasize that workers and their organizations have systematically fought to ensure better worlds of work. In developing their analyses of work under the current stage of capitalism, they remind us that the broader structures of work and employment, as well as the ideologies that bolster these structures, can be located historically and are the result of human action and interaction. For the authors, then, the structures, relations, and ideologies that define paid and unpaid work under contemporary capitalism are outcomes of human agency and are thus changeable, notwithstanding their appearance of solidity and immutability.

REFERENCES

Amin, Ash. 1994. *Post-Fordism: A reader.* Oxford: Blackwell
Armstrong, Pat, and Hugh Armstrong. 1990. *Theorizing women's work.* Toronto: Garamond Press
Bakan, Abigail B., and Daiva Stasiulis, eds. 1997. *Not one of the family: Foreign domestic workers in Canada.* Toronto: University of Toronto Press
Bakker, Isabella, ed. 1996. *Rethinking restructuring: Gender and change in Canada.* Toronto: University of Toronto Press
Bannerji, Himani. 2000. *The dark side of the nation: Essays on multiculturalism, nationalism and gender.* Toronto: Canadian Scholars' Press
Barrett, Michèle. 1980. *Women's oppression today: Problems in Marxist feminist analysis.* London: Verso Editions
Beechey, Veronica. 1977. Some notes on female wage labour in capitalist production. *Capital and Class,* no. 3: 45–66
Beechey, Veronica, and Tessa Perkins. 1987. *A matter of hours: Women, part-time work and the labour market.* Cambridge: Polity Press
Bell, Daniel. 1973. *The coming of post-industrial society.* New York: Basic Books
Boyd, Susan B., ed. 1997. *Challenging the public/private divide: Feminism, law and public policy.* Toronto: University of Toronto Press

Braverman, Harry. 1974. *Labor and monopoly capital: The degradation of work in the twentieth century*. New York: Monthly Review Press

Broad, Dave. 2000. *Hollow work, hollow society? Globalization and the casual labour problem in Canada*. Halifax: Fernwood Publishing

Broad, David, and Wayne Antony, eds. 1999. *Citizens or consumers? Social policy and market society*. Halifax: Fernwood Publishing

Bruegel, Irene. 1979. Women as a reserve army of labour: A note on recent British experience. *Feminist Review*, no. 3:12–23

Burawoy, Michael. 1979. *Manufacturing consent: Changes in the labor process under monopoly capitalism*. Chicago: University of Chicago Press

Burke, Mike, Colin Mooers, and John Shields, eds. 2000. *Restructuring and resistance: Canadian public policy in an age of global capitalism*. Halifax: Fernwood Publishing

Butler, Judith. 1990. *Gender trouble: Gender and the subversion of identity*. London: Routledge

Callinicos, Alex. 1989. *Against postmodernism: A Marxist critique*. Cambridge: Polity Press

Casey, Catherine. 1995. *Work, self and society: After industrialism*. London: Routledge

Cavendish, Ruth. 1982. *Women on the line*. London: Routledge and Kegan Paul

Clement, Wallace. 1981. *Hardrock mining: Industrial relations and technological changes at INCO*. Toronto: McClelland and Stewart

– ed. 1997. *Understanding Canada: Building on the new political economy*. Montreal and Kingston: McGill-Queen's University Press

Clement, Wallace, and Glen Williams, eds. 1989. *The new Canadian political economy*. Montreal and Kingston: McGill-Queen's University Press

Cockburn, Cynthia. 1983. *Brothers: Male dominance and technological change*. London: Pluto Press

– 1985. *Machinery of dominance: Women, men and technical know-how*. London: Pluto Press

Connelly, Patricia. 1979. *Last hired, first fired: Women and the Canadian work force*. Toronto: Women's Press

Creese, Gillian. 1999. *Contracting masculinity: Gender, class, and race in a white-collar union, 1944–1994*. Toronto: Oxford University Press

Crompton, Rosemary. 1999. *Restructuring gender relations and employment: The decline of the male breadwinner*. Oxford: Oxford University Press

Das Gupta, Tania. 1996. *Racism and paid work*. Toronto: Garamond Press

Duffy, Ann, Daniel Glenday, and Norene Pupo, eds. 1997. *Good jobs, bad jobs, no jobs: The transformation of work in the 21st century*. Toronto: Harcourt Brace

du Gay, Paul. 1996. *Consumption and identity at work*. London: Sage

Eagleton, Terry. 1991. *Ideology: An introduction*. London: Verso

Edwards, Richard. 1979. *Contested terrain: The transformation of the workplace in the twentieth century*. New York: Basic Books

Eisenstein, Zillah R., ed. 1979. *Capitalist patriarchy and the case for socialist feminism.* New York: Monthly Review Press

Elger, Tony, and Chris Smith, eds. 1994. *Global Japanization? The transnational transformation of the labour process.* London: Routledge

Engels, Friedrich. 1969 [1845, original German edition]. *The condition of the working class in England.* Toronto: Granada Publishing

Faulkner, Wendy, and Erik Arnold, eds. 1985. *Smothered by invention: Technology in women's lives.* London: Pluto Press

Felstead, Alan, and Nick Jewson, eds. 1999. *Global trends in flexible labour.* London: Macmillan

Feminist Review. 1986. *Waged work: A reader.* London: Virago Press

Fox, Bonnie, ed. 1980. *Hidden in the household: Women's domestic labour under capitalism.* Toronto: Women's Press

Fraser, Nancy. 1989. *Unruly practices: Power, discourse and gender in contemporary social theory.* Cambridge: Polity Press

Friedman, Andrew. 1977. *Industry and labour: Class struggle at work and monopoly capitalism.* London: Macmillan

Gabriel, Christina. 1999. Restructuring at the margins: Women of colour and the changing economy. In *Scratching the surface: Canadian anti-racist feminist thought,* edited by Enakshi Dua and Angela Robertson, 127–64. Toronto: Women's Press

Game, Ann, and Rosemary Pringle. 1983. *Gender at work.* Sydney: George Allen and Unwin

Gannagé, Charlene. 1986. *Double day, double bind: Women garment workers.* Toronto: Women's Press

Gindin, Sam, and Jim Stanford. 2003. Canadian labour and the political economy of transformation. In *Changing Canada: Political economy as transformation,* edited by Wallace Clement and Leah F. Vosko, 422–42. Montreal and Kingston: McGill-Queen's University Press

Hartmann, Heidi. 1979. Capitalism, patriarchy, and job segregation by sex. In Eisenstein 1979, 206–47

Heron, Craig, and Robert Storey, eds. 1986a. *On the job: Confronting the labour process in Canada.* Montreal and Kingston: McGill-Queen's University Press

Heron, Craig, and Robert Storey. 1986b. On the job in Canada. In Heron and Storey 1986a, 3–46

Jenson, Jane. 1986. Gender and reproduction, or babies and the state. *Studies in Political Economy,* no. 20: 9–46

Jenson, Jane, and Mariette Sineau. 2001. *Who cares? Women's work, childcare, and welfare state redesign.* Toronto: University of Toronto Press

Kenrick, Jane. 1981. Politics and the construction of women as second-class workers. In *The dynamics of labour market segmentation,* edited by Frank Wilkinson, 167–91. London: Academic Press

Leisink, Peter, ed. 1999. *Globalization and labour relations.* Northampton, Mass.: Edward Elgar

Lewis, Jane, ed. 1983. *Women's welfare, women's rights.* London: Croom Helm

Littler, Craig R. 1982. *The development of the labour process in capitalist societies.* London: Heinemann Educational Books

Littler, Craig R., and Graeme Salaman. 1982. Bravermania and beyond: Recent theories of the labour process. *Sociology* 16 (2): 251–69

Luxton, Meg. 1980. *More than a labour of love: Three generations of women's work in the home.* Toronto: Women's Press

Luxton, Meg, and June Corman. 2001. *Getting by in hard times: Gendered labour at home and on the job.* Toronto: University of Toronto Press

Mackenzie, Gavin. 1977. The political economy of the American working class. *British Journal of Sociology* 28:244–51

Mantsios, Gregory, and John J. Sweeney, eds. 1998. *A new labor movement for the new century.* New York: Monthly Review Press

Marchington, Mick, Damian Grimshaw, Jill Rubery, and Hugh Willmott, eds. 2005. *Fragmenting work: Blurring organizational boundaries and disordering hierarchies.* New York: Oxford University Press

Marx, Karl. 1967 [1867, original German edition]. *Capital: A critique of political economy.* Vol. 1. New York: International Publishers

Molyneux, Maxine. 1979. Beyond the domestic labour debate. *New Left Review,* no. 116

Munck, Ronaldo. 2002. *Globalisation and labour: The new 'great transformation.'* New York: Zed Books

Murray, Gregor. 2004. Union myths, enigmas, and other tales: Five challenges for union renewal. Forum: Reorganizing unions. *Studies in Political Economy* 74 (Fall/Winter): 157–69

Mutari, Ellen, and Deborah M. Figart. 2001. Europe at a crossroads: Harmonization, liberalization, and the gender of work time. *Social Politics,* Spring, 36–64

Nelson, Margaret K., and Joan Smith. 1999. *Working hard and making do.* Berkeley: University of California Press

Noble, David F. 1977. *America by design: Science, technology, and the rise of corporate capitalism.* Toronto: Oxford University Press

O'Connor, Julia S., Ann Shola Orloff, and Sheila Shaver. 1999. *States, markets, families: Gender, liberalism and social policy in Australia, Canada, Great Britain and the United States.* Cambridge: Cambridge University Press

O'Doherty, Damian, and Hugh Willmott. 2001. Debating labour process theory: The issue of subjectivity and the relevance of poststructuralism. *Sociology* 35 (2): 457–76

O'Reilly, Jacqueline, and Colette Fagan, eds. 1998. *Part-time prospects: An international comparison of part-time work in Europe, North America and the Pacific Rim.* London: Routledge

Peck, Jamie. 1996. *Work-place: The social regulation of labor markets.* New York: Guilford Press

Phillips, Anne, and Barbara Taylor. 1986. Sex and skill. In Feminist Review 1986

Pollert, Anna. 1981. *Girls, wives, factory lives.* London: Macmillan

Porter, John. 1987 [1979]. *The measure of Canadian society: Education, Equality and Opportunity.* Ottawa: Carleton University Press

Preston, Valerie, and Wenona Giles. 1997. Ethnicity, gender and labour markets in Canada: A case study of immigrant women in Toronto. *Canadian Journal of Urban Research* 6 (2): 135–59

Reiter, Ester. 1991. *Making fast food: From the frying pan into the fryer.* Montreal and Kingston: McGill-Queen's University Press

Rinehart, James. 1975. *The tyranny of work.* Don Mills: Academic Press

Rubery, Jill. 1978. Structured labour markets, worker organisation and low pay. *Cambridge Journal of Economics,* no. 2:17–36

Russell, Bob. 1999. *More with less: Work reorganization in the Canadian mining industry.* Toronto: University of Toronto Press

Sargent, Lydia, ed. 1981. *Women and revolution: A Discussion of the unhappy marriage of Marxism and feminism.* Montreal: Black Rose Books

Schwarz, Bill. 1977. On the monopoly capitalist degradation of work. *Dialectical Anthropology* 2:159–67

Skeggs, Beverley. 1991. Postmodernism: What is all the fuss about? *British Journal of Sociology of Education* 12 (2): 255–79

– 1997. *Formations of class and gender: Becoming respectable.* London: Sage

Smith, Vicki. 1994. Braverman's legacy: The labor process tradition at 20. *Work and Occupations* 21: 403–21

Stark, David. 1980. Class struggle and the transformation of the labor process. *Theory and Society* 9: 89–130

Stasiulis, Daiva K., and Abigail B. Bakan. 2005. *Negotiating citizenship: Migrant women in Canada and the global system.* Toronto: University of Toronto Press

Steedman, Mercedes. 1986. Skill and gender in the Canadian clothing industry, 1890–1940. In Heron and Storey 1986a, 152–76

Thompson, Paul. 1989. *The nature of work: An introduction to debates on the labour process.* 2nd ed. London: Macmillan

Thompson, Paul, and Stephen Ackroyd. 1995. All quiet on the workplace front? A critique of recent trends in British industrial sociology. *Sociology* 29 (4): 615–33

Thompson, Paul, and Eddie Bannon. 1985. *Working the system: The shop floor and new technology.* London: Pluto Press

Thompson, Paul, and Chris Warhurst. 1998. *Workplaces of the future.* Basingstoke: Macmillan

Thrift, Nigel. 1999. Capitalism's cultural turn. In *Culture and economy after the cultural turn,* edited by Larry Ray and Andrew Sayer. London: Sage

Vosko, Leah F. 2000. *Temporary work: The gendered rise of a precarious employment relationship.* Toronto: University of Toronto Press

Walby, Sylvia. 1986. *Patriarchy at work: Patriarchal and capitalist relations in employment.* Cambridge: Polity Press

Warhurst, Chris, Irena Grugulis, and Ewart Keep, eds. 2004. *The skills that matter.* Basingstoke: Palgrave Macmillan

West, Jackie, ed. 1982. *Work, women and the labour market.* London: Routledge and Kegan Paul

Westwood, Sallie. 1984. *All day, every day: Factory and family in the making of women's lives.* London: Pluto Press

Wood, Ellen Meiksins, Peter Meiksins, and Michael Yates. 1998. *Rising from the ashes? Labor in the age of "global" capitalism.* New York: Monthly Review Press

Wood, Stephen, ed. 1982. *The degradation of work? Skill, deskilling and the labour process.* London: Hutchinson & Co.

– ed. 1989. *The transformation of work? Skill, flexibility and the labour process.* London: Unwin Hyman

Zeytinoğlu, Isik Urla. 1999. *Changing work relationships in industrialized economies.* Amsterdam: John Benjamins

Zimbalist, Andrew, ed. 1979. *Case studies on the labor process.* New York: Monthly Review Press

2

Methodological Considerations: Thinking about Researching Work

WALLACE CLEMENT

The great thinkers of the social sciences have had much to say about work. In the classic era, Karl Marx wrote about the modes and relations of production and Max Weber wrote about bureaucracy and the modes of administration. In the revival period, C. Wright Mills's remarkable *White Collar* (1951) and Harry Braverman's era-marking *Labor and Monopoly Capital* (1974) were modern classics.

The labour process is a set of factors that combine when work occurs. It is a process in the sense of a chain transforming goods and/or services whereby labour is applied. Labour is the exertion of physical or mental effort towards some conscious end. The conditions and characteristics of labouring are complex and not always obvious. It is easy to observe the work that people do in an office or factory for wages or similarly in fields or at sea to obtain products sold as commodities (goods produced for the purpose of sale to others rather than for one's own consumption). Less obvious are all forms of caring work, especially domestic work that is not done directly for payment; yet this work, as well as having its own immediate labour process, is also part of the overall labour process. Labour process research locates work in the context of developments in technology and the organization of work. Work is located in the context of how the resources of society are mobilized and controlled. The labour process is at the heart of class analysis, raising questions about the control and appropriation of society's production. At the personal level, the labour process poses issues concerning how people organize their work and preparation time, cooperate with others, and "make a living." Work is not only a system of production; it is also a source of identity and a basis upon which people are evaluated by others and assess themselves.

As a lens on the social sciences, the study of work is most revealing. The rise of feminism, for example, placed on the agenda the double day or, as captured so prosaically by the Armstrongs, *The Double Ghetto* (1978). In the post-industrial literature, the rise of various forms of service work is seen to be intimately connected to the increasing labour force participation of women and young people.

Methods and methodology are topics that students new to the social sciences often avoid. Similarly, they tend to shy away from theory and theorization as topics of inquiry. They are attracted, instead, to more descriptive accounts and topics. This is because specialists all too often present theory and methods as free-standing rather than integral parts of analysis. The more experienced researchers become, the more attention they pay to the central place of methods in the scholarly research process, whether for their own work or in their assessment of others'.

Methodology's appropriateness depends upon the theoretical questions being asked. Methodology should never lead the research agenda. It determines what sources will be regarded as evidence: that is, how data will be sought and what kinds of data there will be – documentary, officially gathered statistics, survey data, case studies, and so on. Methodology entails both the development of a research agenda or strategy and the ways of carrying out that strategy (methods). Research techniques involve the ways in which various sources of information are organized and utilized, including how that information is communicated in the form of evidence. Theory provides the answers to *why* things are as they are, while *how* offers an account of their organization.

Methods should be regarded as research tools that researchers call upon as demanded by the issue they wish to address in order to produce evidence appropriate to the audience to which they seek to speak. Theories are explanations that attempt to make sense of the world. Sets of theories (and usually accompanying methodologies that specify what is regarded as evidence) that "hang together" are known as paradigms. Effective social science demands the integration of the theoretical, methodological, and substantive. Method is about how issues are framed, while theory is about how they are explained. Framing is what scholars must do to conduct research, to specify what is backgrounded and foregrounded in their account. Without some way to distinguish the context from the text or the background from the main actors, research is not possible; investigations without a foundation of theory and method result in mere description or assertion, not scholarship.

Labour process literature says that those who work, who produce and labour, should be foregrounded as agents and subjects of study. The literature is interested in accounts of how and why labour power is used and controlled. Who works, why, and under what conditions? Ownership, technology, and organizational practices all structure and contextualize such research and enter in various ways into explanations. Feminism's encounter with the labour process revealed entire domains of work that had been rendered invisible in earlier accounts. Most notable were unpaid forms of family labour, domestic work, and volunteering. More than that, so-called secondary labour, or work performed by women, youth, or the elderly, often on a part-time basis, was also in the shadows of analysis.

RESEARCH QUESTIONS

Research questions can be grouped into two types. The first type is concerned with *accounts* of social practices and focuses on four questions: *who* questions include the actors involved in the processes (their gender, ethnicity, generation, class relationships, citizenship status, skills, training, household formation, etc.); *what* questions deal with the subject matter of the research, namely what is investigated (in this case, the subject is work, broadly defined to include formal and informal, paid and unpaid, and their relationships); *where* questions explore the spatial boundaries, scope, or focus of the research and its claims; and *when* questions involve the temporal parameters of the research. Each of these questions is only an entry into deeper and much more rigorous ways of framing research questions. For instance, the *when* questions are about social change, the subject matter of most social science research. They would involve the marking of eras or the periodization of change. Social change is a claim about two or more times being sufficiently distinct as to require being separated. As a methodological issue, these eras or periods require that there be specification about what is distinctive to each and what has changed between them to merit the separation. The spatial questions give a locality to research and a material specificity to the claims. The spaces may be neighbourhoods, cities, provinces, countries, continents, regions, or blocs that are often compared or contrasted. *Where* has also come to mean a physicality to certain claims or developments, such as the importance of locality, environment, and ecology to accounts and explanations.

Research questions of the second type offer *explanations*. *How* questions are about processes – the way things unfold or combine. *How* answers order things in logical sequences or relationships. The *why* question is the largest and least concrete of the questions. It is the foundation of theory. Theories offer explanations; that is, they offer accounts that attempt to make sense of things by clarifying why things happen as they do. Theories reveal and conceal; that is, they signify some features as more important than others by identifying priorities and orders to relationships. Explanations are supported by evidence; otherwise they are assertions. Data dislocated from explanation is description. Dimensions of theories include space (territory, boundaries) and time (social change, direction, and movement). Theories derive from paradigms, which are sets of assumptions about how the world operates, by specifying priorities in the account.

Methods are ways of translating theories into the concrete. They allow researchers to move between levels of abstraction. Here, there are again two dimensions. Big-M Methods focus on the logic of inquiry. They involve questions, logical constructions, concept definitions, and specifications, including identification of appropriate indicators. Small-m methods are research techniques. They are the actual operationalizations, measurements, data gathering, sources, and issues of reliability and validity that give research its credibility. The goal of methodology is to strengthen scholars' ability to move between levels of abstraction, from the most abstract theories to the most concrete, by focusing on how these levels mediate and transform one another.

The point of research is not to simplify but to clarify. All theories, as noted, both reveal and conceal. They specify which of a myriad of factors are claimed as most important in an account. As noted, theory specifies which factors will be foregrounded and which backgrounded or, to use another image, which are text and which are context. Methods are the essential mediators between theories; they offer explanations and the specificity of accounts that identify the relationships between actors and subjects located in time and space.

RESEARCH PRACTICES: THE INSTANCE OF PRECARIOUSNESS

As social scientists, we are in the business of explanation. That means we need to be diligent about mapping issues, such as the who, where, and when questions identified earlier, but also about discovering what is happening and what can be done about it. A good example is the rise of what has come to be known as "precarious employment." First, how has precarious employment come about and why? Answering this could involve our undertaking grounded research on precariousness by abstracting from the experiences of those engaged in precarious forms of employment and attempting to discover what produces the processes that are creating these forms of employment. In doing so, we would want to know why these processes have specific class, gender, generation, racial, and status effects. Accounts need to be more connected; it is not enough simply to assert that precarious employment is due to modernization, globalization, neo-liberalism, technological change, or post-industrialism. These are all very broad and abstract notions that require theorization and specification before they can be used to organize our thinking and methodological strategy. The audience that researchers envision also comes into play in terms of what kinds of evidence will be convincing and useful. It matters whether the intended audience is made up of activists, academics, students, other researchers, or practitioners. There are always assumptions behind research strategies. For example, most research on precarious employment is concerned about the quality, availability, and valuing of work. It typically values a progressive notion of flexible work over insecure or cheap labour. A progressive view would prioritize the flexible-for-whom question, focusing on workers as parents, partners, or citizens rather than as low-cost sources of disposable labour for employers.

Framing the research, which is the essence of methodology, needs to be conducted with clarity, and first of all with clarity of purpose. The precarious employment relationship and precarious work have become the subject of much scrutiny. As a starting point, however, researchers should ask whether their primary interest is in vulnerable workers or precarious jobs. A focus on vulnerable workers leads researchers to concentrate on the characteristics of the workers themselves in terms of gender, age, race, education, experience, and so on. A focus on precarious jobs leads them to concentrate on the characteristics of the jobs, how they are created and rewarded. The strongest research strategy is one that says it is important to know the conditions that produce both precarious jobs and precarious working relationships and understand how these combine under specific conditions. The invoking of a more holistic strategy leads to more nuanced answers. Typically, the full battery of questions will produce a conditional analysis in terms of a specific time and space. Only then can researchers address the conditions and identify the progressive and regressive situations (of course, progressive and regressive for whom) because the interests of employers and employees or the self-employed do not always coincide. As class analysis insists, these interests are relational and at least in tension if not in contradiction with one another.

A CASE STUDY: DESKILLING AND
POST-INDUSTRIALISM

Late in his too short life, John Porter, Canada's pre-eminent socio-
logist and author of *The Vertical Mosaic* (1965), delivered a two-part lecture at York University entitled "Education, Equality, and the Just
Society." He chose this as the concluding paper in his last collection of
essays, *The Measure of Canadian Society* (1987). The title of this book was
meant ironically: both the counting and accounting aspects of measurement were implied. Porter had pioneered the measurement of
various forms of inequality in Canada. In this lecture and essay, he
made a major reverse in his assessment of the post-industrial world and
the so-called knowledge economy, both of which, at the time, were
laden with assumptions about the equalizing force of education and
the expansion of skill-based jobs as the labour market shifted from
industrial to service work. The second part of Porter's major reflection
began by introducing the findings of Harry Braverman presented in
his *Labor and Monopoly Capital: The Degradation of Work in the Twentieth
Century* (1974). Braverman's main thesis was that monopoly capitalism
was transforming labour from a basis of skill to one of science, and that
the productivity of capital was in contradiction with the place of workers in the production process, since this drive involves the separation
of workers from their skills, the separation of conception from execution, and the valuing of monopoly over knowledge by capital, thus
resulting in workers losing control over their labour process, with an
outcome of overall deskilling. This process, Braverman argued, was
also applicable to clerical workers, who were being subjected to a
new labour process involving a technical division of labour based on
routinization and the application of numerical and mathematical control, a process that thereby destroyed the meaning of separating mental
and manual labour. Braverman's work was controversial and provocative, creating a growth industry in labour process research for the next
generation.

Porter was not a Marxist, as Braverman was, but he appreciated
Braverman's insight, which flew in the face of many of the assumptions
Porter had been following: "Why, Braverman asks, has the upgrading
thesis been so firmly entrenched as the conventional wisdom of both
labour economics and sociology? The answer he provides is a difficult
one to refute. Much of the upgrading is a statistical artefact of census
occupational categories rather than changes in the real work world"
(Porter 1987, 266). Porter went on to discuss in some detail the rise of
so-called semi-skilled machine operators and the problems of classifying farmers in occupational schemes. He anticipated a finding of later,

more sophisticated statistical analysis known as "good jobs, bad jobs," observing that "the labour forces of industrial and postindustrial societies are increasingly assuming a bimodal distribution with respect to skill requirements, the highly qualified at one end and the mass of less qualified at the other, creating a polarization which as it increases will have great implications for equality, not only of incomes but of authority and power, thus providing a further dimension to the segmentation of the labour force" (1987, 267). A check of Porter's endnotes reveals that his key reference to Braverman was to what amounted to a methodological appendix added as the book's final chapter, entitled "A Final Note on Skill." It was in the details of Braverman's methodological critique of occupational classification schemes that Porter found his connection with Braverman. More notable, it was in this critique that Porter found the basis on which to make a major theoretical shift in his entire corpus of research, a shift that cast a completely different light on his studies of education, occupation, and mobility. Porter completely rethought his earlier assumptions about the effects of postindustrialism and new forms of technology on the production of inequalities – all because of an essentially methodological insight.

DEFINING THE ISSUES: MATTERS OF PERSPECTIVE

I make the claim that we do not have a crisis of lack of available work (as is usually asserted by those looking at unemployment figures). There is much to do and a great deal to care for – the young, the elderly, the environment, the homeless, the challenged. We have a crisis of the valuing of work, its allocation, and its funding. We can begin in the household, where caring and reproductive work, which can be repressive or rewarding, depending upon its conditions, is essential. And then there are the links between the household and its supports, on the one side, childcare, schools, hospitals, care for the elderly, and so on; and on the other, flexible, supportive paid work – hours, leaves, benefits. A key insight of socialist-feminist analysis into the multifaceted nexus between class and gender, as expressed by the links between the formal and informal economies, paid and unpaid work, and the labour force and the household, remains germane under postindustrial capitalism.

People want to be active and engaged, but under conditions of their choosing and valuing. Many retired people are delighted to assist in childcare and activities for the elderly, and there is much need for them. Many students want to have employment, both to gain experience and to earn money for living and educational expenses. These work experiences, however, should be meaningful and engaging rather than demeaning and exploitative if they are to attract so-called marginal workers.

"Flexible for whom" is a question that needs to be asked for all these cases. A state system striving to reduce health services, clothing manufacturers seeking to compete with Third World wages, and core post-industrial firms cutting their wage bills – that is what "productive" has come to mean. It does not mean productive in the sense of healthy, well-rounded individual workers, households, and societies seeking to reproduce themselves. It does not even mean productive in terms of the work that is produced. Productive has become equated with cheaper and the production of profit, not with quality and value.

The essays in the collection *Good Jobs, Bad Jobs, No Jobs*, edited by Ann Duffy, Daniel Glenday, and Noreen Pupo (1997), provide a good illustration of some of the issues currently under review by Canadian scholars of work. Duffy, for example, addresses the complexity of part-time work for women, youth, and seniors (Duffy, Glenday, and Pupo 1997). The answer to whether part-time work is empowerment or entrapment is, of course, contingent – it depends. The same can be said of part-career work, exemplified by Japanese women's practice of leaving regular employment when children arrive or German men's early exiting from industrial work. These relate to what David Broad calls "the contingent labour force" and the re-casualization of labour that are part of global restructuring, creating a labour market based on flexible production and contingent workers who form a veritable "reserve army of labour" (Duffy, Glenday, and Pupo 1997).

Is telework another form of contingent work? It all depends on the terms of employment. Telework tends to be measurable work, and it places the costs for maintaining an office on the employee. Employees gain in commuting savings and reduced direct supervision, but employers can turn the situation to their advantage by hiring so-called independent contractors, giving them relief from benefits and job security obligations. Telework is an attractive option for some, as Kay Stratton Devine, Laurel Taylor, and Kathy Haryett show, but when it is adopted as an exclusive form of work, teleworkers miss the support of co-workers and unions (Duffy, Glenday, and Pupo 1997). Focus on such work places the link between household work and paid work on the agenda, as does the chapter by Noreen Pupo, who investigates the important issue of women's "double day" (Duffy, Glenday, and Pupo 1997).

The re-engineering of work and revamping of occupations and professions are well represented by Jerry White's study of the inadequacy of health care, a fundamental service, because of government expenditure cuts and the rise of work-related stress levels (Duffy, Glenday, and Pupo 1997). The same could be said of education and housing.

Another excellent example of the social construction of technological change is provided by Vivian Shalla in her study of airline passenger
agents (Duffy, Glenday, and Pupo 1997). The introduction of computerization into airline reservations was used as a way to control employees, facilitating contracting out, often to commission-based travel
agents, and intensifying electronic surveillance (adding to stress). The
process of computerization could have provided a mechanism for
greater coordination of the labour process – ticketing, advising, routing
of luggage – relieving stress while expanding and enriching the services
provided. It was not inherent in the technology but in the social relations of its production and adoption. This is also an industry where
global pressures are highly visible; that is, the employer does not act
autonomously in these developments but is driven by international
competition.

The social construction of the labour market is directly addressed by
Patrick Burman in his provocative chapter (Duffy, Glenday, and Pupo
1997). He documents job losses through plant closures in manufacturing and other goods-producing industries and layoffs in the service
sector through the 1990s and then asks, "What are the obstacles to
employment creation in Canada?" The answer is crucial because, as he
notes, fewer than half of the jobless Canadians today qualify for unemployment insurance (from over four-fifths before the plan was "stream-
lined") and there are a million and a half unemployed "officially" plus
at least another half-million hidden unemployed.

In his chapter, David W. Livingstone addresses where the responsibility rests when he questions what he calls the "credential gap" (people are either over-qualified for their current jobs or under-qualified
for available jobs) (Duffy, Glenday, and Pupo 1997). This question
obviously needs to be related to the "job gap": there are not presently
enough jobs to go around. He addresses the complex relationship
between training and job requirements, especially under conditions of
skill surpluses and the active pursuit of education by members of the
labour force. One difficulty is that there has been more general education and less job-specific training because education is driven by popular demand rather than employer-directed training. A tension exists
between employers' responsibilities to their workers and their socialization of the costs to either the state or individuals. Inadequate
employer-sponsored training continues to be a serious problem in
Canada.

The disconnection between jobs and growth in the Canadian business boom of the 1990s is explored by Jamie Swift (Duffy, Glenday,
and Pupo 1997). The Canadian economy has become more export-
oriented than ever owing to a reduced domestic market because of

high unemployment. Swift challenges the way training dollars are currently being spent. Training is concentrated in the high-skilled, male labour force. Is training the solution as the Economic Council of Canada's influential *Good Jobs, Bad Jobs* report advocated? We must ask whom the training is for and under what circumstances. There are no blanket answers. Training has tended to be invoked so that the blame can be laid on individual skills, qualifications, or adjustments (a liberal solution) rather than on the social response, which should be to provide decent jobs and take collective responsibility for labour market preparations and changes.

The way we tackle these public issues will have a great impact on the future of work in Canada. And the future of work will have a great impact on the quality of life Canadians will experience. It is important that researchers recognize that the way in which the questions are framed has a great impact on what is looked for and what is made problematic. Only then can they devise an appropriate research strategy to pursue evidence relevant to the puzzles posed.

USING DATA

Data is never innocent; nor does it speak for itself. Behind all data lie a myriad of decisions and judgments. Researcher are obliged to find out and know as much as they reasonably can about the data they invoke as evidence. This is especially so for statistical data. When data are used in comparisons between countries, there are more challenges because things can have very different meanings in their national contexts. The issue of rates of unionization provides a good illustration relevant to the world of work. Table 2.1 provides current data from the Organization for Economic Co-operation and Development (OECD), which represents thirty advanced industrial countries. For this table, I selected six countries with which I have research familiarity, but the original table includes all thirty members of OECD. Most comparisons of trade union strength use information about the rates of union membership, by which is meant the share of the labour force that is made up of members of trade unions. This is referred to as trade union density. Collective bargaining coverage refers to the share of the labour force that comes under the terms of the agreements reached between unions and employers.

Table 2.1 vividly reveals the overall but uneven decline of trade union density and coverage from 1980 to 2000. In two of the countries, union coverage is much wider than their membership. In Australia, a national awards system sets the conditions across sectors and is applied to all those working in these sectors whether they are union members or not.

Table 2.1   Trade union density and coverage, 1980–2000 (in percentages)

	Density			Coverage		
	1980	1990	2000	1980	1990	2000
Australia	48	40	25	80+	80+	80+
Canada	35	33	28	37	38	32
Germany	35	31	25	80+	80+	68
Japan	31	25	22	25+	20+	15+
Sweden	80	80	79	80+	80+	90+
United States	22	15	13	26	18	14

Source: Based on OECD, *Employment Outlook, 2004* (Paris, 2004), Table. 3.3, p. 145.

In Germany there has been a tradition of sectoral bargaining. Again, all those working in the sectors are covered by agreements negotiated by the unions and employers, whether they are union members or not. Sweden has nearly universal union membership and union coverage. Despite the breakdown of central bargaining in Sweden (Ahrne and Clement 1992), nearly all workplaces are covered by union agreements. Moreover, membership in Swedish unions is governed by the so-called Ghent system, which includes union-administered unemployment insurance plans, offering workers an added incentive to join. Sweden, Australia, and Germany remain highly unionized countries, at least in terms of coverage by union settlements. Some break in German coverage was evident after reunification, while the Australian developments concerning the weakening of central awards through the national tribunals in favour of enterprise management since the turn of the century are not exposed, although the decline in union density is quite evident. Sweden extended its coverage by 2000 to record levels. With just the union density data, one would conclude that unions have pretty much the same strength in Australia, Canada, Germany, and Japan. Only Sweden stands out as exceptional at one end and the United States as exceptional at the other end.

The United States and Japan show declining membership and coverage over the three decades, while Canada stands very much between the two clusters, not in a league with the broad-coverage countries (Sweden and Australia) but certainly much more protected than either the United States or Japan. The anomaly of lower coverage than density in Japan is explained by the fact that "about 30% of trade union members are not covered by bargaining units" (OECD 2004, 174). With the availability of data on union density and collective bargaining coverage, researchers can much more accurately assess the strength of unions in these different countries. Still, the data really do not produce full answers; rather they suggest more research questions, things to be explained. Why has Australia's density suddenly fallen off in the last decade? Does it matter, since its coverage has remained so high? What has occurred in Germany to explain the decline over the 1990s in density and coverage? Has this all been the effect of reunification or have there been other developments as well? What is to be made of the erosions in Japan and, to a lesser extent, Canada? Are both countries drifting towards a U.S.-style low unionization pattern? Statistical data are not in and of themselves evidence. It requires framing, explanation, and illumination.

GETTING DATA

There are many sources for data, especially for statistical information. Statistics Canada is the most obvious general source in Canada (www.statcan.ca). Comparatively, there is the OECD (www.oecd.org), already mentioned; the International Labour Organization (ILO), which provides a wealth of information about work for over a hundred countries (www.ilo.org); and the frequently cited Luxemburg Income Survey and its associated Employment Survey (www.lisproject.org). Sometimes these sources are difficult to access and use. The Gender and Work Data Base (www.genderwork.ca) is a new source for data in Canada. It is an on-line, user-friendly website maintained at York University, and it covers a wide range of areas organized by modules. These include, for Canada, health care, migration, precarious employment, rural-urban, technology, unions, unpaid work, and comparative perspectives for various industrialized countries. In addition to statistics, the website offers documentation on concepts and discussion papers that help frame the topics covered. Moreover, users can manipulate many of the statistics in order to customize the information to their specific subject.

COMPARATIVE FRAMINGS:
WHAT QUESTIONS ARE ASKED

There has been an extensive enterprise around comparative welfare state research since the early 1990s. Gøsta Esping-Andersen's classic work on welfare capitalism identified three regimes: the *liberal* regime, where services are provided by markets, which means they vary according to individual successes in labour markets; the *conservative* regime, where subsidies, not services, are provided to the needy, thus making it difficult for women to participate in the labour force and promoting principal male breadwinners; and the *social democratic* regime, which promotes social rights and women's labour force participation by way of providing services for care work. Esping-Andersen's recent work

(1999) offers an institutional framework of welfare regimes character-ized by the interaction of composite parts: labour markets, the family, and the welfare state. According to him, all nations have combinations of each part, but with different accents: the liberal Anglo-Saxon nations are "market-biased," the southern European or Japanese are "powerfully familialist," and then there are the Scandinavian welfare states.

O'Connor, Orloff, and Shaver's book on four liberal societies, *States, Markets, Families: Gender, Liberalism and Social Policy in Australia, Canada, Great Britain and the United States* (1999), extends the analysis beyond welfare states per se to "social policy regimes," which include reproductive rights. For these authors, regime "indicates something broader than the 'welfare state,' connoting the full range of domestic policy interventions as well as broader patterns of provisioning and regulation," including "sexual and reproductive relations" (1999, 28). Foremost, they argue that questions about gender should be at the forefront of such analyses, but they also contend that there are major differences within these "liberal" regimes that challenge the integrity of the Esping-Andersen categorization.

Offering another intervention into the dilemmas of comparative welfare state classifications, Giuliano Bonoli (1997) focuses on con-ceptual and methodological limitations to such research. He begins by making a distinction between two European traditions of welfare state policy. Under the Bismarckian model, the focus is on income mainte-nance, benefits are earnings-related, eligibility is determined by con-tributions, and coverage is for employees. Under the Beveridgean model, the focus is on poverty prevention with flat-rate benefits, eligi-bility is based on need, and coverage is financed through taxation for the entire population. Bonoli pairs this dichotomy with spending lev-els by the welfare states to create a new typology. Most interesting are the reservations he identifies at the end, namely, "the non-comparabil-ity in quantitative terms of welfare states based on different models ... Bismarckian and Beveridgean social policies are not only two different kinds of social policy: they are two different policies because their objectives are different. Both policies can be measured in quantitative terms, but the result will fail the test of comparability, since in one case we will have a measure of a country's effort put into poverty prevention and in the other case the measure will tell us how much is spent for the purpose of income maintenance." This leads Bonoli to call for com-parative studies into "definitions of concepts which are used in cross-national comparisons. The simple comparison of economic indicators can be misleading since they sometimes refer to different things in dif-ferent countries" (369–70). Insightful advice.

FRAMING MY RESEARCH:
RELATIONAL ANALYSIS[1]

My primary argument is that to understand and explain the social, cultural, political, and economic relationships associated with the transformation of post-industrial societies, it is essential to locate them within the triangulation of connections between households, labour markets, and welfare states. The main relationships I seek to take into account are those of class, gender, and generation. The combination of these three analytical sites, together with their overall connection, reveals the essentially holistic nature of these relationships and their practices with respect to our understanding of the way work is constructed in advanced societies. This is not an approach that begins with a particularly elaborate model of classes, gender relations, and generations. Rather, it is an approach that attempts to reveal these relationships through its account of the three sites of households, states, and labour markets. A part of the claim of this research is that classes, genders, and generations have been transformed by post-industrialism, not singularly but in combination. There are distinctive and distinct expressions of these relationships across countries.

My approach to the study of work focuses on the practices of social welfare, paid work, and unpaid work as located in the relation between citizenship entitlements, markets, and households. Within each practice and through its relationships with the others, I seek to discover the class-gender nexus. I think of three levels of abstraction: relations of reproduction, relations of production, and welfare state regimes at one level, corresponding to domestic labour, paid labour, and citizenship at an intermediate level, and concretely located in households, labour markets, and social practices.

Beyond extending traditional analysis further than the institutions of the labour market and the state into the household, my claim to novelty is embodied in the methodology of relational analysis. The three sites of labour markets, welfare states, and households are not specifically studied as institutions, policies, or practices (although they rely heavily upon such studies). Rather it is the matrix of relations between these sites that yields our understanding of class, gender, and generation. Class, gender, and generation are themselves relational concepts that are given meaning in terms of how they unfold in the intricacies of these fundamental relationships. Space and time are crucial to the yielding of variations and transformations in these relations. Relations can never be static; they must continually be sustained and adjusted. They are not the same everywhere; spatial context matters. And they are subject to change; time matters.

Generation provides a strong reminder of this, since one's generation is embedded in time and life stage, defined relationally. Generation involves the intersection of individuals with their context. Children are dependent upon others for their support; youth are between sexual maturity and economic independence; adults are economically independent; the elderly are mature people retired from full labour market dependence. Generation includes several levels of analysis, such as the following: the relative weights of numbers of one set compared to the others (are there sufficient adults to sustain the others?); the relationship between the generations (who will care for the children and elderly?); and the problems of transition (what are the conditions for youths to attain economic independence and for the elderly to attain freedom from the labour market?). Households include the "long family," which extends across generations from childhood to pensioners, and the notions of living under the same roof and sharing obligations through common roots. Labour markets include the active period of paid employment but also work-based pensions and all forms of "leaves" that follow.

The six relationships between the three sites are not boundaries but blurred and interconnected spheres that I call the "intersections triad." *Households* include domestic labour, families, and unpaid community work (volunteers). They are associated with the relations of reproduction and maintenance/supply-side. *Labour markets* include paid work (market work) and relations of production/demand-side. *Social policy* involves citizenship entitlements, communities, and welfare state regimes/regulation. All three sites are classed and gendered but in different ways – that is, in ways that enhance or undercut the class-gender nexus. They can be identified as associated with three types of claims, entitlements, or rights: family-status claims, market citizenship entitlements, or social citizenship rights.

This leads to questions about whether such investigations reveal distinct work-life regimes. Are there distinct, identifiable regimes of gender, capital, labour, and state relations? And how have they experienced change in this era of restructuring at the end of the twentieth century? What effects do these regimes have on labour market regimes?[2] The answers to such questions would help us understand not only a social-democratic model as exemplified by Sweden, but also how the social-democratic regime itself is being transformed and with what implications for work.

Work-life regimes are clusters of power that include institutions, practices, and ideologies; labour market profiles are combinations of factors that influence who works and under what conditions. Included in labour market profiles are the following: the relationship between school and work (when people leave school, whether they work while in school either part-time or part-year); the relationship between home and work (especially relevant for part-time work, the careers of women workers); the age of retirement and whether retired workers continue to work; restrictions on workers by citizenship requirements; the recruitment of labour through immigration practices; and systems of unemployment compensation, for discouraged workers, and for others. Age has become a key labour market factor, one that includes child labour (minimum age) and retirement as parameters of the labour market. Child labour covers "baby-sitting" minimum ages (say twelve years), the exploitation of children in sweat shops or sweat fields, and, in between, the way work and schooling are combined.

Much of what we refer to as post-industrial work involves transformations in households. As Nancy Folbre and Julie Nelson say, there is an "intertwining of 'love' and 'money.'" They claim: "[T]he shift of caring activity from family to markets represents an enormous social change. Markets on their own are unlikely to provide the particular volume and quality of 'real' care that society desires for children, the sick, and the elderly" (2000, 138).

Labour markets everywhere are socially constructed, not simply based on an abstract supply and demand for labour. Countries vary enormously in student work – both during the school year and during vacations – and in the practice of retirement. Important variations also occur in paid versus unpaid work, especially childcare and care of the elderly, and in the use of low-paid workers. Addressing these issues is fundamental to calculations of unemployment rates, working time, work-life transitions, and youth and women's labour force experiences. They all form part of a nation's work-life regime.

Working time, who works, and under what conditions have become newly recontested issues under post-industrial capitalism. During this period of major transformations in work-life regimes, it is particularly important that we understand how work is organized and distributed. Of interest are the conditions (such as class formations; gender relations; the influence of age, race, and ethnicity; immigration policies; and labour market policies) upon which different labour market outcomes are contingent.

DOES THE HOUSEHOLD MATTER FOR UNDERSTANDING PAID WORK?

Research on work has typically focused on the labour market of paid work and, quite frequently, on its relationship to state policies and practices. Much less common is the focus on households and their

Table 2.2   Non-employment among single parents (in percentages)

	Single-Parent Non-employment, 2001	Poverty Rates* Single Parents, 1993–95	
		Non-working	Working
Australia	57	57.1	9.3
Canada	49	72.5	26.5
Germany	34	61.8	32.5
Sweden	13	24.2	3.8
United States	23	93.4	38.6

* Percentage of persons living in households with incomes below 50 per cent of the median-adjusted disposable income of the entire population.

Table 2.3   Women's employment and the presence of children, 2000 (in percentages, persons 25 to 54)

	No Children		One Child		Two or More	
	Employment	Gender Gap	Employment	Gender Gap	Employment	Gender Gap
Australia	69	16	55	33	43	48
Canada	77	6	75	15	68	24
Germany	77	7	70	21	56	36
Sweden	82	0	81	10	82	9
United States	79	7	76	17	65	29

Source: OECD, *Employment Outlook, July 2002* (Paris, 2002), Table 2.4, p. 77.
Note: Gender gap is the percentage-point difference between the employment rates of men and women.

impact on work. Two brief illustrations will show the importance of locating work in relation to households. They will also demonstrate how these relationships are not universal but particular to national practices, which themselves require examination. Gender inequalities are worked out differently in various countries.

Table 2.2 shows the major variations in national practices with respect to the employment of single-parent mothers. While nearly all single parents have employment in Sweden and the United States (though obviously under very different conditions, since few working single parents live in poverty in Sweden but more than a third do in the United States), about half the single parents in Canada and over half those in Australia are not employed. This has implications for the poverty rates experienced by these single parents. While there is virtually no poverty among working single parents in Sweden and the poverty rate for working single parents is low in Australia as well, these rates are highest in the United States, even higher than for non-working single parents in Sweden. Nearly all non-working single parents in the United States live in poverty, and while there is variation, the poverty rates for unemployed single parents in all the countries are very high. Even in Sweden, a quarter of non-working single parents live in poverty. These statistics illustrate that working matters and availability for work matters, given the child-rearing obligations of single parents. Table 2.3 pushes this point further.

Even without children present, there is a large gender gap in terms of employment in Australia, although there is much less in the other countries (in fact, none in Sweden). As soon as children are added to households, the gap increases and, aside from Sweden, the number of children present also matters. Sweden, with record levels of women's employment, is the notable exception, regardless of the presence of children. Findings like this are what makes Sweden such an interesting place for those who study work. Australia is also of interest, but for the opposite reason. Its low levels of women's employment are even lower than those of Germany, which has long had the reputation of being a country where women's place is in the home. There is little difference evident between Canada and the United States in this respect.

While comparative statistics can point to issues that require explanation, it is the detailed case study of each country and the actual practices and policies that really make sense out of the puzzles produced by the statistical data. Such studies often require extensive reading and literature searches for writings on the specific topics for each country. With the use of search engines and the Internet, we now have much more information on specialized topics at our fingertips. While there is no substitute for spending time in the countries in question, that is not always possible or even necessary for us to gain access to extensive information (especially since English is the *linga franca* of the Internet). Random searches, however, do not constitute research. Research first requires an identification and framing of the subject. It then requires the researcher to devise a way of interrogating the subject and theorizing about explanations and accounts. Without these foundations, reams of information and data are just descriptions, not evidence. It is much easier for researchers to produce volumes of noise than writings with insights.

A FINAL CASE STUDY: THE STRUGGLE TO ORGANIZE

A good deal of the research on work, particularly studies with a labour process focus, has used case studies of particular industries or workplaces. I have done some case studies myself, most notably on the mining[3] and fishing industries.[4] Both studies were theorized within a class and property framework. The mining study concentrated on how miners retained their real autonomy within the labour process even when formally subordinated to their employers. The study on fishing demonstrated that even though many fishers are not formally subordinated to employers, they in fact experience real subordination of labour. In both studies, I had to undertake detailed investigation to move beyond appearances to reveal the underlying power relationships. Here I can only hint at how this research was conducted for my study on the fisheries.

Briefly, capitalist relations generally create the proletarianization of labour whereby workers are transformed into wage labourers in the employ of capital, losing their own means of realizing their labour (control over their means of production). By theorizing ownership relationships in terms of legal (or formal) ownership on one side and real ownership divided into economic ownership (directing the use of production and disposal of products) and possession (the immediate labour process) on the other, I was able to break through the appearances of independence attributed to many fishers. Among other forms, I identified capitalist or proletarian relations, independent commodity production, and dependent commodity production. In the final form, there is an appearance of formal ownership by fishers, but capital appropriates economic ownership while labour retains possession, producing a kind of disguised proletariat behind a veil of self-employment. That is to say, fishers nominally owned their own boat and means of production and they directed their own immediate labour process, but capital controlled economic ownership through control over monopolized markets or through financial debt. Armed with this theoretical insight, I was able to explain the class content and behaviour of various organizations within the fishery. I could show why some unions acted like cooperatives, some associations acted like unions, and some cooperatives acted like capitalist firms. In so doing, I addressed the issues of race and gender within the fisheries that impacted on the culture, ideology and politics of the industry. The material bases of ideologies that have themselves led to various political practices could be explained in terms of property relations. I gave weight to issues of time and space, as they were meaningful in how people explained their actions and acted within this complex area. Parenthetically, I neglected to give sufficient weight to ecological issues and the limitations imposed by the decline of fish stocks, which have wreaked havoc on fishing communities. Only through the detail of case studies was I able to move beyond the appearances and puzzles of the fisheries to provide explanatory insights into what was really happening and with what implications. Had I either simply theorized the issues of class and property relations or only engaged in detailed empirical investigations, I could not have developed the explanations so essential to scholarly insights. It is the mediation between the levels of analysis of the abstract and the concrete that methodology offers. Not only does methodology translate theories into the concrete, but it mediates back from the empirical to modify the theory. Methodology is the engine that drives scholarly enquiry at both the empirical and abstract levels.

METHOD OF PRESENTING RESEARCH

Research has two phases: the process of discovery and the mode of presentation. This has mostly to do with the way material is organized and presented. Scholars begin the process of discovery by identifying the subject itself as an area, field, or topic of investigation. After immersing themselves in the relevant literature, researchers latch on to a research question. This becomes the basis for framing the inquiry. As the question and its tentative answer begin to form, researchers develop an argument or position within this literature. Then there is the systematic gathering of information and data that will be transformed into evidence to address the argument. Once that is done, researchers draw their conclusions and refine their argument. This, however, is only half the process. All too many stop here and simply record their results by writing their paper. What they should now work on is the mode of presentation. They should begin with the conclusions just reached that now have the status of claims about the research. Next they restate the research question and locate it again vis-à-vis the literature (so the literature is now read in light of their claims, not as a summary review). Then researchers present the evidence to convince the reader about the conclusion. This can be done judiciously and to great effect because the evidence is sustaining a clearly articulated position. Finally, researchers restate their conclusion and its implications. If this all seems quite modern, read the following quotation written in 1873: "Of course the method of presentation must differ in form from that of inquiry. The latter has to appropriate the material in detail, to analyse its different forms of development, to trace out their inner connexion. Only after this work is done, can the actual movement be adequately described." These are the enduring thoughts of Karl Marx (1967, 19).

NOTES

1 I have discussed this ongoing research in three published places from which the following section draws: "Comparing Households, Labour Markets and

Welfare States in Canada, Japan and Beyond," *Journal of Economics Quarterly* (Hokkai-Gakuen University) 51, no. 1 (June 2003): 43–57; "Revealing the Class-Gender Connection: Social Policy, Labour Markets and Households," *Just Labour: A Canadian Journal of Work and Society* 4 (summer 2004): 42–52; and www.justlabour.yorku.ca/Clement.pdf.

2 For a comparison of the same six countries, see Wallace Clement, "Who Works? Comparing Labor Market Practices," in *Reconfigurations of Class and Gender*, edited by Janeen Baxter and Mark Western (Stanford: Stanford University Press, 2001). John Myles and I pioneered comparative relational analysis of class and gender in *Relations of Ruling: Class and Gender in Postindustrial Societies* (Montreal and Kingston: McGill-Queen's University Press, 1994).

3 For mining, the main study is *Hardrock Mining: Industrial Relations and Technological Changes at Inco* (Toronto: McClelland and Stewart, 1981), with two essays, including one entitled "The Subordination of Labour in Canadian Mining," which is included in my collection *Class, Power and Property: Essays on Canadian Society* (Toronto: Methuen, 1983).

4 For fishing, the main study is *The Struggle to Organize: Resistance in Canada's Fishery* (Toronto: McClelland and Stewart, 1986), with two essays, including one entitled "Canada's Coastal Fisheries: Formation of Unions, Co-operatives and Associations," which is included in my collection *The Challenge of Class Analysis* (Ottawa: Carleton University Press, 1988).

REFERENCES

Ahrne, Göran, and Wallace Clement. 1992. A new regime? Class representation within the Swedish state. *Economic and Industrial Democracy: An International Journal* 13 (4): 455–79

Armstrong, Pat, and Hugh Armstrong. 1978. *The double ghetto: Canadian women and their segregated work.* Toronto: McClelland and Stewart

Bonoli, Giuliano. 1997. Classifying welfare states: A two-dimension approach. *Journal of Social Policy* 26:3

Braverman, Harry. 1974. *Labor and monopoly capital: The degradation of work in the twentieth century.* New York: Monthly Review Press

Duffy, Ann, Daniel Glenday, and Noreen Pupo, eds. 1997. *Good jobs, bad jobs, no jobs.* Toronto: Harcourt Brace Canada

Folbre, Nancy, and Julie A. Nelson. 2000. For love or money – or both? *Journal of Economic Perspectives* 14:4

Esping-Andersen, Gøsta. 1999. *Social foundations of postindustrial economies.* Oxford: Oxford University Press

Marx, Karl. 1967. Afterword to the second Germany edition of Karl Marx, *Capital* (unabridged edition of the first volume). New York: International Publishers

Mills, C. Wright. 1951. *White collar: The American middle class.* New York: Oxford University Press

O'Connor, Julia, Ann Orloff, and Sheila Shaver. 1999. *States, markets, families: Gender, liberalism and social policy in Australia, Canada, Great Britain and the United States.* Cambridge: Cambridge University Press

OECD (Organization for Economic Co-operation and Development). 2004. *Employment outlook, 2004.* Paris: OECD

Porter, John. 1965. *The vertical mosaic: An analysis of social class and power in Canada.* Toronto: University of Toronto Press

– 1987 [1979]. *The measure of Canadian society: Education, equality and opportunity.* Ottawa: Carleton University Press

3

Gendered Labour Market Insecurities: Manifestations of Precarious Employment in Different Locations

LEAH F. VOSKO

"Precarious employment" is an apt label for the state of work and labour in tumultuous times. Although it is a defining feature of labour markets in liberal industrialized countries, precarious employment takes shape in different ways in different contexts. The common assumption is that precarious employment corresponds with forms of employment and work arrangements that differ from the so-called standard employment relationship – or with forms that deviate from the norm of the full-time permanent job with benefits. This assumption is somewhat misleading, for less recognized is the manner in which precarious employment is also manifest in the deteriorating quality and character of full-time permanent employment itself.

This chapter paints a comparative portrait of precarious employment in Australia, Canada, and the United States, with attention to the gender dimension. It develops a "thick account" (Clement 2001) of the diverse manifestations of precarious employment, as well as of policies attempting to deal with them, in three countries with similar economic, political, and legal institutions and traditions. And it sketches the contours of an alternative approach to limiting gendered labour market insecurities.

The chapter unfolds in four sections, beginning in the first section by introducing the analytic concepts framing the discussion and its guiding methodological approach.

Moving to the body of the chapter, the second section describes two manifestations of precarious employment – in Australia and Canada – that are characterized by deviation from the standard employment relationship. This section sketches the nature and character of precarious part-time employment in Australia and precarious self-employment in Canada, exposing the regulatory gaps permitting their expansion and the politics behind these gaps.[1] In Australia, precarious employment takes particularly sharp expression in part-time ongoing casual employment. A disproportionate number of Australian women, many with young children, fall into this category. In Canada, a form of precarious employment that grew in significance in the 1980s and 1990s is full-time solo self-employment. A large segment of women, many of whom engage in this form of employment to fulfil caregiving responsibilities, falls in this group. In both Australia and Canada, attempts, at a policy level, to limit precarious employment centre on minimizing deviation from the standard employment relationship, either by curtailing the expansion of certain forms of work or by improving their quality and conditions. They conceive of this normative model of employment as a "leaky boat" and seek to plug its most serious leaks.

Shifting emphasis, the third section considers the deteriorating character of full-time permanent employment in the United States. In this context, many full-time permanent employees lack the certainty of continuing work, social benefits, such as employer-provided health-care coverage, and protections afforded by a collective agreement. Many also confront low income. Moreover, women, especially single women with young children, are highly vulnerable to precarious employment. The U.S. case illustrates the manner in which dimensions of precarious employment characterize the form of employment corresponding most closely to the standard employment relationship and thus the limits of focusing too narrowly on upholding a singular employment norm in efforts to mitigate gendered labour market insecurities.

After synthesizing the country-level findings, the fourth section sketches the contours of an alternative approach to curtailing precarious employment, one that offers promise in confronting its multiple and varied manifestations in liberal industrialized countries. The section concludes the chapter with some reflections on how a life-course approach to labour and social protection founded on gender equity could contribute to mitigating gendered labour market insecurities.

I THEORETICAL AND METHODOLOGICAL FOUNDATIONS

Analytic Concepts

A central limitation of the most common approaches to curbing precarious employment, particularly those that focus on forms of work that differ from the employment norm, is the tendency to dichotomize the standard employment relationship, defined by security and durability, and non-standard work, a catch-all term grouping together a wide range of forms of employment and work arrangements typically associated with insecurity and a lack of permanence. There is certainly a correlation between forms of employment (such as part-time temporary paid employment and solo self-employment) and work arrangements (such as multiple jobholding) and labour market insecurity in the Australian, Canadian, and American cases.[2] However, the notion of a standard/non-standard dichotomy is misleading, since it upholds a singular and gendered baseline – that is, the male norm of the standard employment relationship.[3] When we focus too narrowly on deviation from the employment norm, there is a danger that we will overlook or flatten important qualitative differences among employment forms and work arrangements and fail to capture the deterioration of full-time permanent employment.

To steer clear of these problems, this chapter focuses on *precarious employment* – that is, on forms of work involving limited social benefits and statutory entitlements, job insecurity, low wages, and high risks of ill health. Precarious employment is shaped by employment status (i.e., self-employment or paid employment), form of employment (i.e., temporary or permanent, part-time or full-time), and dimensions of labour market insecurity as well as social context, such as occupation, industry, geography, and social location (Vosko 2006). Employing this concept thereby opens space for probing both complex forms of deviation and the quality and character of employment that corresponds to the employment norm.

Another analytic concept framing this chapter that captures the interplay between the social norms and governance mechanisms linking work organization and the labour supply is the *normative model of employment* (Deakin 2002, 179; Supiot 2001). The standard employment relationship epitomizes this norm in liberal industrial democracies. First emerging in the 1920s and 1930s and reaching its apogee in the post–World War II period, it is a full-time continuous employment relationship where workers have one employer, work on the employer's premises under their direct supervision, normally in a unionized sector, and have access to social benefits and entitlements that complete the social wage (Mückenberger 1989). The contours of the standard employment relationship are similar in Australia (Owens 2002; Paterson 2003), Canada (Fudge and Vosko 2001b; Lowe and Schellenberg 2001), and the United States (Hyde 2000; Piore 2002), and this norm organizes labour and social policy in each instance.

The standard employment relationship was first limited primarily to male blue-collar workers, but it eventually extended to white-collar workers, also primarily men but including some women in the public sector (see, especially, Fudge 2002). However, as a norm, it exists independently of individuals and encompasses prescriptive and descriptive elements. Indeed, the social wage model integral to the standard employment relationship assumes that statutory benefits and entitlements, and employer-sponsored extended benefits, are best distributed to workers and their dependants via a single earner. This employment norm thus shapes familial obligations and household forms as well as the organization of the labour force. Historically, the standard employment relationship has also been linked to a particular *gender contract* – the final core concept in this chapter – or normative and material basis around which sex/gender divisions of paid and unpaid labour operate (Rubery 1998, 23). Alongside the emergence of this employment norm, a male breadwinner/female caregiver gender contract grew to dominance. This contract, however, is increasingly unstable in Australia, Canada, and the United States, albeit in different ways.

Methodological Approach

The distinct manifestations of precarious employment in Australia, Canada, and the United States call for a *thick comparison* of gendered labour market insecurities. Thick comparisons involve an in-depth and intensive analysis of the processes and policies that produce different or similar outcomes in specific comparative case studies (Clement 2001). They combine descriptive statistical analysis, analyses of laws and policies on the books and in practice, and other forms of documentary evidence from particular countries' case studies. The utility of a thick comparative analysis, in this instance, is that it allows us to focus on the defining features of each country rather than on a strict comparison.

The point of departure for this thick comparison is a statistical portrait of precarious employment in Australia, Canada, and the United States – one that troubles the standard/non-standard employment dichotomy, whereby non-standard work is treated as a catch-all category – by adopting an alternative approach to conceptualization and measurement.[4] Table 3.1 provides a snapshot of total employment in Australia, Canada, and the United States for 2000 by breaking it down into mutually exclusive categories. This approach aims to capture complex forms of deviation from the standard employment relationship – that is, forms of employment that differ from this norm on multiple bases – as well as the complexity of deviation and, at the same time, to depict the size of full-time permanent employment.

Table 3.1 Composition of total employment, Australia, Canada, and the United States, 2000

	Australia			Canada			United States		
	Men	Women	Both Sexes	Men	Women	Both Sexes	Men	Women	Both Sexes
Total employed	100	100	100	100	100	100	100	100	100
Paid employees	73	85	78	82	89	85	87	92	89
Permanent	55	55	55	72	77	74	84	88	86
Full-time	53	40	47	66	59	63	76	68	72
Part-time	2	15	8	5	17	11	8	20	14
Temporary	18	30	24	10	12	11	3	4	3
Full-time	9	7	8	7	6	7	2	2	1
Part-time	9	23	16	3	6	4	1	2	2
Self-employed	27	15	22	18	11	15	13	8	11
Solo	15	8	12	11	8	10	8	7	8
Full-time	13	3	8	9	5	7	7	4	5
Part-time	2	5	4	2	4	3	1	3	3
Employers	10	5	8	7	3	5	5	1	3
Full-time	9	3	7	7	2	5	5	1	3
Part-time	1	2	1	0	1	0	0	0	0

Sources: Survey of Employment Arrangements and Superannuation, 2000, Special Request, Australian Bureau of Statistics; Labour Force Survey, 2000, Public Use Microdata File Custom Tabulation, Statistics Canada; Current Population Survey and Contingent Worker Supplement, 2000, Public Use File Custom Tabulation, United States Bureau of Labor Statistics.

To reflect the diversity in the forms of employment differing from the standard employment relationship, Table 3.1 first elevates employment status by differentiating between paid employees and the self-employed. It then divides the self-employed into those without employees (solo self-employed) and those who employ others (employers). In parallel, it separates permanent and temporary employees. Finally, it splits each subgroup of employees and the self-employed by full-time and part-time status.

Breaking down total employment at a country level in this way links forms of employment differing from the norm to dimensions of precarious employment such as control over the labour process, employment certainty, and degree of regulatory protection (Rodgers 1989, 3–5). The first order of distinction in Table 3.1 (i.e., between employees and the self-employed) reflects workers' capacity to exercise control over the labour process and their degree of regulatory protection.

This is because labour and social protections extend most fully to workers with an identifiable employment relationship. Furthermore, in Australia, Canada, and the United States, few self-employed people have access to collective representation through a union (Cranford et al. 2005; Clayton and Mitchell 1999; Piore 2002).

The second order of distinction reflects the degree of certainty of continuing employment by grouping employees according to job permanency and distinguishing between the solo self-employed and employers. In each of the three countries, the solo self-employed are more vulnerable to uncertainty than employers (Fudge, Tucker, and Vosko 2002; Hyde 2000; O'Donnell 2004). Among employees, the category "permanent" signifies durability in the employment relationship, indicated normally by an indefinite contract of employment, while the category "temporary" approximates uncertainty. In Canada and the United States, all forms of temporary employment fall, as one would expect, within the temporary category.[5] The terminology is employed somewhat differently in Australia, however, where this category includes all casual employment[6] as well as employment on a fixed-term contract or paid by an agency. As Anthony O'Donnell (2004, 18) argues, a strong case can be made for "aggregating those jobs which, regardless of their extended tenure (or prospect for extended tenure), grant relatively unfettered power to the employer to terminate by virtue of their regulatory designation."[7] Consistent with a thick approach, the grouping together of all casual employment, employment on a fixed-term contract, and employment paid by an agency makes it possible to compare Australia with Canada and the United States.[8]

The third and final order of distinction also addresses access to social and regulatory protection in these countries, since eligibility for and/or level of certain social benefits is often pegged to hours of work.

Comparing countries, this portrait illustrates that the form of employment corresponding most closely to the standard employment relationship is quite fragile – especially in Australia and Canada, where only 48 and 63 per cent of people in the labour force held full-time permanent jobs in 2000 respectively. These percentages are lower than in the United States, where 72 per cent held full-time permanent jobs that year.

More than half of total employment in Australia and over one-third of that in Canada deviate from the employment norm. However, these deviations take different forms in each country. Part-time ongoing casual employment is dominant in Australia. In Canada, in contrast, full-time solo self-employment is prevalent and much of it is precarious, although sizable percentages of the workforce engage in permanent part-time employment and temporary full-time employment. Conversely, in the United States, almost three-quarters of total employment is full-time and permanent – the closest proxy for the norm – but much of it is precarious.

II PRECARIOUS EMPLOYMENT AS DEVIATION

How does precarious employment manifest itself in Australia and Canada? What social, political, and legal structures, institutions, and practices lie behind its central manifestations? Where are the regulatory gaps? And on what bases do the Australian and Canadian policies that seek to limit precarious employment operate?

Part-Time Ongoing Casual Employment in Australia[9]

In Australia, part-time ongoing casual employment, a highly gendered form of part-time employment, is a prime manifestation of precarious employment. Nearly half of all women work part-time in Australia as opposed to 28 and 26 per cent in Canada and the United States respectively. The importance of part-time employment to women reflects historical patterns in Australia, where women's low level of participation in full-time employment has remained constant since the 1930s.[10]

The composition of part-time employment in Australia is also unique. Part-time employment is more than twice as likely to be temporary in Australia than in Canada and over five times more likely to be temporary than in the United States. Breaking part-time employment into its core components provides greater insight into a prime manifestation of precarious employment in Australia. Accordingly, Figure 3.1 divides part-time employment into its six dominant forms: permanent paid employment; ongoing casual paid employment; fixed-term[11] casual paid employment; fixed-term non-casual paid employment; solo self-employment; and employer self-employment. Just 27 per cent of all those who work part-time are permanent employees. The remaining group is composed of those either employed on a casual or a fixed-term basis or self-employed.

Considering part-time employees, only one-third are permanent but nearly two-thirds are both ongoing and casual, while the remainder are fixed-term casual and non-casual (Figure 3.2). A disproportionate percentage of part-time employees fall into the ongoing casual category.[12]

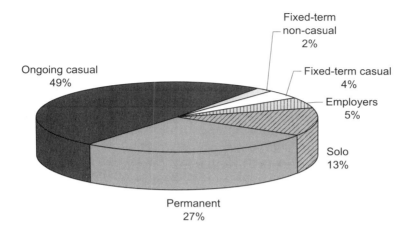

Figure 3.1 Composition of part-time employment, self-employed included, Australia, 2000

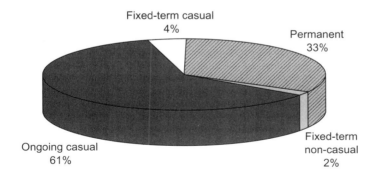

Figure 3.2 Composition of part-time employment, self-employed excluded, Australia, 2000

Part-time ongoing casuals are by far the largest group of part-time employees in Australia, and women are over-represented in this group. Out of all female part-time employees, one-quarter are on-going casuals, a sharp contrast to the just over one-tenth of all men. Furthermore, over two-thirds of part-time ongoing casuals are women as opposed to under one-third of men. In Canada and the United States, part-time work is primarily the domain of women with young children and some (primarily young) men pursuing education (Applebaum 2002a; Armstrong and Armstrong 1994; Duffy and Pupo 1992; Rosenfeld 2001; Vosko 2002). These patterns exist in Australia as well. However, the large proportion of female employees with young children who are part-time ongoing casual makes Australia unique. Out of all female employees with young children, approximately one-third are in this group.

Industrial and occupational segregation by sex also reflects the gendered character of this category. Female-dominated industries have the highest levels of part-time ongoing casual employees – accommodation, cafes, and restaurants followed by retail trade and cultural and recreational services.[13] Patterns are similar by occupation, although women in clerical, sales, and service occupations, a female-dominated group, are particularly likely to be engaged on a part-time ongoing casual basis.

The significance of part-time ongoing casual employment, and especially its gendered character, relates to the distinct social, legal, and political meaning of casual employment in Australia. In Australia, casuals normally work under a contract of employment, but they lack the full range of labour and social protections enjoyed by permanent employees. They rarely have entitlements that provide them with a modicum of income security, such as sick leave, annual leave, severance pay, maternity leave, and, in most instances, protection against unfair dismissal (O'Donnell 2004, 26).[14] Under Australia's awards system,[15] a key component of its rapidly declining system of centralized bargaining, casuals are defined as people who are normally paid at the end of each engagement. In exchange for being paid on the basis of supposedly limited engagements and the consequent uncertainty, casuals receive "casual loadings" or payments in lieu of entitlements (Campbell and Burgess 2001, 177; Owens 2001). Because of their low wages, many casuals rely on this compensatory premium (normally around 20 per cent) to bolster their income. However, this "precarity pay" does not remedy the gender income gap among ongoing part-time casuals, who have the largest differential among all part-time employees.[16] Casuals also have historically had less protection against unfair dismissal than their permanent counterparts; for example, whereas the probationary period was normally three months for non-casuals, casuals had to be employed for twelve months before they were protected from unfair dismissal under the Workplace Relations Act (1996) (Regulation 30 B (1) (d)). The increase in casual employment, which accounted for two-thirds of the growth of total employment between 1990 and 2001, was attributable partly to provisions under the Act.[17] Unpaid parental leave has also historically been accessible to a very limited group of casuals. In the early 2000s, casuals covered by certain federal awards who had worked for an employer on "a regular and systematic basis" over a period of at least twelve months and who had "a reasonable expectation of ongoing employment on that basis" had access to this statutory entitlement (s. 53 (1), (2) and s. 57).[18]

Casuals are employed under various types of contracts, including on "once-off" bases, where many labour protections do not apply, and on fixed-terms, where access to such protections depends on the length of the term (Stewart 1992). But a sizable number are in ongoing relationships where extensive labour and social protections should apply. These ongoing casuals do not have leave entitlements, have less protection against unfair dismissal than their permanent counterparts,[19] and have historically lacked entitlements to parental leave. As Rosemary Owens (2001, 18) contends, ongoing casual employees thus represent a "distinct class" in Australian society.

Several policies and practices have fostered the growth of part-time ongoing casual employment in Australia, especially among women. Most central is what Barbara Pocock, John Buchanan, and Iain Campbell (2004, 20) characterize as the "conjunction of permissive regulation of casual work with strict regulation of part-time work." In Australia, awards in key female-dominated occupations and industries rarely provide scope for expanding the number of part-time permanent employees. In contrast, awards in male-dominated industries and occupations routinely impose restrictions on the use of casuals,[20] although few awards in female-dominated occupations and industries set such limits. Policies and regulations applicable to female-dominated occupations have contributed to the magnitude of part-time ongoing casual employment by restricting access to permanent part-time employment. Under the South Australian Clerks Award, for example, it only became possible to work part-time hours, other than as a casual, in 1988 (Pocock, Buchanan, and Campbell 2004, 20).

To curb this manifestation of precarious employment, under mounting pressure from unions and social movement groups throughout the 1990s and early 2000s, the pre-Howard federal government (as well as some state governments) lent its support to two types of measures. The first set fostered conversion to permanent employment (full- and part-time) among ongoing casuals in female-dominated occupations. A chief example was the South Australia Clerks Award, which granted ongoing casuals with twelve months service the right to request to become permanent, a request that the employer could not refuse on unreasonable grounds. This approach had definitive limits, however. Instead of the safety net being extended to casuals automatically, workers had to elect to convert, a "choice" that obscured power imbalances between employees and employers (Owens 2002). The desire to limit casual employment to relationships that are genuinely irregular or intermittent nevertheless lay behind this "limitation approach." The perception was that policy-makers, as well as employers and unions, had lost sight of the true meaning of casual. As the argument went, "casual" had not been defined and interpreted properly, resulting in a regulatory gap.

The second set of measures sought to increase the scope for permanent part-time employment. For example, in key policy areas, such as parental leave, there was a movement to extend entitlements to ongoing casual part-time employees on the basis of equal treatment with other part-time employees. These proposals cast part-time employment positively, as enhancing social and economic objectives. Their aim was to construct "a new deal for part-time workers, to improve the quality of their jobs and ensure access to part-time work for parents who need it" (Buchanan and Thornthwaite 2001, 2). Those who supported these measures understood the problem of precarious employment in Australia as a problem of poor-quality part-time jobs. The idea was to improve part-time jobs by *decasualizing* those that are ongoing. By targeting mainly women with family responsibilities, however, such measures risked perpetuating a low-wage segment, mainly in female-dominated service industries.[21]

The fundamental problem with both sets of measures was that they focused narrowly either on limiting deviation from the standard employment relationship (e.g., measures to minimize ongoing casual employment) or on stretching this norm (e.g., measures directed at regularizing part-time employment, especially among women), with scant attention to (gendered) labour market insecurities more broadly. A related problem was that both sets of measures were cast in gendered terms – each was designed to enable *women* to "balance" caregiving and paid employment.

Full-Time Solo Self-employment in Canada[22]

In Canada, part-time permanent employment is the most common form of deviation from the employment norm, and full-time temporary

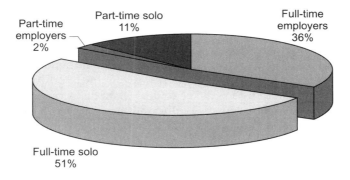

Figure 3.3 Composition of self-employment, both sexes, Canada, 2000

employment is also sizable. However, full-time solo self-employment is the dominant manifestation of complex deviation, and much of it is highly precarious.

Canada has a relatively high proportion of self-employment among OECD countries (15 per cent of total employment in 2000), and it sits at a midpoint between Australia and the United States (Table 3.1). From the late 1970s to 1998, self-employment grew at a faster rate than paid employment. Self-employment in Canada is quite varied, cutting across industry and occupation; it may involve employing others or working by oneself (i.e., solo); and it may be full-time or part-time.

Solo self-employment drove the growth in self-employment in the 1990s and then stabilized at relatively high levels. Moreover, full-time solo self-employment constitutes half of all self-employment (Figure 3.3), and this is the case among both men and women, which is notable since self-employment has historically been a male domain.

Much of full-time solo self-employment resembles paid employment; that is, it does not necessarily coincide with entrepreneurship (Fudge, Tucker, and Vosko 2002, 16; Dale 1991; Rainbird 1991).[23] This resemblance is gendered. Despite the widespread assumption that the self-employed are driven by entrepreneurial values, a substantial core of men (26 per cent) and women (23 per cent) pursue full-time solo self-employment because they cannot find suitable paid work. For many women though, caregiving responsibility is the foremost reason.[24] More women pursue full-time solo self-employment for caregiving reasons, while more men pursue it for entrepreneurial reasons. These patterns highlight the importance of examining the extent to which full-time solo self-employment not only resembles paid employment, but can also be precarious. They also underscore the importance of probing how various aspects of precariousness among this group are gendered.

Access to a full package of social benefits and entitlements akin to the social wage is a feature of high-quality employment. Among the self-employed, a good indicator is extended benefits coverage. In general, those in full-time solo self-employment have low levels of benefit coverage, and men and women lack benefits in equal measure. Indeed, a majority lack extended health coverage, a rate that also holds equally for both sexes. Among those with extended health coverage, coverage via a spouse is quite common, especially among women. Not only do many more women than men in the full-time solo group pursue self-employment because of caregiving responsibilities, many more women than men confront dependency as a consequence. Another indication of the degree to which full-time solo self-employment is precarious is income level,[25] especially when analysed in relation to benefits coverage and source of benefits coverage. One-quarter of all full-time solo self-employed people earn less than $20,000 annually, while only 16 per cent of full-time permanent employees are in this earnings category. And the percentage of women falling into the lowest-income group is almost double that of men.[26] Furthermore, as Figures 3.4 and 3.5 illustrate, almost a third of the full-time solo self-employed both earn less than $20,000 and have no benefits and/or no independent access to benefits, and among women the percentage rises to nearly half. A large segment of full-time solo self-employment not only resembles paid employment but is precarious, and the gender of precariousness, in this instance, is female.

The significance of full-time solo self-employment relates to the wide-ranging relationships that it incorporates – that is, the heterogeneous character of solo self-employment. Itself a blurred category,[27] solo self-employment includes self-employed contractors who normally have multiple clients and may contract for a service or product; this group includes artists and cultural workers of various sorts (MacPherson 1999; Vosko 2005), fishers (Clement 1986), construction workers (MacDonald 1998), and truck drivers (Madar 2000), as well as independent contractors who work directly for a contractor, such as newspaper carriers (Tucker 2005). It also includes so-called disguised employees who may "work for just one company, and whose status may be little more than a device to reduce total taxes paid by the firms and the workers involved" (OECD 2000, chap. 5, 187).

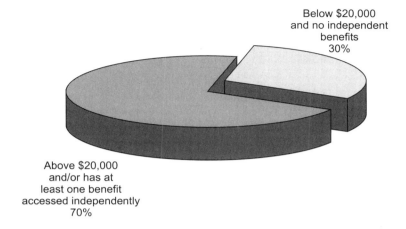

Figure 3.4 Income group and access to benefits among the full-time solo self-employed, both sexes, Canada, 2000

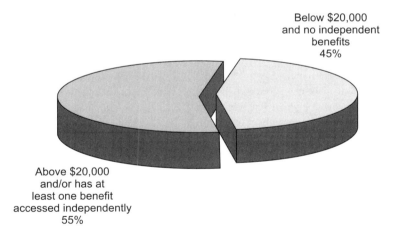

Figure 3.5 Income group and access to benefits among the full-time solo self-employed, women, Canada, 2000

Regardless of the subgroup to which they belong, solo self-employed persons are not necessarily engaged in enterprise self-employment. Yet there is a tendency, at a policy level, to equate self-employment of all sorts with entrepreneurship and to deny the self-employed access to labour protections on this basis (Fudge, Tucker, and Vosko 2002), cultivating dimensions of the precarious such as low levels of regulatory protection. This tendency is exacerbated by the promotion of self-employment as a viable alternative to paid employment in federal social insurance programs, such as Employment Insurance (EI), which includes a self-employment assistance program, and other targeted federal and provincial initiatives geared to increasing women's labour force participation.

At a policy level, there is some recognition that certain groups of self-employed people, especially those engaged in solo self-employment, not only require labour protection but require interventions on the part of the state and other social actors, such as unions, to reduce their precarious status. Accordingly, partly to curb precarious solo self-employment, in the latter part of the twentieth century, many federal and provincial policies, as well as practices of courts and administrative tribunals, emphasized maintaining the employment relationship as the access point for labour protection and, in many instances, they have expanded this concept (Fudge, Tucker, and Vosko 2002, 8; for a detailed review, see England, Christie, and Christie 1998, 2.1).[28] For example, to minimize the significance of the distinction between employees and independent contractors, legislators deemed persons not normally classified as independent contractors to be employees (Fudge, Tucker, and Vosko 2003a). A well-known example is the extension of collective bargaining rights to "dependent contractors," who are reliant economically on their clients, in the Canada Labour Code and various provincial statutes (Arthurs 1965; Bendel 1982; Davidov 2002).

Through such measures, groups such as editors and homecare workers gained access to, for example, collective bargaining rights (Cranford 2005; Vosko 2005). Several Canadian jurisdictions also minimized the salience of the employee/independent-contractor distinction under human rights legislation (e.g., federal, Nova Scotia, and Prince Edward Island), and a majority have done so under occupational health and safety standards (Commission for Labour Cooperation 2003, 14).[29] In the last quarter of the twentieth century, social policies changed as well. The Canada Pension Plan covers independent contractors, and Employment Insurance extends, with slight modifications, to specific groups of workers, such as fishers (Schrank 1998),[30] as well as to barbers, hairdressers, and manicurists who are not employees and some taxi drivers and drivers of other passenger-carrying vehicles (Fudge, Tucker, and Vosko 2002, 81–2).[31] Further-more, at century's end, the federal government introduced new legis-lation on the status of the artist, and parallel legislation emerged in Quebec, extending collective bargaining to independent contractors who are professional artists.

The boldest efforts to address forms of self-employment that resem-ble paid employment in Canada cater to specific groups of contrac-tors, such as artists, fishers, and owner-drivers, while the remainder (and indeed the majority) are concerned with limiting so-called dis-guised employment. The more dominant approach is to maintain the employee/independent-contractor distinction while simultaneously extending coverage, through other means, to workers resembling paid employees who would otherwise fall out of this definition. Virtually no attention has been paid to the pivotal question of whether labour pro-tection should extend primarily to employees. This is the central weak-ness of Canada's approach to curbing this manifestation of precarious employment. However, as Judy Fudge, Eric Tucker, and I (2002, 119–21) argue elsewhere, there is no principled reason for excluding from protection any persons who are dependent on the sale of their capacity to work, thereby providing openings for precarious self-employment, unless there is a compelling rationale.[32]

A related weakness of Canada's approach is its neglect of the gendered effects of piecemeal efforts to curb precarious employment, which, in the case of full-time solo self-employment, retain a male norm of not only employee status but entrepreneurship. A sizable pro-portion of full-time solo self-employment is precarious, and women in this category experience dimensions of precariousness disproportion-ately. Granted, there is growing recognition that many more women than men in self-employment endure financial hardship. In 2003, the Prime Minister's Task Force on Women Entrepreneurs proposed that maternity leave benefits be extended to self-employed women (Can-ada 2003, Recommendation 4.01). It also observed that "many [women] are in lower income categories than their male counter-parts" and that their socio-economic situation unfairly compromises their ability to save for retirement (Canada 2003, Recommendation 12.06). But recognizing – and seeking to redress – only the most seri-ous "leaks" in the normative model of employment is inadequate to the task of remedying gendered labour market insecurities.

III PRECARIOUS EMPLOYMENT AS DETERIORATION

How does precarious employment take expression in the United States, where three-quarters of total employment resembles the stan-dard employment relationship?

Full-Time Permanent Work in the United States[33]

In the United States, the magnitude of full-time permanent employment remains significant. Although part-time permanent employment represents 14 per cent of total employment and one-fifth of all employed women hold part-time permanent jobs, there is a much larger share of full-time permanent employment in the United States than in both Australia and Canada (Figure 3.6); furthermore, as a percentage of total employment, full-time employment has declined least in the U.S. context over time (Figure 3.7). But while the standard employment relationship is associated with durability, continuity, and security, full-time permanent employment – its closest proxy – does not necessarily reflect these characteristics in the United States.[34]

In the United States, "contingent work" is a common moniker used to connote temporary or transitory employment (Polivka 1996) – and for good reason.[35] The use of this concept – and its focus on a lack of permanency – relates to social and legal customs and conventions, and it provides clues as to the nature of precarious employment in this context, specifically, the deterioration of employment resembling the employment norm. In the face of high levels of full-time permanent employment, the focus on contingency reflects the virtual absence of legislation on unjust dismissal at the national and state levels. The United States has never had either a broad protection against unfair dismissal or discharge without just cause or a requirement for any period of notice through the common law or by statute. Rather, employment at will prevails – an employee can be discharged legally at any time "without notice for good reason, bad reason or no reason" (Commission for Labor Cooperation 2003, 26).[36] What this means, as Clyde Summers (2000, 69) argues, is that while permanent employment is *indefinite* employment, "indefinite employment [is], by definition employment at will."

The effects of employment at will on the security and durability of full-time permanent employment have varied over time, shaped by the rise and decline of a particular version of the standard employment relationship, fostered by the growth of internal labour markets (Doeringer and Piore 1971; Edwards, Gordon, and Reich 1982) and large vertically integrated firms (Hyde 1998; Stone 2001), and a particular version of the male breadwinner/female caregiver contract (Applebaum 2001; Fraser 1997). After World War II, implicit contracts for lifetime employment were common,[37] especially among white men. While employment at will did not disappear, employers "routinely entered into contracts in which people were effectively guaranteed lifetime employment" (Hyde 1998, 3). The postwar period was

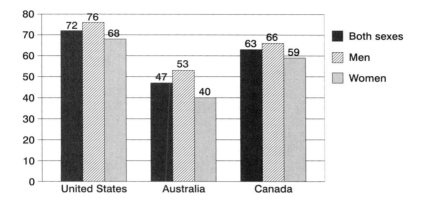

Figure 3.6 Full-time permanent employment, the United States, Australia, and Canada, 2001 (percentages)

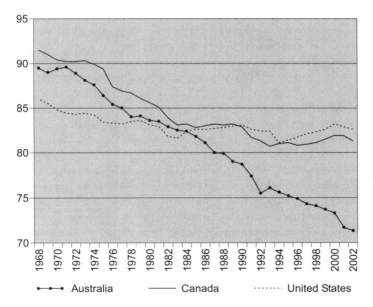

Figure 3.7 Decline of full-time employment, Australia, Canada, and the United States, 1968–2002 (percentages)

characterized by an implicit bargain between workers and employers that firms would invest in workers' acquisition of skills, provide workers with a range of social benefits and entitlements, including back-loaded benefits such as pensions, and increase workers' wages incrementally – all in exchange for workers' loyalty over the long term (Jacoby 1985; Stone 2001). After the early 1970s, however, with the contraction of internal labour markets, the breakup of vertically integrated firms, falling real wages, and declining rates of unionization, the lifetime employment model waned.[38] Americans endured "sharply accelerating rates of job separation" such that there were significant "increases in those responding to surveys [who reported] that they were involuntarily terminated and [in] the new phenomenon of intentional decreases in the size of the workforce previously found only in troubled companies" (Hyde 1998, 101; see also Block and Roberts 2000, 293). With the decline of job stability (Swinnerton and Wial 1995), protection against unfair dismissal has become more limited in the United States than in either Canada or Australia. Many American unions continue to negotiate collective agreements prohibiting dismissal without just cause, but even where these provisions exist, enforcement is a major challenge.[39] Consequently, a negligible percentage of total employment is temporary. Employment at will shapes the social meaning of *permanency* fundamentally and thereby the character and quality of full-time permanent employment.

Full-time permanent employment is surrounded by a high level of uncertainty in the United States. Yet what are its other characteristics? Medical benefits are the foremost social benefits historically linked to employment in the United States, in contrast to countries like Canada, where core medical coverage is not attached to either the contract of employment, the employer, or the workplace.[40] Most Americans with medical coverage (i.e., medical care, prescription drug, dental, and vision coverage) access it through plans provided by their employers and requiring employee contributions.[41]

Full-time permanent employees have significantly higher levels of independently accessed medical coverage than their part-time counterparts (Jacobs and Gerson 2004; USDOL 1999), but their rates of coverage provided by an employer are declining. Between 1989/90 and 1998/99, their coverage rate declined from 83 to 68 per cent (Figure 3.8). In private industry, where coverage is highest in white-collar occupations and lowest in service occupations and where large establishments are more likely than smaller ones to offer medical insurance, an even higher percentage of full-time permanent employees lack such coverage (44 per cent). The deterioration of full-time

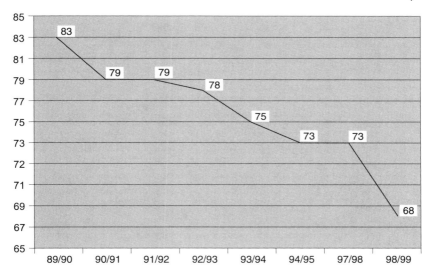

Figure 3.8 Medical-care coverage for full-time permanent employees, the United States, 1989/90–1998/99 (percentages)

permanent employment highlights the consequences of delivering such vital benefits primarily via the contract of employment.

Union membership, another feature identified with the standard employment relationship, is highly correlated with decent wages and social wage protections in the United States. It has also long served as a primary means of securing protection against unfair dismissal or discharge without just cause. Yet union membership declined dramatically in the post-1970 period, particularly in the 1980s and the 1990s, such that the proportion of all private sector non-agricultural employees who are union members in the current period is less than one-third of the proportion covered in the 1950s. Among all wage and salary workers, union membership declined from 20 per cent in 1983 to just 13 per cent in 2002 (Figure 3.9). The pace of decline was especially dramatic for men, whose membership rates dropped from 25 to 15 per cent, although women's membership rates still remain lower, standing at 12 per cent in 2002. Even among full-time permanent employees, rates of union membership are very low; only 14 per cent had the protection of a collective bargaining agreement in 2003.[42]

Alongside the decline in union membership in the United States, wages stagnated in the last quarter of the twentieth century. While real hourly earnings rose by more than half for production and non-supervisory workers in private sector non-agricultural industries after World

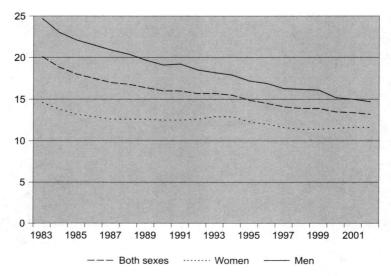

Figure 3.9 Union membership among wage and salary employees, the United States, 1983–2002 (percentages)

War II, when the male breadwinner/female caregiver contract reached its height at over half of all married couples, most of this growth occurred in the 1950s and 1960s (Figure 3.10). After peaking in 1973, real hourly earnings fell or stagnated for two decades, and they only began to stabilize in 1998. Wage inequality also grew in the 1980s and 1990s; according to the U.S. Department of Labor (USDOL 1999, 19), "after forty years of narrowing inequality, the high-to-low wage ratio[43] increased by 19 per cent between 1979 and 1999 (from 3.7 to 4.4), largely because low-wage workers' earnings fell dramatically [in the 1980s]."

Among all full-time permanent employees, average weekly wages stood at $788.70 in April 2004. Despite rising hours of work among this group, particularly among women, men earned $873.40 on average while women earned just $681.80 – a weekly wage gap of 78 per cent (Figure 3.11). There is a strong relationship between average weekly earnings of men and women, marital status, and presence or absence of young children. Among full-time permanent employees, average weekly wages are lower than the national average for both married and single people with children under six years of age. This is especially the case for women. The average weekly wages of women in full-time permanent employment who are married with children under six are lower than the average for all women ($675.60), and

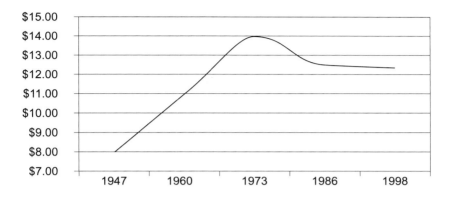

Figure 3.10 Average hourly earnings, the United States, 1947–1998 (in 1998 dollars)

Figure 3.11 Average weekly wages for full-time permanent employees, the United States, April 2004

Figure 3.12 Average weekly wages with children under age 6 by marital status,
full-time permanent employees, the United States, April 2004

they are lowest for single women with children under six ($424.30),
who comprise the majority of single parents in the United States (Figure 3.12).

Not only do many full-time permanent employees lack the protection
afforded by a collective agreement, along with the formal protections
against unjust dismissal and social wage benefits flowing normally from
such protection, but they earn hourly wages that leave them in poverty.[44]
An hourly wage of $8.70 or less is a conservative measure of low income
in the United States, as it amounts to $18,100 annually, the current offi-
cial poverty level for a family of four (Schulman 2003). Exploring low
income and union status together, Figure 3.13 depicts the percentage
of full-time permanent hourly employees that are not unionized and
earn less than $8.70/hour. In April 2004, 20 per cent of all full-time
permanent hourly employees were in this situation. One-fifth of all full-
time permanent hourly employees – and fully a quarter of women –
experience precariousness on these two dimensions.

In the United States, precarious employment takes sharp expression
in the deterioration of work that closely resembles the employment
norm. Employment that is full-time and permanent still dominates.
However, many full-time permanent employees lack the certainty of
continuing work, social benefits, such as employer-provided health-
care coverage, and protections afforded by a collective agreement.
Many also confront low income, and women, especially single women

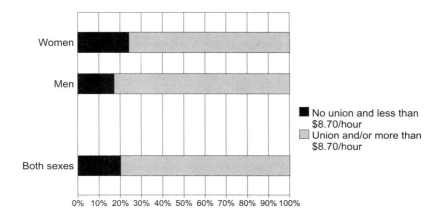

Figure 3.13 Percentage of full-time hourly permanent employees by union status and low-wage status, men and women, the United States, April 2004 (percentages)

with young children, are highly vulnerable to precariousness. The U.S. case highlights the complex character of precarious employment in liberal industrialized countries: not only is the standard employment relationship declining numerically, its quality is deteriorating and its meaning is shifting.

Despite the magnitude of full-time permanent employment, American efforts to curtail precarious employment primarily involve regularizing terms and conditions of work surrounding forms of employment deviating from the norm. The main recommendations of the Dunlop Commission on the Future of Worker-Management Relations (1994a), a joint commission of the U.S. Secretaries of Labour and Commerce that explored goals for the twenty-first-century American workplace, reflect this emphasis. The commission's recommendations included a proposal for adopting a single definition of employer and a single definition of employee "for all workplace laws based on the *economic realities* of the employment relationship," akin to the notion of the "dependent contractor" that exists in Canada in the federal labour code and in several provinces, and the "worker concept" in the United Kingdom (Dunlop Commission 1994a, 12, emphasis added; Freedland and Davies). However, it has not been taken up.[45]

Calls are also mounting for parity for workers in "non-standard jobs" with respect to hourly pay and pro-rated benefits regardless of employment status, proper classification of employees (including the prevention of the misclassification of temporary workers and independent contractors), and more good part-time jobs (Applebaum 2001, 26; Tilly 1996). And efforts to regulate market-mediated relationships, such as temporary-help work at the federal and state levels, have met with some success. For example, in March 2003, the U.S. House of Representatives passed a bill to limit the practice of misclassifying employees as independent contractors or temporary agency workers in order to deny them access to health, pension, leave, and other social benefits (U.S. House of Representatives 2003; Gonos 2001).

Despite this overriding emphasis on plugging the most serious leaks in the employment norm, some initiatives for change address deterioration more squarely, especially as it relates to instability in the gender contract. Initiatives among the most promising relate to working time, specifically to the length of work hours. Jerry Jacobs and Kathleen Gerson (1998, 466) make three proposals that could curtail the declining quality and character of full-time permanent employment in this context. Their first proposal is to extend the Fair Labour Standards Act (1938), which sets out federal minimum employment standards, to employees who are professionals and managers. These groups presently do not fall under this Act and are therefore not subject to existing wage and hours legislation. In practice, this means that employers are not required to pay them for overtime work. Since professional and managerial employees are at high risk of excessive weekly hours, Jacobs and Gerson argue that extending this Act would reduce overwork among salaried workers. Their second proposal is that the standard workweek be shortened slightly – to thirty-five hours – for all employees. Government could do this by providing tax incentives for employers to adopt shorter hour weeks, such as reduced payments into mandatory employer contribution systems. Jacobs and Gerson's third, and final, recommendation involves the introduction of mandatory pro-rated benefits for all employees. While the proposal relates to the American context, it has potential applications beyond it. Its goal is twofold: to discourage excessively long hours among salaried employees and to reduce working-hours polarization. The idea is to provide all employees with basic benefits that accrue on the basis of hours of work. As it stands, full-time workers do not receive additional increments in benefits if they work more than forty hours per week. At the same time, even if they work close to a full-time or standard workweek, part-time employees often do not receive any benefits. If implemented, this change could reduce the tendency among employers to require salaried employees to work excessive overtime, since there would be no cost savings in the provision of benefits. It would also improve the situation of part-time employees, many of whom work weekly hours equivalent to definitions of a full-time workweek in Canada or Australia. Using pro-rated benefits to limit excessive hours of work could curb deterioration and foster gender equity. Such proposals nevertheless fail to alter the baseline itself.

IV LIMITING PRECARIOUS EMPLOYMENT: PATHWAYS OF CONTINUITY AND CHANGE

The deterioration of full-time permanent employment in the United States and the prevalence of complex forms of deviation, such as part-time ongoing casual employment in Australia and full-time solo self-employment in Canada, highlight the magnitude of the challenge of limiting gendered labour market insecurities in liberal industrialized societies. There are, however, paths to follow that go beyond piece-meal efforts that address only the most serious leaks in the employment norm.

Labour and Social Protection: A Typology of Models

Approaches to limiting precarious employment may be conceptualized by developing a typology of models of labour and social protection defined by two intersecting continua – a continuum of mechanisms of protection and a continuum of different configurations of the gender contract. Figure 3.14 depicts this typology. Briefly, the horizontal axis depicts mechanisms that govern labour and social protection as they intersect with social norms. It distinguishes between approaches based on the employment relationship at one pole and the life-course at the other pole. The employment relationship approach organizes labour and social protection around the standard employment relationship. Under this approach, social benefits and statutory entitlements are accrued not only on the basis of participation in employment but, especially, on the basis of full-time permanent employment.

At the opposite pole, the life-course approach adopts a vision of labour and social protection that includes all people, regardless of their labour force status, from birth to death, in periods of training, employment, self-employment, and work outside the labour force, including voluntary work and unpaid caregiving (Supiot et al 2001). It is concerned with spreading social risks and is attentive to transitions in the life cycle, such as movements from paid employment to retirement and from school to work; it also values civic engagement (Gazier 2002; Schmid 2002). This approach assumes, moreover, that every worker, over the course of his or her lifetime, should maintain regular working hours in key periods, but should have access to reductions in working hours, as needed, while retaining access to comprehensive labour and social protections, as well as income supports (Applebaum 2002b, 142). The life-course approach conceives of working-time adjustments in a flexible manner to accommodate shorter working hours in periods of weak demand, ongoing voluntary community activities, periodic skills upgrading, phased-in retirement, and extended leaves, such as maternity and parental leave.

The intersecting vertical axis delineates the gender contract. This continuum is defined by an unequal-work/undervalued-care gender contract at one pole and a shared-work/valued-care gender contract (Applebaum 2002b) – or the universal caregiver model (Fraser 1997) – at the other pole. The unequal-work/undervalued-care gender contract places a high premium on labour force participation. The male breadwinner/female caregiver model is one version of this gender contract, as it assumes a primary male breadwinner with access to a standard employment relationship and a female caregiver principally performing unpaid work, often undervalued, and receiving social protection indirectly through her spouse. Yet there are other variations of this combination where dual earning is assumed, while caregiving is virtually ignored, perpetuating *de facto* (and highly marginalized) female caregiver norms.

The shared-work/valued-care contract at the opposite end of this continuum aims, in contrast, to reshape the behaviours, goals, and values of men and women and the social norms that they engender by limiting employers' ability to make demands on employees and by rewarding care, learning, and civic participation. Shared work encompasses a fairer distribution of paid work among people through shortened workweeks, limits to overtime, graduated benefits for part-time workers, flexible scheduling, and job-sharing associated with "family-friendly" working-time reforms (Applebaum 2002a, 95; Jacobs and Gerson 2004; Rosenfeld 2001). One central aim is to improve access to the labour force for those (mainly women) who conventionally bear the responsibility for children and other family members requiring care. Another is to foster a more equitable distribution of unpaid work between the sexes within and outside households, especially domestic labour and the care of children, and of other socially necessary unpaid work between households and communities. The flip side of this contract is socially valued care, which is linked, on the one hand, to giving people greater control over their time and, on the other hand, to improving caregiving as well as the terms and conditions of those who provide it (both paid and unpaid). For some, valued care entails enabling people to "negotiate the flexibility they need to meet their *individual responsibilities*" (Applebaum 2002a, 95, emphasis added). However, the sense in which it is used here entails both increased social responsibility for care (Eichler 1997) and an expansion of the public provision of services for those requiring care, with the attendant commitment to improve and expand public sector employment for caregivers to be more in line with countries such as Denmark (Esping-Andersen 2002, 120; Jackson 2006) and Sweden (Anxo 2002, 102, 104).

Locating Australia, Canada, and the United States

Australia, Canada, and the United States occupy distinct locations within this typology, positions that reflect the manifestation of precarious employment dominant in each context. The scale and gender of precarious part-time employment places Australia in the bottom right-hand quadrant of the typology of approaches (Figure 3.14). Reflecting complex deviation, part-time ongoing casual employment, a grouping populated principally by women, is sizable in this context. As a result, many women, especially women with young children, are unable to accrue entitlements to income security such as sick leave, annual leave, severance pay, maternity leave, and, in many cases, protection against unfair dismissal. In this instance, the policy direction gaining most prominence involves fostering the growth of permanent part-time employment for women through measures ranging from conversion for part-time ongoing casuals to interventions compensating this group more fully for their precarious situation and providing greater access to protections such as parental leave to more people (Buchanan and Thornthwaite 2001; Junor 1998; Pocock, Buchanan, and Campbell 2004). This modified approach sheds protective relics of an older order, but while it stretches the standard employment relationship to bring more women into the labour force, it retains this male norm.

In contrast to Australia, Canada sits closer to the life-course end of the labour and social protection continuum. Canada's location on this axis relates partly to its somewhat superior maternity and parental leave policies, especially for those eligible for paid leaves under Employment Insurance (still mainly employees with a considerable number of accumulated hours), although its policies compare very poorly with those of most European countries (Kamerman 2000; Vosko 2003). The recommendation of the Prime Minister's Task Force on Women Entrepreneurs to extend parental and maternity leave entitlements to self-employed workers reflects this orientation. And it attests to the greater social openness in Canada to displacing the male breadwinner/female caregiver gender contract in an attempt to move towards shared work and, to a lesser degree, valued care, evidenced by the growing commitment to measure unpaid work and

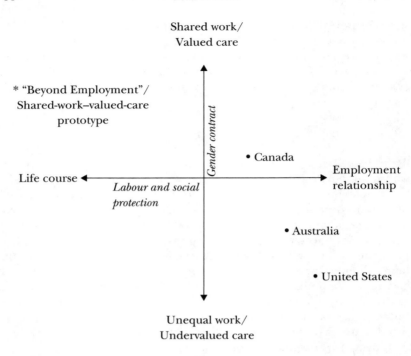

Figure 3.14 Models of labour and social protection: A typology

value it in key policy areas (e.g., pensions, caregiving for people with disabilities) (Bakker 1998; Townson 1997; Zukewich 2003). Still, Canada's focus on limiting "disguised employment," rather than extending comprehensive labour and social protections to a broader group of self-employed workers, places Canada at the employment relationship end of the labour and social protection continuum. Moreover, its placement along the gender contract continuum reflects growing tensions in public policy: without sufficient support for caregiving, the promotion of entrepreneurship among women positions Canada at a midpoint on this axis (Figure 3.14).

Among the three countries, the United States is situated at the farthest point on the employment relationship end of the labour and social protection continuum, given the size and character of full-time employment and the policy emphasis on employment as the primary route to economic security in this context. And it is positioned closer to Australia than to Canada on the gender contract continuum (Figure 3.14). In practice, however, the gender contracts in the United States and Australia are qualitatively distinct: in contrast to the bifurcation evident in men's and women's patterns of labour force participation in Australia, full-time permanent employment is increasingly common among women as well as men in the United States. Still, its dominance for both sexes has failed to dislodge female caregiving norms, since this form of work encourages all workers to behave as though they are not encumbered by responsibilities outside the labour force.[46]

CONCLUSION: TOWARDS AN ALTERNATIVE PARADIGM

Australia, Canada, and the United States occupy distinct locations in the typology of alternative models. However, all three countries uphold the standard employment relationship as a baseline, albeit to different degrees, and assign limited social value to caregiving. Their positions within the typology, however, are not fixed, nor need they be. Rather, despite the different manifestations of precarious employment prevailing in these three contexts, it is possible to envision approaches to curbing precarious employment that move "beyond employment" by building on proposals in the European Union (Supiot et al. 2001), where individuals are encouraged to share work and place value on activities outside the market.

The greatest promise for an alternative paradigm lies in the top left quadrant of the typology, where it is possible to envisage a "beyond employment"/shared-work–valued-care prototype (Figure 3.14). Drawing inspiration from *Transformation of Labour and Future of Labour Law in Europe* (European Commission 1998), this prototype embraces a broad concept of work that covers all people "in both periods of inactivity proper and periods of training, employment, self-employment and work outside the labour market," where "work outside the labour market" includes training at one's own initiative, voluntary work, and care for others (Supiot et al. 2001, 55). The prototype calls for replacing the paradigm of employment with a paradigm of labour market membership based on the notion of *statut professionel*, or the idea that "an individual is a member of the labour force even if he or she does not currently have a job" (Supiot et al. 2001, x). More consistent with a life-course approach, the idea is to allow for breaks between jobs as well as life cycle changes, to reject a linear and homogeneous conception of working life tied to the employment contract (Supiot et al. 2001, C.1).

Rather than treating "regular" part-time employment as a valid variation on the norm and calling for an extension of benefits, advocates of this prototype support reducing working time for all people over the course of their lives and reorganizing production for the market to reflect its different phases. They embrace "worker-time" to reconcile occupational and personal life, encourage genuinely work-centred flexibility, and promote the redistribution of employment (Supiot et al. 2001, 84; for a similar proposal for Canada, see Fudge and Vosko 2001a). This type of working-time adjustment resembles developments in Germany[47] and the Netherlands,[48] influenced partly by the European Commission's *Directive on Part-Time Work* (1997), that have met with some success.

Social drawing rights are a hallmark of this prototype. They are a means of facilitating or easing labour market transitions without the loss of essential protections. These public rights are essentially "a new type of social right related to work in general (work in the family sphere, training work, voluntary work, self-employment, working the public interest, etc.)" that are based on a prior contribution to the labour force, but are "brought into effect by the free decision of the individual and *not as a result of risk*" (Supiot et al. 2001, 56, emphasis added). On the question of the employment relationship as a gateway to labour protection, this prototype also casts as of central importance people's need for freedom to work under different statuses without forfeiting social rights and entitlements (Supiot et al. 2001, 10). Adding to arguments for collapsing the distinction between employees and the self-employed, it is concerned less with quantitative changes than with qualitative changes across the employment relationship.

Advocates of moving beyond employment in Europe devote scant attention to exploring ways to foster greater sharing of unpaid caregiving among men and women. However, they acknowledge a significant danger, namely, that the emerging social and legal system of production "will be built along strongly biased gender lines, discriminating against women from the standpoint of economic independence and professional careers; and against men with respect to the developments of bonds of affection and family relations" (Supiot et al. 2001, 180). Proposals for moving beyond employment reject a policy direction that would compel workers to trade off precarious conditions for the type of flexibility necessary if they were to engage in unpaid caregiving, volunteer work, training, or other activities in the public interest. But to advance genuine change in the gender contract, both high-quality opportunities for training and employment for men and women and a greater emphasis on socially valued and shared caregiving are needed – in sum, a contract characterized by universal earning, learning, and caregiving. For this type of gender contract to be assured, new and modified rights and entitlements must be public; that is, these social rights and entitlements must be derived from one's presence in a community (be it local, subnational, national, or supranational) and made meaningful through effective state policies and supports. It is critical that analysts be cognizant of the risk of privatization (or marketization). Such rights and entitlements derived beyond employment, like those flowing from the standard employment relationship dominant in the late twentieth century and its associated citizenship norm, are not, by definition, incontrovertible. Maintaining them in the service of gender equity thus requires devising appropriate policy mechanisms as well as engaging in continuous struggles to anticipate potential regulatory gaps (broadly conceived) and attempts to exacerbate these pitfalls.

Although it is an ideal type, the "beyond employment"/shared-work–valued-care prototype offers a paradigm for moving forward in curtailing precarious employment in liberal industrialized countries. By shifting away from a singular employment norm and opening space for a plurality of employment forms and work arrangements, it has the potential to counter both the deterioration of full-time permanent employment and the complex forms of deviation. At the same time, by recognizing the need to share caregiving and assign it greater social value, the prototype shows greater promise than the piecemeal approaches that plug only the most serious leaks in the boat.

NOTES

Author's Note: The research for this chapter was made possible by the Social Sciences and Humanities Research Council of Canada (Grant # 410–2000–1362). I also benefited from the support provided by the Law Commission of Canada for a related project on gender and the international regulation of precarious work. I am grateful to the editors of this volume, Wallace Clement and Vivian Shalla, for their incisive comments on an earlier version of this text, and to Kate Laxer and Kim McIntyre for their able research assistance. The Australian case study covers developments to March 2006. Changes to Australian labour policy introduced under the federal government's Work Choices legislation shortly thereafter make several risks of casualization posed by the magnitude of part-time ongoing casual employment in Australia – and identified in this chapter – realities. All errors and omissions are my own.

1 In this chapter, I conceive of regulatory gaps or failures in a socio-legal sense. They are understood to flow from disparities of treatment between workers in precarious employment and workers with greater security, gaps in legal coverage, and a lack of compliance and enforcement, as well as the interaction between labour market position and social location (for an overview of this interdisciplinary conception of regulatory failure, see Bernstein, Lippel, Tucker, and Vosko 2006).

2 For studies of Australia that highlight this correlation, see Pocock, Buchanan, and Campbell 2004; Burgess and Campbell 1998; O'Donnell 2004; Owens 2002. For studies based on the Canadian case, see Fudge 1997; Hughes 2003; Krahn 1995. For similar evidence from the United States, see Jacobs and Gerson 2004; Polivka 1996.

3 For country-specific examples exhibiting the limitation of this distinction and especially how it upholds this baseline, see Campbell 1995; Cranford, Vosko, and Zukewich 2003; Owens 2002.

4 This approach was first developed by the author, along with Nancy Zukewich and Cynthia Cranford, as a critique of traditional approaches to conceptualizing and measuring non-standard work and contingent work in Canada (see Vosko, Zukewich, and Cranford 2003). The discussion that follows applies this approach to Australia and the United States and develops it further (see especially Table 3.1).

5 In Canada, temporary work includes seasonal, contract, casual, and "other temporary" work, including work through a temporary agency. In the United States, it includes all employees that describe their employment situation as temporary.

6 Casual employment is defined by the Australia Bureau of Statistics (ABS) as all paid employment lacking leave entitlements (both sick leave and paid annual leave). Following Joo-Cheong Tham (2003, 3), I therefore use the lack of leave entitlements to define casual employment to reflect the long tradition in Australia's industrial relations system.

There is a growing movement to redefine the category "casual" in ABS surveys to conform to what O'Donnell (2004) labels its "vernacular" meaning – that is, intermittent, irregular, or on-call. This tendency is evident in recent surveys that permit analysts to adopt the concept "self-identify casual," such as the Forms of Employment Survey and the Survey of Employment Arrangements and Superannuation, to capture the so-called true casual. However, this approach is questionable because the vernacular conception of true casual has very little meaning at either a contractual or regulatory level. The significance of the category "casual" and its legal meaning are discussed at length below.

7 See also Campbell 1998 (108), which highlights the similarities between casual employment in Australia and temporary employment in the EU.

8 This grouping is also consistent with that used by the OECD in defining temporary employment in Australia for the purpose of comparison.

9 The statistical profile of precarious part-time employment in Australia in this section is based on a special request from the Survey of Employment Arrangements and Superannuation, 2000, Australian Bureau of Statistics.

10 As Belinda Probert (1997, 186) illustrates, in 1933, 25.2 per cent of women were in full-time employment and, in 1994, the figure was just 27.1 per cent.

11 The category "fixed-term" is used to refer to employment either on a fixed-term basis or paid by an agency, since the latter is such a small group.

12 The statistical category "part-time ongoing casual" includes all part-time employees who lack leave entitlements (i.e., are not entitled to paid holiday or sick leave) and are neither on a fixed-term contract or paid by an agency. Among this group, 74 per cent expect to be with their current employer in twelve months time. This definition is inspired by the findings of other earlier studies that reveal the long job tenure of many casuals in Australia (e.g., Campbell 1998, 72; Owens 2001).

13 Furthermore, in the two industries with the highest levels, a majority of women employees hold part-time ongoing casual positions.

14 Except where noted otherwise, the ensuing discussion of the status of casual employees at the regulatory and contractual levels refers to federal examples.

15 In Australia, awards have historically represented the primary mechanism of centralized collective bargaining. Long dominant at both the federal and state levels, they set basic terms and conditions of employment in a given sector or occupation across a specified jurisdiction. This system is under challenge, especially after the introduction of the Work Choices Act in 2006.

16 On a weekly basis, female part-time ongoing casuals earn 88.2 per cent of that earned by their male counterparts.

17 Under this Act, the power of the Australian Industrial Relations Commission to make or vary industrial awards was curtailed – the commission could no longer limit the number or proportion of employees that an employer may employ in "a particular type of employment" (s. 89 A (4)). With the introduction of the Work Choices Act in spring 2006, the federal government limited unfair dismissal protection for all workers employed in firms of less than one hundred. This casualization of the entire labour force was nevertheless accompanied by lesser access to unfair dismissal protections for ongoing casuals.

18 At the state level, the movement to grant casuals family leave has also been incremental. For example, the Queensland Industrial Relations Act (s. 16, 39 (2), 40) extends family leave, caregiver's leave, and bereavement leave to ongoing casuals, defined as "a casual employee engaged by a particularly employer on a regular and systematic basis, for several periods of employment during the period of at least a year" (s. 15 (A)). Yet many other states still exclude casuals from access to parental leave (e.g., South Australia and Western Australia).

19 Enforcement has historically been a major obstacle in gaining access to protection against unfair dismissal because, as Joo-Cheong Tham asserts (2003, 8), "more often than not, the employer and the casual employee would not have expressly adverted to this question [i.e., whether their relationship is ongoing]. In these circumstances, it becomes a nice question of fact where the casual employee is engaged on an ongoing contract."

20 The South Australian Clerks Award and the Metal, Engineering and Associated Industries Award are cases point. For an incisive commentary on these awards, see Owens 2001. Furthermore, half of the eighty-six awards in manu-

facturing set maximum periods of engagements for casuals of two to four weeks and over two-thirds set eight-week maximums (Pocock, Buchanan, and Campbell 2004, 24).

21 As Ann Junor (1998) and Belinda Probert (1995, 1997) argue, the promotion of part-time permanent employment as a strategy for women had enabled employers to avoid overtime because in Australia part-time employees can be asked to work up to full-time without supplemental pay.

22 The statistical profile of precarious self-employment in Canada in this section is based on a special request from the Survey of Self-employed, 2000, Public Use Microdata File Custom Tabulation, Statistics Canada. Elements of this section build conceptually on research conducted by the author in collaboration with Judy Fudge and Eric Tucker on the legal concept of employment (Fudge, Tucker, and Vosko 2002) and with Nancy Zukewich on gender and precarious self-employment (Vosko and Zukewich 2006).

23 The solo self-employed, more broadly, are more likely to receive some kind of support from their clients than their employer counterparts – 40 per cent reported receiving support from their clients in 2000 (Delage 2002, Table B.7). And many have few clients – fully 51 per cent had five or fewer clients in 2000 (Lowe and Schellenberg 2001, Table 4.2).

24 A third of women in full-time solo self-employment cite "balancing work and family" and "work from home" as their main reason for self-employment – five times the number of men.

25 The Survey of Self-Employment allows for analysis of income by four major income groups: less than $20,000; $20,000–$40,000; $40,000–$60,000; and $60,000 plus. The ensuing analysis considers the full-time solo self-employed with incomes under $40,000. It also considers those with incomes of under $20,000, since this group is unequivocally precarious along the dimension of income level.

26 This figure is consistent with other studies. For example, although they do not break down self-employment by type, Lin, Yates, and Picot (1999) reveal that almost three-quarters of self-employed women (72 per cent) earned less than $20,000 in 1994 compared to 48 per cent of women employees.

27 Data indicate that the number of solo self-employed may, in practice, be larger than is often estimated, since conventional measures fail to capture the degree to which people move between solo and employer forms. The self-employed who do not hire others in a given reference year are normally classified as solo self-employed, while the self-employed who hire others are considered employers.

28 This has often involved moving from tests resting on control and subordination to tests centring on economic dependence, a tendency growing in the post-1960 period (Arthurs 1965; Bendel 1982; Davidov 2002).

29 For a broader discussion of legislation focusing on social justice, see Fudge, Tucker, and Vosko 2002, 65–73.

30 Fishers' EI is financed by self-employed fishers and designated employers and qualifying requirements are organized on the basis of earnings rather than hours.

31 Among these groups, Employment Insurance is extended to those who are not employees and who neither own nor operate the business, nor own more than 50 per cent of the vehicle, and who are provided supports, such as tools, equipment, and other resources, by the business operator. In these cases, contributions are split between the owner or operator of the business and the self-employed person.

32 We include the following areas of labour regulation in our recommendations: anti-discrimination law, pay and employment equity legislation, occupational health and safety legislation, minimum standards legislation, collective bargaining legislation, and social wage and social revenue legislation. Yet we acknowledge that there may be relevant distinctions between different groups of workers that should be taken into account in the design of instruments to provide labour protections to all workers regardless of the type of income they receive.

33 The statistical profile of full-time permanent employment in this section is based on Figure 3.6 (whose sources were, for Australia, the 2000 Survey of Employment Arrangements and Superannuation, Special Request, Australian Bureau of Statistics; for Canada, the 2000 Labour Force Survey, Public Use Microdata File Custom Tabulation, Statistics Canada; and for the United States, the February 2000 Current Population Survey and Contingent Worker Supplement, Public Use File Custom Tabulation, United States Bureau of Labor Statistics), Figure 3.7 (whose sources were OECD Labour Force Statistics: Indicators), Figure 3.8 (whose source was William J. Wiatrowski, 26 May 2004, "Documenting Benefits Coverage for all Workers," Compensation and Working Conditions Online, USDOL), Figure 3.9 (whose source was "Women in the Labor Force: A Databook," USDOL, February 2004, 70–1), Figure 3.10 (whose source was futurework: *Trends and Challenges for Work in the 21st Century*, 1999, USDOL), and Figures 3.11, 3.12, 3.13a–c (whose source was April 2001 Current Population Survey, Public Use File Custom Tabulation, United States Bureau of Labor Statistics).

34 Owing to data limitations, the proxy used for full-time permanent employment in the ensuing analysis is full-time employment. Aside from the technical reasons, there is a good rationale for adopting this proxy: full-time temporary employment accounts for just 1 per cent of total full-time employment.

35 The U.S. Bureau of Labour Statistics classifies contingent workers as people who expect their job to end (some with a predetermined end-date), many of whom are employees and the rest of whom are self-employed or independent contractors. Three definitions dominate, each pivoting on certainty: the first includes all wage and salary workers who do not expect their job to last. This

definition corresponds with the Canadian definition of temporary work. The second definition narrows the focus to employment of very limited duration by including only those wage and salary workers who expect to work in their current job for one year or less and who have worked for their current employer for less than one year. The third definition broadens the second by including self-employed workers who expect to be, or have been, in their current employment situation for one year or less (Vosko, Zukewich, and Cranford 2003, 17; see also Belman and Golden 2002; Polivka 1996).

36 Where the gender contract is concerned, this means that "workers in the US can be – and frequently are – fired if their family responsibilities interfere with their jobs" (Applebaum 2002b, 94).

37 I borrow the term "lifetime employment" from Alan Hyde (1998), although similar concepts are used by Stone (2001) and Jacoby (1985).

38 In the face of the decline of this model, to cushion the potentially severe effects of employment at will, three judicially created exceptions emerged: the public policy exception, the handbook rule, and an exception based on the covenant of good faith and fair dealing, "an implied obligation in every contract" (Summers 2000, 72). State courts gradually recognized these means of challenging employee discharges, but these measures did not forestall the growing uncertainties surrounding permanent employment. Furthermore, the positive impacts for employees of judicially created exceptions on unfair dismissal became weaker in the 1990s. Some judicial exceptions still prevail but Montana remains the only state that provides to all non-union employees broad legal protection against wrongful dismissal (Commission on Labor Cooperation 2003).

39 Two pieces of federal legislation seek to remedy this problem. The federal Worker Adjustment and Retraining Notification Act (1989) requires large employers (i.e., those employing 100 or more full-time employees or a 100 of more full-time and part-time employees who work an aggregate of at least 4,000 hours per week, exclusive of overtime) to provide sixty days advance notice of planned plant closings and mass layoffs. The Consolidated Budget Reconciliation Act (1985) requires employers that provide a group health insurance plan (excluding churches, public employers, and employers that normally employ fewer than twenty employees) to offer participating employees and their spouses and dependent children the chance to continue coverage when they are discharged, except for "gross misconduct"; such coverage may continue for 18–36 months.

40 In Canada, while there are various means of extending labour and social protections, medical care and health insurance flow from what Brian Langille (2002, 140) aptly labels a "citizenship platform," which provides social infrastructure regardless of an individual's labour force status.

41 Public health insurance is available to the elderly through Medicare. It is also provided to a segment of people with low-incomes through Medicaid. The

remainder of the population must either secure benefits through an employer, self-insure (a practice common among the self-employed), or go without these benefits altogether. In 1997, 17 per cent of non-elderly U.S. residents did not have access to either public health insurance or employer-based plans.

42 These trends are also gendered: 13 per cent of women, in contrast to 15 per cent of men, were unionized that year.

43 The wage ratio is measured by the Bureau of Labor Statistics as the ratio of a high-wage worker's earnings (in the 90th percentile of the wage distribution) to that of the low-wage worker's earnings (in the 10th percentile). The figures cited here reflect weekly earnings ratios.

44 The ensuing discussion focuses on full-time permanent hourly employees for technical reasons. In order to be able to generalize the analysis to all full-time permanent employees, I use indicators of a lack of control over the labour process and a low income level suitable for both salaried and hourly employees. I also omit employee-sponsored health-care benefits from the analysis, since they are more common among salaried than hourly employees (Jacobs and Gerson 1998, 461).

45 Notably, since the federal Fair Labour Standards Act and the Occupational Health and Safety Act already employ this approach.

46 The Family Medical Leave Act is an improvement in the United States that works somewhat against the grain. However, few men and women employees can access such leaves, including those who are part-time and/or temporary and those who work in small firms (Kamerman 2000). Leaves are also unpaid, unless employers subsidize them, and the career penalties for people who take breaks from employment are often great due to the structure of weekly hours and high levels of wage inequality.

47 The German Act on Part-Time Work and Fixed-Term Contracts (2001) confers a right to reduced work time to all employees (full-time and part-time) with six months continuous service whose employer regularly employs more than fifteen people (section 8). Employers, however, may deny employees this right by invoking "business reasons," and there are few checks to police this provision (Burri, Opitz, and Veldman 2003, 322). The objective of this measure is to lessen unemployment and to allow employees to fulfil family responsibilities and/or to engage in unpaid voluntary work, training, apprenticeship, or educational programs (Burri, Opitz, and Veldman 2003). The Act also grants part-time employees who fulfil these criteria to extend their working time (section 9) and compels the employer to "give preference to an interest [in] an extension of working time unless this would conflict with *urgent* operational reasons or requests of other part-time employees." This measure aims to cultivate greater equality between men and women by fostering a better gender balance not only among those who work part-time but also among those who work full-time.

48 Even stronger than its German counterpart, the Dutch Working Time
Adjustment Act (2000) grants employees a statutory right to both reduce and
extend working time unless an employer can demonstrate that serious business reasons preclude the granting of such a request. In this way, Dutch
legislation challenges dominant definitions of regular weekly hours (Burri
2001).

REFERENCES

Abraham, K.G. 1990. Restructuring the employment relationship: The
growth of market mediated employment relationships. In *New developments
in the labour market,* edited by K. Abraham, 86–120. Boston: MIT

Anxo, D. 2002. Time allocation and the gender division of labour of France
and Sweden. In *The future of work, employment and social protection: The
dynamics of change and the protection of workers,* edited by P. Auer and C.
Daniel, 99–108. Geneva: Ministry of Social Affairs, Labour and Solidarity;
France: International Institute for Labour Studies

Applebaum, E. 2001. Transformation of work and employment and new
insecurities. In *The future of work, employment and social protection: The
dynamics of change and the protection of workers,* edited by P. Auer and B.
Gazier, 17–36. Geneva: Ministry of Social Affairs, Labour and Solidarity;
France: International Institute for Labour Studies

Applebaum, E. 2002a. Introductory remarks: Shared work/valued care: New
norms for organizing market work and unpaid care work. In *The future of
work, employment and social protection: The dynamics of change and the protection
of workers,* edited by P. Auer and B. Gazier, 93–6. Geneva, Ministry of Social
Affairs, Labour and Solidarity; France: International Institute for Labour
Studies

Applebaum, E. 2002b. Synthesis of *The future of work, employment and social
protection: The dynamics of change and the protection of workers,* edited by P.
Auer and B. Gazier, 141–5. Geneva: Ministry of Social Affairs, Labour and
Solidarity; France: International Institute for Labour Studies

Armstrong, P., and H. Armstrong. 1994. *The double ghetto: Canadian women
and their segregated work.* Toronto: McClelland and Stewart

Arthurs, H.W. 1965. The dependent contractor: A study of the legal problems
of countervailing power. *University of Toronto Law Journal* 16:89–117

Bakker, I. 1998. *Unpaid work and macroeconomics: New discussions, new tools for
action.* Ottawa: Status of Women Canada

Belman, D., and L. Golden. 2002. Which workers are non-standard and
contingent and does it pay? In *Flexible work arrangements: Conceptualizations
and international experiences,* edited by I.U. Zeytinoğlu, 241–68.
Netherlands: Kluwer Law International

Bendel, M. 1982. The dependent contractor: An unnecessary and flawed development in Canadian labour law. *University of Toronto Law Journal* 32:374–411

Bernstein, S., K. Lippel, E. Tucker, and L.F. Vosko. 2006. Precarious employment and the law's flaws: Identifying regulatory failure and securing regulatory effectiveness for workers. In Vosko 2006, 203–20

Block, R., and K. Roberts. 2000. A comparison of labour standards in the United States and Canada. *Relations Industrielles/Industrial Relations* 55 (2): 293–317

Buchanan, J., and L. Thornthwaite. 2001. *Paid work and parenting: Charting a new course for Australian families.* Sydney: University of Sydney

Burgess, J., and I. Campbell. 1998. The Nature and Dimensions of Precarious Employment in Australia. *Labour and Industry* 8 (3):5–21

Burri, S. 2001. Part-time work in the Netherlands: Towards policies on differentiation of working time during one's lifetime? *EuroAS* 11:208–17

Burri, S.D., H.C. Opitz, and A.G. Veldman. 2003. Work-family policies on working time put into practice: A comparison of Dutch and German case law on working time adjustment. *International Journal of Comparative Labour Law and Industrial Relations* 19 (3): 321–46

Campbell, I. 1998. *Labour restructuring and the growth of casual employment in Australia, 1982–1996.* Melbourne: University of Melbourne, Australia

Campbell, I., and J. Burgess. 2001. Casual employment in Australia and temporary employment in Europe: Developing a cross-national comparison. *Work, Employment and Society* 15 (1): 171–84

Canada. 2003. *Prime-Minister's Task Force on Women Entrepreneurs.* Ottawa: Ministry of Supply and Services

Clayton, A., and M. Mitchell. 1999. *Study on the employment situations and worker protection in Australia: A report to the International Labour Office.* Melbourne: Centre for Employment and Labour Relations Law at the University of Melbourne

Clement, Wallace. 1986. *The struggle to organize : Resistance in Canada's fishery.* Toronto: McClelland and Stewart

– 2001. Who works? Comparing labor market practices. In *Reconfigurations of class and gender,* edited by Janeen Baxter and Mark Western, 55–80. Stanford: Stanford University Press

Commission for Labor Cooperation. 2003. *The rights of nonstandard workers: A North American guide.* Washington, D.C.: Secretariat of the Commission for Labor Cooperation

Cranford, C. 2005. From precarious workers to unionized employees and back again? The challenges of organizing personal-care workers in Ontario. In Cranford et al. 2005

Cranford, C., J. Fudge, E. Tucker, and L.F. Vosko. 2005. *Self-employed workers organize: Law, policy, and unions.* Montreal and Kingston: McGill-Queen's University Press

Cranford, Cynthia, Leah F. Vosko, and Nancy Zukewich. 2003. The gender of precariousness in the Canadian labour force. *Relations Industrielles/Industrial Relations* 58 (3): 454–82

Dale, A. 1991. Self-employment and entrepreneurship: Notes on two problematic concepts. In *Deciphering self-employment*, edited by R. Burrows, 35–51. London and New York: Routledge

Davidov, G. 2002. The three axes of employment relationships: A characterization of workers in need of protection. SJD dissertation, University of Toronto

Deakin, S. 2002. The many futures of the contract of employment. In *Labour law in an era of globalization: Transformations, practices and possibilities*, edited by J. Conaghan, M. Fischl, and K. Klare, 177–96. London: Oxford University Press

Delage, B. 2002. Results from the survey of self-employment in Canada. Hull, Que.: Human Resources Development Canada

Doeringer, P.B., and M.J. Piore. 1971. *Internal labor markets and manpower analysis*. Lexington, Mass.: Heath Press

Duffy, A., and N. Pupo. 1992. *Part-time paradox: Connecting gender, work and family*. Toronto: McClelland and Stewart

Dunlop Commission on the Future of Worker-Management Relations. 1994a. *The Dunlop Commission on the future of worker-management relations: Final report*. Washington, D.C.: Secretary of Labor and Secretary of Commerce

– 1994b. *Fact finding report: Commission on the future of worker-management relations*. Washington, D.C.: Secretary of Labor and Secretary of Commerce

Edwards, R., D. Gordon, and M. Reich. 1982. *Segmented work, divided workers : The historical transformations of labor in the United States*. New York: Cambridge University Press

Eichler, M. 1997. *Family shifts: Families, policies, and gender equality*. Toronto: Oxford University Press

England, G., I. Christie, and M. Christie. 1998. *Employment law in Canada*. Toronto: Butterworths

Esping-Andersen, G. 2002. Towards a post-industrial gender contract. In *The future of work and social protection: The dynamics of change and the protection of workers*, edited by P. Auer and B. Gazier, 109–28. Geneva: International Institute for Labour Studies

European Commission. 1998. *Transformation of work and the future of labour law in Europe*. Luxembourg: Office for Official Publications of the European Communities

Fraser, N. 1997. *Justice interruptus: Critical reflections on the 'postsocialist' condition*. New York: Routledge

Fudge, J. 1997. *Precarious work and families*. Toronto: Centre for Research on Work and Society, York University

- 2002. From segregation to privatization: Equality, the law, and women public servants, 1980–2001. In *Privatization, law and the challenge to feminism,* by J. Fudge and B. Cossman, 86–127. Toronto: University of Toronto Press

Fudge, J., and L. F. Vosko. 2001a. By whose standards? Re-regulating the Canadian labour market. *Economic and Industrial Democracy* 22:327–56

- 2001b. Gender, segmentation and the standard employment relationship in Canadian labour law and policy. *Economic and Industrial Democracy* 22 (2): 271–310

Fudge, J., E. Tucker, and L.F. Vosko. 2002. *The legal concept of employment: Marginalizing workers.* Ottawa: Law Commission of Canada

- 2003a. Changing boundaries in employment: Developing a new platform for labour law. *Canadian Labour and Employment Law Journal* 10 (3): 361–99

- 2003b. Employee or independent contractor? Charting the legal significance of the distinction in Canada. *Canadian Journal of Labour and Employment Law* 10 (2): 193–230

Gazier, B. 2002. Introductory remarks: Labour markets & transitions. In *The future of work, employment and social protection: The dynamics of change and the protection of workers,* edited by P. Auer and B. Gazier, 25–32. Geneva: Ministry of Social Affairs, Labour and Solidarity; France: International Institute for Labour Studies

Gonos, G. 2001. Fee splitting revisited: Concealing surplus value in the temporary employment relationship. *Politics and Society* 29 (4): 589–611 (December)

Hughes, K. 2003. Pushed or pulled? Women's entry into self-employment and small business ownership. *Gender, Work and Organization* 10 (4): 433–54

Hyde, A. 1998. Employment law after the death of employment. *University of Pennsylvania Journal of Labor and Employment Law* 1:1–19

- 2000. Classification of U.S. working people and its impact on worker protection: A report submitted to the International Labour Office

Jackson, A. 2006. Regulating precarious labour markets: What can we learn from new European models? In *Precarious employment: Understanding labour market insecurity in Canada,* edited by L.F. Vosko, 277–300. Montreal: McGill-Queen's University Press

Jacobs, J., and K. Gerson. 2004. *The time divide.* Boston: Harvard University Press

- 1998. Toward a family friendly and gender-equitable work week. *University of Pennsylvania Journal of Labor and Employment Law,* 457–72

Jacoby, S.M. 1985. *Employing bureaucracy: Managers, unions, and the transformation of work in American industry, 1900–1945.* New York: Columbia University Press

Junor, A. 1998. Permanent part-time work: New family-friendly standard or high intensity cheap skills? *Labour and Industry* 8 (3): 77–95

Kamerman, S.B. 2000. Parental leave policies: An essential ingredient in early childhood education and care policies. *Social Policy Report* 14 (2)

Krahn, Harvey. 1995. Non-standard work on the rise. *Perspectives Canada,* Catalogue no. 75–001E

Langille, B. 2002. Labour policy in Canada – new platform, new paradigm. *Canadian Public Policy* 28:132–42

Lin, Z., J. Yates, and G. Picot. 1999. *Rising self-employment in the midst of high unemployment: An empirical analysis of recent developments in Canada.* Research Paper Series. Ottawa: Statistics Canada, Analytical Studies Branch

Lowe, G.S., and G. Schellenberg. 2001. *What's a good job? The importance of employment relationships.* Changing Employment Relationships Series, CPRN Study no. W05. Ottawa: Renouf Publishing Co.

MacDonald, D. 1998. The new deal model of collective bargaining and the secondary labour market. SJD dissertation, Department of Law, Policy and Society, Northeastern University

MacPherson, E. 1999. Collective bargaining for independent contractors: Is the status of the artist a model for other industrial sectors? *Canadian Labour and Employment Law Journal* 7:355–89

Madar, D. 2000. *Heavy traffic: Deregulation, trade, and transformation in North American trucking.* Vancouver: University of British Columbia Press

Mückenberger, U. 1989. Non-standard forms of work and the role of changes in labour and social security legislation. *International Journal of Sociology of the Law* 17:267

O'Donnell, A. 2004. "Non-standard" workers in Australia: Counts and controversies. *Australian Journal of Labour Law* 17:89–116

OECD (Organization for Economic Co-operation and Development). 2000. *Employment outlook: The partial renaissance of self-employment.* Paris: OECD

Owens, R. 2001. The "long-term or permanent casual" – an oxymoron or a "a well enough understood Australianism" in the law? *Australian Bulletin of Labour* 27 (2): 118–36

– 2002. Decent work for the contingent workforce in the new economy. *Australian Journal of Labour Law* 15:209–34

Paterson, W.A. 2003. Desire for social justice: Equal pay, the International Labour Organization, and Australian government policy, 1919–1975. Doctoral dissertation, Schools of Humanities and Liberal Arts, Faculty of Education and Arts, University of Newcastle

Piore, M. 2002. The reconfiguration of work and employment relations in the United States at the turn of the 21st century. In *The future of work, employment and social protection: The dynamics of change and the protection of workers,* edited by P. Auer and B. Gazier, 171–90. Geneva: International Institute for Labour Studies

Pocock, B., J. Buchanan, and I. Campbell. 2004. *Securing quality employment: Policy options for casual and part-time workers in Australia.* Adelaide: Chifley Research Centre

Polivka, A. 1996. Contingent and alternative work arrangements, defined. *Monthly Labour Review,* October: 3–9

Probert, B. 1995. *Part-time work and managerial strategy: Flexibility in the new industry relations framework.* Canberra: AGPS

– 1997. Gender and choice: The structure of opportunity. In *Work of the future: Global perspectives,* edited by P. James, W.F. Veit and S. Wright, 181–97. Sydney: Allen and Unwin

Quebec. 1990. Detailed study of Bill 97. National Assembly, Permanent Committee on Social Affairs, 28/11/1990

Rainbird, H. 1991. The self-employed: Small entrepreneurs or disguised wage-labourers? In *Farewell to flexibility,* by A. Pollert, 200–14. Oxford: Blackwell

Rodgers, G. 1989. Introduction to *Precarious jobs in labour market regulation: The growth of atypical employment in Western Europe,* by G. Rodgers and J. Rodgers, 1–16. Geneva: International Institute for Labour Studies

Rooney, J., et al. 2002. *Self-employment for women: Policy options that promote equality and economic opportunities.* Ottawa: Status of Women Canada

Rosenfeld, R.A. 2001. Employment flexibility in the United States: Changing and maintaining gender, class, and ethnic work relationships. In *Reconfigurations of class and gender,* edited by J. Baxter and M. Western, 105–30. Stanford, Calif.: Stanford University Press

Rubery, J. 1998. *Women in the labour market: A gender equality perspective.* Paris: OECD Directorate for Education, Employment, Labour and Social Affairs

Schmid, G. 2002. Employment insurance for managing critical transitions during the life cycle. In *The future of work, employment and social protection: The dynamics of change and the protection of workers,* edited by P. Auer and B. Gazier, 63–82. Geneva: Ministry of Social Affairs, Labour and Solidarity; France: International Institute for Labour Studies

Schrank, W.E. 1998. Benefiting fishermen: Origins of fishermen's employment insurance in Canada, 1935–1957. *Journal of Canadian Studies* 33 (1): 61–85

Schulman, B. 2003. *The betrayal of work: How low-wage jobs fail 30 million.* New York: The New Press

Stewart, A. 1992. Atypical employment and the failure of labour law. *Australian Bulletin of Labour* 18:217–35

Stone, K.V.W. 2001. The new psychological contract: Implications of the changing workplace for labour and employment law. *UCLA Law Review* 48:519–622

Summers, C. 2000. Employment at will in the United States: The divine right of employers. *University of Pennsylvania Journal of Labor and Employment Law* 3: 65–86

Supiot, A., et al. 2001. *Beyond employment: Changes in work and the future of labour law in Europe.* Oxford: Oxford University Press

Swinnerton, K., and H. Wial. 1995. Is job stability declining in the U.S. economy? Reply to Diebold, Neumark and Polsky. *Industrial and Labor Relations Review* 48 (2): 293–304

Tham, J.-C. 2003. Legal conceptions of casual employment. In *The Proceedings of the 17th AIRAANZ Conference: Refereed Papers,* edited by P. Holland. Melbourne: AIRAANZ

Tilly, C. 1996. *Half a job: Bad and good part-time jobs in a changing labor market.* Philadelphia: Temple University Press

Townson, M. 1997. Non-standard work: The implications for pension policy and retirement readiness. Ottawa: Women's Bureau, Human Resources Development Canada

Tucker, E. 2005. Star wars: Newspaper distribution workers and the possibilities and limits of collective bargaining. In *Self-employed workers organize: Law, policy, and unions,* by C. Cranford, J. Fudge, E. Tucker, and L.F. Vosko. Montreal and Kingston: McGill-Queen's University Press

United States. 1938. *Fair Labor Standards Act.* Available at www.dol.gov/esa/whd/flsa/

– 1985. *Consolidated Omnibus Budget Reconciliation Act.* Available at www.dol.gov/dol/topic/helathplans/cobra.htm#doltopics

– 1989. *Employment and Training Act.* Available at www.dol.gov/dol/allcfr/ETA/Title_20/Part_639/toc.htm

– 1989. *Worker Adjustment and Retraining Notification Act.* Available at www.dol.gov/dol/allcfr/ETA/Title_20/Part_639/toc.htm

U.S. Department of Labor. 1999. *futurework: Trends and challenges for work in the 21st century.* Washington

U.S. House of Representatives. 2003. *Employee Benefits Protection Act of 2001,* HR 1397, 20 March

Vosko, L.F. 2002. Rethinking feminization: Gendered precariousness in the Canadian labour market and the crisis in social reproduction. Annual Robarts Lecture, John P. Robarts Centre for Canadian Studies

– 2003. Gender differentiation and the standard/non-standard employment distinction in Canada, 1915 to the present. In *Patterns and processes of social differentiation: The construction of gender, age, 'race/ethnicity' and locality,* edited by D. Juteau, 25–80. Toronto and Montreal: University of Toronto Press/University of Montreal Press

– 2005. The precarious status of the artist: Freelance editors' struggle for collective bargaining rights. In Cranford et al. 2005

– ed. 2006. *Precarious employment: Understanding labour market insecurity in Canada*. Montreal and Kingston: McGill-Queen's University Press

Vosko, L.F., and N. Zukewich. 2006. Precarious by choice? Gender and self-employment. In *Precarious employment: Understanding labour market insecurity in Canada*, edited by L.F. Vosko, 67–89. Montreal and Kingston: McGill-Queen's University Press

Vosko, L.F, N. Zukewich, and C. Cranford. 2003. Precarious jobs: A new typology of employment. *Perspectives on Labour and Income* (Statistics Canada, Ottawa), October, 16–26

Zukewich, N. 2003. Unpaid informal caregiving. *Canadian Social Trends* 70 (autumn): 14–18

4

Employment Strain, Precarious Employment, and Temporary Employment Agencies

WAYNE LEWCHUK, ALICE DE WOLFF,
AND ANDY KING

"I'm stressed out every day."
– Temporary agency worker

1 INTRODUCTION

As standard employment and its protections erode in Canada, different health issues are emerging for workers. These are not new issues. In the 1800s and early 1900s, many employees worked under precarious employment relationships, and they lacked the legal protections, benefits, pensions, health care, and social programs that unions and social reformers fought for and won after World War I. Since the 1980s, employers have demanded increasingly flexible forms of employment, and consequently a growing number of contemporary workers do not have stable employment, are not protected by employment legislation or social programs, and receive few of the benefits associated with permanent employment. This chapter reports the findings of a study we undertook of workers in southern Ontario that explored the stress associated with precarious employment. The study opens up a new area of concern about this form of employment: that precarious employment relationships can contribute to poor health among workers.[1]

In this chapter, we develop the concept of "employment strain" to describe the cumulative effect of workers' uncertainty over access to work or its terms and conditions, the effort, or workload, associated with finding and maintaining employment, and the extent to which workers have workplace or household support. These issues are of particular concern to young workers, women, and ethnic minorities, who are often forced into various types of precarious employment. Using this framework, we describe the working conditions and health concerns associated with several types of precarious employment relationships, focusing particularly on the working conditions and concerns of workers hired through temporary employment agencies. The study indicates that employment through temporary agencies is particularly precarious and exposes employees to the greatest employment strain.

2 WORK AND HEALTH

Because of the distressing history of workplace injuries, illnesses, and deaths, and because of the successful efforts of unions and other worker advocates to publicize and change unsafe working conditions, it is widely recognized that workplace equipment, materials, environments, and safety practices can have an effect on workers' health. The Industrial Revolution brought with it new occupational risks associated with exposure to dangerous machinery, long hours of work, and fatigue. Early efforts to regulate workplaces under various forms of factory acts and the early twentieth-century push for workers' compensation systems were largely driven by the increase in health problems related to these new physical risks and were supported by a wave of occupational health and safety research on these subjects (Tucker 1990). With the increased use of new materials and new chemical processes after World War II, another wave of research was undertaken into occupational health and safety issues related to exposure to dangerous substances. Irving Selikoff's research into the risk associated with exposure to asbestos and the recognition of the health hazards associated with coal dust in West Virginia mines gave rise to a worker-led movement around work and health issues in the 1970s (Selikoff 1964; Smith 1987).

While exposure to physical risks and dangerous substances has received the attention of labour activists, unions, and researchers, there is less recognition of the connection between the way that jobs are organized and workers' health – in essence, how employment relationships themselves create health risks. A third wave of occupational health and safety research suggests that the organization of work itself may be an underappreciated source of work-related health risks. In their recent publication *The Changing Organization of Work and the Safety and Health of Working People*, the United States National Institute for Occupational Safety and Health stated, "There is growing appreciation that the organization of work has broad implications for the safety and health of workers" (NIOSH 2002).

Much of this new interest in the organization of work has emerged from the path-breaking work of Michael Marmot and his colleagues in Britain. In a project begun in 1967 and referred to as the Whitehall studies, Michael Marmot and his colleagues discovered an age-adjusted social gradient in death rates and absenteeism in a study involving tens of thousands of British civil servants. Civil servants in the highest employment grade (administrative) had from one-third to one-half the incidence of mortality of those in the lowest grade (clerical) (Marmot et al. 1984; Marmot et al. 1991; Marmot 1994; Marmot 2000). These workers were not heavily exposed to traditional health risks, such as physical risks, dangerous substances, or biomechanical hazards associated with manufacturing. Equally important, the health impact of poverty was largely removed from the equation, as even the lowest-paid employment grade enjoyed a comfortable material standard of living.

What explains the causes of this social health gradient? Subsequent research indicated that lifestyle explained only a small component of this difference. In their Whitehall II study, begun in 1985, Marmot and his colleagues began exploring the role of work organization as an explanation of this gradient. Work organization is the complex set of practices that shape the physical and social organization of workplaces. Together, these practices define how people interact with their physical environment and how they interact with each other.

Research into work organization and health by Robert Karasek (Karasek and Theorell 1990) has shown that workers experience stress and ill health when their jobs are characterized by high demands and by low levels of control over how the work is performed. This condition has come to be known as "job strain." Studies show that workers exposed to job strain are more likely to be exhausted, depressed, and dissatisfied with their job, and to have stress-related illness and cardiovascular disease (Belkic et al. 2000; Karasek and Theorell 1990; Marmot 2000). Other studies have shown that chronic exposure to job strain increases blood pressure (Schnall et al. 1992; Schnall et al. 1998; Landsbergis et al. 1994; Laflamme et al. 1998).

The Effort Reward Imbalance (ERI) model (Siegrist 1996; Siegrist and Peters 2000) offers a second approach to understanding how work organization affects health. Johannes Siegrist argues that an imbalance between costs and gains at work (i.e., high effort/low reward condition) results in a state of emotional distress and associated strain reactions. When effort and rewards are imbalanced, workers are stressed and in the long run are more likely to experience negative health outcomes. The evidence supporting the significant role of effort-reward imbalance in determining health outcomes at work is becoming increasingly compelling. Siegrist (1996) shows that the risk of acute myocardial infarction, sudden cardiac death, and coronary heart disease was most elevated in those with at least one indicator of high effort and at least one indicator of low reward. More recently, the Whitehall II study has uncovered a significant relationship between effort-reward imbalance and increased risk of alcohol dependence, psychiatric disorder, long spells of sickness, absence, and poor health functioning (Stansfeld, Head, and Marmot 2000).

These studies provide a useful point of departure for our study of precarious employment and health. However, they are limited because they analyse only the workplace organization of the production of goods and services. Karasek developed his analysis in the early 1970s in a world where, at least for most white men, the standard employment relationship was the norm. The studies do not investigate the links between health and the employment relationship itself – how people acquire work, how they keep work, and how they negotiate the terms and conditions of work. It is on these aspects of work and particularly these aspects of precarious employment relationships that we focus.

3 AN INTRODUCTION TO THE EMPLOYMENT STRAIN SURVEY

Between 2002 and 2004, the research team surveyed 800 workers in southern Ontario on the characteristics of their employment relationship. The fixed-response, self-administered survey was designed to measure employment strain, other work organization characteristics, and health outcomes. Questions on employment strain were developed for this project. Questions on job strain and health outcomes were taken from an existing survey that members of the research team used with workers employed in the manufacturing sector. One of the challenges of the study was finding a sample of workers in precarious employment. The sample that was chosen was composed of respondents to ads placed in newspapers, employees of temporary agencies, homecare workers, university workers, community workers, and a diverse group found through employment agencies and worker-based groups in Toronto.[2] In addition, a sub-sample of those completing our survey participated either in focus groups or individual interviews.[3] We use this detailed information to confirm the findings from our survey data and to deepen our analysis.

The survey results make it possible to compare the experience of several groups of precarious workers – temporary agency workers, short-term workers, and on-call workers – with the experience of full-time workers. On most measures, the temporary agency workers experienced greater uncertainties, more effort finding and maintaining work, and less support at work and in their households. Those who had high levels of employment strain were also the most likely to report high levels of pain and discomfort at work, stress, and ill health.

Of the 800 individuals who completed our survey, many reported having acquired work through a complex set of different work arrangements. It was common for individuals to be simultaneously self-employed, working part-time, and seeking work through a temporary employment agency. To convey an accurate sense of the conditions under each form of precarious employment, we limited sections 3–9 of this chapter to an analysis of the employment relations of the 391 respondents who found work through a single source. A total of 281 respondents reported either working only through a temporary agency, working on-call, or having short-term contracts that were not likely to be renewed. In these sections, we explore the differences between each cluster and compare them to the 110 respondents in the sample who reported working only in a full-time position. In section 10 we focus on the overall work experience of individuals and their health outcomes using a set of work organization descriptors we have developed. We use the entire sample of 800 respondents for this analysis.

Table 4.1 reports the socio-economic characteristics of each cluster of respondents discussed in sections 3–9 of this chapter. The survey respondents were notable because they did not conform to common assumptions about who is in precarious employment. Our sample did not consist of mainly young students working at precarious jobs. Less than one-fifth of the respondents were below the age of twenty-five, and less than 10 per cent were full-time students. Nor was this a poorly educated sample. Ninety per cent had completed secondary school, and 70 per cent had some college or university education. One-sixth of the sample had completed university.

Temporary agency workers are workers who are placed in work assignments by temporary services agencies. In our sample, these workers were in their mid-working life, with an average age of 36.3 years. Two-thirds were male, and half were not white, making them the most racially diverse of the four clusters. One in four was a recent immigrant. Eighty-six per cent had incomes under $25,000 a year, and two-thirds lived in low income households. More than half did not receive employment benefits such as medical, dental, or drug benefits, about double the frequency reported by full-time workers. While they were as educated as the full-time workers in the study, the majority (60

Table 4.1 Socio-economic characteristics of sample by employment type

| | Types of Precarious Employment | | | |
	Temporary Agency	Short-Term Contract	On-Call	Full-Time Employment
Average age (years)	36.3	33.2	48.6	36.5
Female (%)	36	53	94	58
White (%)	52	62	83	70
Lived in Canada < 5 years (%)	25	12	1	9
Some university (%)	28	43	7	28
Own income < $25,000 (%)	86	82	83	42
Household income < $35,000 (%)	69	76	50	34
No employment benefits (%)	60	61	44	28
Full-time student (%)	6	18	1	5
Union member in all workplaces (%)	1	18	82	28
Occupation/Sector:				
Factory work (%)	60	18	2	29
Clerical (%)	21	27	4	20
Education (%)	0	26	1	26
Health (%)	2	14	92	10
Number of observations	85	68	128	110

per cent) were employed in factory work. Almost none of them were protected by a union.

The short-term contract employees in the sample found work on their own and did not rely on an agency. We restricted this group to those who did not expect their current employer to offer more work. They were earlier in their working lives than the other groups and were evenly split between men and women. Just over one-third were not white, and 12 per cent were recent immigrants. They had the highest education of the clusters and the largest proportion of full-time students. More lived in poor households, fewer of them than any other group earned employment benefits, and four of five earned less than $25,000 a year.

On-call workers were primarily older, white, female homecare workers. They had a permanent relationship with an employer but did not have a guarantee of hours of work or pay. Few had university-level education. While the percentage earning less than $25,000 a year was similar to temporary and short-term contract workers, they were more likely to live in households with marginally higher incomes. Even though most were unionized, just over half had benefits.

Full-time workers in this study were employed permanently and expected to work at least thirty hours per week. Just over half were female. Thirty per cent were not white, and 9 per cent were recent immigrants. Of all the groups, full-time workers were the least likely to report having low incomes or living in low-income households, and more had employment benefits than the other clusters.

4 THE TEMPORARY SERVICE INDUSTRY

Before discussing the survey and interview findings in detail, we must provide some context for the experiences of our respondents. Since the mid-1980s, more mid-career men in the industrial sector, women of all ages, recent immigrants, and youth have become temporary workers (Vosko, Zukewich, and Cranford 2003). This growth is a predictable outcome of employment strategies and policies of both private sector employers and governments seeking flexibility and new ways of controlling costs (Herzenberg, Alic, and Wial 1998). Together, business and government have restructured employment so that increasing numbers of workers are "free agents" in a weakly regulated labour market. They have created a climate where employers have permission to break the implicit and explicit agreements associated with standard employment relationships. They have created new levels of uncertainty for workers who must continually search for work and renegotiate the terms and conditions of their employment. Further, through exclusions from social and labour protections, governments and employers are downloading to workers many of the costs associated with production as well as the costs of social reproduction (medical benefits, family-related leaves, pensions, unemployment insurance, etc.).

The temporary employment service industry is a key enabler of the increase in labour market flexibility/precariousness. Its services have expanded from the traditional provision of short-term temporary replacements and day labour in office work and construction to the provision of long-term and short-term workers in all occupations and sectors, as well as to the delivery of partial or full human resource services. Some employers contract temporary agencies to handle all human resource functions – recruiting, hiring, payroll, supervision, firing – in situations where the demand for workers is project based (the film industry, the RRSP industry, etc.). Contracting out all human resource functions is an option taken up by companies that are downsizing and by smaller companies that decide not to develop an in-house capacity.

Table 4.2 Temporary employment in Canada by sex, 1989 to 2002 (workers on temporary contracts, including workers hired through temporary agencies)

Employees	% Total Employment				% Female Employment				% Male Employment			
	1989	1994	1997	2002	1989	1994	1997	2002	1989	1994	1997	2002
Temporary full-time	4	5	6	7	3	3	4	6	4	5	6	7
Temporary part-time	3	3	4	4	4	4	3	6	2	2	3	3

Source: Cranford, Vosko, and Zukewich 2003, based on Statistics Canada General Social Survey, 1989 and 1994, and Labour Force Survey 1997 and 2002.

Employers use agencies to screen, hire, and take potential new employees through a probationary period; to handle fluctuating demand and just-in-time production; and to test the viability of a new division or project. More agencies are specializing in one occupation. High-tech workers, accountants, teachers, homecare workers, nurses, models, early childhood education workers, or hotel workers can all find on-call work, short-term assignments, and sometimes full-time jobs through specialized agencies.

Between 1993 and 2002, Canadian employment services agencies increased in number from 1,191 to 3,966. Their revenues increased from $1.5 billion in1993 to $5.6 billion in 2002. Temporary placements generated 78 per cent of these revenues, and temporary workers generated 218 million billable hours in 2002 (Statistics Canada 2004a, 2004b). It is difficult to identify accurately the number of temporary workers who are employed through employment agencies on the basis of the regular Statistics Canada labour force data, but it is clear that there has been a significant increase in the number of temporary workers across the country. Table 4.2 shows that 11 per cent of Canadian workers were in full-time and part-time temporary work in 2002 and that the proportion of full-time temporary workers increased from 4 per cent of the labour force to 7 per cent between 1989 and 2002. The increase was more significant for men than for women.

The temporary agency employment relationship is significantly different from the single employer employment relationship. Three parties are involved in the former: the agency, the client company, and the worker. Wages, benefits, agency fees, transportation costs, and responsibility for training, health and safety, supervision, and finder's fees for permanent hirings and rehirings are all negotiated between the agency and the client company. Although temporary agencies are

usually understood to be the primary employer, each contract is different. Employees can be left with poor or confused access to the
protections that should be available to all workers because of gaps in
the contracts or uncertainty about who is responsible. Prior to 2001,
the temporary agency industry in Ontario was regulated. Industry
practices before World War I and the resulting protests of unions and
immigrant groups led governments to attempt to limit the profits that
could be made and the abuses that could be practised by those selling
someone else's labour (Vosko 2000). In Ontario, the remains of these
regulations have been lifted, leaving the industry to self-regulate during this period of expansion and reorganization.

Several people we interviewed expressed their vulnerability as
agency workers. One experienced manufacturing worker said, "They
don't really protect you. They claim that they do, they send you news-
letters and stuff. They claim that they are like a paternal type of agent,
but they're not ... They're trying to pawn off a lot of their crud jobs ...
They always say to you 'how low will you go [in wages]?'" A construction worker observed: "You're replaceable. You're there for them, not
for you. You're there to make them money. They're giving you 9 bucks
an hour and the employer is paying them 15 bucks an hour."

A growing segment of the Canadian workforce has come to rely on
temporary agencies for employment. The remainder of this paper will
assess the conditions of precarious employment in general and in particular work associated with temporary employment agencies as well as
the relationship between precarious employment and health status.

5 EMPLOYMENT RELATIONSHIP UNCERTAINTY: WORKING AS A TEMP

> "Your wage fluctuates from high to low to low to very low, so you
> don't know how much you're making. It's totally unstable."
> – Temporary manufacturing worker

Employment relationship uncertainty is the control dimension in our analysis of "employment strain." It measures the extent to which workers
have control over access to employment, earnings, and scheduling.
Employment relationship uncertainty has three components. *Work
uncertainty* measures the level of control over future employment and
the frequency with which employment terms are renegotiated. It
assesses respondents' perceived uncertainty about whether current
employers will offer more work, and also assesses average contract
length. *Earnings uncertainty* measures the level of control that workers
have over future earnings. It includes responses to survey questions

Table 4.3 Employment relationship uncertainty (average scores)

	Types of Precarious Employment			
	Temporary Agency	Short-Term Contract	On-Call	Full-Time Employment
Employment relationship uncertainty	58.0	51.7	40.6	26.5
Work uncertainty	51.2	49.7	7.9	6.7
Earnings uncertainty	60.1	59.2	49.5	33.9
Scheduling uncertainty	58.4	37.8	47.9	25.0

Note: Index scores range from 0 to 100 where higher scores indicate higher levels of uncertainty.

about the worker's ability to predict future earnings, the existence of written pay records, whether unemployment insurance and government pensions are deducted from earnings, whether workers are paid when they are sick, whether they are paid on time, and whether they have disability insurance and pension entitlements. *Scheduling uncertainty* measures the control that workers have over when and where they will work. It is constructed from questions about the length of advance notice of work schedules, hours to be worked, and work location.

Table 4.3 shows us that temporary agency workers had higher levels of work, earnings, and scheduling uncertainty than any of the other clusters of workers. Short-term workers had slightly less scheduling uncertainty. On-call homecare workers could count on a long-term relationship with their placement agency, but had little control over how often they would work, how much they earned, or when they would work. Temporary agency and short-term contract respondents in our survey experienced twice the levels of employment relationship uncertainty as full-time workers.

Workers who participated in interviews and focus groups provided us with glimpses of how they experience these uncertainties. The temporary employment agency relationship is almost by definition unpredictable, having a multitude of uncertainties. Concerns about unpredictable work, low wages, pay inequality, and scheduling surfaced early in most of our conversations. Very few temporary agency workers can predict their income. One woman who had two full-time stable assignments over the previous five years told us that even though the work had been remarkably stable and her relationship with the agency was good, she still could not count on it. "The company hires us through the agency so that they can let us go with almost no notice. They are experimenting with new services and have reorganized at least twice. There are rumours all the time. We could be gone next week." On the other end of the stability spectrum, a manufacturing temporary agency worker who had five assignments in the previous six months reported that he could not even rely on the wage he agreed to at the beginning of an assignment: "Sometimes they will say we have a job for you and we think it's around $10 or $12 an hour. They say 'I think.' And then you get your pay cheque stub and it's not like that." Even the unionized homecare workers with an agency who were classified as "full-time permanent employees," could not predict how much they would be paid. "They can't promise you hours. I either log in 60 hours a week for three months straight with no breaks, or I've worked 20 hours a week. I have even gone down to 15 hours."

Temporary workers constantly have to make decisions about whether and where to work. The temporary employment agency industry, as well as some researchers, suggest that this is a way for workers to take control over their work lives (Cooper 2002). The workers involved in our study, however, reported that their choices were most often about having to choose one bad situation over another. A short-term contract community service worker described this dilemma: "I was told last month that I had a contract but I haven't seen a contract yet. Should I start the work or not? Why should I work without a contract and not know if the employer is going to change their minds and then I have to go to small claims court to get paid?" An office worker talked about trying to take more control over the quality of her work, but because she needs the money, she often overworks because she has overlapping contracts or she takes jobs that do not use her skills. A manufacturing worker said that his choices were often between no work and jobs that paid $8 or $10 an hour but would have cost him $20 a day in transportation. A laid-off technical design worker observed that his experience looking for work had taught him that there were few labouring jobs in his region; in fact, he was aware that several large plants had announced layoffs, so he expected that there would be even fewer choices. He had a $12-an-hour assembling job and was afraid that he would not find another labouring job, let alone a job in his field. "I told my wife if I find another job that pays the type of money I was earning [as a technical designer] I will not go into it unless I've got an absolute guarantee for six months minimum."

The wages for this group of temporary agency workers were very low, which makes the uncertainty particularly difficult. As one of them said, "I worked fifteen hours a week and it took me two weeks to earn my rent ... and the other two weeks was my food and car payments. Then you see people coming in and throwing away $100 on a bottle of wine or whatever, and life isn't fair." When $1 an hour might make the difference between being able to pay the rent or not, or having to go to a food bank or not, disparities between workers are keenly noticed. A construction worker told us that he often works beside people doing the same job who earn considerably more than he does. A hotel worker saw particularly large wage gaps when she was in unionized hotels. "Other people in the hotel are working the same job as I do, right? And they are $18 an hour and I got $8 or $8.50, but we are doing exactly the same job." These pay inequities make workers angry and can erode their sense of self-worth and competence.

Scheduling uncertainties, even when they are not linked to income uncertainty, are significant stressors in precarious workers' lives. Schedules are generally based on the employer's need for flexibility, and in situations where workers are most vulnerable, schedules can be unfair. A replacement daycare worker told us that she did not know until 7:30 each morning whether she would be working. The hotel worker described getting calls at 7:00 a.m. and travelling an hour and a half to the workplace to which she had been assigned, sometimes to find that there was little or no work. A homecare worker described her very long and broken-up day: "I start at 7:00 a.m. and then I have a two-hour break, then I have an hour, then I travel [by bus or walking], then I travel back to other clients. Some days my day doesn't end until 5:30 so I am up at 5:00 a.m. and get in the house at 6:00 p.m." A recently married manufacturing worker bluntly described the impact of irregular scheduling: "Number one, sex life. If you are on two different schedules entirely, you just never see the person." He also said, "If I'm trying to volunteer and all of a sudden they need me for night shift and it pays well, then I have to shuffle everything." Women workers with children reported significant disruption in childcare arrangements when they did not know their schedule at least a week in advance. An older worker described his preference for schedules that gave him some ability to keep up his social contacts during the afternoon and evening, and he talked about his sense of isolation when he could not work these shifts. Because some schedules are worse than others, scheduling can be used as a form of discipline. One worker told us that in her workplace "casual employees were all afraid that if you said anything you would end up on nights."

6 EMPLOYMENT RELATIONSHIP WORKLOAD: GETTING AND KEEPING WORK

Employment relationship workload captures four concerns for precarious workers: the amount of time and effort spent getting new work; getting to, being functional in, and maintaining relationships in multiple work sites; being continually evaluated; and dealing with harassment at

Table 4.4 Employment relationship workload (average index scores)

	Types of Precarious Employment			
	Temporary Agency	Short-Term Contract	On-Call	Full-Time Employment
Employment relationship workload	41.5	37.2	33.7	24.7
Effort getting work	45.9	47.8	7.1	9.3
Multiple employers/ worksites effort	35.2	30.0	32.1	16.9
Constant evaluation effort	48.6	32.8	38.8	27.0
Harassment/ Discrimination effort	49.5	48.7	34.3	36.2

Note: Index scores range from 0 to 100 where higher scores indicate higher levels of workload.

work. *Effort getting work* measures time spent looking for work. *Multiple employers/worksites effort* combines questions about the number of employers, supervisors, and work locations; unpaid time spent travelling between jobs; frequency of working with new sets of co-workers in unfamiliar locations; and conflicts arising from having multiple employers or work locations. *Constant evaluation effort* includes questions about the extent to which attitude and performance evaluations affect future assignments or contracts or the kinds of work assigned. *Harassment and discrimination effort* includes questions about the level of harassment and discrimination in the work relationship, the effect it has on future assignments or schedules, and the frequency with which one is asked to do things unrelated to work.

Table 4.4 shows us that temporary agency workers spent the most effort trying to maintain a relationship with their current employer and looking for future work. Short-term contract workers also spent significant effort getting new work and handling harassment or discrimination in their workplaces. The on-call homecare workers expended less effort looking for work than even full-time workers, but regular evaluation from clients and supervisors, given its effect on the need to schedule more work, was a continuous concern for them.

Several workers in our sample told us that they expended two different kinds of effort in getting new work: first, finding the best possible temporary assignments, and second, looking for permanent work that suited their skills and background. One experienced worker told us that he had learned to recognize from regional agency ads those client companies, and consequently temporary jobs, that were most likely to have decent working environments. He also readily recognized what he described as "scams," like pyramid marketing schemes or minimum wage customer service. He and several other workers said that they checked websites or papers daily. Several workers said that, in comparison with other employment services, government websites were not well maintained and made the effort of job search more difficult.

The search for permanent work generally takes more effort. None of the temporary agency workers that we spoke with thought they were doing what they wanted to do; they either wanted permanent work in the same occupation or wanted work in another occupation better suited to their skills and background. Many reported being underemployed and disappointed and disillusioned with their work life. A trained community worker said, "I walk home, especially from my cleaning job, I go to the living room, sit and watch TV for a few minutes. Right above the sofa that faces my TV there is my college diploma and I look at it and I'm like, that's there and I am doing something else that is not even close to it and all that gets me really stressful." The search for better work takes more time and requires more personal and financial resources.

The experienced manufacturing worker told us that he was invited to an interview at a unionized auto plant for a job that would have paid up to $25 an hour: "These are five part interviews. I had taken four days off from work … I lost $420 plus gas, so $450, $460 going to this place because I had to book it off work because it was during the week. Didn't get hired. It's a risk. You have to take it." Another worker took a college computer course in the hope that it would supplement his experience: "I called up three different agencies and asked which programs would you recommend. They said it changes, you have to decide for yourself. So I have taken a course that has proven to be in effect useless." Workers who want to change their occupation often try to mask the type of work they are in. Several spoke about not being able, or not wanting, to make or take phone calls from potential employers at their current jobs. One woman wondered about borrowing a friend's cellphone so that she could make calls during her breaks (she was not able to afford one herself). A childcare worker who planned to get out of supply teaching said, "I have to cut up my credit card, not use it and save over the next six months so that I can get high speed Internet, so I can start my on-line business."

Workers' efforts to find better jobs that are also permanent can be derailed by the contracts between temporary agencies and client companies. Contracts often include a finder's fee if the client company wants to offer the worker a permanent position. Finders fees, which can be substantial, are often a deterrent. A construction worker told us, "All these people want to hire me, but they sign this contract … No one wants to pay the fee to hire me. They told me it was two or three thousand dollars."

There are many moments in the temporary agency employment relationship when workers are selected for placements, tasks, and schedules, and consequently there are more opportunities for discrimination in this relationship than in permanent employment relationships (Nunes and Seligman 1999). Among the people we interviewed, workers of colour, older workers, women workers, and workers with disabilities reported that they had experienced some form of discrimination. The temporary agency workers in this survey were a racially diverse group who reported high levels of discrimination and harassment. Discrimination can show itself not only in what is said to workers, but in the types of placements offered by the agency, by the number of times a worker is called, or by the kind of information that does not get communicated – "You never know why you don't get called." As well as dealing with the resulting anger and humiliation, workers who experience discrimination can find themselves doing the hardest or the most dangerous jobs. One worker was particularly angry about the situations he had seen: "The white people had more power in the warehouse because they can speak English. They assume the responsibility so that when immigrants come in, they talk down to them, make them work in the bad areas, don't train them, isolate them out … One guy from Romania was injured recently, because what they got him to do was all the crouching and doing the wrapping of the skids. So when you wrap skids you have to be in this position and you have to go very fast. Of course all the white people in the company who are strong, they couldn't do it, but because he's the immigrant who speaks the least English, he did it all. And he injured his back."

7 JOB STRAIN

Our survey does not show a consistent difference in job strain between precarious and full-time workers. Job strain occurs when workers have low levels of control and heavy workloads in their jobs. As Table 4.5 illustrates, both full-time and short-term contract workers had higher levels of control and lower levels of physical workload. Both groups were employed across industrial sectors and occupations, so this result is not related to either of these variables. Temporary agency workers and on-call workers had lower levels of control and heavier physical workloads, which may reflect the similarities in the two employment relationships. However, cognitive workload does not significantly differ across the four clusters.

Our findings are consistent with other studies that have not found consistently high levels of job strain among precarious workers. Analysts have suggested that low levels of control are offset by lower work-

Table 4.5 Job strain indicators (average index scores)

	Types of Precarious Employment			
	Temporary Agency	Short-Term Contract	On-Call	Full-Time Employment
Control at work	47.1	56.0	52.3	65.9
Physical workload	40.5	27.4	42.7	32.9
Cognitive workload	46.2	41.4	42.5	45.0

Note: Index scores range from 0 to 100 where higher scores indicate higher levels of control/workload.

loads in some forms of precarious employment (Goudswaard and Adries 2002; Parker et al. 2002). Others have suggested that while precarious workers are more likely to have heavy physical or cognitive workloads (Dauba-Letournex and Thébaud-Mony 2002), this is offset by their ability to control whether and where they will work. Our results suggest that job strain measures a different set of risk factors than employment strain and that workers in precarious employment relationships do not necessarily face more job strain. The risks that capture the differences between full-time and precarious workers appear to be particularly associated with employment strain rather than with job strain.

8 SUPPORT: WORKPLACE AND SOCIAL SUPPORT AND HOUSEHOLD INSECURITY

Other studies have suggested that support at the workplace, along with household and community support outside of the workplace, can lower workers' stress (Johnson 1991). For precarious workers, household support may be particularly important. Households that have sufficient resources, for example, can provide a buffer for the stress related to employment strain, while those with insufficient resources may add to the stress.

In our study, *household insecurity* combines responses to questions regarding individual and household earnings, household benefit coverage (drug, medical, dental, eye, life), and the presence in the household of children eighteen or younger. Low levels of household insecurity may make it easier for a worker to handle the low levels of control and high levels of effort associated with their particular employment relationship. *Workplace support* combines responses to questions about the availability of help with a job, assistance at work if a worker is stressed, and the presence and effectiveness of a union. *Social support* combines questions about whether an individual has

Table 4.6 Support (average index scores)

| | Types of Precarious Employment | | | |
	Temporary Agency	Short-Term Contract	On-Call	Full-Time Employment
Household insecurity	72.7	71.2	57.9	34.0
Workplace support	18.2	23.6	44.1	30.6
Social support	35.1	42.5	58.3	57.0

Note: Index scores range from 0 to 100 where higher scores indicate higher levels of insecurity/support.

access to someone who provides emotional, practical, or financial support in a crisis situation, and questions about whether they can draw on the support of friends, family, and people in their neighbourhood or community to deal with problems they might face.

As illustrated in Table 4.6, temporary agency workers were the most isolated, with the least access to resources that might mediate the precariousness of their employment relationship. This predominantly male and racially diverse group lived in the most insecure households and had the least employment and social support. By contrast, although they did not have the same support as full-time workers, the almost exclusively older white, female, on-call homecare workers in our study had greater household security and greater employment relationship support than the full-time workers in the sample.

Several people we interviewed spoke about their social isolation. One said, "Eventually I found that I just got disconnected from my friends. They worked Monday to Friday during the day … family and friends just stopped asking me to join them." It is hard to maintain any other significant involvement. It was even a complicated process to set up our one-time interviews with this group because most did not know when or whether they were working. An older worker described how he could not easily keep up his friendships or make new contacts because he could not phone from work, and he said that his household can no longer afford to entertain as it did when he had a full-time job.

Part of the isolation is related to greater household insecurity. The temporary agency workers lived in households with very low incomes and few benefits. One worker said, "I don't care if I have to dig ditches to bring an income in. At least I brought an income in, though it has been terribly low, and I find that I am disgusted with it. How in the world is anybody supposed to survive on what I am earning? And yet, people do. We try to spend no more than $100 on groceries a week." He described an afternoon when he and his wife gave themselves a

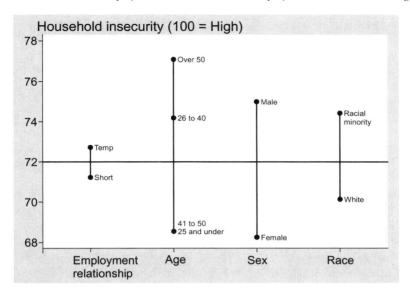

Figure 4.1 Household insecurity of workers employed by temporary agencies and on short-term contracts by sex, race, and age (average scores)

break from their tight budget to go "shopping." "I said that we should pretend that we had $100 to spend, and we spent the afternoon in the mall figuring out how we would spend it, if we had it."

Figure 4.1 shows levels of household insecurity in more detail, focusing on short-term and temporary agency workers. We looked closely at the experience of these two groups because they exhibited a number of similarities and were the most likely to report high levels of employment strain. The results reported in Figure 4.1 are the average scores for the groups with the characteristics indicated. Among them, workers in the twenty-six to forty age group, who are more likely to be having and supporting children, and workers over the age of fifty lived in less financially secure households. Women in these two groups were less likely to live in financially insecure households than men. While our indicators do not measure the extent to which the household is supportive beyond income and benefits, other studies indicate that the type of effort that workers invest in maintaining households continues to fall heavily on women (Statistics Canada 2003). While the women in our study had slightly more household economic support, it is likely that they experienced their households as places where they support others. Our findings echo studies that show that race correlates with lower household incomes (Galabuzi 2001) and suggest that precarious employment may be a significant component of lower incomes among racial minorities.

Table 4.6 reports findings related to how much support workers had at work. The on-call homecare workers had much more support than other precarious workers or even the full-time workers in the sample. They had access to union stewards and regular union meetings and had a relatively consistent relationship with supervisors, nurses, and other workers in the agency. Because they were not replacement workers, no group of permanent workers resented or excluded them, and because of the demands of their occupation, they received training and new information with some regularity.

In comparison, temporary agency and short-term workers had very little support from supervisors or other co-workers. Very few are unionized, and few assignments are long enough for workers to develop consistent relationships with supervisors or co-workers. Temporary workers are often considered the lowest in the workplace hierarchy and can be actively resented, rather than supported, by more permanent workers. One worker described a recent situation where the employer consistently gave temporary and part-time workers more overtime, which upset the full-time union members and ultimately led to a strike. Temporary workers do, of course, develop supportive connections with each other, but they are challenged in many different ways. A factory worker told us that he and a co-worker were strong enough friends to swap shifts with each other, but other co-workers had given them trouble. "A lot of the temps got upset because we did that because they coveted the morning shift." Temporary agencies are rarely prepared to help sort out difficulties raised by employees. This same worker told us: "If you complain, or try to take up someone else's fight, they'll say well, you're making a complaint, we'll look into it. You're working for the same temp agency and most of us won't push too hard because you'll get known as a complainer/troublemaker. It's not going to go anywhere."

One worker observed that temporary workers are treated better at unionized workplaces than at non-unionized workplaces. "If the union members go to a safety committee meeting, the temps go to the safety committee meeting." It is by no means the norm, but collective agreements can cover all aspects of temporary workers' employment relationships, from inclusion in committees to wages and seniority.

Interactions between employment relationship uncertainty, employment relationship effort, and employment relationship support generate employment strain. Figure 4.2 summarizes how an employment relationship can lead to employment strain. All employment relationships generate a level of employment strain. What this chapter has

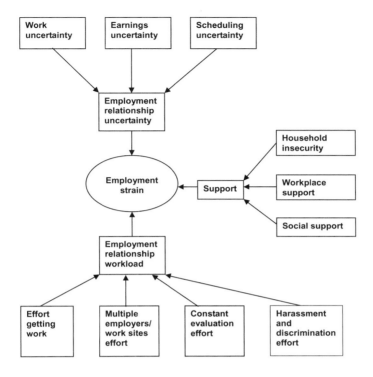

Figure 4.2 The components of employment strain

revealed is that precarious employment relationships, and in particular employment found through temporary employment agencies are associated with higher levels of employment strain.

9 PRECARIOUS EMPLOYMENT AND HEALTH

Our study also examined the physical and emotional health of workers in different employment relationships. We used the standard question in Canada's National Population Health Survey to assess general health; we also asked workers how much time they spent working in pain, how often they were tense at work or exhausted after work, and to what extent they found everything an effort. The study revealed that workers employed by temporary agencies were in poorer health than those in full-time employment. We tested the relationship between our measures of work organization and workers' health status using a multivariate regression analysis. This allowed us to control for age, sex,

Table 4.7 Health status by employment relationship (average scores)

| | Types of Precarious Employment | | | |
	Temporary Agency	Short-Term Contract	On-Call	Full-Time Employment
Self-reported health worse than very good	48.8	53.0	55.2	44.0
Pain at work half the time or more	32.9	13.8	25.8	22.6
Exhausted after work most days	36.5	25.4	28.1	34.5
Tense at least half the time at work	41.2	39.7	16.0	33.6
Everything an effort most of the time	25.0	17.6	15.3	15.5

Note: Index scores range from 0 to 100 where higher scores indicate poorer health status.

race, physical working conditions, and pre-existing health problems. Overall we found that increases in employment relationship uncertainty and employment relationship workload were correlated with poorer health outcomes and that increases in employment relationship support were correlated with better health outcomes. We discuss these findings below. The details of this analysis are included in the technical appendix at the end of the chapter.

Table 4.7 shows the health status of respondents in each employment relationship. Temporary agency workers report high levels of stress. They were the most likely to report that there was tension at work and that everything was an effort. They were also the most likely to report working in pain. The on-call homecare workers reported considerably less tension at work; this could be related to their stronger occupational identity (discussed below) and to the extent that their union supports them. These on-call workers were also less likely to be exhausted after work. Short-term workers reported working in pain less frequently than any other cluster and were less likely to be exhausted after work than full-time workers. Taken together, these results suggest that the most significant health differences between precarious and full-time employment may be related to stress and tension rather than to the physical risks associated with work.

Figures 4.3 and 4.4 explore health outcomes in more detail for temporary and short-term contract employees only. Figure 4.3 reports findings on the prevalence of tension at work by employment relationship, sex, race, and age. In general, younger workers and men were more likely to report being tense at work half the time or more frequently. Figure 4.4 reports findings on the prevalence of working in

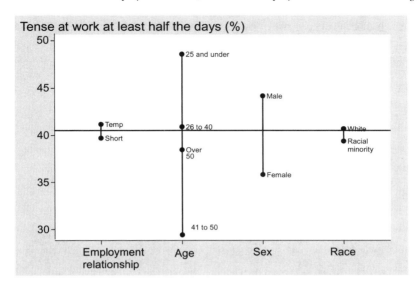

Figure 4.3 Tense half the time or more by employment relationship, sex, race, and age (%) (average scores)

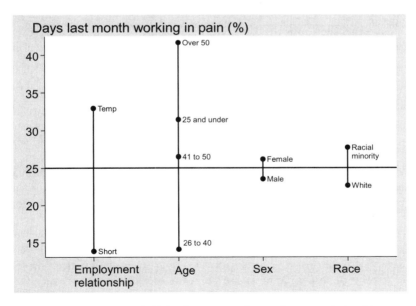

Figure 4.4 Working in pain half the time or more by employment relationship, sex, race, and age (%) (average scores)

pain half the time or more by sector, sex, race, and age. Older workers were more likely to report working in pain. The differences between men and women and between workers of colour and white workers were relatively small. Workers employed by temporary employment agencies were more likely to report working in pain than those in short-term contracts.

Table 4.7 and Figures 4.3 and 4.4 suggest that precarious workers, and especially temporary agency workers, are in poorer health than those in full-time employment. There are also some important age, sex, and race differences. Older workers report more pain but less tension. Men report more tension. The differences between people of colour and white people were relatively small.

10 DETAILED ANALYSIS OF EMPLOYMENT STRAIN AND HEALTH OUTCOMES

Our study allows us to explore with more precision the relationship between health outcomes and employment relationship characteristics. We used a multivariate logistic regression analysis that controlled for characteristics such as sex, age, and race. We also controlled for differences in the physical hazards at work (poor air, noisy environment, uncomfortable temperatures) and for whether an individual was forced into a precarious job because of a prior injury or illness. Because our focus in this section is on the relationship between specific work organization characteristics and health outcomes, rather than on the characteristics of a particular form of employment relationship, we are able to use the entire sample in the analysis.

Here we discuss the broad findings of this exercise. The details are reported in the technical appendix. In general, greater uncertainty in workers' employment relationships and, in particular, the greater uncertainties related to scheduling and earnings were correlated with poorer self-reported health, more frequent tension at work, and more frequent reporting that everything was an effort. A 10 percentage-point increase in employment relationship uncertainty increased the likelihood that workers would report less than excellent health, tension at work, or everything being an effort at work to about the same degree. Greater employment relationship uncertainty was not, however, significantly correlated with the frequency of pain at work or the frequency of exhaustion. This supports our argument that the employment relationship may be more relevant to explaining stress-related health outcomes than pain and exhaustion at work.

Increases in the effort workers invest in the employment relationship, especially effort having to do with multiple employers/sites, constant evaluation, and harassment/discrimination, are associated with poorer health status. The association was particularly strong between employment relationship effort and workers' experience of tension at work. A 10 percentage-point increase in employment relationship effort increases the likelihood of workers' reporting tension at work by 40 percentage points.

Increases in the support workers receive in the workplace were significantly correlated with better health outcomes on all the measures of health status except the "everything an effort most of the time" indicator. Increases in workers' household insecurity were correlated with poorer self-reported health and more frequent pain at work.

These results suggest that even after correcting for differences in age, sex, race, physical work hazards, and prior health problems, those characteristics of the employment relationship that are associated with precarious employment, and especially with temporary agency work, are correlated with poorer health outcomes. Higher levels of employment relationship uncertainty and higher levels of employment relationship workload are correlated with poorer health status, particularly with tension at work. Improvements in workplace support and reductions in household insecurity are correlated with better health status.

We have examined the study's data for the impact of age, sex, and race on health outcomes in different employment relationships. In general we found that differences in health status are not statistically different across gender and racial lines and that the type of employment relationship is a much more critical factor. Increased age was correlated with some increased frequency of pain but with decreased frequency of exhaustion after work and tension at work. People of colour were slightly more likely to report that everything was an effort. Women were less likely to report tension at work.

Information gleaned from our interviews and focus groups supports the argument that precarious employment relationships lead to stress and poor health outcomes. Many of those interviewed described a sense of disappointment and disillusionment with their employment, the long-term implications of which can be depression and related ill health. Large European surveys report low levels of job satisfaction among non-permanent workers (Benach, Gimeno, and Benavides 2002; Benavides and Benach 2000), suggesting a similar phenomenon. None of the temporary agency or short-term workers we spoke with were working at tasks or were in employment relationships that they had expected or hoped for, and most were upset and angry about it. One worker said, "I had planned that I wanted to buy a home. When I lost my full-time job, I started working two jobs because I wanted to buy a home. I wanted to have my mortgage paid down so that I would be ready to have a child. With the uncertainty of my job there is no way. I can't buy a home and I'm not going to bring a child into the world if I can't take care of it properly … As I turn thirty-five that's really kind of hit home – time is running out." Another short-term worker said, "I am kind of angered by the line that everyone fed us: everything is going to be okay once you grow up and get a job. Once I grew up and had a job I was so disappointed." Two interviewees told us that although they were generally positive people, they had considered suicide because they could not see a different future.

Several workers spoke about their generally unexpressed anger, both about their disillusionment and about how they were being treated. One agency worker said, "I block it in. It gets to the point at times that it explodes and that's not good, blocking things in. I always have something to say and I'll say it if it is very, very important, but most of the time I just block it in. That's probably what causes my breathing problems." She and three others had some form of breathing problem that included a chronic sore throat and shortness of breath. Several women spoke about temporary assignments, disrupted schedules, and low income making it difficult to eat and exercise regularly. A temporary agency worker described what happened when she began to take enough assignments to support herself: "I'm in a rush, eat burgers. The only day I can actually have a nice homemade meal is if I don't work Saturdays. I've noticed that I've been gaining a lot of weight." A construction worker told us that he had lost his temper several times in workplaces and that those incidents had hurt only him, so he had seen counsellors about anger management. Several women felt that their reproductive problems were related to stress from their employment situation. One had had a miscarriage that she attributed to the demands of her job and the stress of not knowing when she would be working or how far she would have to travel each morning. Both men and women reported sleep disruption resulting from regular but long or overnight shifts as well as from irregular assignments.

On-call homecare workers construct their occupational identity differently, and consequently their health issues appear to be different. Homecare is a female-dominated caring profession that relies on the workers' capacity to pay attention to others' needs. This group was generally dedicated to their work, took a certain pride in it, and felt that their efforts were valued by their clients if by no one else. They told us that they felt it was "unprofessional" to talk about their own health-related problems. At the end of one session during which all participants had said they had no problems with their health, we learned that one had angina and heart problems, several had severe back problems, and another could not stand for any length of time.

They did, however, speak about the emotional stress of working with people who were very ill or dying. "I just go for a brisk walk afterwards to release some of the stress, but it can bother you for a little bit, if they are going through a rough time. You know them and you worry about them so they become like family members and it's very hard to separate."

None of the precarious workers in our study were paid for sick days – "If I don't work I don't get paid." Only a few precarious workers receive basic medical benefits. European studies have shown that non-permanent workers are absent from work less frequently than permanent workers (Benach, Gimeno, and Benavides 2002). People in this study reported that they worked when they were sick and that there were very few illnesses or injuries that would keep them away from work. Even the homecare workers, who were constantly working around illness and communicable diseases, were not paid for sick days. A factory worker told us that when he injured his eye, the doctor told him to stay off work for a week, but he went back to work in two days because he needed the money. An office worker described how an old traffic injury caused a level of pain that meant she could work only if she took anti-nausea medication, which she did daily. Many people reported not being able to look after various aspects of their health – not going to the dentist, not exercising, not eating well – the neglect of any of which could have a cumulative health effect if continued over a long period.

Our study also suggests that risk of injury and ill health related to the production process is about the same for permanent and precarious workers. About 20 per cent of the those who work through an agency, on-call homecare workers, and full-time permanent employees suffered discomfort due to air, noise, and temperature problems most days. Short-term contract workers reported a marginally lower frequency of discomfort.

Michael Quinlan suggests that precarious workers are more likely to experience injury or ill health related to the production process because of three factors: the organization of contracts and rewards (competition, long hours, piecework); the disorganization of the work (ambiguity of rules, splintering occupational health and safety management systems); and the increased likelihood that laws do not apply to these employment relationships (Quinlan 1999; Quinlan and Mahew 1999). A forklift operator illustrated these types of concerns with this story: "There's supposed to be nobody within twenty feet of a forklift drop because a load could drop and fall on someone. When I was working on this line I would back off, but you would have the forklift doing a drop and you'd have these guys – all recent immigrants – all here picking and packing. I told them the law is twenty feet. But they're afraid to stop, and the supervisors would say they're not going fast enough." Workers in this instance and other temporary agency workers we interviewed told us that they received some health and safety training (particularly Workplace Hazardous Materials Information System training) from their agencies, but were often in situations where they were given no information by the client company about workplace-specific hazards and safety measures. They reported that they were not certain about how workers' compensation legislation and protections applied to them; some thought these protections changed depending on the assignment, others did not feel able to assert their rights to health and safety protections before either the client company or the agency.

Precarious workers, like full-time workers, are exposed to various physical risks at the workplace. However, it is unlikely that these risks alone explain the poorer health status of precarious workers compared to full-time workers. It has been suggested that an expanded notion of employment control might help account for the uneven health effects found among workers in different types of precarious employment (Quinlan, Mayhew, and Bohle 2001). The concept of employment strain developed in this chapter is one way of exploring how control issues relate to work-related health outcomes. If, as the findings here suggest, the forms of the employment relationship, particularly precarious forms of employment, create new types of health risks, then the existing system of workplace health and safety regulations needs to be re-examined. Existing forms of regulations do not address health issues related to uncertainty over access to work, the effort or workload associated with maintaining employment, or low levels of workplace or social support.

11 THE STRAIN OF PRECARIOUS EMPLOYMENT RELATIONSHIPS AND EFFORTS TO CHANGE AND RESIST

This study indicates that those precarious workers who work through agencies, those who are on short-term contracts, and those who work on-call experience considerable uncertainty in employment relationships, and consequently low levels of control, and expend considerable effort maintaining these relationships. They also tend to have higher levels of household insecurity and less workplace and social support than full-time workers. The combination of greater uncertainty and increased workload creates high levels of what we call employment strain. Several aspects of employment strain are strongly associated with poorer health and stress. These include the uncertainties of scheduling, the efforts workers must make to handle performance evaluations, which affect future employment, and the efforts they must make to handle workplace harassment and discrimination.

It is not easy for precarious workers to act collectively to bring about changes in these conditions, either at work or in the rest of their lives. As we have seen in this discussion, the most precarious workers are the most likely to be isolated and to receive little support in their employment relationship. Individuals' involvement in organizing initiatives can make them even more vulnerable to harassment, discrimination, and job termination. Low incomes keep many focused on daily survival, and isolation makes the effort to find others in the same situation difficult. But even in the face of these barriers, individual workers do stand up for themselves and each other, and organizing efforts among precarious workers are increasing. Both community groups and trade unions are experimenting with a range of strategies to organize temporary agency workers and others in precarious forms of employment (Cranford and Ladd 2003). Since the mid-1990s, formal union organizing has taken place in Canada among garment workers, farm workers, homecare workers, rural route mail carriers, and university contract teachers, to name a few. This list includes the homecare workers who participated in our survey. Community-based organizing is also taking place in Toronto and Montreal, where groups of workers and community supporters are tackling the issues by educating the general public, creating space for leadership to develop among workers, and challenging employers and legislation. These initiatives are part of a growing international movement of workers' groups that is challenging the global phenomenon of increased labour flexibility.[4]

This study contributes to the growing evidence that there are increased health risks for workers as well as social and economic costs associated with the deregulation of labour markets and increased flexibility in employment relationships. This needs to be discussed and acted on by community-based advocates and unions concerned about working conditions and by those who make health policy. Our findings suggest that larger studies, including more extensive group and individual interviews, could further isolate the employment relationship variables that influence health outcomes, the interactions among these variables, and the interaction between employment strain and job strain. All these constitute a genre of risks and costs that must be recognized by employers and included in contemporary legislative and public insurance protections for workers.

APPENDIX
MULTIVARIATE ANALYSIS OF RELATIONSHIP
BETWEEN WORK ORGANIZATION CHARACTERISTICS
AND HEALTH

Table 4.8, below, reports results from the study's multivariate logistic regression analysis where health outcomes were the dependent variable and work organization characteristics and a series of control variables were the independent variables. Each cell represents a separate regression between one health outcome and one work organization characteristic. The health outcome variables are all binary variables. The work organization variables are indices with values from 0 to 100. Each model is controlled for age, sex, and race. We also controlled for differences in physical work environment using as an indicator discomfort at work owing to poor air, noise, and temperature extremes. We also controlled for prior health status using as an indicator whether or not an individual left a permanent job because of an injury or illness. The reported coefficients are odds ratios and represent the change in the likelihood of reporting the health outcome in question associated with a 10-point increase in the relevant work organization indices. The stars in Table 4.8 represent the degree of statistical significance. The more stars there are, the more statistically significant the result. We used the full sample of 800 observations. The number of observations per regression varies with the frequency of missing responses to specific questions. The numbers reported can be interpreted as follows: the number 1.11 in the cell representing *employment relationship uncertainty* and *health worse than very good* means that the odds of reporting *health worse than very good* increases 11 per cent for each 10-point increase in the *employment relationship uncertainty* index. Numbers greater than 1 indicate that increases in the work organization index are correlated with poorer health outcomes. Numbers less than 1 indicate that increases in the work organization index are correlated with better health outcomes.

Table 4.8 Multivariate analysis of relationship between work organization characteristics and health

	Health Less Than Very Good	Pain Half the Time or More	Exhausted after Work Most Days	Tense Half the Time or More	Everything an Effort Most of the Time
Employment relationship uncertainty	1.11 **	1.07	1.07	1.11 **	1.13 **
Work uncertainty	1.04	0.98	0.99	1.01	0.98
Earnings uncertainty	1.11 **	1.05	1.01	1.07	1.11 **
Scheduling uncertainty	1.05 **	1.05 **	1.07 **	1.06 **	1.07 **
Employment relationship effort	1.13 **	1.20 **	1.28 ***	1.39 ***	1.14 **
Effort getting work	1.02	1.02	1.01	1.02	1.05 **
Effort multiple employers/ sites	1.01	1.08 *	1.19 ***	1.21 ***	1.09 **
Constant evaluation effort	1.04 *	1.05 **	1.06 **	1.07 **	1.05 **
Harassment/ Discrimination effort	1.13 ***	1.16 ***	1.15 ***	1.24 ***	1.02
Household insecurity	1.09 **	1.10 **	1.01	1.04	1.03
Workplace support	0.82 ***	0.86 ***	0.92 **	0.80 ***	0.94
Social support	0.91 ***	0.99	0.93 **	0.92 ***	0.95 *
Control at work	0.89 ***	0.85 ***	0.82 ***	0.83 ***	0.89 **
Physical workload	1.08 **	1.22 ***	1.32 ***	1.27 ***	1.14 ***
Cognitive workload	1.13 ***	1.35 ***	1.41 ***	1.43 ***	1.15 **
Relations with management	0.88 ***	0.87 ***	0.86 ***	0.82 ***	0.92 **

*** p < .001; ** p < .05; * p < .10

Number ranges from 645 to 729.

Model health index = f (age, sex, white, left job due to injury, physical work quality, work index)

NOTES

Authors' Note: The authors would like to thank Nicki Carlan, Simon Enoch, Cindy Gangaram, Brian Gibson, Erika Khandor, Michael Polanyi, and Syed Naqvi for their contributions to the research on which this paper is based. The research was funded by the Social Sciences and Humanities Research Council (SSHRC) Community University Research Alliance (CURA) program. Lewchuk received further assistance from a SSHRC Initiative on the New Economy (INE) grant. Wayne Lewchuk teaches in the Labour Studies Program at McMaster University. Andy King is on staff at the United Steelworkers. Alice de Wolff is currently a researcher with the employment strain group at McMaster University. All are members of the Alliance on Contingent Employment housed at York University.

1 The study is based on survey responses from 800 workers, three focus groups, and ten interviews. It took place in southern Ontario between 2002 and 2004 and is described in detail in this chapter.

2 Response rates from the different groups varied significantly, from close to 100 per cent among homecare workers, to 12 per cent among agency workers, to 7.4 per cent among university workers.

3 We interviewed a total of ten individuals in three separate focus groups. Individuals were selected on the basis of their responses to the survey. We selected individuals from a range of employment relationships and with moderate to high levels of employment strain. Seven women and three men were interviewed.

4 Toronto Organizing for Fair Employment, Au Bas de L'Échelle in Montreal, the Migrant Agricultural Workers Support Centre in southern Ontario, and INTERCEDE, which champions domestic workers, all use different approaches to organizing precarious workers. The North American Alliance for Fair Employment (NAFFE) is a coalition of over seventy unions and community-based organizations that actively organize among precarious workers. Information about NAFFE members and current campaigns can be found at www.fairjobs.org.

REFERENCES

Belkic, K., et al. 2000. Psychosocial factors: Review of the empirical data among men. In *The workplace and cardiovascular disease* (issue title), edited by P.L. Schnall, K. Belkic, P. Landsbergis, and D. Baker. *Occupational Medicine: State of the Art Reviews* 15:24–46

Benach, J., D. Gimeno, and F.G. Benavides. 2002. *Types of employment and health in the European Union.* Dublin: European Foundation for the Improvement of Working and Living Conditions

Benavides, F.G., and J. Benach. 2000. *Temporary employment and health-related outcomes in the European Union.* Dublin: European Foundation for the Improvement of Working and Living Conditions

Cooper, C.L. 2002. The changing psychological contract at work. *Occupational Environment Medicine* 59:355

Cranford, C., and D. Ladd. 2003. Community unionism: organising for fair employment in Canada. *Just Labour* 3:46–59

Cranford, C., L. Vosko, and N. Zukewich. 2003. Temporary employment in the Canadian labour market: A statistical portrait. *Just Labour* 3:6–22

Dauba-Letournex, V., and A. Thébaud-Mony. 2002. *Work organization and health at work in the European Union.* Dublin: European Foundation for the Improvement of Working and Living Conditions

Galabuzi, G.E. 2001. *Canada's creeping economic apartheid.* Toronto: Centre for Social Justice Foundation for Research and Education

Goudswaard, A., and F. Adries. 2002. *Employment status and working conditions.* Dublin: European Foundation for the Improvement of Working and Living Conditions

Herzenberg, Stephen A., John A. Alic, and Howard Wial. 1998. *New rules for a new economy: Employment opportunity in post-industrial America.* Ithaca: IRL Press

Johnson, J.V. 1991. Collective control: Strategies for survival in the workplace. In *The psychosocial work environment: Work organization, democratization and health,* edited by J. Johnson and G. Johansson. Amityville: Baywood Publishing Company

Karasek, R., and T. Theorell. 1990. *Healthy work: Stress, productivity and the reconstruction of working life.* New York: Basic Books

Laflamme, N., C. Brisson, J. Moisan, A. Milot, B. Masse, and M. Vezina. 1998. Job strain and ambulatory blood pressure among female white-collar workers. *Scandinavian Journal of Work, Environment and Health* 24 (5): 334–43

Landsbergis, P.A., P.L. Schnall, K. Warren, T.G. Pickering, and J.E. Schwartz. 1994. Association between ambulatory blood pressure and alternative formulations of job strain. *Scandinavian Journal of Work, Environment and Health* 20 (5): 349–63

Marmot, M.G., 1994. Social differentials in health within and between populations. *Daedalus* 123: 197–216

– 2000. Social class, occupational status and CVO. In *The workplace and cardiovascular disease,* edited by P.L. Schnall, K. Belkic, P. Landsbergis, and D. Baker. *Occupational Medicine: State of the Art Reviews* 15:46–49

Marmot, M.G., et al. 1984. Inequalities in death-specific explanations of a general pattern. *Lancet* 1:1003–6

– 1991. Health inequalities among British civil servants: The Whitehall II study." *Lancet* 337:1387–93

NIOSH (National Institute for Occupational Safety and Health). 2002. *The changing organization of work and the safety and health of working people.* Cincinnati: NIOSH

Nunes, A., and B. Seligman. 1999. *Treatment of Caucasian and African-American applications by San Francisco Bay area employment agencies.* San Francisco: Impact Fund

130 Wayne Lewchuk, Alice de Wolff, and Andy King

Parker, S., et al. 2002. Effects of temporary contracts on perceived work
characteristics and job strain: A longitudinal study. *Personnel Psychology*
55:689–708

Quinlan, M. 1999. The implications of labour market restructuring in
industrialized societies for occupational health and safety. *Economic and
Industrial Democracy* 20:427–60

Quinlan, M., and C. Mahew. 1999. The effects of outsourcing on
occupational health and safety: A comparative study of factory-based
workers and outworkers in the Australian clothing industry. *International
Journal of Health Services* 29:83–107

Quinlan, M., C. Mayhew, and P. Bohle. 2001. The global expansion of
temporary employment, work disorganization, and consequences for
occupational health: A review of recent literature. *International Journal of
Health Services* 31:335–414

Schnall, Peter L., J.E. Schwartz, P.A. Landsbergis, K. Warren, and T.G.
Pickering. 1992. Relation between job strain, alcohol, and ambulatory
blood pressure. *Hypertension* 19 (5): 488–94

– 1998. A longitudinal study of job strain and ambulatory blood pressure:
Results from a three-year follow-up. *Psychosomatic Medicine* 60:697–706

Selikoff, Irving et al. 1964. Asbestos exposure and neoplasia. *Journal of the
American Medical Association* 188:22–6

Siegrist, J. 1996. Adverse health effects of high effort/low reward conditions.
Occupational Health Psychology 1:27–41

Siegrist, J., and R. Peters. 2000. The effort-reward imbalance model. In *The
workplace and cardiovascular disease* (issue title), edited by P.L. Schnall, K.
Belkic, P. Landsbergis, and D. Baker. *Occupational Medicine: State of the Art
Reviews* 15:83–7

Smith, Barbara Ellen. 1987. *Digging our own graves: Coal miners and the struggle
over black lung disease.* Philadelphia: Temple University Press

Stansfeld, S.A., J. Head, and M. Marmot. 2000. *Work related factors and ill-
health: The Whitehall II study.* Norwich: Her Majesty's Stationary Office

Statistics Canada. 2004a. CANSIM Table 361-0001 – Summary statistics for
employment services (all establishments), by NAICS #5613

– 2004b. Employment services industry. *Daily,* 29 March

– 2003. Number of persons aged 15 and over, by number of unpaid hours
doing housework, Canada, 1996 and 2001. In *2001 Census. Release 6,*
February 11. Ottawa

Tucker, Eric, 1990. *Administering danger in the workplace.* Toronto: University
of Toronto Press

Vosko, Leah F. 2000. *Temporary work: The gendered rise of a precarious employment
relationship.* Toronto, University of Toronto Press

Vosko, Leah F., Nancy Zukewich, and Cynthia Cranford. 2003. Precarious
jobs: A new typology of employment. *Perspectives,* October, 16–26

5

Contradictions of Labour Processes and Workers' Use of Skills in Advanced Capitalist Economies

DAVID W. LIVINGSTONE AND
ANTONIE SCHOLTZ

INTRODUCTION

In this chapter we will argue that Canadians' opportunities to utilize their knowledge is significantly related to their class position within the capitalist labour process, and specifically to the level of control and autonomy a worker has. To assess accurately the type and scope of workers' learning practices and the extent to which their knowledge and skills match current job requirements, we will use a more inclusive conception of learning, one that includes not just formal schooling and adult or further education, but also informal training (such as mentoring) and non-taught informal learning. While the conflict between capitalists and workers cannot explain all social change, class analysis remains a primary explanatory tool for understanding the dynamic processes that affect the experiences and learning practices of a majority of workers.

There is an inherent contradiction in the relations between capitalist business owners and their actual and prospective employees in advanced capitalist economies. Capitalists need to hire workers who are sufficiently knowledgable and versatile to produce and sell frequently changing forms of commodities, while simultaneously ensuring that these employees do not gain enough uniquely specialized knowledge and autonomy in the production process to demand wages and benefits that could jeopardize competitive product prices and profits. This struggle over wages and profits underlies much of the recent public and scholarly debate over a "knowledge-based economy" (KBE) versus the "deskilling of workers."

The dominant theme in current public discourse about changing work patterns and learning needs is the emergence of the KBE, where new information technology developments are assumed to demand more educated, highly skilled, and self-motivated workers. This view tends to generalize from a small proportion of privileged workers to the labour market as a whole, largely ignoring the concentration of economic power in the hands of corporate elites. Within capitalist organizations, asymmetrical power relations continue to lead to the subordination of most workers, who often find their existing skills both unrecognized and underutilized. The access to and utilization of knowledge has been a point of conflict in almost all class-based economies, but this conflict has been particularly intense under capitalism. The gap between workers' knowledge and their ability to apply it in the workplace has been a growing problem since modern industry began to flourish in the early part of the nineteenth century.

Today, the contradictions inherent in the capitalist labour process exacerbate the underemployment of many workers. Workers have access to and are pursuing formal education at a higher rate than ever before. At the same time, capitalist firms are compelled to exploit workers' knowledge through various means, including by routinizing and deskilling jobs, in order to reduce production costs so as to realize profits. As more and more workers seek to upgrade their education and skills in an economic environment where the actual skill requirements for work appear to be increasing gradually and unevenly at best, underemployment worsens and the contradictions become clearer.

Our later analysis will distinguish several classes that are based on production relations, including ownership classes, intermediate hired employees (notably managers and professionals), and working classes (see Livingstone and Mangan 1996). We will assess differential profiles of learning and determine how such learning corresponds with job skill requirements. For introductory purposes, we need only note that our analysis will pay particular attention to working-class people, who are posited to experience the greatest barriers to formal education, enjoy little recognition of informal learning, and be most affected by the underutilization of skill and knowledge.

Chapter Outline

The chapter begins with a short review of knowledge-based economy theories, with a focus on assumptions of rapid technology-driven increases in skill requirements. Then, we suggest a perspective on workers' learning that includes learning beyond the walls of "authorized" educational institutions. Next, to begin to identify why and to what extent skill requirements have actually changed in the current economy, we provide some working definitions before looking back at the development of labour process theory. From Braverman 1974 onward, this research has traditionally focused on capitalists' inherent drive to control and make ever more efficient production processes, whether through the use of technology or the detailed division of tasks. We then examine how labour process theory has moved from its classical Marxist roots and how emerging research on subjectivity, gender and race, and management control strategies allows us to construct a more complex and accurate picture of job-related skill requirements in the current capitalist job market. Then we offer a more substantial discussion of why class analysis remains a key to understanding employment-related learning. We test these arguments with data collected from recent national surveys and related case studies of formal and informal learning related to employment. The section on underemployment in Canada explores the implications of these findings. We argue that rapidly increasing learning activities among all Canadian employees, coupled with only gradual increases in job skill requirements, have led to widespread underemployment, particularly among the working classes. Finally, we summarize our findings and briefly make a case for economic reforms to address this education-jobs gap.

THEORIES OF A KNOWLEDGE-BASED ECONOMY

The notion of underutilization of workers' knowledge is not often entertained within the current dominant discourse. Rather, a large body of writing claims that capitalism is undergoing a fundamental shift in what and how it produces, in the type of commodities that will sustain economic growth, and in the nature of paid employment in this new environment. Various theorists argue that, via the diffusion of information technologies, knowledge is the new raw material of production. In this supposed post-industrial (Bell 1973) or knowledge-based economy (OECD 1996, 2002), employment is seen to be transcending monotonous, low-skill manual labour, moving instead towards more rewarding intellective or knowledge work that involves complex planning and design activity (Neef 1999; Stewart 1997). It is assumed that authoritarian management strategies will have to be dismantled and companies will have to become "learning organizations" if they are to extract value from their labour forces and remain profitable (Senge

1994). The result of these changes is a growing demand for a new type of worker, one who is highly educated, with versatile skills, and who can take responsibility for more decision-making within the enterprise (Kleinman and Vallas 2001).

The current archetype for this new type of employee is the much vaunted knowledge worker (scientists, engineers, computer analysts, and other creative design workers) whose superior educational credentials are augmented by a necessary commitment to work-related lifelong learning (Cortada 1998; Drucker 1993). Theorists of a knowledge-based economy often assume that the shift to knowledge work has already been substantial, an assumption that has permeated almost every level of public discussion, including government policy setting and educational reform (Livingstone 2004). The logical extension is that all workers must increase their knowledge if the country is to meet the demand for highly skilled workers now and in the future. Implicit in much of the public discourse regarding skills and education is the belief that workers are currently not well enough educated for the available work and not yet committed to lifelong learning. While the theories and assumptions of the KBE will be critiqued throughout the chapter, it should immediately be noted that such theories allude to the notion that learning is an ongoing, lifelong activity that includes but is not bound to state-sanctioned institutions. This allusion to multiple forms of learning, however, remains significantly under-documented.

A MORE INCLUSIVE VIEW OF LEARNING

One of the most distinguishing features of the human species is our continuing acquisition of knowledge and skills. This learning does not occur merely within the bounds of formal educational institutions or under the direction of authorized instructors. The learning practices of workers, and other adults, can be distinguished in terms of who controls the learning and how pre-organized the subject matter is.

Only government-sanctioned schooling and adult or further education have typically been acknowledged or studied. Other forms of learning and training have tended to be marginalized because they are harder to study and/or they are grounded in the experiential knowledge more relevant to subordinated workers (Gereluk, Briton, and Spencer 1999; Burns 1999). Our studies have distinguished four broad types of learning (Livingstone 2005):

1 *Formal schooling.* A pre-established body of knowledge is used to construct a required curriculum, which is then taught to learners by an

authorized teacher. Examples include K to 12 schooling, college, and university.

2 *Further or adult education.* Learners willingly acquire knowledge or skill relating to their interests by studying with a teacher who uses an organized curriculum. Examples include adult night school courses, workshops, various distance education courses.

3 *Informal education or training.* Here teachers or mentors work with learners without sustained reference to any specific curriculum, often in more incidental and spontaneous learning situations. On-the-job training by more experienced workers is a prime example.

4 *Non-taught individual or collective informal learning.* Learning is undertaken either individually or as part of a group without direct reliance on a teacher or an externally organized curriculum. These forms of learning can be of the intentional sort, as focused on in this chapter, or more tacit, where learning is coterminous with life experience itself.

Overall, informal learning complements rather than replaces more formal types of learning. It is sometimes difficult to separate these types of learning. For example, a self-directed learner may acquire and follow quite closely an institutionally approved curriculum. But the key point is that narrow formal conceptions of learning tend to reproduce existing inequitable and hierarchical knowledge/power structures. To equate workers' intellectual capacities with formal educational attainments is to ignore the informal modes of learning that are often more essential to the development of their working knowledge (Livingstone and Sawchuk 2004).

However, before we undertake a class-based analysis of learning or examine the correspondence of worker capabilities and job skill requirements in more detail, it is important that we understand how skill has been conceptualized and if and why skill requirements have changed in current capitalist labour processes. Recent research from the labour process perspective provides helpful insights on issues of control in the employer-employee relationship, technological innovation, and shifting trends in skill utilization.

WORKING DEFINITIONS

As a first step into the labour process debate, we need to specify a number of key concepts that feature prominently throughout the rest of the chapter. Concepts central to our analysis of the capitalist labour process include the mode of production, the means of production, the forces and relations of production, the division of labour, and skills. In

Marxist terms, a historical *mode of production* is the totality of means and relations of production constituting the economic structure of society, which is shaped by the development of the material forces of production and provides the most general conditions for social, political, and intellectual life. The *means of production* include natural resources, raw materials, and instruments of production. The *forces of production* are the things we use to produce what we need, including the means of production and labour power (both physical and mental capacities). The *relations of production* are the relations of power and control between people and productive forces.

Each mode of production is distinguishable by a primary form of extraction of labour from direct producers by ownership classes. In the slave mode, plantation owners owned the slaves outright; in feudalism, lords exacted days of free labour from serfs tied to their lands. In the capitalist mode of production, capitalists own the major means of production (including tools and production sites such as factories, stores, offices) as their private property, hiring and firing workers according to the amount of surplus value they can extract from their labour power and realize as profit through the sale of goods and service commodities. Those who do not possess sufficient means of production to initiate a production process are forced to sell their labour power as a market commodity in order to survive and to strive to ensure their continuing marketability.

Capitalist enterprises are driven by both inter-firm competition in commodity markets and class conflict between owners and workers over profits and wages/benefits to continually modify the means of production in order to reduce costs and maximize profits. Capitalism encourages scientific and technological development in aid of more profitable production with less labour cost. The forces of production, including tools and techniques and their combination with the capacities of labour, have experienced extraordinary growth during the short history of industrial capitalism. Such technological developments as the hand mill, the steam engine, electrical generators, and interconnected electronic networks have all served to expand commodity production and exchange while also socializing, or making very widely accessible, diverse forms of knowledge (via such forums as the public library, public radio and television, and now the Internet). At the same time, private ownership of the means of production and the attendant wealth have become increasingly concentrated in a small number of large corporations, from the joint stock companies of the 1880s to the massive global corporations of the present. The contradictions between the socialization of the forces of production and the privatization of ownership of the means of production are most evident in the capitalist labour process, where owners strive to control production techniques for their own benefit, while workers have ever greater access to diverse sources of knowledge that is relevant for production.

The *division of labour* is not simply the identification and separation of the different technical components of a task. The division of labour is also a social phenomenon, where decisions are made about the complexity (or simplicity) of the work that individuals will carry out. In other words, the division of labour is about the specialization of workers. At its negative extreme this specialization can lead to individuals performing a single, simple task with no need for them to understand the entire process of which they are a part (Braverman 1974; Murphy 1993; Noble 1984). Discussions about the division of labour are closely related to notions of skilled and unskilled labour.

Skill denotes the power to perform any given activity competently, as in "he is a skilled carpenter." It also refers to the ability to use one's knowledge effectively and readily in performance. Often the definition of skill is omitted in discussions of work. This lack of attention to the complexity of "skill" has led to a number of serious problems, including (1) the conflating of workers' educational attainments with the skill requirements of jobs, (2) a narrow focus on technical requirements, and (3) an uncritical acceptance of politicized definitions of skill. It is worth elaborating on these points.

First, approaches exemplified by human capital theory take the view that skill exists in the worker, that it is a set of competencies that can be carried from job to job. Such a conceptualization prevents any measure of skill increase or decrease in the labour process per se, misleadingly equating the rapid increase in workers' educational attainments in the last century with a rising demand for job-related skills (Spenner 1983; Pankhurst 2004). We shall later extend this criticism to the theories of an emerging knowledge-based economy.

Second, notions of skill have frequently been simplistic and one-dimensional, focused on the increase or decrease of easily identified technical tasks. We argue that technical and social relations of production engender different but interrelated types of skills. Skill, in other words, is multidimensional; in studying skill as purely technical mastery, one ignores the learned ability to interact socially within a hierarchical system. Here, Kenneth Spenner's distinction between "skill as substantive complexity" and "skill as autonomy-control" is a useful one (Spenner 1984, 828). Spenner defines the *substantive complexity of skill* as "the level, scope and integration of mental, interpersonal, and manipulative tasks in a job" and *autonomy-control* as "more or less room for the worker to initiate and conclude action, to control the content, manner, and speed with which a task is done" (828). Spenner notes that the latter dimension of skill is not the same as formal authority or supervision, which involves one's place in the organizational hierarchy or network; rather, autonomy-control is the discretion a worker is permitted within a defined role.

We argue that autonomy-control is discretion and more: it is the tacitly or actively acquired set of skills for performing and responding to authority. It can occur in a fairly passive manner, where the employee simply knows how to interact with "superiors," or it can be in a more active manner, where the employee works within the power structure to establish control over a given work "space" (physical or intellective). It is difficult to deny that understanding power relations, especially how to resist or manipulate them, is a skill separate from technical requirements. This distinction between the technical complexity of the task and the discretionary control one has over one's job is crucial for understanding how paid work has been changing in today's economy, particularly in light of the KBE claims that the relationship between workers and management is currently undergoing a fundamental shift.

The third barrier to a comprehensive conception of skill is the often overtly political identification of skill. Employees use power gained via organization (e.g., professional association, trade union) to define their work as highly skilled (Cockburn 1991). They do this in conflict with the employer and sometimes in conflict with other groups of workers. In negotiations between unions and employers, the actual skill required to perform a job can be less important than the relational values attached to given tasks.

Workers with substantial power are able to argue that their work is more skilled and should be compensated as such. While some workers and their jobs may be (over)valued, the work and skills of others are undervalued, artificially depressed in the dynamic hierarchy of skills. This devaluation and marginalization of some workers and their skills often occurs along the lines of gender and race.

THE LABOUR PROCESS DEBATE: IDENTIFYING CURRENT SKILL REQUIREMENTS

Braverman: Critiques and Extensions of the Work Degradation Thesis

The current labour process debate emerges primarily from Harry Braverman's *Labor and Monopoly Capital* (1974). As discussed in greater depth in the introduction to this book, Braverman's critical Marxist analysis examined the historical relationship between capitalists and workers, in particular the philosophy and tactics used by management to increase the efficiency of the labour process in order to maximize profits. One of the results of this drive for profit, as Braverman saw it, was a gradual decline in skill requirements via routinization and automation. Rather than accepting technological change as deterministic (Foster 1994), however, Braverman placed issues of control, profit, and the division of labour squarely at the centre of transformations in skill requirements and organizational structure.

Braverman's conclusion – that the technical division of labour was being used by management to separate "conception from execution" (Braverman 1974, 79) in order to increase control and profit, literally subdividing human beings (51) – evoked an immediate response. Research supporting, reworking, and rejecting his assertions continues to the present day (Zimbalist 1979; Meiksins 1994; Smith 1994; Wardell 1999). It is argued that Braverman's analysis ignores the patriarchal (Cockburn 1991) and racialized (Madamba 1998; Vallas 2003) assumptions on the basis of which predominately white, male management and workers' organizations restrict women and minorities to lower-wage and supposedly less-skilled work. The over-representation of women and minorities/immigrants in less powerful, less-unionized sectors, where work is often part-time and/or contingent and vulnerable to routinization, means that these groups' jobs are especially prone to outsourcing and susceptible to intensification (Huws 2003; Burris, 1998).

Braverman's apparent preoccupation with employer control may have led him to neglect not only race and gender but also the ways in which subjectivity (Hochschild 1983; O'Doherty and Willmott, 2001) and class struggle shape the labour process as well (Zimbalist 1979). For example, Michael Burawoy, in his study (1979) of how employers acquire workers' consent to the conditions of production, found that most labour processes are negotiated and often reflect an anti-managerial, if not anti-capitalist, form of workers' resistance (see also Smith 1994; Meiksins 1994). Others have noted that scientific management and worker-employer conflict are not ubiquitous, that profit and not control is the prime motivator within capitalism (Cohen 1987).

In many cases, humanistic managerial strategies coexist with more-controlling approaches, with less-centralized operating structures allowing for upskilling and greater employee discretion (Edwards 1979; Meiksins 1994; Smith 1994; Zimbalist 1979), or what has been called "responsible autonomy" (Friedman 1977). Some, such as Paul Adler (2006), believe that, regardless of the approach used, the labour process within capitalism inadvertently socializes the forces of production. Other research has examined the ways managers and highly educated and/or specialized workers have used their power in the labour market to maintain control over their knowledge and work processes, forcing enterprises to be more sensitive to the autonomous space of these professionals (Larson 1980).

Technology and Control in the Labour Process

Any discussion of control in the current capitalist epoch must address the development of information technologies (IT). Much of the work around the purported shift to a post-industrial or knowledge-based economy, for instance, has looked upon technology as a crucial or determining factor in altering control in the labour process (Bell 1973; Hirschhorn 1984). Technology, it is assumed (and/or hoped), will demand both a greater variety and an average increase of skills among the workforce. Automating technology is believed to reduce repetitious factory work significantly and allow a large number of workers to move into more complex knowledge or service work. In this new workplace, workers (and managers) are no longer encumbered by traditional hierarchies, learning becomes the new form of labour, and time-space constraints on intellective work are broken down as IT allows tasks to be performed remotely (Zuboff 1984). The point here is not a neo-Luddite complaint that such a future is not possible or desirable, it is only to argue, first, that technological development does not have some life outside of the social, and second, that excitement over the potentialities of technology should not blind us to the possibility that the power relations and autonomy within the labour process may not have changed as much as post-industrial theories would have us believe.

In his study of the post–World War II "military-industrial-educational-complex" in the United States, David Noble made clear the social, highly political nature of scientific research and innovation (Noble 1994, 20). More recently, A. Aneesh (2001) has identified how Taylorist rationalizing principles can find their way back into IT-intensive labour processes that integrate rather than fragment tasks. Arguing that a focus on up-skilling or deskilling misses the more important rationalization that is occurring regardless of technical skill requirements, Aneesh proposed a theory of "skill saturation," a "phenomenon characterized by an absolute predictability of procedure and outcome, resulting from an exhaustive ordering of various components of skills, and the elimination of irregular spaces of work" (363).

Ursula Huws (2003), like Aneesh and others (see also Kraft 1977; Hennessy and Sawchuk, 2003), found that increasingly generic and integrated software networks have been applied to jobs that were formerly resistant to standardization and routinization. This trend, where professional judgment is minimized by "intelligent" systems, has created a new group of "process" knowledge workers who support the labour of a select few creative or originating knowledge workers. The convergence and standardization of skills have enabled managers in the fields of knowledge work, service, and data processing – under enormous pressure to reduce costs – to outsource work via digital networks, a trend felt most intensely by women, minorities, and others marginalized in the current labour process.

Socio-economic Trends: The Canadian Context

Within the Canadian economy, as in most advanced capitalist economies, a number of broad trends are widely recognized: (1) job growth has been primarily in the service sector, with increased numbers also in managerial, professional, and semi-professional occupations; (2) most adult females, including those with young children, are now in the labour force; (3) contingent work has increased, notably part-time work with low benefits and little security; and (4) computer-based technologies have been increasingly adopted in the labour process, which has both created (information management, programming, data processing) and reduced (clerical, goods-producing) jobs within different sectors of the economy (Clement 1981; Heron and Storey 1986; Livingstone 2002; Krahn and Lowe 2002; Russell 1999).

In the wake of fading manual jobs, new information technologies and worldwide digital networks are supposed to turn rapidly growing numbers of Canadians into knowledge workers. The reality in Canada, however, is that while new technologies have been rapidly and widely incorporated by capitalist enterprises, knowledge workers make up less than a quarter of the labour force by the most optimistic estimates (Statistics Canada 2003; cf. Lavoie and Roy 1998). This leaves three-quarters of Canadians still working in jobs that involve the routinized transmission of data, the processing of goods, and the delivery of services. The impact of new technologies has only led to a gradual increase in job skill requirements (Leckie 1996; Barton 2000; Handel 2000). Indeed, according to the General Social Survey (GSS), Canadians continue to acquire more computer skills (or computer literacy) than they have the chance to use in their work (Lowe 2000).

Continuity, then, rather than change, appears as the dominant trend in skill requirements, workforce composition, and the social relations of production. The fact is that the new economy has not transcended old class divisions. Countries like Canada may be developing post-industrial economies, but we are certainly not post-conflict. Class antagonisms cannot explain all social change or conflict, but the idea of class remains vital for any analysis of the labour process, work-related learning, and economic change.

CLASS POSITIONS

Global capitalism, in its ever-expanding search for profit, is now working at a frenetic pace, with goods and services circulating around the globe. Capitalist commodification has pushed further and further into the domestic and community spheres of life, seeking "profit niches." Simultaneously, the same types of capital-intensive technology are generally available to all competitors in a given sector, and thus they offer each competitor diminishing chances of a competitive edge via technology. Many investments in technology now provide little return, existing essentially as a capital expenditure to keep a firm in the game. Consequently, capitalists and their managers are under enormous pressure to extract the maximum amount of value from human labour if they want to remain profitable.

As the economies in advanced capitalist countries shift away from manual labour, the emphasis is less on appropriating physical labour, through such practices as scientific management, and more on appropriating workers' knowledge. As noted earlier, a recent management mantra has centred on the creation of workplaces that are less hierarchical and promote learning, where workers are motivated and/or coerced, first, to become lifelong learners and, second, to share their knowledge for the good of the company. While the reality of working conditions may have diverged sharply from this ideal of power diffusion throughout the enterprise, there is little doubt that workers are becoming more knowledgeable and that capitalist firms are striving to exploit this knowledge to increase productivity in the name of profit.

To delve more deeply into these issues, we need to identify class positions in the capitalist production process more specifically and assess available empirical evidence. We distinguish eight major class groupings in production relations (Livingstone and Mangan, 1996):

1 *Corporate executives* own large assets and employ many others.
2 *Small employers* own their own businesses but have relatively few employees.
3 *Self-employed* survive through businesses based on their own labour; they have no employees.
4 *Managers* are hired by larger private enterprises and public organizations to control the enterprise's regular operations.
5 *Professional employees* perform various specialized functions semi-autonomously.
6 *Supervisors* are employees in larger or more dispersed organizations to whom managers delegate some operational control.
7 *Industrial workers* produce goods.

8 *Service workers* provide various clerical and sales services (they include workers previously identified as process knowledge workers and data processors).

In the traditional Marxist binary of capital and labour, the owners of capital (businesses, land, substantial financial assets), including corporate executives, small employers, and the self-employed, are distinct from the rest of the labour force, the proletariat, those who do not own and are alienated from the means of production. However, managers, professionals, and supervisors do not fit cleanly into such a binary; rather, as employees who carry out the will of their employers over subordinate employees, they have more intermediate class positions. Manual and service wage workers, whom we can more clearly call working class, are the most subordinated workers within the capitalist framework, enjoying little input into the firm's labour process. It must be noted here that this class analysis ignores large numbers of people entirely excluded from production relations, the "lumpen class" in Marx's terms.

So, formally recognized discretionary control in the use of skills and knowledge (for example, in job descriptions) is, in general, significantly diminished for workers lower in this class hierarchy. For the most part, corporate executives and small employers possess the greatest amount of control over the direction of their enterprises, labour processes, and what skills they will utilize. The self-employed are generally considered outside of the class struggle; although they control their own enterprises, theirs is a tenuous existence and they can easily slide into various employee positions or climb into the position of small employer. Managers and professional employees have a relatively significant amount of discretionary power, but as noted above, this occurs within the confines of carrying out the instructions of owners. Supervisors usually have little power in the labour process, mainly following the directions of managers or senior professionals. Often supervisors are drawn directly from the firm's wage workforce and thus experience some of the most intense "lived" contradictions between capital and labour. Industrial and service workers, who form the core of the working class, generally experience the least amount of control regarding how and when they will utilize their skills within the enterprise.

As the scope and scale of capitalist production expanded, owners increasingly turned to managerial and professional employees for assistance in coordinating and designing general labour processes. Over the past century, these intermediate, contradictory class positions – those holding them performing part of the capitalist owners' role while remaining hired employees – have increased considerably. Various theorists have argued for and against including such contradictory occupational groups in the working classes. Barbara and John Ehrenreich (1979) believe that advanced capitalism has effectively created a new class. They argue that the professional-managerial class (PMC) consists of "salaried mental workers who do not own the means of production and whose major function in the social division of labor may be described broadly as the reproduction of capitalist culture and capitalist class relations" (12). This PMC is relational rather than categorical, fluid rather than rigid, encompassing individuals in a broad range of jobs, skill sets, income levels, power, and status.

To debate the validity of the professional-managerial class as a new class is outside the scope of this chapter; for our purposes, it is not necessary to verify whether a new class has been created, only to emphasize that capitalism continues to produce contradictions as effectively as it produces goods and services. Acknowledging such contradictions also brings us back to our earlier discussion about the definition of skill and the social and technical relations of production. Unlike engineers and other professional employees who bridge the gap between the social and technical relations of production, managers generally possess only familiarity with technical tasks, not mastery. Managers, in a sense, are oriented less to "skill as substantive complexity" and more to "skill as autonomy-control" (Spenner 1984, 828). It seems fairly evident that managers manage and that their technical knowledge may not be as developed as those they direct. This relationship, then, is imbued with a certain inherent tension, with management constantly in a struggle to legitimize their workplace authority over a working class that may have more technical skill than they have.

Workplace ethnographies have documented complex repertoires of hidden knowledge among workers in many occupational groups that are never acknowledged by employers and managers or even by most labour unions (Kusterer 1978; Livingstone and Sawchuk 2004; Rose 2004). Even in the most highly automated production processes, machine operators retain significant uncaptured control. The informal training provided by more experienced operators remains essential to any novice wanting to perform the job. For example, a young rolling mill operator in a unionized steel mill, now on the job for several years, describes his experience:

Reading the tolerances in molten steel is *all* eyeball because we burn wood against it, it makes an impression, and each mark on the impression dictates what you need to do. That was the hardest part about the job, learning how to read that wood ... The guy who trained me ... told me that *sound* would save my life there one day. And I wear earmuffs, and I wear earplugs. And when I was there for the first couple of weeks, I just looked at him like he was from outer space, because I had no idea what he was talking about. I hear things now that I shouldn't hear ... That mill, when it changes speed, I know. I know where it changed speed, if the bar is loose somewhere I can hear it, if it breaks out somewhere – the sound plays that much of a role ... I think I'm probably a year away from proficiency, to the point where I'll never be questioned ever again [by supervisors] on what I do.[1]

Many working-class employees retain some discretionary control over their jobs. Indeed, the most automated and computerized labour processes may depend more directly than earlier industrial processes on the monitoring attention of workers, and may thereby enhance the potential collective economic power of the diminishing numbers of directly productive labourers (cf. Mallet 1975). Beyond this, case studies conducted at employment sites in cooperation with labour unions have shown that many assembly line workers have developed informal learning networks to teach themselves how to use personal computers. Some of these workers have become competent computer programmers, even though they have had no employer encouragement and no immediate opportunities to use these skills in their jobs (Sawchuk 2003).

Generally, employees who belong to unions or similar types of associations tend to enjoy more power within the workplace than unorganized workers. Working-class union members, whom we might call the most powerful among the least powerful, are often in a better position to bargain for workplace rights and greater skill designation for their jobs. As noted in the discussion of skill definition, political power plays a significant role in distinguishing high-skill from low-skill jobs. The broader point here is that power within and between work-based groupings, as in society at large, is dynamic, negotiated, struggled over, historical, and lived. It is in this context that workplace training and learning are sought and acquired. To examine learning and knowledge acquisition without acknowledging class and differential access to power is to presume a highly idealized environment. Class struggle does not determine learning choices or outcomes, but it is likely to have a strong influence on whether and where that learning is recognized. To paraphrase Marx, we make our own history but not in circumstances of our choosing.

CLASS AND LEARNING

A large and increasing majority of people now regard an advanced education as very important to getting along in society (Livingstone,

Hart, and Davie 2003). As human capital theorists have argued, the correspondence between formal educational credentials and income is a strong one. However, a focus on this relationship alone masks both the factors influencing access to formal education and the substantial learning that occurs outside recognized educational institutions. Employers, and many workers, tend only to recognize credential-based learning, privileging the efforts of those who have the financial resources necessary to afford the cost of and time for extensive formal education. This is not, of course, to say that formal educational attainments are in any way negative. It is good news when we find that Canadians are among the most educated people in the world, with approximately 50 per cent of the population aged twenty-five to sixty-four having achieved a post-secondary credential (Statistics Canada 2000). Participation rates in both advanced schooling and adult education have increased geometrically since the 1960s among Canadians, including those from working-class origins (Livingstone and Stowe 2003).

The fixation on formal credentials within capitalist social relations has served to marginalize less formal types of learning often pursued by individuals from working-class and other less advantaged backgrounds. It is well documented that youth from working-class origins are streamed into programs that offer them relatively little chance of going on to pursue a post-secondary education (Curtis, Livingstone, and Smaller 1992). Young adults from working-class backgrounds remain persistently under-represented in higher education, while those from privileged class origins are much more likely to obtain a post-secondary degree. This serious waste of talent is only exacerbated when employers fixate on formal education credentials, denying any recognition of other prior learning.

The fact that informal learning is usually unrecognized in employment-related discussions about a person's learning attainment is especially important to those in working-class jobs. Workers are often presumed to be "stuck" in their jobs because they lack commitment to lifelong learning. While it is true that working-class people continue to experience persistent barriers to acquiring formal learning, most theorists have failed to recognize that the general population, especially less powerful social groups, have benefited significantly from the increased availability of free voluntary forms of knowledge production, such as public libraries, various educational media, trade union schools, and electronic information networks. Not only are working-class and subordinated groups enabled to build their job-related and general knowledge bases, these socialized forces of knowledge production directly challenge attempts to commodify knowledge.

Recent survey research has found that although industrial and service workers are generally much less formally schooled than corporate executives, managers, and professional employees, they are just as likely to devote time and energy both to informal job-related learning, ranging from computer literacy to health and safety, and to informal learning related to unpaid domestic and community work and other general interests (Livingstone 2002). While much of this general knowledge may be irrelevant to the immediate objective of enhancing firms' profitability, it is directly applicable in other socially useful and fulfilling household and community work and, potentially, in jobs redesigned to use workers' growing repertoire of skills more fully. This opposition between the *socialized* forces of knowledge production and the *privatized* relations of knowledge production is a fundamental contradiction of knowledge development in capitalist economies (Livingstone 2004).

National surveys conducted in 1998 and 2004 provide relevant recent data on both participation in various learning activities and class positions in production relations for the employed Canadian labour force. As Table 5.1 summarizes,[2] the differences in completion of the most advanced credential programs, as indicated by university degrees, are very substantial between occupational classes in the active labour force. The vast majority of corporate executives and nearly half of all managers and professionals have university degrees, while less than 10 per cent of all wage workers do, including about 3 per cent of industrial workers. But around 20 per cent of industrial workers now have community college diplomas. Class differences in the incidence of participation in adult education are less marked and appear to be decreasing. About half of the employed labour force, including over a third of industrial workers, took a course or workshop of some duration in the previous year. Participation in diverse forms of informal learning, including job-related learning, unpaid work-related learning, and general interest learning, is widespread and of similar incidence across all classes and most other social background groups. The incidence of total self-reported informal learning among wage workers is as great as among more affluent and highly schooled classes, and these learning activities are far more extensive than participation in adult education (Livingstone 1999). As Table 5.1 summarizes, the time devoted to informal job-related learning on a weekly basis is also much the same across the class positions. There appears to be a massive and more egalitarian informal learning society hidden beneath the pyramidal class-structured schooling system and the somewhat less hierarchical array of further-education programs.

The evidence suggests that Canadian workers are already lifelong learners, whether they have achieved a high level of formal education

Table 5.1 Schooling, further education, and incidence of job-related informal learning by occupational class, employed Canadian labour force, 1998 and 2004

Occupational Class		University Degree (%)	Course/ Workshop Last Year (%)	Informal Job-Related Learning (median hrs/week)
Corporate executives*	1998	70*	20*	*
	2002	81*	38*	*
Small employers	1998	22	51	4
	2004	22	44	2
Self-employed	1998	15	45	3
	2004	23	49	2
Managers	1998	34	71	4
	2004	39	67	3
Professionals	1998	58	61	3
	2004	63	52	2
Supervisors	1998	12	60	3
	2004	13	63	2
Service workers	1998	8	50	2
	2004	8	48	2
Industrial workers	1998	3	31	4
	2004	3	41	2
Total (N = 928)	1998	16	49	3
(N = 5720)	2004	20	51	2

Sources: Livingstone 1999, 2005.

*Estimates for Ontario corporate executives in 1998 and 2002 from Livingstone, Hart, and Davie 1999, 2003; no comparable data are available on their job-related informal learning, but self-reported total informal learning is very similar to that of other class groups.

or not. While learning input does not always equal successful learning output, and a less capable learner may have to spend considerably more time to achieve a successful outcome, it must also be emphasized that self-reported learning surveys may very substantially underestimate the total amount of informal learning that people do because of the embedded and taken-for-granted character of their often tacit learning.

These data also suggest that the supply of educated workers may not be a significant general problem in the Canadian economy (despite a chronic shortage of workers in the skilled trades, largely as a consequence of an underdeveloped apprenticeship system). But a core assumption of KBE theories is that job skill requirements in general are increasing more rapidly than the knowledge and skill acquisition of the labour force. That educational attainments among Canadian workers are increasing cannot be denied. Predictably, in the wake of higher attainment levels, the charge that the quality of mass education has deteriorated has been widely promoted, complete with literacy panics (Livingstone 2004). But the central implicit and often explicit claim of KBE advocates remains that this economy is rapidly creating more highly skilled jobs than can be filled. Is the commitment to learning shown so far by Canadian workers not enough to meet the demand? To address this question, we must assess how successfully current labour processes utilize the existing skills of workers.

UNDEREMPLOYMENT IN CANADA

Admittedly, some mismatches between employer demand and the supply of job seekers are to be expected within a dynamic, competitive capitalist labour market. However, the aggregate demand for certain skills, on the one hand, and the aggregate supply of workers with certain skill sets, on the other hand, should not be construed as a system always tending towards equilibrium. As noted above, the formal educational attainments and adult education participation rates of Canadians have been rapidly increasing since the 1960s, and Canadians have also continued to pursue a vast amount of informal adult learning related to both jobs and other interests. However, the continued routinization and standardization tendencies in the name of efficiency and profit, even in purportedly highly skilled jobs, make it doubtful that the incremental growth in skill requirements found by recent researchers is likely to accelerate. At least in overall terms, it is increasingly clear that the cumulative employment-related knowledge and skills of the labour force now exceed the capacity of the current labour market to provide adequate numbers of corresponding sorts of jobs. Labour shortages in Canada have not been as persistent as KBE proponents would have us believe; rather, aside from the chronic skilled-trades shortage, any undersupply of workers has been occasional and almost always limited to short-term shortages in other specializations.

Underemployment in capitalist economies refers to the underutilization of the knowledge and skills that potential workers bring to the labour market. Underemployment includes both time-based complete or partial exclusion from employment and skill-based underutilization of capabilities in employment (Livingstone 2004). The multiple dimensions of underemployment include the following:

- *Conventional unemployment* refers to people who actively seek employment without success, as well as to "discouraged workers," who have given up active search.
- *Involuntary temporary employment* includes those who hold part-time jobs but who would prefer to have full-time jobs.

- *Credential underemployment* includes those who have jobs with entry requirements significantly lower than their formal education and skill certification.
- *Performance underemployment* includes job holders whose achieved levels of skills and knowledge significantly exceed the levels actually required to do their job, regardless of what entry credentials may be required.
- *Subjective underemployment* refers to people who believe that they are overqualified for the jobs they have been able to get.

Canada appears to be one of the more extreme cases of under-employment among advanced capitalist economies. Numerous studies have documented some of the dimensions of underemployment (Tandan 1969; Statistics Canada 1999; Livingstone 2004).

Conventional unemployment and involuntary temporary under-employment are both extremely serious conditions for millions of Canadians, and the pervasiveness of these time-based forms of under-employment are often hidden by official unemployment statistics (Livingstone 2004). However, for the purposes of this chapter, we will focus on the latter three skill-based forms of underemployment. Before addressing underemployment by occupational class specifically, we should note a few general findings from recent national surveys, as summarized in Table 5.2.

In terms of their subjective assessment of the extent of the correspondence between their qualifications and their job's requirements, most Canadians believe they have adequate qualifications for their jobs. About a quarter feel that they are overqualified, while less than 10 per cent feel underqualified. Sentiments of overqualification or underemployment may have increased somewhat in the past few years. The match between the entry credentials required and the actual educational credentials attained by job holders is somewhat more mixed. About half report that they have credentials that match entry requirements. About a third report educational credentials that exceed current entry requirements for their jobs by at least one level – for example, community college graduates in jobs requiring only a high school diploma. Less than 20 per cent report credentials that are less than those required for entry; these are mostly older workers who entered their jobs before credential requirements were raised, or inflated in some cases, and who otherwise indicate adequate job performance. The credential gap may also have increased marginally in recent years. However, in contrast to KBE assumptions, both measures find the extent of underemployment to be greater than the extent of under-qualification. Both employed workers and employers may under-

Table 5.2 Dimensions of education-job requirement matching, total employed Canadian labour force, 1998 and 2004

		Underemployed (%)	Matched %)	Underqualified (%)	Total
Self-assessment	1998	20	75	5	100
	2004	26	65	9	100
Credential gap	1998	30	49	21	100
	2004	34	48	18	100
Performance gap	1998	31	28	41	100
	2004	28	33	39	100

Sources: Livingstone 1999, 2005.

estimate under-employment in terms of self-assessments and entry requirements because of tendencies to rationalize the status quo and accept credential inflation. While self-reports of the adequacy of qualifications for current jobs may produce somewhat optimistic levels of matching attainments and requirements, both measures offer profiles in which underemployment now exceeds underqualification by a ratio of about 2:1.

Independent assessments of the relationship between the knowledge and skill levels attained by workers and the skill actually needed to perform any given job have been a more controversial and extremely complex issue since at least the 1960s (Livingstone 2004; Pankhurst 2004). This is where the dispute over upgrading or deskilling has been centred in empirical research. Typically, independent rating experts have used general educational development (GED) scores to estimate the *performance gap*. This method has completely ignored the informal experiential learning and accumulated practical knowledge of the current labour force and, as noted earlier, often confounds job skill requirements per se with the skills workers themselves have attained and may or may not use in this job. Despite this inherent underestimation, several measures of job performance requirements find that around half of the Canadian and American employed labour forces are now underemployed (Livingstone 2004). The most optimistic measures now assume that virtually all jobs require high school completion – an assumption that may be more a reflection of a pervasive supply of high school graduates than a conclusion based on direct expert ratings of increased performance requirements – and therefore may overestimate the extent of underqualification and underestimate the extent of underemployment in less skilled jobs.

According to one of the most optimistic measures,[3] around 30 per cent of the currently employed Canadian labour force still have job-related skills and knowledge that exceed the estimated performance requirements of their current jobs, while about a third have skill levels that basically match imputed performance requirements. Around 40 per cent apparently have less skill than their jobs now require for adequate performance. If these ratings were valid, the majority of the employed Canadian labour force would still remain well qualified to perform their jobs. Most of those designated underqualified on this measure are found in this survey to be involved, along with other workers, in significant continuing learning activities. It is somewhat counterintuitive to infer that such a large proportion of current job holders do not have sufficient skills to do their jobs. In any case, we will proceed to use this conservative measure to examine performance underemployment in a class analysis. Table 5.3 provides further insight into how underemployment is experienced by occupational class.

The most consistent finding on all three measures is that corporate executives, who wield the most economic power to define their own and others' jobs, are least likely to be underemployed. Hardly any corporate executives consider themselves to be overqualified for their jobs, and their incidence of underemployment on other measures is significantly lower than that of most other class groupings. Both small employers and the self-employed are somewhat more likely to assess themselves as underemployed and to be so assessed on more independent performance measures; however, their credential-based measures produce the highest underemployment ratings of all classes. This is probably because these ratings are occupation-based. The occupational composition of these proprietary positions is very diverse, and the occupational requirements may be very loose because the main criteria for entry are based on capital assets rather than skills. Among all those who depend on their own hired labour, clear majorities of over 60 per cent in all class positions feel that they are adequately qualified, while around a quarter assess themselves as underemployed and generally less than 10 per cent feel underqualified.

As for the credential gap, professional employees, who rely most essentially on credentials for entry into their positions (Collins 1979), are most likely to have matched credentials and requirements and least likely to be underemployed. Managers are more likely to be chosen for their posts on the basis of other, less tangible criteria, such as leadership skills, as well as for their educational credentials, and therefore have higher underemployment levels than professionals but lower underemployment levels than either supervisors or wage labourers.

A similar but more pronounced pattern is found on the performance gap measure that estimates the full array of skills actually required to do the job. Managers and professional employees have the

Table 5.3 Incidence of underemployment by occupational class, employed Canadian labour force, 1998 and 2004

Occupational Class		Self-assessment (%)	Credential Gap* (%)	Performance Gap (%)
Corporate executives*	1998	2	9	14
	2002	2	10	13
Small employers	1998	16	40	19
	2004	28	46	25
Self-employed	1998	14	47	20
	2004	25	45	19
Managers	1998	22	25	14
	2004	20	26	13
Professionals	1998	13	18	14
	2004	19	15	16
Supervisors	1998	20	31	40
	2004	28	33	30
Service workers	1998	30	30	51
	2004	32	40	49
Industrial workers	1998	19	28	35
	2004	29	31	39
Total labour force	1998	20	30	31
	2004	26	34	28

Sources: Livingstone 1999, 2005.

*Estimates for Ontario corporate executives in 1998 and 2002 from Livingstone, Hart, and Davie 1999, 2003.

lowest underemployment levels, under 20 per cent. Service workers and industrial workers have much higher levels of underemployment, around 50 per cent for service workers. Supervisors have intermediate levels, with around a third underemployed.

In any case, the overall orderings of results on each of these measures by class position are generally consistent with the prediction that underemployment is directly related to class power. Both self-assessments and credential measures find that most workers' educational attainment and educational job requirements correspond, but that underemployment consistently outweighs underqualification. Using these same measures, further analyses of these two national surveys and other data sources indicate that visible minorities and recent immigrants tend to be highly underemployed (Expert Panel on Skills 2000). Some of the more severe measures of performance requirements do find underqualification to be generally more prevalent than underemployment (Livingstone 2004). But again it is working-class positions that have the highest levels of underemployment and that are much more likely to be underemployed than to be underqualified for their jobs. There is scant evidence, even if the most optimistic measures of skill requirements are used, that the Canadian working class is being consistently deskilled. However, there is substantial evidence of considerable "relative deskilling" of many jobs in relation to the knowledge the working class brings to these jobs.

To summarize underemployment in another way, we could say that Canada is already a knowledge society even if it is not yet a knowledge-based economy.

CONCLUSION

Debunking Theories of a Knowledge-Based Economy

In this chapter we have begun to deconstruct some of the key assumptions on which the theories of a knowledge-based economy are founded. Against the boosterism and technology-based optimism of these evolutionary theories, our research allowed us to reach some solid conclusions.

- A large segment of the working population remains outside the boundaries of knowledge work, which continues to constitute less than a quarter of all jobs. Overall, technical skill requirements have increased gradually, but changes to autonomy-control–related skills remain more difficult to measure.
- Canadians' learning activities have been expanding rapidly over the last forty years. This growth has included huge leaps in post-secondary completion and participation in adult education courses, as well as people of all social statuses spending much more time in a variety of informal learning activities.
- The mismatch between Canadians' learning achievements and the requirements of their jobs continues to be a significant problem. In this context, underemployment is more prevalent than under-qualification, especially for those in working-class positions.
- Occupational class continues to be a primary influence on which types of learning are recognized and who has discretionary control over how learning is applied in the paid workplace.

Government policy responses to employment problems in Canada and other advanced capitalist economies have tended to focus on educational and training solutions. Recent government employment policies have been based on a perceived need to rectify a widespread skills shortage if Canada is to make a successful transition to a knowledge-based economy. Generalizing from chronic shortages in some specialized fields to aggregate skill levels, and from knowledge work to broad occupational shifts, public discourse and policy responses have predominantly ignored the existence and growth of underemployment. Such employment policies make the error of generalizing from a few exceptions. A candid recognition of the extent and increasing incidence of underemployment could expose the inherent contradictions of the capitalist system and stimulate thought and action about economic alternatives as responses to current employment problems. The cumulative body of empirical evidence on the education-employment relationship surely provides some support to reverse the dominant optic and begin to seriously consider economic reforms with comparable interest. But to concede that there is widespread underemployment would be to undermine appeals to workers to resolve their own unemployment problems by overcoming skill deficits. Similarly, while much attention has been paid to the proliferation of the Internet, its positive impact on the ongoing knowledge acquisition of workers and, more generally, the socialization of the forces of knowledge production continue to be largely ignored in educational discourse, which remains fixated on learners' deficiencies. While progressive educational reforms are always welcome, they will do little to resolve the already substantial underemployment of workers' current skill levels.

Another main failure of KBE theories as explanatory models of change is an overconfidence in the power of information technologies to democratize the social and technical relations of production. With profit as the primary goal, it has rarely been in the interest of capitalist firms to recognize and subsequently reward workers' informal learning. The contradictions between persistent practices seeking to sustain profitability largely via the routinization and fragmentation of work and a generous rhetoric of employee discretion and participation are becoming increasingly untenable from a working-class standpoint.

Looking to the Future

The learning achievements of workers and disadvantaged groups in particular are making more apparent the contradictions within the capitalist labour process. Gradual increases in the skill requirements of jobs in the face of rapid increases in the knowledge acquisition of workers increasingly illuminate the *relative* deskilling that Braverman (1974) noted was occurring alongside *absolute* deskilling (see also Zimbalist 1979, xv). This level of increased knowledge and latent competency has the potential to lead, as Adler put it, to "greater intellectual sophistication, broader worldviews, and sharpened expectations of justice" (2006, 8). Increasingly educated workers may be less likely to accept their place in a rigidly rationalized labour process. Various surveys of working people's attitudes in advanced capitalist economies are finding that growing majorities appear to be becoming less deferential to employers and more distrustful of government and dominant social institutions (Freeman and Rogers 1999). More generally, the rapidly growing non-hierarchical interconnectivity of communication, transportation, and energy networks is enabling unprecedented popular mobilization of marginalized and alienated people, as shown by the worldwide antiwar demonstrations of 15 February 2003 (Mitchell 2003, 207–11). While continual changes in the social and technical relations of capitalist production mean that old industries die and new industries are born, the changes in the knowledge, expectations, and orientation to authority of workers give hope that old structures are losing their effectiveness and more genuine democratic practices and organizational philosophies can arise.

From a historical materialist (or Marxist) perspective, those who are most exploited within capitalist economies – those forced to sell their labour power – have the most potential to change the mode of production. Globally, nearly a billion people are now unemployed or underemployed (International Labour Organization 2003), while similar numbers go to sleep hungry every night (International Forum on Globalization 2002). Even as capitalism pushes commodification ever further into our lives, these problems, together with environmental degradation, demonstrate the limits to unfettered capitalist expansion. Of course, progressive change is always possible within the dominant economic system. Capitalist logic is not all-encompassing and workers' struggles have had significant positive results in the past (reductions in the working day/week, unemployment benefits). Growing numbers of Canadian companies and labour organizations are taking steps to better recognize workers' skills and learning, and various job redesign initiatives – job rotation, job enrichment, incentive pay, work teams, and flexible scheduling – have emerged to address quality of work concerns (see Lowe 2000). These initiatives may allow more participatory decision-making and discretion, but they do not necessarily change the culture of the capitalist firm, its inner workings, its relations of production; these remain at best stakeholder rather than shareholder versions of the capitalist mode of production.

Among the feasible economic alternatives, *economic democracy* is emerging as the most likely option to effectively address both underemployment and alienation as well as environmental degradation (International Forum on Globalization 2002; Livingstone 2004). Genuine democratic participation in the workplace allows workers to make decisions on work redistribution, job matching, and learning recognition that take into account social cohesion, fair production and distribution processes, and ecological preservation and sustainability. Where economic democracy has been practised, as it has been on a small scale for generations, community sustainability has come to prevail over profit maximization. In contrast to the private markets that drive capitalism or the authoritarian central planning that has failed in many Communist countries, economic democracy is based on a socialized market model. This model considers that communities as well as individuals are economic actors with vested interests, that social costs (and benefits) should be accounted for in economic decisions, and that all members of society should have a voice and be granted the right to vote in these decisions (see Livingstone 2004, chap. 6, for a more detailed discussion).

Economic democracy may sound radical in advanced capitalist economies today, where neo-liberal practices and free markets appear omnipresent. But capitalism at its birth was no less radical an idea, emerging as an enclave from within the then dominant feudal mode of production. In any case, the processing of information rather than materials within capitalism has not yet made many labourers into knowledge workers in the sense of their having greater control over the conception and planning of their paid work. Indeed, the prospect of greater exploitation of intellectual labourers is growing because of the impossibility of limiting the length of their working day (Rikowski 2004). Whether many ever become knowledge workers – given their expanding knowledge – may be one of the most important questions for the future of our species and the sustainability of the ecosystem.

NOTES

Authors' Note: The data reported on in this chapter were gathered in 1998 and 2004 national surveys funded by the Social Sciences and Humanities Research Council. For further information on these surveys and related research networks, see the websites www.nall.ca and www.wallnetwork.ca.

1 Interview with rolling mill operator, local steel mill, Toronto, May 2004.
2 The tables in this paper are based on data from the New Approaches to Lifelong Learning (NALL) survey in 1998 and the Changing Nature of Work and Lifelong Learning (WALL) survey in 2004. Details on both surveys are found at www.wallnetwork.ca.
3 The performance measure applied in this analysis is based on Ivar Berg's fifth alternative measure of GED-level years of schooling equivalencies (Berg 1970, 44, 50). This measure reduces a six-point scale into three levels: it collapses the lowest three categories into one standing for eleven or fewer years

of schooling; it equates the fourth and fifth categories with everything from high school completion to college diplomas and three years of university; and, like most equivalency schemes, it treats a university degree as the highest level. It should be noted that worker self-reports of performance requirements produce much lower estimates of underqualification. For further discussion, see Livingstone 2004 (78–85).

REFERENCES

Adler, P.S. 2006. From labour process to activity theory. In *Critical perspectives on activity: Explorations across education, work and everyday life*, edited by P. Sawchuk, N. Duarte, and M. Elhammoumi. New York: Cambridge University Press

Aneesh, A. 2001. Skill saturation: Rationalization and post-industrial work. *Theory and Society* 30:363–96

Barton, P.E. 2000. *What jobs require: Literacy, education and training, 1940–2006*. Princeton, N.J.: Educational Testing Service

Bell, D. 1973. *The coming of post-industrial society*. New York: Basic Books

Braverman, H. 1974. *Labor and Monopoly Capital*. New York: New York Monthly Review Press

Burawoy, M. 1979. *Manufacturing consent: Changes in the labor process under monopoly capitalism*. Chicago: University of Chicago Press

Burns, G. 1999. Dichotomization of formal and informal education, the marginalization of elders and problems of Aboriginal education and Native studies in the public educational system. In *Exploring human potential: New directions in facilitating growth in the new millennium*, edited by P. Gamlin and M. Luther. Toronto: Captus University Press

Burris, B.H. 1998. Computerization of the workplace. *Annual Review of Sociology* 34:141–55

Clement, W. 1981. *Hardrock mining: Industrial relations and technological changes at Inco*. Toronto: McClelland and Stewart

Cockburn, C. 1991. *Brothers: Male dominance and technological change*. Concord, Mass.: Pluto Press

Cohen, S. 1987. A labour process to nowhere? *New Left Review* 165:34–50

Collins, R. 1979. *The credential society*. New York: Academic Press

Cortada, J.W. 1998. Introducing the knowledge worker. In *Rise of the knowledge worker*, edited by J.W. Cortada, xii–xix. Boston: Butterworth-Heinemann

Curtis, B., D.W. Livingstone, and H. Smaller. 1992. *Stacking the deck: The streaming of working-class kids in Ontario schools*. Toronto: Our Schools/Our Selves Education Foundation

Drucker, P.F. 1993. *Post-capitalist society*. New York: HarperCollins

Edwards, R. 1979. *Contested terrain: The transformation of the workplace in the twentieth century.* New York: Basic Books

Ehrenreich, B., and J. Ehrenreich. 1979. The professional-managerial class. In *Between labor and capital,* edited by P. Walker, 5–45. Boston: South End Press

Expert Panel on Skills. 2000. *Stepping up: Skills and opportunities in the knowledge economy.* Presented to the Prime Minister's Advisory Council on Science and Technology Expert Panel on Skills. Ottawa: Industry Canada. Available at http://acst-ccst.gc.ca

Foster, J.B. 1994. 'Labor and monopoly capital' twenty years after: An introduction. *Monthly Review* 46 (6): 1–13

Freeman, R., and J. Rogers. 1999. *What workers want.* New York: Russell Sage Foundation

Friedman, A. 1977. *Industry and labour: Class struggle at work and monopoly capitalism.* London: Macmillan

Gereluk, W., D. Briton, and B. Spencer. 1999. *Learning about labour in Canada.* Working Paper no. 7. Retrieved 12 October 2004 from the Ontario Institute for Studies in Education of the University of Toronto, Research Network on New Approaches to Lifelong Learning (NALL) website: www.oise.utoronto.ca/csew/nall/index.htm

Handel, M. 2000. *Trends in direct measures of job skill requirements.* Working Paper no. 301, Jerome Levy Economics Institute. Available at www.levy.org/does/wrkpap/papers

Hennessy, T., and P. Sawchuk. 2003. Worker responses to technological change in the Canadian public sector: Issues of learning and labour process. *Journal of Workplace Learning* 15 (7/8): 319–25

Heron, C., and R. Storey. 1986. *On the job: Confronting the labour process in Canada.* Montreal and Kingston: McGill-Queen's University Press

Hirschhorn, L. 1984. *Beyond mechanization: Work and technology in a postindustrial age.* Cambridge, Mass.: MIT Press

Hochschild, A.R. 1983. *The managed heart: Commercialization of human feeling.* Berkeley: University of California Press

Huws, U. 2003. *The making of a cybertariat: Virtual work in a real world.* New York: Monthly Review Press

International Forum on Globalization. 2002. *Alternatives to economic globalization: A better world is possible.* San Francisco: Berrett-Koehler Publishers

International Labour Organization. 2003. *Global employment trends.* Geneva: ILO

Kleinman, D.L., and S.P. Vallas. 2001. Science, capitalism, and the rise of the "knowledge worker": The changing structure of knowledge production in the United States. *Theory and Society* 30:451–92

Kraft, P. 1977. *Programmers and managers: The routinization of computer programming in the United States.* New York: Springer-Verlag

Krahn, H.J., and G.S. Lowe. 2002. *Work, industry and Canadian society.* 4th ed. Scarborough: Nelson Canada

Kusterer, K. 1978. *Know-how on the job: The important working knowledge of "unskilled" workers.* Boulder, Colo.: Westview Press

Larson, M. 1980. Proletarianization and educated labor. *Theory and Society* 9 (1): 131–75

Lavoie, M., and R. Roy. 1998. *Employment in the knowledge-based economy: A growth accounting exercise for Canada.* Ottawa: Applied Research Branch, Human Resources Canada

Leckie, N. 1996. On skill requirement trends in Canada, 1971–1991. Research report for Human Resources Canada and Canadian Policy Research Networks

Livingstone, D.W. 1999. Exploring the icebergs of adult learning: Findings of the first Canadian survey of informal learning practices. *Canadian Journal for the Study of Adult Education* 13 (2): 49–72

– 2002. *Working and learning in the information age: A profile of Canadians.* Toronto: Canadian Policy Research Networks

– 2004. *The education-jobs gap: Underemployment or economic democracy.* Aurora, Ont.: Garamond Press

– 2005. *Exploring adult learning and work in advanced capitalist society.* PASCAL International Observatory, October 2005, PASCAL Hot Topic (www.obs-pascal.com/hottopic.php)

– 2006. Informal learning: Conceptual distinctions and preliminary findings. In *Learning in places: The informal education reader,* edited by Z. Bekerman, N. Burbules, and D. Silberman, 203–28. Berlin: Peter Lang

Livingstone, D.W., D. Hart, and L.E. Davie. 1999. *Public attitudes towards education in Ontario (1998): The twelfth OISE survey.* Toronto: OISE Press

– 2003. *Public attitudes towards education in Ontario (1998): The fourteenth OISE survey.* Toronto: OISE Press

Livingstone, D.W., and J.M. Mangan, eds. 1996. *Recast dreams: Class and gender consciousness in Steeltown.* Toronto: Garamond Press

Livingstone, D.W., and P. Sawchuk. 2004. *Hidden knowledge: Organized labour in the Information Age.* Toronto: Garamond Press

Livingstone, D.W., and S. Stowe. 2003. Class and learning in Canada: Intergenerational patterns of inequality. In *Yesterday's dreams: International and critical perspectives on education and social class,* edited by A. Scott and J. Freeman-Moir, 121–35. Auckland: Canterbury University Press

Lowe, G. 2000. *The quality of work: A people-centred agenda.* Don Mills: Oxford University Press

Madamba, A.B. 1998. *Underemployment among Asians in the United States: Asian Indian, Filipino, and Vietnamese workers.* New York: Garland Publishing

Mallet, S. 1975. *The new working class.* Nottingham: Spokesman

Meiksins, P. 1994. 'Labor and monopoly capital' for the 1990s: A review and critique of the labor process debate. *Monthly Review* 46 (6): 45–60

Mitchell, W.J. 2003. *Me++: The cyborg self and the networked city.* Cambridge, Mass.: MIT Press

Murphy, J.B. 1993. *The moral economy of labor: Aristotelian themes in economic theory.* New Haven, Conn.: Yale University Press

Neef, D. 1999. *A little knowledge is a dangerous thing: Understanding our global knowledge economy.* Boston: Butterworth-Heinemann

Noble, D. 1984. *Forces of production – A social history of industrial automation.* New York: Oxford University Press

O'Doherty, D., and H. Willmott. 2001. Debating labour process theory: The issue of subjectivity and the relevance of poststructuralism. *Sociology* 35 (2): 457–76

OECD (Organization for Economic Co-operation and Development). 1996. *The knowledge-based economy.* Paris: OECD

– 2002. *Towards a knowledge-based economy: Country readiness assessment report: Concept, outline, benchmarking and indicators.* Paris: OECD

Pankhurst, K.V. 2004. Overview of research and policy issues. Paper presented at Human Resources and Skills Development Symposium on Essential Skills, October

Rikowski, R. 2004. On the impossibility of determining the length of the working-day for intellectual labour. *Information for Social Change* 19:52–60

Rose, M. 2004. *The mind at work: Valuing the intelligence of the American worker.* New York: Viking

Russell, B. 1999. *More with less: Work reorganization in the Canadian mining industry.* Toronto: University of Toronto Press

Sawchuk, P. 2003. *Adult learning and technology in working-class life.* New York: Cambridge University Press

Senge, P.M. 1994. *The fifth discipline: The art and practice of the learning organization.* Toronto: Doubleday/Currency

Smith, V. 1994. Braverman's legacy: The labor process tradition at 20. *Work and Occupations* 21 (4): 403–21

Spenner, K.I. 1983. Deciphering Prometheus: Temporal change in the skill level of work. *American Sociological Review* 48 (6): 824–37

Statistics Canada. 1999. *Adult Education and Training Survey 1998.* Catalogue no. 81C0045. Ottawa: Statistics Canada

– 2000. *Education indicators in Canada: Report of the Pan-Canadian Education Indicators Program.* Ottawa: Statistics Canada

– 2003. *Knowledge workers in Canada's economy, 1971–2001.* Ottawa: Statistics Canada

Stewart, T.A. 1997. *Intellectual capital: The new wealth of organizations.* Toronto: Doubleday/Currency

Tandan, N. 1969. *Underutilization of manpower in Canada.* Special Labour Force Studies no. 8. Ottawa: Dominion Bureau of Statistics

Vallas, S.P. 2003. Rediscovering the color line within work organizations: The "knitting of racial groups" revisited. *Work and Occupations* 30 (4): 379–400

Wardell, M. 1999. Labor processes: Moving beyond Braverman and the de-skilling debate. In *Rethinking the labor process,* edited by M. Wardell, T.L. Steiger, and P. Meiksins. New York: SUNY Press

Zimbalist, A.S. 1979. *Case studies on the labor process.* New York: Monthly Review Press

Zuboff, S. 1984. *In the age of the smart machine: The future of work and power.* New York: Basic Books

6

Industrial Work in
a Post-Industrial Age

CHARLOTTE YATES AND
BELINDA LEACH

INTRODUCTION

Industrial work, in particular work in the manufacturing sector, is pivotal to our understanding of the postwar period and the Fordist regime. Mass production and mass consumption, the twin pillars of Fordism, were primarily defined in terms of the mass production of goods, not services. Economic expansion in the postwar period up to the 1970s was fuelled by investment and expanded employment opportunities in productive manufacturing capacity. Just as the resource sector dominated Canadian innovations in collective bargaining practices and employment institutions in the interwar period, so labour in the industrial sector struggled and reshaped these practices and institutions in the postwar period. The 1950 pact between General Motors and the United Auto Workers (UAW), known as the Treaty of Detroit, symbolized this shift. Throughout the postwar period, arguably to the present day, labour-management relations in the automotive industry – and the unionized manufacturing sector more broadly – have set the gold standard for collective agreements and established patterns and innovations in wages and working conditions. Hence it was primarily through employment in the manufacturing sector that the postwar dream of a car, house, and TV for every family was realized. The centrality of manufacturing work to postwar development was demonstrated by analysts and historiographers whose stories of work and labour focused on white men employed in the manufacturing sector.

But the centrality of manufacturing work to postwar Canada and elsewhere was also evident in the ways that this sector was integrated into postwar models of economic growth and, ultimately, culture. Economic development models, conceived in the 1950s and 1960s to explain why some countries were more developed than others and how lesser-developed economies could be shifted onto the path of development, identified manufacturing for mass consumption as the final stage of development (Rostow 1960). Policies ranging from export-led development to Keynesianism were aimed at harnessing and stabilizing national capacities to mass produce goods for mass consumption. Popular culture, transformed by the advent of mass media, became interwoven with the virtues of mass consumption.

If the postwar period was characterized by the centrality of manufacturing work, this model has been turned on its head since the 1980s. This reversal was in part a result of shifts in employment patterns, begun much earlier in the late 1960s, towards employment in the public and private service sectors (Economic Council of Canada 1990). Yet, the popular and scholarly perception that manufacturing in northern developed countries was displaced in economic importance is rooted in much deeper changes in the economy and in our understanding of these changes. The two recessions of 1981–82 and 1990–93 in Canada were marked by plant closures and highly publicized shifts of manufacturing work from Canada to the low-wage U.S. south and the Third World. These trends were reinforced by the economic restructuring that accompanied the negotiation of free trade, first with the United States in 1988 and then, in 1993, an expanded arrangement that included Mexico (Campbell et al. 1999). As these events unfolded, political-economic analysis focused on three themes: the deindustrialization of the United States and Canada (Bluestone and Harrison 1982; Drache 1989; High 2003); the changing international division of labour wherein labour-intensive manufacturing work was becoming concentrated in the South and "knowledge" work in the North; and arguments about the end of Fordism (Holmes and Leys 1987; Piore and Sabel 1984). Government policies aimed at laying the foundation for a knowledge society in a post-industrial era (Bell 1976) reinforced the expectation and assumption that the manufacturing age had come to an end for Canada and the United States.

Many would argue, then, that to study manufacturing work is therefore to study work in Canada's past, not to study the future world of work. In this chapter we take issue with this line of argument. We demonstrate that the manufacturing sector continues to be an important sector for employment and, ultimately, that its study is important for understanding future trends in work and working people's lives and their communities. Notwithstanding downward pressure on wages across the economy, manufacturing offers to many women, racially diverse populations (including immigrants), and youth better employment opportunities and wages than work in other sectors. At the same time, because for years there were few studies of industrial work, with the exception of studies of the fate of older, laid-off workers and of the anomalous experience of work in automotive assembly, there is now a need for a careful examination of the ways in which industrial work has changed. In other words, while we argue that manufacturing work continues to be important, the nature of this work and the characteristics of the workers employed in this sector have changed dramatically over the last twenty years.

The next section of this chapter sketches out our theoretical framework. We then offer a brief discussion of why manufacturing matters in today's post-industrial society. The meat of our argument follows this introductory discussion. Manufacturing companies continue to be important employers, but changes in the nature of manufacturing investment and employment have enormous implications for unions, local communities and economies, and workers, as well as for broader labour market institutions and practices. We examine three important dimensions of change in who works and where they work in manufacturing in Canada. First we examine the spatial dispersion of manufacturing away from unionized establishments in urban centres in the Montreal and Toronto areas, offering examples from the automotive, garment, and food-processing industries. We then discuss the feminization and racialization of the industrial workforce and the implication of these developments for employment relations and working conditions. Throughout the chapter, we draw examples from a range of manufacturing industries, concentrating largely on developments in Ontario, the province that constituted the heart of manufacturing employment in Canada in the postwar period.

CAPITALISM, INEQUALITIES, AND THE SOCIAL RELATIONS OF WORK

We begin our analysis by recognizing capitalism as a historically specific mode of production with distinctive sets of social relations. These social relations are materially grounded in multiple, and occasionally competing, domains of power that arise out of gendered, racialized, and class-based relations of inequality and domination. The specific interplay between gender, race, and class relations and manifestations of (and experiences of) inequality and domination varies across history and place and is dependent upon the actions of capital and states, as well as upon ongoing political resistance and struggle.

Yet, although our historically materialist analysis points to changes in the dynamics of capitalism and the social relations therein, we also note in our examination of work and labour markets a remarkable persistence in the inequalities and dominations experienced by women in relation to men and by racialized groups in relation to white workers. The last two decades have brought considerable change in labour market practices and employers' treatment of workers, largely in response to government and union actions and changing market dynamics. Yet, women and racialized groups continue to be the most exploited and dominated groups in the labour market. They are systematically paid less, they experience explicitly sexist and racist forms of domination, and they are found in the worst jobs in the economy. To understand these labour market dynamics, we have adopted a labour market segmentation approach. Labour market segmentation theorists argue that employers derive advantages in dividing and redividing the workforce. While the labour market was originally conceived as being divided into two distinct segments – a primary segment with decent, often unionized jobs and a secondary segment containing poorer jobs – later versions of the theory posit multiple sources of labour market division (Gordon, Edwards, and Reich 1982; Rubery 1980; Thompson 1983; Peck 1996). These include, at a minimum, skill, gender, race, ethnicity, and age, to which we would add locational characteristics, such as rural and urban, global north and south, and home-based and factory-based, as well as citizenship. Segmentation stratifies the labour market in ways that render workers more easily controllable and susceptible to being pitted against each other in the competition for better jobs. The overall effect is to divide workers and reduce their capacity to improve wages and working conditions across the labour market. Segmentation theory links the operation of labour markets with changes in labour processes at the point of production (Burawoy 1979). Where the organization of work is perceived to be under attack such that skill or pay is threatened, workers are likely to act to protect their positions. Jill Rubery argues that "their most effective tactic is to differentiate themselves from potential competition" (1980, 260), a process in which capital often quite willingly participates. Using this theoretical framework, we examine the ways in which capital continues to invest in manufacturing in Canada, albeit under different conditions than in the past. In so doing, labour supply and demand are segmented in new ways with deleterious effects on wages, working conditions, and labour communities.

MANUFACTURING MATTERS

The discourse of post-industrialism is a powerful one in Canada, as it is in other high-wage countries. Such ideas attained hegemonic status in much of the American literature on industrial change that emerged in the 1980s. Canada's geographic proximity to the United States and its close economic ties led analysts to assume that Canada followed in lockstep with the United States in its decline in manufacturing employment. These ideas have acquired such currency, and indeed such broad-based acceptance as fact, that it is swimming against the tide to suggest a different trajectory for Canada's economy. Yet, as indicated in Table 6.1, manufacturing employment in Canada continued to grow between 1945 and 2003, except for the two recessionary periods since 1980.

Historically, manufacturing mattered most to Ontario and Quebec, where manufacturing investment, facilities, and hence employment were concentrated.[1] The regional dimension of Canada's manufacturing history draws our attention to the way capital makes selective decisions about where to locate different kinds of economic activity, and hence work, thus contributing to the uneven development of the country. Regional disparities have emerged for a variety of reasons. Market factors in part determine patterns of investment. In the late nineteenth century, as manufacturing capacity was taking off in North America, Ontario had the largest markets in Canada for manufactured goods and the greatest pools of capital available for investment in manufacturing; moreover, its industrial areas were closer than those of other provinces to markets in the United States (McCallum 1980). Transportation issues in a massive country like Canada also contributed to the concentration of manufacturing in the Windsor to Quebec City corridor. But the politics and policies of nation-building, and later province-building, have also played their part. The Crow rates, introduced in 1897 as part of a deal between the Canadian Pacific Railway and the Canadian government, established differential railway rates for the movement of goods. These Crow rates made it cheaper for raw materials to be shipped from the West to central Canada and for finished industrial goods to be shipped from central to western Canada. This had the effect of discouraging manufacturing in the West while guaranteeing markets for goods produced in central Canada, henceforth consolidating Ontario's comparative advantage in manufacturing (Fowke 1957). In the 1970s and 1980s, in a bid to diversify their economies, western provincial governments offered firms financial support and other incentives to locate in their jurisdictions (Pratt and

Table 6.1 Employment ('000s) in manufacturing (Canada), by male/female, 1945–2003

	1945	1954	1965	1974	1978	1983	1988	1993	1998	2003
Total employment	2937	5243	6862	9137	9776.2	11,027	12,710.3	12,857.5	14,140.4	15,746
Total employment male	2088	4044	4842	5976	6145.5	6420.5	7178.2	7029.9	7661.4	8406.7
Total employment female	849	1199	2020	3161	3630.7	4606.6	5532.1	5827.5	6479	7339.3
Total manufacturing employment	1062	1326	1636	2024	1859.8	1848.7	2104.3	1786.4	2113.8	2294
Total manufacturing employment male	814	1057	1287	1534	1391.7	1336.7	1522.3	1300	1525.1	1629.5
Total manufacturing employment female	248	269	349	490	468.2	512	582	486.4	588.7	664.5
Female as a % of total manufacturing	23	20.28	21.33	24.20	25.16	27.69	27.65	27.22	27.85	28.96
Manufacturing as % of total female employment	29	22.40	17.30	15.50	12.90	11.10	10.50	8.30	9.10	9.10
Total manufacturing as a % of total employment	27.71	25.29	23.84	22.15	19.02	16.76	16.55	13.89	14.90	14.56

Sources: Statistics Canada. 1945, "Industry Distributions, Persons with Jobs – Paid Workers," *The Labour Force, November 1945–January 1955*, Reference Paper no. 58.
1954, 1965, and 1974, "Civilian Employment, by Occupation and Sex," in Statistics Canada, *Historical Statistics of Canada*, 2nd ed. (Ottawa: Statistics Canada, 1983).
1978, 1983, 1988, 1993, 1998, and 2003, "Labour Force Survey Estimates (Employment) by NAICS, Sex and Age Group, Table 282-0008."
Note: All figures are based on annual unadjusted averages, except for 1945, which is based on figures for November 1945.

Richards 1979). Meanwhile, Quebec advanced its nationalist project by encouraging the growth of Quebec-owned businesses and a francophone entrepreneurial class, using various forms of state economic supports (Gagnon 2004). The transportation giant Bombardier, for example, which manufactures everything from snowmobiles to aircraft, reached its present market position in large part through the actions and financial assistance of the Quebec and Canadian governments (Hadekel 2004).

Manufacturing continues to be especially important for Ontario and Quebec. Between 18 and 19 per cent of total employment in these provinces is based directly on manufacturing, compared to 10 per cent or less in other provinces (Baldwin, Brown, and Vinodrai 2001). In 2003, manufacturing accounted for 18 per cent of Canada's gross domestic product (GDP) and two-thirds of Canada's total exports of goods and services (CME 2004b).

Unlike many high-wage countries, Canada has maintained its manufacturing sector in part because of relatively low wages, a trend reinforced by the low value of the Canadian dollar throughout most of the last twenty years. Lower costs for employee benefits, largely because of Canada's public health care system, further reduce labour costs in Canada relative to the United States. Canada's proximity to the United States has led to additional economic benefits. Canadian workers have some of the highest levels of education of the member countries of the Organization for Economic Co-operation and Development (OECD), and the pay differentials between higher- and lower-educated workers are significantly less than in the United States (Morissette, Ostrovsky, and Picot 2004). This trend has been reinforced by the influx of highly educated immigrants, many of whom end up working in manufacturing for want of other opportunities (Galabuzi 2001; Vrankulj and Yates 2006). There are also lower labour turnover rates in Canada compared to both the United States and Mexico. Multinational companies can therefore hire an educated workforce at a low cost in Canada. It should therefore come as no surprise that foreign direct investment in Canada by multinational corporations engaged in manufacturing increased by almost 50 per cent between 1999 and 2003 (CME 2004b).

Yet, in assessing why manufacturing continues to matter to the Canadian economy and hence to an analysis of employment and work, we have to account not only for the direct economic benefits, but for the indirect ones as well. According to the Canadian Manufacturers and Exporters Association (CME), every dollar of manufacturing output generates $3.05 of economic activity (CME 2004b). Linkages between manufacturing and other sectors of the economy have mutual advantages. Indeed, the service sector draws much of its profit in indirect ways from the production of goods, namely through financial trading and by selling services to those who are supported by manufacturing, whether they be production workers whose wages are above average or firms in search of business services (Cohen and Zysman 1987). These spinoffs have increased in the last ten to fifteen years, as many services that were once made available in-house by manufacturing companies have been outsourced and are now provided by businesses in the service sector.

DYNAMICS OF CHANGE IN MANUFACTURING WORK

In spite of the evidence presented so far about the continued importance of work in manufacturing, the story of industrial work in Canada cannot be told without some discussion of what has been lost in manufacturing and what has changed. Whereas in the 1950s and 1960s the everyday consumer goods of Canadian life – TV, radio, refrigerator, car, bicycle, Mum's Sunday suit, and the makings of Sunday lunch – were manufactured in Canada, by the 1980s this was no longer the case. What happened to Canada's manufacturing capacity?

The recession of 1981–82 hit the manufacturing sector hard (Cameron and Houle 1985). Many factories closed, some because of corporate consolidation and reorganization of their operations,[2] others because of the complete failure of firms.[3] Thousands of workers in manufacturing were laid off. As consumers felt the bite of economic recession, they searched for cheaper alternatives. Many turned to imported goods, a trend that reinforced the loss of manufacturing capacity here in Canada.

The scars of this first recession were deepened by government policy. The high interest rate policy of the early 1980s made it impossible for firms to borrow capital and for consumers to finance the purchase of consumer durables. Meanwhile, the negotiation of free trade with the United States (1988) and later Mexico (1993) opened the Canadian market to greater competition and increasingly tied the hands of government, restricting its use of the policy levers that it had once used to enhance national manufacturing capacity. The 1980s were therefore a volatile time for the manufacturing sector. Analysts assumed that Canadian and U.S. manufacturing operations were doomed to fail in the face of intense international competition. Canada's future, it was argued, rested on becoming a post-industrial knowledge economy in which manufacturing would have a shrinking place. Governments became increasingly concerned with how to redesign policy to catch the wave of high-wage knowledge-intensive employment (Piore and Sabel 1984; Drache 1992).

The end of manufacturing in Canada seemed nigh with the recession of 1990–93. This was an especially deep recession in Canada, and once again manufacturing was hard hit. Some firms replaced labour with capital in their bid to compete; others closed their doors either because of bankruptcy or because their operations were relocated to places where wages were cheaper and unions all but illegal. The Canadian Labour Congress (CLC) reported that in the three years between 1989 and 1992, 7,000 plants closed down and Canada lost 300,000 manufacturing jobs (CLC 2004, 9; Vardy 1991). Once a significant producer of shoes and clothing, agricultural implements, white goods (refrigerators, washing machines), small consumer goods (radios, televisions), and furniture, Canada maintained little if any capacity in these industrial sectors by the end of this second recession.

Yet, sounding the death knell on industrial manufacturing work has been premature. Since the 1990–93 recession, manufacturing has rebounded, with many new firms entering the market. Fully 39 per cent of the plants manufacturing goods in Canada in 1997 were not in operation in 1988 (CLC 2004). By 2003, there were 20,000 more manufacturing facilities in Canada than ten years earlier. Between 1993 and 2003, employment in manufacturing in Canada rose by 500,000 jobs, 95 per cent of which are full-time (CME 2004b). Sectors that continue to grow and employ considerable numbers of workers include food processing, clothing manufacture, wood-product processing (e.g., sawmills or wood veneer production), plastic and rubber products, fabricated metal products (cutlery/tools/nuts and bolts production), machinery, transportation equipment, and furniture (Statistics Canada 2004). In 2003, manufacturing employment stood at 2.3 million persons or 15 per cent of total employment in Canada. Average earnings for jobs in manufacturing are 25 per cent higher than national average earnings. This gap increased over the 1990s. In 1989 the average compensation for a job in the economy as a whole was $28,678; in manufacturing, the average compensation was $32,812; these averages had increased by 1997 to $35,359 and $44,070, respectively (Nadeau 1999; CME 2004b). For these reasons alone, it is important that we look more carefully at what has happened to work in the manufacturing sector. In particular, we should ask, who works in manufacturing, where in Canada does manufacturing take place, and what is the changing nature of wages and employment relations?

SPATIAL DISPERSION

New technologies, changes in the modes of transportation of goods to markets, and the uneven development of the manufacturing sector, driven by intense competition and marked by consolidation and expansion, have resulted in the dispersion of manufacturing employment. We identify three axes of dispersion of manufacturing employment: (1) the dispersion of production from urban centres to suburbs and rural communities; (2) the shift of manufacturing production and employment from large, often unionized establishments to small workplaces; and

(3) a slight regional shift of some manufacturing employment towards the western parts of Canada.

Data collected between 1976 and 1997 point to a shift in manufacturing production from the city cores of Toronto and Montreal to suburban areas adjacent to cities, as well as to rural areas. These shifts have been driven by the greater availability of labour supply and of low-cost land on which to build and by incentives offered by suburban municipalities, including infrastructure servicing of industrial parks (Brown and Baldwin 2003; Baldwin, Brown, and Vinodrai 2001). The expanded use of trucking to ship goods, together with the building of new roadways, has facilitated this dispersion.

These shifts are the most recent in the long history of the spatial reorganization of manufacturing employment associated with the capitalist dynamics of competition and consolidation. In the immediate postwar years, many rural communities were host to small manufacturing operations that served local markets. In particular, food-processing operations – such as mills that refined wheat and dairies that produced butter, ice cream, and other milk products for local markets – offered pockets of manufacturing employment to rural and small-town workers. By the late 1960s, buyouts and cutthroat competition by large multinational corporations (e.g., Kraft) began to eliminate these local operations and centralize production in large urban centres (Winson and Leach 2002).

In the 1990s, new economic imperatives drove manufacturing to disperse once again. Automotive production provides an excellent illustration of these dynamics. Spatial dispersion to "greenfield sites" – namely, land that has not previously been used for building or manufacturing – was not a new strategy for automotive assemblers. In 1951 Ford built and opened a new assembly operation in Oakville with the express intent of avoiding the United Automobile Workers of Canada union (UAW-Canada). This union-avoidance strategy was unsuccessful, however. Within three years of opening, the Ford Oakville automotive assembly plant was unionized. By the end of the decade, Ford had agreed to a master bargaining arrangement whereby all Ford plants bargained together for one master contract, a strategy that limited Ford's capacity to shift work to non-union locations within Canada (Yates 1993).

In the 1980s, governments insisted that Japanese automakers wishing to sell vehicles to North American consumers produce vehicles here. The result was a series of new automobile assembly plants, all of which were built in rural areas of Ontario outside the existing corridor of automotive investment. Toyota built in the outskirts of Cambridge, Honda built in Alliston, and Suzuki joined with General Motors to build a jointly owned factory outside of London, near Ingersoll. With the exception of the latter, these factories are non-unionized. All of them have drawn on new rural supplies of labour from surrounding municipalities and have benefited from expanded transportation links built by provincial governments.

Associated with this dispersion of manufacturing production along the rural-urban dimension is a shift towards employment in small workplaces. Between 1990 and 2001, the average establishment size in manufacturing dropped from 47.3 to 36.6 employees (CLC 2004,10). In 2003–4, 84 per cent of manufacturing facilities in Canada employed fewer than fifty employees compared to 3 per cent that employed 200 or more people (CME 2004b). Two firm-level dynamics have driven this move towards smaller establishments. For some large multinational firms, such as Magna and arguably Linamar, both auto parts producers, small firm size is a business strategy that allows them to locate production close to their clients, facilitates paternalistic strategies of labour control (Lewchuk and Wells 2004), and reflects their involvement in the production of multiple different parts, as well as some sub-assembly, that is most profitably and flexibly undertaken in multiple small plants.

But the growth in small workplaces is also a response to changing demand created by outsourcing and subcontracting, the fragmentation of markets, and the associated opening up of niche markets, into which have crowded many small businesses. The ways in which these changes work themselves out vary from one sub-sector to another. Examples from the automotive, garment, and food-processing industries illustrate these differences. Automotive parts production has shifted from in-house production within large factories owned by assemblers such as Ford and General Motors to production by a chain of subcontractors involved in outsourcing arrangements. The result has been significant growth in the 1990s in small Canadian-owned auto parts producers. They locate in small towns and suburbs within easy travelling distance to the major automotive assembly plants, which themselves have been dispersed. Unionization in the parts industry is lower than in assembly and has not had the same upward, industry-wide effect on wages as seen in auto assembly. Pay scales are significantly lower in automotive parts than in assembly. Whereas starting wages for workers in assembly plants in 2001 were approximately $22/hour plus benefits, starting wages in small auto parts firms ranged from $10/hour and up, with an uneven spread of benefits (Vrankulj and Yates 2006). A new and disturbing trend in Canadian automotive parts production is seen in the move towards "homework." In 2003 there were reports that traditional Mennonite farms were setting up small production facilities in barns and other farm buildings, employing family labour (Stevenson 2003). These kinds of operations put considerable downward pressure on labour costs for the industry as a whole, thus jeopardizing employers' willingness to pay a living wage to workers in more urban locales.

The garment industry offers a slightly different example of the dynamics of change associated with dispersion to small workplaces. At one time in Canada, garments were manufactured in large factories. A considerable part of this industry has been moved from Canada to lower-wage locations such as Taiwan, Turkey, and China. The garment work that remains in Canada, and that in fact increased in the 1990s, is located in a chain of subcontractual relations involving small factories as well as homeworkers (Leach 1993). In 2004 Statistics Canada reported that three-quarters of the firms involved in the Canadian apparel industry, making women's, men's, and children's clothing, employed fewer than fifty employees (Statistics Canada 2004). The actual number of homeworkers employed in garment work in large cities such as Toronto and Vancouver is unknown, although estimates put it conservatively at 5,000 for Ontario in 1998 and 25,000 to 30,000 for Quebec in the early 1990s (Yanz et al. 1999).

Changes in food production reflect the fragmentation of markets and the growing demand for niche products. The beer industry is an interesting illustration of this, as the last decade has seen an explosion of micro- and niche breweries. These small firms have cut deep into the market share of large manufacturers such as Molson's and Labatt's that at one time cornered the market with beer mass-produced in large factories. Again, these shifts in production have significant impacts on work and wages. Whereas large breweries were heavily unionized with excellent wages and benefits, these conditions no longer hold in these small operations.

The third and final dimension of dispersion is the regional dimension. Although manufacturing continues to be concentrated in Ontario and Quebec, there is evidence of a westward shift to Manitoba, Alberta, and British Columbia. The much publicized and hotly debated opening of a large Maple Leaf Foods meat-packing plant in Brandon, Manitoba, is perhaps symbolic of this trend, as food processing has become one of the key manufacturing employers in all of the western provinces (Novek 1992). The expected 2005 closure of a Winnipeg slaughter operation and the consolidated expansion of Maple Leaf's operations in Brandon, combined with the recently announced investment in an organic meat slaughterhouse in Neepawa, Manitoba, are further evidence of the trends towards dispersion of manufacturing. Not surprisingly, the manufacturing sectors that are expanding in the West draw largely on local resource extraction industries and are often aimed at serving markets in Asia or Central America (Maple Leaf Foods 2000).[4] Thus, in addition to Winnipeg's large cluster of aerospace manufacturing, Manitoba's manufacturing growth has been in the agricultural industry, ranging from food processing to some production of agricultural implements. Alberta's growth is concentrated in chemical and petroleum products as well as food processing, while British Columbia's manufacturing capacity is in activities related to wood processing (Vinodrai 2001; Fleming and Rowell 2000). Arguably, industrial expansion in the West has been facilitated by the end to the Crow rates, which for years offered structural disincentives to industrial investment in the West (Fowke 1957; MacLachlan 2001).

How do these multiple dimensions of dispersion affect and interact with work and labour in manufacturing in Canada? Many firms are driven to the suburbs and rural communities in order to avoid unions and extract the maximum work from workers for the least cost. Labour cost reductions are driven by growing competitive pressures from producers in the southern United States, Mexico, and Southeast Asia, where wages are considerably lower than in Canada. Union avoidance is made all the more likely if the shift is to rural and small workplaces where union density is low or to locales such as Alberta where labour laws are viciously anti-union. Firms have hired particular kinds of workers as they disperse, their objective being to avoid hiring those with industrial, and possibly union, experience (Yates and Stoutley 2004). Companies seek to hire employees from new communities of labour who are driven to work hard either through desperation or a strong work ethic. Tony Winson (1997) argues that firms that locate in rural communities tap into an agrarian work ethic where hard work and self-sufficiency are morally sanctified, which satisfies the bottom-line demand of increased productivity at reduced costs. Similarly, as firms disperse, they often tap into new immigrant and racialized communities, identifying them as hard working and highly exploitable because of their limited alternative employment options (Selby 2004; Yates 1998; Leach 1998; Galabuzi 2001). Wages, although generally higher than the private service sector, are low compared to wages in large industrial operations, such as steel mills and auto assembly, and are driven downward by competition. Working conditions have deteriorated as work intensifies. A more elaborate discussion of these effects can be found below, in the section on work and employment relations.

Dispersion of manufacturing employment has reconfigured and reinforced labour market segmentation. We now turn to a discussion of the gendering and racialization of manufacturing employment.

FEMINIZATION

Historical analysis of the industrialization period in Canada stresses the role that women (and children) played in the early days of factory work, when they provided a source of unskilled labour significantly cheaper than that of men. But factory acts of the late 1890s, reinforced by the wider critique of social reformers and underpinned by a growing ideology of female domesticity, marginalized women factory workers into particular areas of factory work, such as the garment industry (Gannage 1986). A pattern of segregation emerged in manufacturing, echoed in practically every other part of the labour market, that persisted into the twentieth century (Sugiman 1994). Manufacturing employment that drew on women's traditional skills, such as sewing or manual dexterity, was identified as women's work, while heavier manufacturing work was associated largely with men.

In the postwar period, attempts to understand the operation of mass production capitalism set off a generation of industrial studies that examined contemporary and historical work in a range of industries, from chemical plants (Nichols and Beynon 1977), automobile assembly (Beynon 1973; Chinoy 1955), and machine shops (Burawoy 1979) to steelmaking. The family wage that characterized much unionized postwar factory work, combined with social policies such as family allowances, allowed many workers in Canada to achieve middle-class status; mothers and wives ceased work in the paid labour force, at least until their children were grown. Although many women continued to work in manufacturing, usually in segregated un-unionized factories, their work was made invisible in postwar analysis, which constructed a profile of industrial work as male dominated (Parr 1990).

In Britain, this perception was partially corrected in the 1970s and 1980s as the women's movement gathered momentum and focused attention on all facets of women's lives. The result was a series of landmark British ethnographic studies of women-dominated factories. These included Sallie Westwood's *All Day, Every Day: Factory and Family in the Lives of Women* (1985), Ruth Cavendish's *Women on the Line* (1982), and Anna Pollert's *Girls, Wives, Factory Lives* (1981).

The interplay between the women's movement and analyses of women's place in the political economy produced a different emphasis in Canada. The publication of *The Double Ghetto* (Armstrong and Armstrong 1978) marked a watershed in studies of women and work, drawing attention to the issues of gendered segregation in the Canadian labour market and the centrality of women's unpaid work in their labour market experience. Hugh Armstrong and Pat Armstrong demonstrated that women's rising labour market participation rates were accompanied by the concentration of women in certain occupations, notably clerical, nursing, cleaning, sewing, and related jobs. By 1991, women in these occupations accounted for about 50 per cent of all women workers. While attention was increasingly paid to women's work (Armstrong and Armstrong 1975; Connelly 1978; Steedman 1997), Canadian scholars paid more explicit attention to the connections between women's paid work and the unpaid work they carried out in the home (Fox 1980; Luxton 1980; Meissner et al. 1979; Morton 1972; Seccombe 1979). This focus contributed to the growing understanding that women's segregation in specific kinds of work was related to their ongoing household responsibilities. Thus, with few exceptions, little scholarly attention was paid to women's experience in manufacturing work. More recently, analyses of women's manufacturing work tend to focus on the newly industrializing countries.

Manufacturing, however, continues to be a vital sector of the economy, and it employs a considerable number of women. Women's employment as a percentage of employment in manufacturing has risen from 21.1 per cent in 1954 to 29.3 per cent in 2003 (see Table 6.1), although only about 10 per cent of the total female labour force is employed in manufacturing, compared to 19 per cent for men. A big increase in women's employment in manufacturing came in the 1970s and, to a lesser extent, the 1990s. Women were hard hit with layoffs, as were men, by the 1981–82 and 1990–93 recessions. As in the broader economy, women tend to be employed in those sectors or occupations within manufacturing that draw on their special "talents" (Jenson 1989) – their perceived greater dexterity, nimbleness (making it easier for them to work in small work areas), and ability to pay more attention to detail. The manager of a temporary staffing agency that places workers in the auto parts industry identified the contemporary dynamics of segregation with these words: "I think that a lot of our clients still tend to want males, maybe, versus females. It's a pretty good split. And it depends on the companies. There are certain companies or certain departments that it's all men, basically, that can work there because of lifting issues, those sorts of things. But anything to do with smaller parts, then they'd rather have women doing that because the dexterity in women is typically better. But it's probably about a 50–50 split" (Yates and Stoutley 2004).

Within the automotive parts industry, where women constitute a growing proportion of the workforce, women tend to be concentrated in plastics and upholstery, whereas men are more likely to be found where greater physical strength is required, such as stamping and engines. The latter jobs, in part for historic reasons, including higher rates of unionization, and in part because of greater rewards for the "skills" of men than for the "talents" of women, tend to pay more per hour (Jenson 1989). Although garment manufacture represents a relatively small proportion of manufacturing employment today, women continue to be concentrated in this industry, and they make up the entire home-working population. Similarly, gender segregation runs deep within food processing. Whereas men predominate in meat slaughterhouses and beer factories, for example, women predominate in the manufacture of candy and the processing of chickens. A recently released study of time-series census data by Sam Vrankulj and Charlotte Yates points to considerable local variations in women's employment. In areas such as Brantford, Ontario, for example, where unemployment has historically been higher than the provincial average and many industrial workers have been laid off, starting wages are depressed and women are being pushed out of manufacturing jobs by men seeking work. Thus, the number of women employed in manufacturing in Brantford is in decline. In contrast, in Stratford, Ontario, women and men tend to remain segregated in long-term historical patterns, and women's rates of employment in manufacturing are proportionally greater (Vrankulj and Yates 2005).

Work in the manufacturing sector has long represented "good" work for working-class women, as it is more likely to offer full-time status, higher wages, and a chance at unionization, which is associated with greater job security and benefits. Access to manufacturing employment as good work may become more important for women who are now more likely to be the sole support of a family and as attacks on the welfare state reduce the good jobs available for women in the public sector. At the same time, Charlotte Yates and Belinda Leach (2006), in their study of women employed in auto parts manufacture, have found that manufacturing workplaces, with their long, rigidly scheduled hours of work, the dirt and grime, and the combative and often sexist and racist environment, are hostile workplaces for women. These authors report that many women lamented the poor wages paid in clean, service-type jobs – at Tim Horton's and Zeller's, for example – which they identified as preferable to manufacturing jobs but jobs that could not sustain working women and their families.

RACIALIZATION

Segregation in manufacturing has also involved dynamics of ethnicity and race. In manufacturing, historical studies have shown ethnic and racial stratification in industries such as steel (Heron and Storey 1986) and automotive production (Meier and Rudwick 1979) where workers of different ethnic and racial backgrounds were pitted against each other in the workplace. White workers blamed immigrants and racialized minorities for undermining wages and other gains made by workers over the years. Employers fomented these antagonisms in their pursuit of labour control (Yates 1998), often bringing in immigrants and racialized groups as scabs during industrial disputes. Scholarly work on racialization in the labour force has examined the connection between immigration policies and labour market needs, focusing especially on the vulnerability of the most marginalized immigrant workers, such as domestic workers on temporary visas (Abu-Laban and Gabriel 2002; Arat-Koc 1990), the growing numbers of racialized workers in contingent and precarious work (Cranford, Vosko, and Zukewich 2003), and the struggles of immigrants and racialized groups to unionize. Other studies have pointed to the growing income gap between racialized groups in the Canadian labour force and other Canadians. In 1996 Canadians from racialized groups made 23 per cent less per year than other Canadians (Galabuzi 2001,15). Yet, in Canada, little scholarly attention has been paid to the experiences of immigrants and racialized groups in manufacturing work.

Much as it is for women, manufacturing is an important point of entry to the labour market for immigrants and racialized groups. Grace-Edward Galabuzi reports that in 1996, while 7 per cent of the Canadian population overall worked in manufacturing and processing, 15.5 per cent of recent immigrants were working in these jobs (2001, 50). Women of colour are twice as likely as the national average to be employed in manufacturing. Overall, 27 per cent of the manufacturing workforce is immigrant (CLBC 2004, 7). Immigrants are over-represented in low-wage manufacturing sectors such as clothing and textiles and under-represented in the better-paying industries, such as automotive assembly (Galabuzi 2001, 53). In clothing, more than half the labour force is immigrant, and over a quarter of these have only recently come to Canada (CLBC 2004, 7). Between 35 and 38 per cent of the labour force in electronics, furniture, electrical, and textiles are immigrants (CLBC 2004, 8). Even more striking, 63 per cent of manufacturing workers in Toronto and 49 per cent in Vancouver are immigrants (CLBC 2004, 8).

Thus, for immigrants and racialized groups, manufacturing is a particularly important source of jobs, albeit often for quite different reasons. For many racialized and immigrant women, such as Philippine domestic workers, the manufacturing sector offers a step up in the labour market once they have completed their two-year domestic residency requirement. The wages are better, the hours are more predictable, and the isolation and powerlessness experienced in the home-as-workplace are lessened. Humanitarian immigrants – those arriving in Canada as family-class immigrants or as refugees – take the least desirable menial jobs and have often moved up the labour market ladder into better-paid, more secure manufacturing jobs (Satzewich and Wong 2003, 365). However, moving into these better manufacturing jobs is becoming more difficult (Satzewich and Wong 2003, 380). Other immigrant and racialized workers look at jobs in the manufacturing sector as stepping stones while they attempt to gain recognition in Canada for foreign academic training and professional qualifications. Finally, migrant workers are increasingly being brought in to address labour shortages in the industries where employers refuse to pay adequate wages.

Immigrant workers bring to Canada highly desirable human capital (Satzewich and Wong 2003, 365). In 1996, 34 per cent of immigrants between the ages of twenty-five and forty-four had a university degree, compared with only 19 per cent in the comparable Canadian population (Galabuzi 2001, 69). Yet, these well-educated immigrants are much more likely than Canadian-born workers to be working in low-paid jobs (Jackson et al. 2000). In manufacturing, 26 per cent of immigrant workers have university degrees and a further 24 per cent have college or trade diplomas (CLBC 2004, 8). Such a highly qualified immigrant workforce in manufacturing allows employers to increase productivity by taking advantage of the skills and knowledge of workers while paying low wages. Such practices become more widespread as rates of unionization in manufacturing decline.

Finally, and in contrast to the trends that identify manufacturing as a way up in the labour market, those who get trapped in homework manufacturing, such as Chinese immigrant women in Toronto, experience manufacturing as a labour market ghetto. Woefully inadequate wages, poor working conditions, and highly exploitative employment practices are borne by these workers whose labour market alternatives are few given the racism and sexism in the public labour market and the limitations imposed by weak English-language skills (Leach 1996).

The feminization and racialization of work frequently operate together, doubly disadvantaging women of colour, who are concentrated in the more unstable industries and kinds of jobs (Brand 1988; Das Gupta 1996). Grace-Edward Galabuzi (2001, 7) notes that the racialized members of the labour force who are stuck in low-end jobs are far more likely to be women than men, especially when they are working in manufacturing sweatshops or as homeworkers. Segmentation occurs not just at the industry level, but at the firm level where particular racialized and/or gendered groups of workers are concentrated in particular workplaces. This is partly the result of employer hiring practices that ascribe certain "natural" talents or abilities to specific groups and use family and community networks to tap into a labour supply. Charlotte Yates and Andrew Stoutley (2004) have found that these patterns of labour market segmentation are reinforced by temporary help agencies' efforts to find workers who "fit" best within the existing workplace, a practice that often involves finding women to work on small manufacturing operations that require dexterity, "big strong guys" to do heavy lifting, and Punjabi workers to work with other Punjabi workers. At the root of labour market segmentation lies the drive by employers to exploit the existing labour market inequalities experienced by women and racialized groups, as well as a deep-seated historically constituted racism and sexism that associates certain groups of workers with certain traits and capabilities.

The story of the Brandon Maple Leaf Foods pork-processing plant illustrates many of the dynamics of the racialization of manufacturing. Meat packing has undergone massive restructuring in the face of intense competition, the result being steep wage cuts and intensification of work, along with an increasing concentration of corporate ownership (MacLachlan 2001). In 2003, 1,300 workers were employed by Maple Leaf in Brandon. They were paid $9.45/hour, while the minimum wage was $6.75. Management's response to absenteeism and high turnover rates of between 80 and 100 per cent each year was to introduce attendance bonuses of $1/hour that could be earned for perfect attendance over the course of a month. Injury rates are high among workers. As one worker commented about the work, "Every job at Maple Leaf is hard. It's messy, brutal work. You work eight hours a day, five days a week and your body is going to wear out" (*Globe and Mail*, 28 November 2003). The dreadful working conditions and below-poverty-level wages, together with Brandon's tight labour market, have exacerbated labour shortages. The company's response has been to draw into the workforce two racialized groups, Aboriginal Canadians and migrant workers from Mexico and Central America. According to a Maple Leaf press release, currently 29 per cent of the workforce is Aboriginal and 5 per cent are foreign migrant workers (Maple Leaf Foods 2003). The "success" of this employment strategy speaks to the vulnerability of workers who end up sticking it out at Maple Leaf Foods. Most of the Mexican workers brought in by Maple Leaf returned home within months, owing to the poor wages that could not sustain a decent standard of living in Brandon. Only those migrant workers brought from war-torn El Salvador remained, desperate to leave their troubled country even if it meant injury, low wages, and dreadful work. For their part, Aboriginal Canadians are another vulnerable population owing to high unemployment rates and poor economic life chances. Not surprisingly, Maple Leaf has increased its recruitment from local Aboriginal communities.

Maple Leaf is not exceptional in this industry for its exploitation of racialized workers. A recent dispute between Lakeside Packers (a branch of the giant American multinational corporation Tyson) and its workers in Brooks, Alberta, revealed similar patterns of exploitation of racialized populations (Selby 2004). In this case, Sudanese workers engaged in a wildcat strike to protest being forced to work while injured, being forbidden to take bathroom breaks, and the company's practice of not rehiring women to their same job after maternity leave. Although food processing may offer some of the starkest examples of the exploitation of race and gender in manufacturing, these patterns are becoming increasingly widespread throughout the manufacturing sector.

CHANGING WORK AND EMPLOYMENT RELATIONS IN MANUFACTURING

The final dynamic of change in manufacturing work that we want to examine in this chapter revolves around the changing nature of work itself and the transformation of employment relations in the manufacturing sector. Work organization in manufacturing has been transformed by intense competitive pressures, new technologies, and changing consumer demand. Capital's responses to these pressures vary. Labour-intensive manufacturing operations whose products can be easily shipped long distances are most vulnerable to competition from locales with low labour costs. For this reason, the post-industrial literature predicted that operations like these in Canada would close and/or relocate to cheaper production localities. Although such deindustrialization has occurred, there is a surprising persistence of low-wage manufacturing employment in Canada, ranging from small garment to auto parts manufacture. Many of the low-wage manufacturers are relatively new; many are small, non-union operations that adopt low-technology solutions to production. New sweatshops have emerged that rely on the exploitation of new immigrants who have few other job opportunities. Public policy changes, such as reductions to unemployment insurance and welfare, wage subsidies for the hard to employ, and welfare-to-work programs that drive down wages in the lowest tiers, facilitate the survival of low-wage manufacturing by making available a ready supply of desperate workers. Low costs combined with proximity to markets provide these operations with their competitive edge.

Capital-intensive firms are more likely to compete through investment in new technologies. According to a Canadian Manufacturers and Exporters report (CME 2004a), technological innovation by Canadian manufacturing operations will accelerate over the next five years. In 2002, the report says, 20 per cent of manufacturing operations used robots, 47 per cent used numerically controlled machines, and 34 per cent adopted cell-based work organization, whereby machines or work processes of different types performing different operations were organized in a tight sequence, typically U-shaped, to facilitate quicker flow of work and flexible deployment of human resources by means of multi-machine working. The CME expects the adoption of these technologies to increase to 35 per cent, 57 per cent, and 48 per cent respectively by 2007 (CME 2004a).

Whether labour or capital intensive, manufacturing firms have sought to compete by pushing workers to work harder and longer for poorer wages and benefits. Average hours of work in the manufacturing sector have crept upwards since the early 1980s. Although workers in the manufacturing sector are more likely to be paid for overtime than workers in the private or public service sectors (Jackson et al. 2000, 84–5), this trend is likely to decline as rates of unionization drop. Work intensity in manufacturing has also increased. Just-in-time production combined with work reorganization processes, such as cell-based work organization, has led to the elimination of precious seconds of downtime. Work in many parts of the automotive sector, for example, is designed so that fifty-seven seconds of every minute of labour time are productively deployed. For workers, the consequences are higher stress, greater likelihood of injury, and overall deterioration in the quality of work life (Stewart, Lewchuk, and Yates 2001; Yates, Stewart, and Lewchuk 2001).

In the past, workers in the manufacturing sector have relied on unions to protect them from these and other changes in wages and working conditions. The positive impact of unions on wages, working conditions, and workers' rights on the job are well documented (Jackson et al. 2000; Yates 2001), but it is worth noting that unions have an especially positive effect on the wages, benefits, and working conditions of women and racialized groups. Grace-Edward Galabuzi's research demonstrates that unions help to reduce the wage gap between white and racialized workers. Non-union racialized workers earn 30 per cent less than non-unionized white workers, while there is only an 8 per cent wage difference between racialized and white unionized workers (Galabuzi 2001). Not surprisingly, women and racialized groups are currently more supportive of unionization.

Yet, unionization in the manufacturing sector has dropped precipitously, with significant negative effects on wages and working conditions. In Canada it has dropped from 44 per cent in 1976 to 30 per cent in 2002, measured as the percentage of workers employed in the manufacturing sector who are members of a union. This dramatic drop in unionization is the result of several changes in the industry. Plant closures in the 1981–82 and 1990–93 recessions disproportionately affected unionized facilities. Lost unionized jobs were not regained once manufacturing employment began to grow in the 1990s, as most new manufacturing firms and facilities tended to be small, non-union operations. Over the last decade, unions have attempted to organize workers in this sector (Yates 2001), and while they have been relatively successful in Ontario, they have been unable to keep pace with employment growth in manufacturing. This is partly a consequence of the difficulty unions face in organizing small, often rural workplaces, but it is also a consequence of the intense anti-union campaigns mounted by employers. Felice Martinello and Charlotte Yates (2004) demonstrate that, of all employers, those in the manufacturing sector mount the most sustained anti-union campaigns when confronted with an organizing drive.

Workers and work in the manufacturing sector have been transformed in the last ten to fifteen years as a result of rapid restructuring and intense competition. Although 95 per cent of manufacturing jobs are full-time and international indicators demonstrate that job tenure has not changed noticeably over the last decade, workers express a growing sense of risk and insecurity in their jobs. Feelings of insecurity and risk are heightened by the growing use of temporary workers in factories, usually hired through temporary help agencies (Yates and Stoutley 2004). They are further reinforced by a pervasive culture of competition that encourages workers to pit themselves against other workers, most often from Mexico and China, in a bid to keep their jobs.

CONCLUSION

Even as the institutions and practices of the "golden age" of mass consumption and production are displaced, employment in manufacturing continues to matter. It matters because more than two million Canadian workers are employed directly in this sector, with tens of thousands of other jobs indirectly dependent upon manufacturing. It also matters because, although manufacturing jobs continue to be better than most other work in the private sector, downward pressures on wages and working conditions in manufacturing means the loss of the postwar gold standard of wages, benefits, and collective bargaining innovation.

Work and workers in manufacturing have changed. Almost a half of current manufacturing employers were not in business in Canada fifteen years ago. Work is more likely to take place in small enterprises located outside large urban centres. The working day has gradually been lengthened and the pace of work intensified. After decades of dense representation by unions, only one in three workers in manufacturing today is likely to be represented by a union. Consequently, wages and benefits have declined and employment contracts have undergone significant change. Canadian manufacturing is increasingly made up of low-wage, labour-intensive firms. Just as manufacturing work is no longer the jewel in the crown of the postwar economy, men have either been pushed out of or abandoned this employment in favour of better jobs elsewhere. And thus, an increasingly educated workforce made up of a growing number of women and immigrants, especially racialized minorities, have been drawn into manufacturing establishments.

What does this mean for Canadian workers and the labour market and what are the possible alternatives? Downward pressure on wages and working conditions in manufacturing has a ripple effect throughout the labour market. Rather than fulfilling the promise of a knowledge economy, Canadian employers and governments have chosen a low-wage path to competitiveness, preventing workers from reaping the rewards of working harder and attaining a higher education. With the feminization and racialization of low-paid manufacturing work, Canada's model of development is converging with those of several poorer, dependent countries whose growth and competitiveness lie in exploiting the most exploited.

As to the possibilities for change, there are several. A reversal of declining rates of unionization in manufacturing is a key strategy for change. Unions have a significant positive effect on wages and working conditions, and they also offer avenues through which workers' interests can be represented and greater workplace democracy realized. At present, there exist high levels of support for unionization among women and racialized workers in Canada. Unions need to work hard at organizing these workers, something that could be facilitated by changes in labour laws across Canada. Despite popular rhetoric to the contrary, governments still have the capacity to regulate work through such measures as restrictions on overtime and better enforcement of minimum standards to ensure that workers are better protected, both at work and in their attempts to balance family and work. The federal government's 2003 introduction of the Compassionate Care Benefit for workers who need time off to look after a dying relative is one small step in the right direction (www.sdc.gc.ca/en/ei/types/compassionate _care.shtml), as are expanded parental leave opportunities. Governments could also play a stronger role in upholding existing regulations governing working conditions and basic human rights – recall the

Lakeside Packers workers dispute with their employer, discussed above. These and other such changes, however, only happen as a result of considerable political and economic pressure being brought to bear on employers and governments. It is for this reason that we must look closely towards and support the mobilization of labour and social movements, as to date these have been the most important agents of change for working people.

NOTES

Authors' Note: This chapter is based on research on workers and social cohesion funded by a Social Sciences and Humanities Research Council of Canada grant.

1 Through this discussion, we do not pretend to offer an exhaustive history of manufacturing in Canada; rather our discussion is constructed as a response to contemporary arguments about the end of manufacturing in North America. For this reason, we do not discuss the rise and fall of manufacturing in Atlantic Canada; nor do we offer an exhaustive explanation for the changing dynamics of manufacturing in all of Canada.

2 A prime example of this can be seen in the agricultural implement industry. Canada was a world leader in the manufacture of agricultural implements. Massey-Ferguson was perhaps the best-known Canadian firm in this industry, but by the early 1980s it was in serious trouble, the result of which was a restructuring of its operations in 1987. Under its new name, Varity Corporation, it specialized in the manufacture of automotive components, diesel engines, and some agricultural implements. By the 1990s, little farm equipment was manufactured in Canada.

3 In 1899 the Canada Cycle and Motor Company (CCM) began producing bicycles in the Weston area of Toronto. Once a Canadian household name, in 1983 this company declared bankruptcy.

4 Manitoba is the largest hog-producing province in Canada.

REFERENCES

Abu-Laban, Yasmeen, and Christina Gabriel. 2002. *Selling diversity: Immigration, multiculturalism, employment equity and globalization.* Peterborough: Broadview Press

Arat-Koc, Sedef. 1990. Importing housewives: Non-citizen domestic workers and the crisis of the domestic sphere in Canada. In *Through the kitchen window,* by M. Luxton, Harriet Rosenberg, and S. Arat-Koc. Toronto: Garamond Press

Armstrong, Hugh, and Pat Armstrong. 1975. The segregated participation of women in the Canadian labour force 1941–1971. *Canadian Review of Sociology and Anthropology* 12 (4): 370–84

– 1978. *The double ghetto: Canadian women and their segregated work.* Toronto: McClelland and Stewart

Baldwin, John, Mark Brown, and Tara Vinodrai. 2001. Dynamics of the Canadian manufacturing sector in metropolitan and rural regions. Statistics Canada Research Paper Series no.169. Ottawa, November

Bell, Daniel. 1976. *The coming of post-industrial society: A venture in social forecasting.* New York: Basic Books

Beynon, Huw. 1973. *Working for Ford.* Harmondsworth: Penguin

Bluestone, Barry, and Bennett Harrison. 1982. *The deindustrialization of America: Plant closings, community abandonment, and the dismantling of basic industry.* New York: Basic Books

Brand, Dionne. 1988. Black women and work. Pt 2. *Fireweed* 26:87–93

Brown, Mark, and John Baldwin. 2003. The changing geography of the Canadian manufacturing sector in metropolitan and rural regions, 1976–1997. *Canadian Geographer Summer* 47:116–35

Burawoy, Michael. 1979. *Manufacturing consent: Changes in the labour process under monopoly capitalism.* Chicago: University of Chicago Press

Cameron, Duncan, and François Houle. 1985. *Le Canada et la nouvelle division internationale du travail/Canada and the new international division of labour.* Ottawa: University of Ottawa Press

Campbell, Bruce, et al. 1999. *Pulling apart: The deterioration of employment and income in North America under free trade.* Ottawa: Canadian Centre for Policy Alternatives

Cavendish, Ruth. 1982. *Women on the line.* London and Boston: Routledge and Kegan Paul

Chinoy, E. 1955. *Automobile workers and the American dream.* Garden City: Doubleday

CLBC (Canadian Labour and Business Centre). 2004. *Workforce profile of the manufacturing sector.* March. Available at www.clbc.ca/Research_and_Reports/Archive/report06080401.asp

CLC (Canadian Labour Congress). 2004. *Economy* 14 (3)

CME (Canadian Manufacturers and Exporters). 2004a. *Global trends in manufacturing.* Report from CME series entitled "Canadian Manufacturers and Exporters20/20 Building our Vision for the Future." Available at www.cme-mec.ca/mfg2020/globaltrends.pdf

– 2004b. *The importance of manufacturing in Canada.* Report from CME series entitled "Canadian Manufacturers and Exporters20/20 Building our Vision for the Future." Available at: http://www.cme-mec.ca/mfg2020/Importance.pdf

188   Charlotte Yates and Belinda Leach

Cohen, Stephen, and John Zysman. 1987. *Manufacturing matters: The myth of the post-industrial economy.* New York: Basic Books

Connelly, Patricia. 1978. *Last hired, first fired.* Toronto: Women's Press

Cranford, Cynthia, Leah Vosko, and N. Zukewich. 2003. Precarious employment in the Canadian labour market: A statistical portrait. *Just Labour: A Canadian Journal of Work and Society* 3:6–22

Das Gupta, T. 1996. *Racism and paid work.* Toronto: Garamond Press

Drache, Daniel. 1989. *The deindustrialization of Canada and its implications for labour.* Ottawa: Canadian Centre for Policy Alternatives

– 1992. *Getting on track: Social democratic strategies for Ontario.* Ottawa: Canadian Centre for Policy Alternatives

Economic Council of Canada. 1990. *Good jobs, bad jobs – Employment in the service economy.* Ottawa: Research Report for Economic Council of Canada

Fleming, Neil, and Allan Rowell. 2000. Canadian manufacturing activity: A geographical perspective. Research paper for the Manufacturing Construction and Energy and Geography Divisions. Available at www.statscan.ca/english/research/31F0028XIE/cmagp.pdf

Fowke, Vernon. 1957. *The national policy and the wheat economy.* Toronto: University of Toronto Press

Fox, Bonnie, ed. 1980. *Hidden in the household: Women's domestic labour under capitalism.* Toronto: Women's Press

Gagnon, Alain. 2004. *Quebec: State and society.* Peterborough: Broadview Press

Galabuzi, Grace-Edward. 2001. *Canada's creeping economic apartheid.* Toronto: Canadian Centre for Social Justice

Gannage, Charlene. 1986. *Double day, double bind: Women garment workers.* Toronto: Women's Press

Gordon, D.M, R. Edwards, and M. Reich. 1982. *Segmented work, divided workers.* Cambridge: Cambridge University Press

Hadekel, Peter. 2004. *Silent partners: Taxpayers and the bankrolling of Bombardier.* Toronto: Key Porter Books

Heron, Craig, and R. Storey. 1986. Work and struggle in the Canadian steel industry 1900–1950. In *On the job: Confronting the labour process in Canada,* edited by C. Heron and R. Storey. Montreal and Kingston: McGill-Queen's University Press

High, Steven. 2003. *Industrial sunset: The making of North America's rust belt, 1969–1984.* Toronto: University of Toronto Press

Holmes, John, and Colin Leys. 1987. *Frontyard, backyard: The Americas in the global crisis.* Toronto: Between the Lines

Jackson, Andrew, et al. 2000. *Falling behind: The state of working Canada.* Ottawa: Canadian Centre for Policy Alternatives

Jenson, Jane. 1989. The talents of women, the skills of men: Flexible specialization and women. In *The transformation of work?* edited by Stephen Wood. London: Unwin Hyman

Leach, B. 1993. Flexible work, precarious future: Some lessons from the Canadian clothing industry. *Canadian Review of Sociology and Anthropology* 30 (1): 64–82

– 1996. Behind closed doors: Homework policy and lost possibilities for change. In *Rethinking restructuring: Gender and change in Canada,* edited by I. Bakker. Toronto: University of Toronto Press

– 1998. Industrial homework, economic restructuring and the meaning of work. *Labour/Le Travail* 42 (Spring): 97–115

Lewchuk, Wayne, and Don Wells. 2004. Management strategies and labour markets: Gaining worker commitment to management goals in auto parts plants in Canada. Paper presented to Auto21 conference "Workers and Labour Markets in the Global Automotive Industry," Hamilton, Ontario, 22–23 October

Luxton, Meg. 1980. *More than a labour of love: Three generations of women's work in the home.* Toronto: Women's Press

McCallum, John. 1980. *Unequal beginnings: Agriculture and economic development in Quebec and Ontario until 1870.* Toronto: University of Toronto Press

MacLachlan, Ian. 2001. *Kill and chill: Restructuring Canada's beef commodity chain.* Toronto: University of Toronto Press

Maple Leaf Foods. 2003. Salvadorean workers celebrate one year anniversary at Brandon facility. Maple Leaf Press Release, 4 December 2003. Available at http://investor.mapleleaf.ca/phoenix.zhtml?c=88490&p= irol-newsArticle&ID=547940&highlight=

– 2000. Interim report to shareholders for the first quarter ended March 31, 2000. Available at www.mapleleaf.com/Investor/PublicFilings/ quartely_reports/1Q2000eng.pdf

Martinello, Felice, and Charlotte Yates. 2004. Union and employer tactics in Ontario organising campaigns. In *Advances in industrial and labor relations,* edited by David Lewin and Bruce Kaufman, 13:157–90. New York: Elsevier

Meier, August, and Elliott Rudwick. 1979. *Black Detroit and the rise of the UAW.* New York: Oxford University Press

Meissner, Martin, Elizabeth W. Humphreys, Scott M. Meis, and William J. Scheu. 1979. No exit for wives: Sexual division of labour and the culmination of household demands. *Canadian Review of Sociology and Anthropology* 12 (4): 424–39

Morissette, Rene, Yuri Ostrovsky, and Garnett Picot. 2004. Relative wage patterns amongst the highly educated in a knowledge-based economy. Catalogue #11F0019MIE – no.232, research paper. Ottawa: Business and Labour Market Analysis Division of Statistics Canada. Available at

www.statcan.ca/english/research/11F0019MIE/
   11F0019MIE2004232.pdf
Morton, Penny. 1972. Women's work is never done. In *Women Unite!*
   Toronto: Women's Press
Nadeau, Serge. 1999. The role of industrial structure in Canada-U.S.
   manufacturing labour productivity gap. Presentation to the 1999
   Canadian Economic Association Meetings, Micro-economic Policy Analysis
   Branch, Industry Canada
Nichols, T., and H. Beynon. 1977. *Living with capitalism: Class relations in the
   modern factory.* London: Routledge
Novek, J. 1992. The labour process and workplace injuries in the Canadian
   meat packing industry. *Canadian Review of Sociology and Anthropology* 29 (1):
   17–37
Parr, Joy. 1990. *The gender of breadwinners.* Toronto: University of Toronto
   Press
Peck, Jamie. 1996. *Work-place: The social regulation of labor markets.* New York:
   Guilford Press
Piore, Michael, and Charles Sabel. 1984. *The second industrial divide.* New
   York: Basic Books
Pollert, Anna. 1981. *Girls, wives, factory lives.* London: Macmillan
Pratt, Larry, and John Richards. 1979. *Prairie capitalism: Power and influence in
   the New West.* Toronto: McClelland and Stewart
Rostow, W. 1960. *The stages of economic growth.* Cambridge University Press
Rubery, Jill. 1980. Structured labour markets, worker organization and low
   pay. In *The economics of women and work*, edited by A. Amsden.
   Harmondsworth: Penguin
Satzewich, V., and L. Wong. 2003. Immigration, ethnicity and race: The
   transformation of transnationalism, localism and identities. In *Changing
   Canada: Political economy as transformation*, edited by Wallace Clement and
   Leah Vosko, 363–90. Montreal and Kingston: McGill-Queen's University
   Press
Seccombe, W. 1979. The housewife and her labour under capitalism. *New
   Left Review* 83:3–24
Selby, Jim. 2004. Organizing Lakeside Packers. *Labour News: Alberta's Voice for
   Working People.* Available at www.afl.org/labour-news/
   afl-news.cfm?newsid=270
Statistics Canada. 2004. Business information by sector. Available at
   strategis.gc.ca
Steedman, M. 1997. *Angels of the workplace: Women and the construction of gender
   relations in the Canadian clothing industry.* Toronto: Oxford University Press
Stevenson, Mark. 2003. Bending their way. *Global and Mail*, 2 August, F1,
   F4–F5

Stewart, Paul, Wayne Lewchuk, and Charlotte Yates. 2001. From hegemony to despotism? An international study of the quality of life at work in the automobile industry. *New Technology, Work and Employment* 16 (2): 72–87

Sugiman, P. 1994. *Labour's dilemma: The gender politics of auto workers in Canada, 1937–1979.* Toronto: University of Toronto Press

Thompson, Paul. 1983. *The nature of work: An introduction to debates on the labour process.* Basingstoke: Macmillan

Vardy, Jill. 1991. Manufacturing bears brunt of job casualties. *Financial Post,* 7 December, 1, 20

Vinodrai, Tara. 2001. A tale of three cities: The dynamics of manufacturing in Toronto, Montreal and Vancouver, 1976–1997. Statistics Canada Research Paper Series no.177. Ottawa, November

Vrankulj, Sam, and Charlotte Yates. 2005. Supply meets demand in Canada's auto parts labour market: A critical examination of labour market trends. Policy paper, Labour Studies, McMaster University

Westwood, Sallie. 1985. *All day, every day: Factory and family in the making of women's lives.* Urbana: University of Illinois Press

Winson, A.R. 1997. Does class consciousness exist in rural communities? The impact of restructuring and plant shutdowns in rural Canada. *Rural Sociology* 62 (4)

Winson, A.R., and B. Leach. 2002. *Contingent work, disrupted lives: Labour and community in the new rural economy.* Toronto: University of Toronto Press

Yanz, Lynda, Bob Jeffcott, Deena Ladd, and Joan Atlin. 1999. *Policy options to improve standards for women garment workers in Canada and internationally.* Ottawa: Status of Women Canada

Yates, Charlotte. 1993. *From plant to politics: The Autoworkers Union in postwar Canada.* Philadelphia: Temple University Press

– 1998. Defining the fault lines: New divisions in the working class. *Capital and Class,* no. 66:121–49

– 2000. Staying the decline in union membership: Union organizing in Ontario, 1985–1999. *Relations Industrielles/Industrial Relations* 55 (4): 640–74

– 2001. *Making it your economy: Unions and economic justice.* Toronto: Centre for Social Justice and Ontario Federation of Labour

Yates, Charlotte, and Belinda Leach. 2006. Why "good" jobs lead to social exclusion. *Economic and Industrial Democracy* 27 (3): 343–71

Yates, Charlotte, Paul Stewart, and Wayne Lewchuk. 2001. Empowerment as a Trojan horse: New systems of work organization in the North American automobile industry. *Economic and Industrial Democracy* 22 (4): 517–41

Yates, Charlotte, and Andrew Stoutley. 2004. Temping in the auto parts industry. Unpublished paper

7

Racializing Work/Reproducing White Privilege

GILLIAN CREESE

INTRODUCTION

It would have come as no surprise to Canadians in the first half of the twentieth century that race and gender matter in the labour market. Employers, workers, trade unions, and politicians of various stripes shared the assumption that different people were fit for different kinds of work. On rare occasions when men and women of different racialized backgrounds worked side by side, different wage scales were invoked to maintain the higher value of white men relative to other men, all men relative to women, and white women relative to other women (Creese 1987, 1988, 1988–89, 1999). Much has changed in the last fifty years, and assumptions about appropriate gender roles, the meanings of race, and the nature of Canadian society have shifted dramatically (Mackey 2002). Legal barriers that denied women and some racialized groups access to particular jobs and educational programs have long been dismantled. In fact, legal discrimination has been replaced by policies designed to facilitate equal treatment in the labour market. Pay equity and employment equity legislation, for example, has been enacted in many jurisdictions across the country (Fudge and Vosko 2003). And yet, as this chapter demonstrates, racialization remains central to the organization of a gendered labour market, and white men continue to monopolize choice jobs and earn a premium compared to other groups.

In this chapter, I explore contemporary processes involved in the racialization of paid work in Canada. I begin by locating the chapter in

the context of feminist post-colonial theories and outlining the historical context that one needs to be familiar with to understand contemporary trends in the labour market. Next, I provide an overview of
racialization patterns in the labour market and explore how economic
restructuring affects these trends. Finally, I turn to research that
explores some of the complex processes that reproduce racialized-
gendered work in Canada.

CONCEPTUALIZING RACIALIZATION AND WORK IN CANADA

Racialization refers to the social significance attached to perceived
phenotypical and/or cultural differences among groups of people
(Miles 1989). It is an ongoing and fluid process that changes across
time and space within specific material contexts, power relations, and
cultural imaginations, creating different conceptions of race in different historical and national contexts. Racialization embodies all subjects, not only those identified as racially "other," including members
of dominant groups who may be treated as the "unraced" standard
against which others are judged. So, for example, "whiteness" is a
racialized category that has been central to the development of power
relations in Canada and the United States but has often been invisible
to those who embody it. Moreover, the constructions and meanings of
whiteness (like other racialized constructions) have changed over time
as some European groups – people from Ireland, for example – shifted
from non-white to white in the North American cultural imagination
(Jacobson 1998), while others from Europe – Portuguese immigrant
women, for example – continue in many ways to be racialized as non-
white (Giles 2002).

As post-colonial feminist scholars point out,[1] racialization processes
are linked not only to the histories of colonization within different
national contexts, but also to interconnections with gender, sexuality,
and class relations (Anthias and Yuval-Davis 1992; Bannerji 2000;
Calliste and Dei 2000; Collins 1990; Dua and Robertson 1999; Hooks
1984; Ng 1990; Razack 1998, 2002; Stasiulis and Yuval Davis 1995). In
the labour market, for example, jobs are clearly divided along class
lines, inscribed with varying definitions of skill, formal educational
requirements, prospects for advancement, levels of control, workplace
autonomy, and associated income levels (Clement and Myles 1994).
The labour market is also fundamentally gendered, with most work
still being done predominantly by either men or women, internal gender divisions existing in jobs that employ both sexes, and women's
paid work being systematically lower valued than men's (Armstrong

and Armstrong 2001). Jobs are also associated with gendered, sexual-ized, and racialized workplace cultures (Creese 1999). For example, many traditional men's jobs are associated with forms of hegemonic heterosexual masculinity (Connell 1995). In such contexts, homopho-bic, sexist, and racist discourses may form part of everyday workplace cultures in sites as diverse as auto plants (Corman and Luxton 1991, 2001), garment factories (Das Gupta 1996), or the training sites for medical students (Beagan 2001). Racialized, gendered, and sexual-ized workplace cultures also permeate areas of traditional women's work, such as hospital nursing (Das Gupta 1996; Calliste 2000) and clerical work (Creese 1999; Pringle 1988). Rosemary Pringle (1988) shows, in the Australian context, how assumptions about the nature of work become inscribed on particular bodies, such that secretaries have come to be naturally equated with the white, heterosexual, work-ing-class women typically hired as secretaries. Similarly, scholars have shown how Filipina women have been constructed as ideal nannies and domestic workers (Bakan and Stasiulis 1997; Pratt 2004).

We can trace racialization processes in Canada to colonialism and the subsequent projects of nation-building. Both colonial exploitation and settlement, marked by ongoing waves of immigration, worked to marginalize Aboriginal peoples from land and resources and position different groups of immigrants in hierarchical imaginings of race (Abele and Stasiulis 1989; Green 2003). Nation-building was tied to British and French capitalist expansion, embedded first in exploiting resources in the colony and later in attempts to construct a white/British and French Canada in which British economic, political, and social structures, cultural values, and immigrants would predominate (Stasiulis and Jhappan 1995). Assumptions about British (and French) racial superiority, as well as about appropriate heterosexual gender roles, were as central to Canadian nation-building as were the eco-nomic and political institutions transported from Europe (Abu-Laban 1998a; Arat-Koc 1997; Perry 2001). Thus, nation-building processes placed racialization within a web of social relations that were simulta-neously gendered, sexualized, and classed.

The "imagined nation"[2] of Canada was soon embedded in images of whiteness in spite of the continued vitality of First Nations communi-ties and the fact that immigration always included some people from outside Europe, including, by the late nineteenth century, significant populations whose origins were in Africa and Asia (Li 2003). The result, by the mid-twentieth century, was characterized by John Porter (1965) as a "vertical mosaic," an ethnic and racialized hierarchy of class, power, and privilege that crossed all major social institutions. According to Porter, those of British origin were at the top of the social hierarchy, followed by those of northern, central, and southern European origin, with those from Asia, Africa, and Aboriginal populations in the bottom tiers. Of course, as Roberta Hamilton (1996) points out, not only was this mosaic structured by class and race, it was also gendered and sexualized. By the late twentieth century the vertical mosaic was no longer so clear or uncomplicated, but neither had it disappeared (Lautard and Guppy 1990; Li 1998; Lian and Matthews 1998). Lian and Matthews argue that "while our traditional 'vertical mosaic' of ethnic differences [among European groups] may be disappearing, it has been replaced by a strong 'coloured mosaic' of racial differences in terms of income rewards and income benefits" (1998, 476).

   In the last quarter of the twentieth century, nation-building processes became more complex and contradictory, unsettling these historical imaginings of community (Satzewich and Wong 2003). The introduction of the points system in 1967 shifted immigration away from Europe and towards other parts of the world, particularly Asia; multiculturalism replaced Anglo-conformity as official policy in the 1970s; the growth of the women's and civil-rights movements created a climate in which issues of gender and racial equality were placed on the public agenda; and the recruitment of immigrant investors, entrepreneurs, and professionals altered the class dynamics of immigration processes. New discourses of nationhood emerged, with a pluralist multicultural Canada at the centre (Mackey 2002). As Eva Mackey (2002) argues, however, discourses of multiculturalism contain and regulate difference and are based on the resilient foundation of an imagined white community. By the dawn of the twenty-first century, then, it might be argued that although the imagined nation, with associated material structures of privilege, has been destabilized and complicated by recent trends, it retains a white centre that is evident in the labour market and elsewhere.[3]

RACIALIZATION AND THE CANADIAN LABOUR MARKET

Canadians do not have equal access to jobs in the labour market. Some differences in access are linked to where people live, with more opportunities in larger urban centres than in smaller cities or rural areas and more access in some regions (like Alberta and Ontario) than in other parts of the country (like the Territories or Atlantic Canada). Other differences in access to jobs are linked to variations in human capital possessed by different workers – for example, differences in levels of education or specific occupational experience. Human capital theory suggests that once we take regional development differences into account, the labour market evaluates people on the basis of their human capital investments and rewards them accordingly (Li 2003). However, as we shall see, differences in individual human capital do not account for persistent racial differences in the Canadian labour market. Instead, there is evidence to suggest that the evaluation of human capital is coloured by race and gender and that the labour market constitutes an ongoing site of racialization that reproduces white privilege.

One way to begin to map out racialization in the labour market is to compare employment trends and income differences among groups. This section presents some broad statistical trends, comparing employment patterns of Aboriginal and non-Aboriginal, visible minority and non–visible minority, and immigrant and non-immigrant women and men. The categories used in this survey of labour force trends are drawn from the Canadian census, which collects data for Aboriginal (First Nations), visible minority (people of colour), and immigrant (foreign-born) populations.[4] Owing to shifts in immigration patterns, there is considerable overlap among people in the visible minority and immigrant groups. Changing patterns of racialization in the labour market are related to changing immigration flows in the postwar period. Older immigrants are more likely to be white (or European in origin), while more recent immigrants are more likely to be people of colour (or visible minorities). In 1996, for example, 44 per cent of all immigrant women were of visible minority background, and 56 per cent were of European background (Statistics Canada 2000, 191). As of 2001, 18.4 per cent of the total population were of immigrant background, or people who were born outside of Canada, although the vast majority of immigrants – 84 per cent – are also Canadian citizens (Statistics Canada 2003a, 5; Statistics Canada 2000, 192; Tran, Kustec, and Chui 2005, 10).[5] Immigrants make up one-fifth (3.2 million) of Canada's total labour force. During the 1990s, they accounted for 70 per cent of the growth in the labour force, and this trend is expected to continue (Statistics Canada 2003b, 12).

There has been a threefold increase in the visible minority population since 1981, from 1.1 million to 4 million; people of colour now constitute 13.4 per cent of the total population (Statistics Canada 2003a, 10). Among immigrants who arrived between 1990 and 2000, 73 per cent are of visible minority background: 58 per cent came from Asia, 20 per cent from Europe, 11 per cent from the Caribbean and Central and South America, 8 per cent from Africa, and 3 per cent from the United States (6, 10). Most immigrants settle in the major urban centres, especially Toronto, Vancouver, and Montreal, and thus visible minorities are concentrated in these centres. In 2001, for example, immigrants made up 44 per cent of the population of Metropolitan Toronto and 37.5 per cent of Greater Vancouver, and 37 per cent of the population of both cities were identified as people of colour (28–9, 35). At the same time, it should be remembered that three out of every ten people of colour in Canada were born in Canada, and many can trace their Canadian heritage back several generations (10).

Racialized patterns of employment and unemployment suggest that some groups are more disadvantaged in the labour market than others. Aboriginal women have the lowest levels of employment among all groups, with only 41 per cent of women over 15 employed in the labour market compared to 48 per cent of Aboriginal men, 53 per cent of non-Aboriginal women, and nearly 66 per cent of non-Aboriginal men (Table 7.1). Visible minority Canadians also have lower employment rates than non–visible minorities. The women of visible minorities have lower participation rates than the men, and both genders have labour force participation rates 10 per cent lower than their white counterparts (Table 7.1). Employment rates for immigrants and non-immigrants also vary in their peak employment years (25–44 years of age): women who are recent immigrants (arriving within the last five years) have the lowest participation rates (56 per cent), followed by (all) immigrant women (68 per cent), non-immigrant women and recent immigrant men (77 per cent), (all) immigrant men (84 per cent), and non-immigrant men (86 per cent) (Table 7.2).

Groups with lower rates of employment also have higher rates of unemployment. In 1996 Aboriginal men had an unemployment rate two and a half times that of non-Aboriginal men; Aboriginal women did not fare much better, with twice the unemployment rate of non-Aboriginals (Table 7.1). Unemployment rates among visible minorities are not as high as those of Aboriginal workers, but they are consistently higher than those of white workers (Table 7.1). Unemployment rates are also significantly higher for recent immigrants. In 2001 recent immigrant men had an unemployment rate nearly double the rate of non-immigrant men, and recent immigrant women nearly two and a half times the rate of non-immigrant women (Table 7.2).

Racialized patterns of employment are also evident in the way people are distributed across different occupational sectors of the labour market. Across all differences of aboriginality, immigrant status, and race is the prevalence of a gendered labour market where the majority of women in all racialized groups are concentrated in traditional sectors of female employment (Tables 7.3, 7.4, and 7.5). At the same time, white native-born women are privileged compared to other women. Aboriginal women are less likely than other women to be employed in managerial, professional, and clerical jobs, and much

Table 7.1 Employment/Unemployment patterns for Aboriginal, non-Aboriginal, visible minority, and non–visible minority populations, 1996

	Per Cent Employed	Per Cent Unemployed
Aboriginal women	41	21.1
Non-Aboriginal women	53.1	9.7
Aboriginal men	48	26.5
Non-Aboriginal men	65.6	9.9
Visible minority women	53	15.5
Non–visible minority women	63.3	9.4
Visible minority men	64.6	13.2
Non–visible minority men	74.1	9.9

Source: Statistics Canada 2000, 243–6, 265–8.
Note: Statistics Canada uses different age cut-offs for each category of worker. For Aboriginal and non-Aboriginal categories, data includes everyone over the age of 15; for visible minority and non–visible minority categories, data includes everyone between 15 and 64 years of age.

Table 7.2 Employment/Unemployment patterns for immigrant, recent immigrant, and non-immigrant populations, 2001

	Per Cent Employed	Per Cent Unemployed
Recent immigrant women	55.6	14.4
All immigrant women	68.4	8.9
Non-immigrant women	77.4	6.1
Recent immigrant men	77.4	10.1
All immigrant men	83.6	6.9
Non-immigrant men	86.3	6.6

Source: Statistics Canada 2003b, 34.
Note: Recent immigrants refer to those who arrived in Canada during the five years prior to the census (in this case 1996 through 2000). This table includes only those between 25 and 44 years of age.

more likely to be in sales and service positions (Table 7.3). Women of colour and immigrant women are twice as likely as white and non-immigrant women, respectively, to be in manual occupations (Tables 7.4 and 7.5). And recent immigrant women are three times as likely to be in manual occupations, much more likely to be in sales and service, and much less likely to be employed as professionals or in clerical work and administration than other women (Table 7.5).

Similar patterns exist among men, with Aboriginal and recent immigrant men concentrated more in lower-paying and lower-status occu-

Table 7.3 Occupational distribution of Aboriginal and non-Aboriginal women and men, 1996

	Aboriginal Women	Aboriginal Men	Non-Aboriginal Women	Non-Aboriginal Men
Managerial				
Senior	1.0	1.7	0.4	1.5
Other	4.2	4.4	5.9	10.1
Total	5.1	6.2	6.4	11.6
Professional				
Business and finance	0.8	0.5	1.7	1.9
Science/Eng./Math	0.9	3.4	2.0	7.7
Teaching	4.8	1.6	5.5	2.9
Social sc./Ed./ Government	7.5	3.6	3.4	2.2
Doctors/Dentist/Health	0.2	0.1	1.1	1.0
Nursing/Other health	5.4	0.7	7.8	1.0
Art/Culture/Sport	2.8	2.2	3.2	2.3
Total	22.4	12.1	24.7	19.0
Clerical/Administrative	23.4	5.4	28.4	8.0
Sales/Service	40.1	19.8	31.4	20.4
Primary industry	2.4	13.4	2.2	6.7
Trade/Transport	3.2	34.3	1.8	24.2
Processing/Manuf./Utilities	3.4	8.7	4.9	9.9
Total	100%	100%	100%	100%

Source: Statistics Canada 2000, 266.

Table 7.4 Occupational distribution of visible minority and non–visible minority women and men, 1996

	Visible Minority Women	Visible Minority Men	Non–Visible Minority Women	Non–Visible Minority Men
Managerial	5.2	10.0	6.1	11.1
Professional	13.4	14.8	16.1	12.0
Clerical/Administrative	23.8	9.8	27.3	7.2
Sales/Service	36.4	26.6	33.9	20.3
Manual	13.4	21.6	6.5	22.8
Other	7.8	17.2	10.1	26.5
Total	100%	100%	100%	100%

Source: Statistics Canada 2000, 245.

Table 7.5 Occupational distribution of immigrant, recent immigrant, and
non-immigrant women and men, 1996

	Women			Men		
	Immigrant	Recent Immigrant	Non-Immigrant	Immigrant	Recent Immigrant	Non-Immigrant
Managerial						
Senior	0.3	0.2	0.4	1.1	0.8	1.1
Middle/Other	6.0	4.3	6.3	10.0	7.7	10.0
Total	6.4	4.6	6.8	11.1	8.5	11.1
Professional	15.7	12.7	18.6	15.6	16.2	12.8
Semi-prof./ Technician	5.9	5.2	7.3	6.4	5.3	6.6
Supervisor	1.4	0.9	1.6	1.2	1.0	1.2
Supervisor – trades	0.8	0.7	1.1	3.3	2.2	5.3
Clerical/ Administrative						
Admin./Senior clerical	8.5	6.2	11.4	1.3	1.0	1.4
Clerical	17.2	13.5	18.8	6.7	7.0	5.9
Total	25.7	19.7	30.1	8.0	8.0	7.4
Sales/Service						
Skilled	4.3	4.0	4.4	6.4	7.1	4.7
Intermediate	15.6	19.8	15.4	6.6	6.5	7.2
Other sales/ service	10.7	14.9	7.9	7.1	10.5	5.1
Total	30.6	38.7	27.8	20.1	24.1	16.9
Skilled craft/ Trades	1.1	1.1	0.8	12.1	9.8	15.6
Manual						
Semi-skilled	9.2	11.4	4.3	17.4	19.1	17.7
Other manual	3.3	5.2	1.6	4.7	5.8	5.4
Total	12.4	16.6	5.8	22.1	24.9	23.1
Total	100%	100%	100%	100%	100%	100%

Source: Statistics Canada 2000, 215.

pational sectors. Aboriginal men are much less likely than other men to be in managerial or professional occupations and much more likely to be employed in primary industries and in trade and transportation (Table 7.3). Visible minority men are much more likely than other

Table 7.6 Employment income (full-year, full-time) for visible minority, non–visible minority, immigrant, and non-immigrant workers, 1996

	Women	Men
Visible minority	27,508	36,088
Non–visible minority	30,479	43,200
Recent immigrant	21,944	29,201
All immigrant	28,693	38,202
Non-immigrant	30,709	41,295

Source: Statistics Canada 2000, 199–217, 243–6, 265–8.

men to be employed in sales and service and much less likely to be employed in "other" occupations (Table 7.4).[6] The occupational distribution of immigrant and non-immigrant men is fairly similar, but recent immigrant men are concentrated at the lower ends of sales and service, are less likely to be managers, trades supervisors, or in skilled trades, and are more likely to be professionals (Table 7.5).

There are significant gaps in average incomes between women and men in general and for Aboriginal workers, visible minorities, and recent immigrants. When we compare full-time, full-year employment for 1996, we see that women earn significantly less than men across all categories (Table 7.6). Within genders, white women earn nearly 10 per cent more than women of colour, and Canadian-born women earn nearly 7 per cent more than immigrant women and nearly 30 per cent more than recent immigrant women (Table 7.6). Similar patterns appear for men: white men earn 15 per cent more than men of colour, and Canadian-born men earn nearly 10 per cent more than immigrant men and 30 per cent more than men who are recent immigrants (Table 7.6). Income differences are even greater between Aboriginal and non-Aboriginal Canadians. The average total income for Aboriginal women is 69 per cent of that for non-Aboriginal women, while Aboriginal men earn only 58 per cent of what other men earn (Statistics Canada 2000, 265–8).[7] There is also considerable income inequality among Aboriginal groups. Employment income for 1995 ranged from just under $17,000 for status Indians (62 per cent of non-Aboriginal incomes) to nearly $21,000 for non-status Indians (77 per cent of non-Aboriginal incomes) (Maxim et al. 2001).[8]

Not surprisingly, there are also significant differences in labour market distribution and income between different visible minority groups. Nearly a third (30 per cent) of people of colour were born in Canada; about one-third arrived in the 1990s;[9] and the rest, though born abroad, have been established in Canada for many years (Statistics Canada 2003a, 10). Some communities are predominantly Canadian-born (65 per cent of those of Japanese origin and 45 per cent of those who identify themselves as black), while other communities are largely composed of immigrants (83 per cent of those of Latin American and Korean origin) (10). Some groups include significant numbers of business immigrants and entrepreneurs (e.g., Chinese from Hong Kong and Taiwan), others include significant numbers of refugees (e.g., Vietnamese and Latin Americans) or domestic workers who came through the Live-in Caregiver Program (e.g., Filipina). These diversities in country of origin, length of time in Canada, and class of immigration, as well as differences in educational levels and fluency in English and/or French, are reflected in variations in occupational distribution and income levels among people of colour. In a study that explored patterns of ethnic labour market segmentation in Montreal, Toronto, and Vancouver, Daniel Hiebert (1999) shows that some groups experience more occupation segmentation than others. Overall, those of British origin are the least segmented, while visible minorities are the most highly segmented (particularly Filipinos and Vietnamese) (355). He observes that "immigrant and visible minority women receive fewer benefits from education than they should; men and women of colour occupy more than their share of secondary occupations; and immigrant women of color are frequently locked into the least-paid, least secure jobs" (364).

The largest employer for women of colour, regardless of their ethnic community, is the sales and service sector, followed (for most) by clerical and administration, a pattern similar to that for white women (see Tables 7.7 and 7.4). There is also evidence that some women of colour are drawn to specific niches in the labour market. Some are much less likely than others to be managers (e.g., black, Filipina, Latin American, Southeast Asian), professionals (e.g., Filipina, Latin American, Southeast Asian), or employed in clerical work and administration (e.g., Latin American, Southeast Asian, Korean) (Table 7.7). The most distinctive employment patterns are among Southeast Asian women, who are nearly three times as likely to be employed in manual occupations; Korean women, who are three times as likely to be managers and least likely to be in manual occupations; and Filipinas and Latin American women, nearly half of whom are employed in sales and service and who have among the lowest levels of managerial and professional employment (Table 7.7). Average employment incomes for women of colour also vary significantly, from a high of $36,000 for women of Japanese origin to a low of just under $23,000 for women from Latin America, a difference of more than one-third (Table 7.8).[10]

To summarize, broad patterns of racialization in the labour market are reflected in lower rates of employment, higher rates of unemploy-

Table 7.7 Occupational distribution of selected visible minority women, 1996

	Chinese	Black	Filipina	Latin American	Southeast Asian	Korean
Managerial	6.8	3.3	2.6	3.4	3.9	19.2
Professional	15.7	14.3	11.5	8.1	9.3	12.6
Clerical/Admin.	26.2	24.1	20.1	18.0	13.8	14.5
Sales/Service	30.8	38.7	49.7	46.5	32.6	43.2
Manual	13.2	10.9	8.5	16.3	31.8	4.8
Other	7.4	8.8	7.5	7.8	8.8	5.6
Total	100%	100%	100%	100%	100%	100%

Source: Statistics Canada 2000, 245.

Table 7.8 Average employment income for women (full-year, full-time), by visible minority group, 1996

Japanese	36,020
Chinese	29,024
Arab/West Asian	28,084
South Asian	27,833
Black	27,585
Filipina	25,234
Southeast Asian	24,182
Korean	22,942
Latin American	22,773

Source: Statistics Canada 2000, 230.

ment, concentration in less desirable jobs in the gendered labour market, and lower incomes for Aboriginal workers, people of colour, and recent immigrants. Moreover, a growing body of research shows that these inequalities have deepened as a result of uneven processes of restructuring in the 1980s and 1990s. Processes of restructuring appear to coalesce with heightened exclusionary practices with respect to immigrants to create increasing levels of disadvantage for recent immigrants of colour.

RESTRUCTURING AND RACIALIZATION

A number of scholars have tried to assess the impact of economic restructuring on racialized divisions in the labour market, particularly as it affects immigrants of colour. Daniel Hiebert and Ravi Pendakur, for example, address changes in the racialized division of labour that occurred between 1971 and 1996 (Hiebert and Pendakur 2003). They argue that economic restructuring in the 1980s and 1990s has disproportionately affected poorly paid sectors of the labour market associated with "ethnic niche economies,"[11] and thus has disproportionately affected immigrants, particularly those from non-European countries. Not only were more immigrants of colour employed in these niche industries by 1996, but there was evidence of an increasing wage gap between these and other industries, a drop experienced not only by recent immigrant workers, but also by entrepreneurs in the niche sector (19). In the restaurant industry, for example, where one in ten recent immigrants are employed, the gap was considerable: "Among new immigrants of non-European background, for example, workers in restaurants earned 40 per cent of the average labour market income, while the self-employed earned 60 per cent" (21). The income gap experienced by recent immigrant entrepreneurs in the niche sector is important, because it suggests that the growth of self-employment among recent immigrants may not provide the anticipated economic buffer against low wages in the labour market (Reitz 2004).

Valerie Preston and Winona Giles (1997) document the loss of manufacturing jobs between 1981 and 1991 in Toronto, when the city lost about 40 per cent of its manufacturing capacity. Because the jobs lost were concentrated in light industries – like food and beverage processing and garment factories – that employed large numbers of immigrant women (137), immigrant women bore the brunt of restructuring in manufacturing. Researcher Roxana Ng (2000) notes that restructuring in the garment industry led to widespread layoffs of immigrant women of colour, the de-unionization of the sector,[12] and a shift to homeworking as sewing machine operators worked at home on a piece-rate system (230). These trends have lowered wages, worsened working conditions, and "deepened the isolation and exploitation of immigrant women" (231). Ng argues that this process is part of the "recolonization" of women from the global south such that "globalization has created 'Third World' enclaves within the geographic boundaries of the 'First World'" (239).

The increasing emphasis on labour market flexibility, the growth of non-standard work (part-time, contracted-out, temporary, multiple-jobs, and self-employment), and state deregulation all form central parts of neo-liberal restructuring. The resulting polarization of the labour market, with sharper differentiations between good jobs and bad jobs, is inherently gendered and racialized (Cohen 1997; Das Gupta 1996; Fudge and Vosko 2003; Gabriel 1999; Galabuzi 2001; Krahn and Lowe 1998; Zeytinoğlu and Muteshi 2000). Women have long formed the bulk of non-standard workers, but recent immigrants, most of whom are visible minorities, now "comprise a disproportionate number of workers in non-standard work," including self-employment (Fudge and Vosko 2003, 204; Reitz 2004). Jane Badets and Linda Howatson-Leo (1999) liken the situation of recent immigrants to that of youth, with the majority of both (68 per cent of youth and 58 per cent of recent immigrants aged 25–44 years) working part-time or part-year (21). In addition to the loss of manufacturing jobs, the increase in non-standard service sector jobs, and the increase in home-work in some industries, a decade of restructuring in the public sector has eliminated many previously good, relatively secure, and well-pay-ing standard jobs held by women in the public sector. These job losses are concentrated among the most recently hired, a disproportionate number of whom are workers of colour (Gabriel 1999, 137; Creese 1999, 163–201).

A recent study by Grace-Edward Galabuzi (2001) characterizes the increasing polarization of the labour market, and the consequent racialization of poverty, as a form of "economic apartheid":

Income, sectoral occupation, and unemployment data show that a racialized labour market is an endemic feature of the Canadian economy. Characteristic of the racial and gender labour market segmentation is the overrepresenta-tion of racialized[13] (particularly women) members in low paid, low end occu-pations and low income sectors, and also temporary work. They are especially overrepresented in low end service sector jobs and precarious and unregu-lated temporary or contingent work. Conversely they are underrepresented in high paying occupations and high income sectors. The racialized employment gap is observable both among low income earners and high income earners. It persists among those with low and high educational attainment (among those with less than high school education and also among those with university degrees). It only diminishes to single digits when you compare racialized and non-racialized unionized workers. (2)

Other research on the racialization of poverty shows that the highest poverty levels in Canadian cities are concentrated among Aboriginal people and recent immigrants from Asia, Africa, and Latin America (Kazemipur and Halli 2000, 2001).

As this research suggests, the position of workers of colour, espe-cially immigrant women, has worsened in the last two decades. During this same time period, it should be noted, the education gaps between immigrant and Canadian-born workers and between visible minority and white workers have grown to widen the overall *educational advan-tage* of immigrants and people of colour. In 1990, for example, only 16 per cent of Canadian-born men but 25 per cent of recent immigrant men had a university degree; by 2000, these percentages had risen to 19 per cent for Canadian-born men and 44 per cent for recent immi-grant men (Frenette and Morissette 2003, 4). This educational advan-tage should, according to human capital theory, privilege immigrants and workers of colour in the labour market.[14] However, comparing immigrant cohorts who arrived in 1981, 1991, and 1996, Badets and Howatson-Leo (1999) found that the prospects for immigrants were considerably worse in the 1990s than in the 1980s even though "these newcomers had higher educational levels and better language skills than those who had arrived in the 1980s" (18). Economic restructuring in the 1990s produced a more precarious labour market generally, but "opportunities for immigrants have deteriorated more significantly" than for others (17).

Chui and Zietsma (2003) explore differences between the 1981, 1991, and 1996 cohorts of immigrants in terms of their economic performance over their first five years in Canada. A majority of immigrants in 1981 were of European or North American origin, while most arriving in 1996 were of Asian origin; the latter also had higher levels of education and official language skills than the former (25). In spite of higher levels of education and language skills, and after controlling for these landing characteristics, the 1996 cohort of men, after five years in Canada, had earnings 16 per cent below those of their 1981 counterparts (27–8). Earnings for immigrant women after five years were the same for the 1981 and 1996 cohorts (27–8). These outcomes were better for the 1996 than the 1991 cohort, who bore the brunt of economic restructuring (and experienced a 30 per cent income gap for men and a 6 per cent gap for women), but the earnings of men who arrived in 1996 remained substantially below those of earlier immigrant groups.

Another recent study (Tran 2004) explores the differences between the long-term economic changes for visible minority Canadians and Canadian-born white men and women. In 1981 visible minority immigrant men had better employment and unemployment rates than Canadian-born white men; by 1996 a wide gap developed to the disadvantage of immigrant men of colour, a gap that narrowed slightly but still existed in 2001. This gap persisted even though visible minority immigrant men were more likely to be university educated than native-born white men and the educational advantage of men of colour grew through the 1990s (Tran 2004, 8–9). Similarly, although Canadian-born men of colour are twice as likely as white Canadian-born men to be university educated and this educational advantage grew between 1981 and 2001, Canadian-born visible minority men witnessed "a small but growing disadvantage in employment rates during the 1990s" (10). Women of colour faced similar increasing disadvantages in spite of higher levels of education. In 1981 immigrant women of colour had the highest employment rate among women aged 25–54; by 2001 they had the lowest rate and were the only group of women to see their labour force participation rates decrease, even through they were more highly educated than white native-born women (11).[15] Canadian-born women of colour are the most highly educated group of women, nearly twice as likely to be university educated as white Canadian-born women; yet, contrary to expectations, they did not enjoy an advantage and had similar rates of unemployment as white Canadian-born women (11).

RACIALIZATION AND HUMAN CAPITAL

To learn more about the processes involved in producing racialized differences in the workplace, we must distinguish between processes of racialization and the effects of education, experience, and other factors on job prospects for everyone. Several studies have set out to do this by comparing the employment outcomes of men and women, by immigrant, visible minority, and Aboriginal status, while holding constant differences in educational levels, occupation, years of experience, age, English/French language ability, and the size of the urban environment in which people live. Pendakur and Pendakur (1998), for example, found that in 1991 there were "substantial earnings differentials between visible minority and white workers" in Toronto, Montreal, and Vancouver even after controlling for education and other human capital (542). These monetary differences existed between immigrant and Canadian-born workers and also between whites and visible minorities born in Canada.[16] In a more recent study, Pendakur and Pendakur (2004) evaluate labour market outcomes for Canadian-born visible minorities, Aboriginal people, and whites between 1971 and 1996. Their study found a pattern of improving relative earnings through the 1970s and 1980s and declining relative earnings in the 1990s. After controlling for personal characteristics, they found that "Canadian-born visible minority and Aboriginal people face a significant earnings penalty compared to whites," with larger differences among men than among women (24).[17] Overall, Pendakur and Pendakur conclude, Aboriginal men and women fare the worst in the labour market relative to their human capital (32).

Peter Li (2000, 2003) also examines racialized earning gaps in 1996, focusing on differences between immigrant and native-born workers within the same racialized groups and genders: "[W]hen variations in human capital, experience, and other individual differences in work-related characteristics and immigrant experience are taken into account, along with differences in urban scale, immigrant population size and unemployment rate, all immigrant groups earned less than their native-born counterparts" (2000, 289–90).

Visible minority immigrant women and men had the greatest disadvantages in the labour market, with women the most disadvantaged of all (2000, 299–302). The extent of these earnings differentials ranged from just over $3,000 a year less for immigrant men of colour in rural areas to more than $8,000 a year less for immigrant women of colour in medium-sized cities (2003, 109–10). This research suggests, Li concludes, that immigrants face unequal opportunities in the labour market and the evaluation of one's human capital is neither gender- nor race-blind (2000, 290, 294).

The persistent and growing gap in immigrant incomes over the last two decades has become even more evident now that researchers can compare census data from 1981 through 2001 (Aydemir and Skuterud 2004; Frenette and Morissette 2003; Picot and Hou 2003). Garnett Picot and Feng Hou (2003) found that low-income rates among immigrants (relative to the Canadian-born) rose consistently between 1980 and 2000, a phenomenon that crosses all age groups, family types, language groups, and education levels, and is concentrated among groups with the largest share of recent immigrants, notably those from "Africa, South Asia, East Asia and West Asia" (19). Moreover, contrary to the assumptions of human capital theory, "the gap in low-income rates between the Canadian-born and recent immigrants was highest among [university] degree holders, particularly those with engineering and applied science degrees" (Picot and Hou 2003, 19). Frenette and Morissette (2003) examined the decreasing earnings of immigrants compared to those of Canadian-born when they enter the labour market and assessed whether the incomes of recent immigrants will eventually converge with those of Canadian-born workers over time, as they did for immigrants who arrived in the 1970s. In the last two decades, the entry wage gap between recent immigrants and the Canadian-born has doubled for both men and women, and fifteen years after arrival immigrants still have "substantially lower earnings than Canadian-born workers" (7–8). Frenette and Morissette argue that this suggests that a much longer time period and "abnormally high" (and therefore highly unlikely) income increases are needed for the immigrants to catch up to their native-born counterparts (13–15). Aydemir and Skuterud (2004) try to explain why the deterioration of earnings among new immigrants has occurred. They argue that three factors, in more or less equal measure, account for the decreased entry earnings of new immigrants over the last two decades: (1) the declining value employers award to foreign labour market experience that occurs "almost exclusively among immigrants from Eastern regions, including Eastern Europe, Africa and Asia"; (2) the weakening of English and French language abilities associated with shifts away from traditional European countries for sources of immigration;[18] and (3) a broader trend of deteriorating entry-level wages also experienced by young Canadian-born workers (17).

In summary, then, recent research clearly indicates that racialized patterns of work and wages in the labour market have intensified in the last two decades as economic restructuring has created a more polarized economy. Although much of this research has focused on trends among immigrants, partly because the deteriorating economic situation of recent immigrants of colour is so marked, we have seen that racialized inequalities in the labour market also persist among Canadian-born people of colour and First Nations peoples. For all groups, labour market inequalities cross gender, educational, and class lines, and cannot be explained by recourse to human capital theories that remain abstracted from processes of gendering and racialization in the broader society. In the next section, I will explore some of the ways that racialization shapes everyday experiences in the workplace, including how it colours assumptions made about human capital and how the workplace serves as a central site of the reproduction of difference and white privilege.

REPRODUCING DIFFERENCE AT WORK

The economy is embedded within broader social structures and power relations. It would be surprising if general patterns of racialized and gendered inequalities did not affect the operation of the labour market and relations within individual workplaces. As Carol Agocs and Harish Jain (2001) conclude in their assessment of legal cases of employment discrimination in Canada, "[R]acial discrimination in employment is a serious problem that prevents the efficient operation of the labour market and causes significant losses for the national economy in terms of underutilized human resources as well as the personal suffering and loss of fair opportunities to a large segment of the society" (16). Processes that reproduce racialized divisions and tensions in workplaces are not dependent on the prejudiced attitudes of individual employers, managers, or workers. Instead, inequalities in the workplace are "collectively or organizationally induced, reflecting inherently relational processes and patterns of affiliation rather than individually rooted attitudes and traits" (Vallas 2003, 390). Moreover, as Tania Das Gupta (1996) points out, individual attitudes and intentions matter less than outcomes: "Racism is the effect of rather than the intention to cause deprivation to people of colour" (14).

Getting a job is the first hurdle for all workers. As Vallas (2003) has argued in the American context, the "colour line" is reproduced through informal social networks and cultural exclusivism. Social networks and social dynamics among affinity groups affect both initial hiring decisions and workers' ability to find mentors and other social support; not only are managers more likely to hire people like themselves, but a worker's ability to acquire skills on the job is also facilitated or hindered by racialized social networks (Vallas 2003). According to studies in Toronto (Henry and Ginzberg 1985; Henry 1999), prejudices in individual hiring decisions result in systemic forms of discrimination in Canada. Henry and Ginzberg (1985) examined hiring decisions by pairing single-sex teams of black and white job applicants with similar resumés and sending them for job interviews advertised in a Toronto newspaper. They documented a pattern of differential treatment that systematically disadvantaged the black applicants; examples include black applicants being told that a job was filled when it was not, being offered a lower-level job than that applied for, and being treated with a rudeness and hostility not experienced by the white applicants. Henry and Ginzberg concluded that, overall, white job applicants had three job offers for every one offered to a black applicant even though they had equivalent job qualifications. In addition, they tested four accents – Pakistani, Jamaican, Slavic or Italian, and local – through telephone contact with potential employers and found differential screening that significantly favoured those with local accents (most likely presumed to be white Canadian) over all others and the white immigrant over immigrants of colour.

Henry and Ginzberg's original study was conducted in the mid-1980s. Henry did a second study with the same format in the early 1990s (1999). She found similar discriminatory screening on the telephone, but this time black applicants were as likely as white applicants to be offered jobs in person. She argues that this was because of the tight labour market at the time of the second study, when employers were having difficulty filling positions, and the research protocol that specified that the black applicant be the first to apply. The result was that half of the black applicants were offered jobs on the spot, before the employer knew a white applicant was available. When these on-the-spot job offers were removed from the sample, the results again showed that white applicants received significantly more job offers than blacks. Henry thus argues that the later study does not indicate any decrease in racial prejudice in hiring decisions.

The practice of hiring by word of mouth, prevalent in some industries, further reproduces racialized access to different kinds of jobs (Das Gupta 1996). And once a job is attained, management practices are critically important to the reproduction of racialization in the workplace. Das Gupta identifies a range of management practices experienced more often by workers of colour, including targeting, scapegoating, excessive monitoring, marginalization, infantilization, blaming the victim, biased work allocation, underemployment, denial of promotions, segregation, co-optation, and tokenism (35–40). Stephen Vallas's (2003) observations in the United States point to additional processes that are important to an understanding of racialization in Canadian workplaces. Like Das Gupta, Vallas observes how racialized status hierarchies at work are linked to closer supervision of minority workers. He suggests that closer supervision in turn leads to forms of defiance or insubordination, resulting in harsher job evaluations and unfair terminations. In addition, hiring practices that produce spatial segregation in many workplaces – with workers of colour often located in the back offices of factories, hospitals, restaurants, hotels, and the like – reproduce differences in status and power among workers, and these differences in turn reinforce the workers' practice of defending their territorial boundaries.

Racialized workplaces are reproduced through a range of formal and informal means of exclusion, from the way work is organized, to social networks and friendships that develop, to cultural assumptions that predominate, including particular forms of humour. Everyday racism and other "micro-inequities" (like sexism and homophobia) are part of the normal daily forms of exclusion and inclusion practised by dominant groups (Beagan 2001; Das Gupta 1996; Essed 1991). Although these may be part of the normal practices of privilege (in this case white privilege), the result may be a toxic or poisoned environment for workers of colour (Das Gupta 1996). As Beagan (2001) argues, these micro-inequities might seem trivial, but they are experienced within a context of broader power relations: "Individual episodes or instances are experienced in the context of the whole of one's life, in the context of one's own past experiences of racism, in the context of stories of racism experienced by others, and in the context of potential racist violence. The power of the 'trivial' racist joke or assumption is that it may come on top of an unending series of incidents that form an overwhelming pattern" (590).

It has been argued that the ability to hold to democratic ideals of equality while engaging in forms of racial exclusion is a quintessential characteristic of racism in Canada, a form of racism that has been termed "democratic racism" (Henry et al. 1995): "Democratic racism is an ideology in which two conflicting sets of values are made congruent to each other. Commitments to democratic principles such as justice, equality, and fairness conflict but coexist with attitudes and behaviours that include negative feelings about minority groups and differential treatment of and discrimination against them" (21). The concept of democratic racism can help us make sense of the contradictions in the shifting support of/opposition to multiculturalism and immigration in recent years, contradictions that have sent mixed messages to people of colour, suggesting that they are both included in and excluded from the imagined community of Canadians (Abu-Laban 1998b; Creese 2005a, 2005b). In the context of the workplace, this concept also helps to illuminate the politics around employment equity.

Employment equity legislation was implemented at the federal level in 1986 as a direct result of the recommendations of the Royal Commission on Equality and Employment chaired by Rosalie Abella.[19] Employment equity was intended to improve the employment situation of people of colour, Aboriginal Canadians, women, and people with disabilities. Employment equity measures require public sector employers and federal contractors to develop employment equity plans, but there are no mechanisms to ensure the effective adoption of such plans (Abu-Laban and Gabriel 2002; Bakan and Kobayashi 2000). Consequently, employment equity policies have done little to improve the situation of those they were meant to help (Bakan and Kobayashi 2000). Moreover, as Vallas (2003) points out in the American context of even more hotly contested affirmative action measures, employers are unlikely to institute substantive changes of their own accord. The narrow, short-term performance orientation of corporations reinforces their minimal attention to issues of racial (or other) inequality in the workplace beyond those associated with exposure to risk of lawsuits. And so long as legal interventions are based on the fiction of the "legal individual," they will provide only limited individual remedies while ignoring the "collectively generated character of racial inequalities" (Vallas 2003, 390).

In spite of the limited effectiveness of employment equity legislation, a backlash against employment equity in Canada developed in the 1990s, dismissing evidence of racialized (or other) inequality in the workplace and fostering the myth that equity groups are special interest groups who are unfairly advantaged in the workplace (Abu-Laban and Gabriel 2002; Creese 1999). As my study (Creese 1999) of equity struggles in one white-collar union demonstrates, for example, these myths are embedded in the erroneous belief that hiring, training, and promotion practices are already based on the skills and merit of individual workers without regard to gender or race. If we believe that neutral principles of merit are actually working, then taking race, gender, or disability status into account is perceived as a violation of the principle of fairness and merit in the workplace. Ironically, then, campaigns against employment equity in the workplace – often mounted by unions attempting to advance equality on other fronts at the same time – reinforce existing unequal power relations while claiming to foster fairness and equality for workers. Moreover, even when unions do not take an explicit stand against employment equity policies, union traditions that privilege seniority as the key to ensuring fairness and sameness as the only measure of equality of treatment in the workplace often disadvantage those equity groups that are more likely to be recently hired (thus lacking seniority) and may require some form of differential accommodation (rather than the same treatment as everyone else) in order to be assured equality at work (Creese 1999). Finally, the backlash against employment equity undermines the actual accomplishments of workers of colour and other equity groups through the common-place assumption that promotions are based on workers' equity group status rather than on their own merit. In this way, the marked disadvantages in the workplace experienced by people of colour, Aboriginal workers, women, and those with disabilities are quite literally turned upside down to recast such workers as unfairly advantaged at work.

Racialized work is also reproduced through the social construction of skill, experience, and education. Educational credentials, work experience, and job skills receive different values depending on the person to whom they are attached. The notion of skill, for example, has long been recognized as a highly gendered concept (Cockburn 1985). In clerical work, for example, men's jobs tend to be defined as technical and skilled, while women's jobs tend to be defined as non-technical and unskilled (Creese 1999). Similar observations have been made in other sectors, such as the garment industry, where white male pattern cutters are considered skilled workers and women of colour sewing machine operators are considered unskilled (Das Gupta 1996).

The undervaluing of skills, education, and experience on the basis of gender and race is evident in relation to immigrants of colour in Canada (Aydemir and Skuterud 2004; Basran and Zong 1998; Bauder and Cameron 2002; Geddie 2002; Henin and Bennett 2002; Li 2003; Reitz, 2003). Li's research (2003) shows that the undervaluation of university degrees, relative to the value placed on those earned by white native-born Canadians, is greatest for immigrants of colour with foreign degrees (especially for women), but a significant wage gap also exists for immigrants who earned their degrees within Canada (120–1).[20] Similarly, Jeffrey Reitz (2003) demonstrates that immigrants' post-secondary credentials and professional skills are significantly discounted by employers and that this skill discounting has increased over time. Abdurrahman Aydemir and Mikal Skuterud

(2004) show that one-third of the deterioration in the earnings of recent immigrants is due to a failure to recognize foreign labour market experience, a situation that appears "almost exclusively in non-traditional [i.e., non-European] source countries" (3). The consequence of these processes of de-skilling is downward social mobility for highly skilled immigrants, even though the points system used in immigrant selection is specifically designed to recruit skilled and professional labour (Basran and Zong 1998; Bauder and Cameron 2002; Elabor-Idemudia 2000; Geddie 2002; Henin and Bennett 2002). As a recent report by the Standing Committee on Citizenship and Immigration concluded, "The current underutilization of human resources is at odds with the country's immigration goals and, in particular, the goals of our skilled worker and provincial nominee programs. Equally important, the impact on the individuals affected – the PhD who ends up driving a taxi, for example – is profound" (Canada 2003, 13).

Contrary to human capital theory, then, skills, experience, and education are not assessed outside of the broader context of processes of racialization (or gender) that "imagine" belonging in Canada along racialized lines. This fact helps to explain why a degree from a British university will be accepted at face value, while a comparable degree from an English-language university in a Commonwealth country, such as India or Uganda (both of whose systems are modelled on the British educational system), will not be accepted by Canadian employers or professional associations. Issues of credential and skill recognition thus imply much more than the limited transnational knowledge of educational systems possessed by Canadian employers or professional associations; they underline fundamental inequities of belonging and inclusion in Canada (Creese 2005b).

The labour market is a central site through which broader notions of belonging are negotiated as people seek to be recognized as productive citizens. This is true for all Canadians, but it may be more so for immigrants, for whom discourses of the good immigrant/citizen are increasingly cast solely in terms of one's economic contribution (Abu-Laban 1998b; Li 2004; McLaren and Dyck 2004). Negotiating the Canadian labour market involves a disjuncture between multicultural discourses of inclusion and realities of exclusionary practices that suggest shifting boundaries of "Canadianness." Notwithstanding multicultural discourses of diversity, immigrants routinely encounter barriers linked to demands for Canadian work experience and Canadian educational qualifications (Basran and Zong 1998; Bauder and Cameron 2002; Creese 2005a, 2005b; Elabor-Idemudia 2000; Geddie 2002; Henin and Bennett 2002). The strategies immigrants adopt to negotiate these barriers often rely on performing unpaid volunteer work as a prelude to acquiring a paid job in Canada, or undertaking long years of retraining within Canadian educational institutions, though seldom to the level attained prior to immigration (Creese 2005b). Thus, systemic demands for Canadian experience and Canadian credentials help transform skilled immigrants into cheap (indeed, often initially free) and subordinate labour.

The conflation of people of colour with immigrants, even though only one-third of visible minorities arrived in Canada during the last decade,[21] is another commonly observed manifestation of the exclusion of people of colour from Canada's imagined community (Abu-Laban 1998a; Bannerji 2000; Pratt 2004; Razack 1998, 2002). This erasure of birthright (Pratt 2004) means that even people of colour who have the requisite lifelong immersion in "the local" – and therefore have Canadian work experience and education – are nevertheless unable to acquire the same value from their human capital as white native-born Canadians do (Li 2000).

Perhaps not surprisingly immigrants with low levels of language proficiency in English or French fare worse in the labour market than those with high levels of official language proficiency, a phenomenon that is compounded for women and those of colour (Boyd 1999).[22] Moreover, many immigrants who have a high level of official language proficiency, including people who were fluent in English or French before arriving in Canada, experience the effective erasure of their language proficiency through accent discrimination. Having their accent denigrated and construed as foreign appears to be an endemic feature of immigrant experiences in the labour market and elsewhere (Creese and Kambere 2003; Creese 2005a; Henry 1999; Henry and Ginzberg 1985; Miedema and Nason-Clark 1989; Scassa 1994). In Henry and Ginzberg's (1985) research, for example, telephone testers with different accents were instructed to call various employers and use standard English and correct grammar so that fluency in English would not be a factor in their ability to acquire job interviews. Even so, Henry and Ginzberg found that the Jamaican- and Pakistani-accented callers had to make eighteen calls to attain ten potential job interviews, while the Slavic- or Italian-accented callers needed thirteen calls and the locally accented (presumed white) callers needed only eleven or twelve calls to attain the same number of job interviews (Henry and Ginzberg 1985; Henry 1999).

My research (Creese and Kambere 2003; Creese 2005a) with immigrants who migrated from Commonwealth countries in Africa and therefore speak fluent English makes it clear that some extra-local accents (for example, those from African countries) are much more likely than others (for example, those from Britain or Australia) to be considered foreign in ways that affect the ability to get jobs, rent houses, negotiate social institutions, and experience belonging in a wide range of social situations. A foreign accent, itself a socially constructed notion in major cosmopolitan cities, appears to serve as a marker to discount the general competencies of potential employees (Creese and Kambere 2003; Creese 2005a; Miedema and Nason-Clark 1989; Scassa 1994). In the case of women who migrated from English-speaking African countries, for example, the presence of an African accent serves to discount English language proficiency in ways that cannot be separated from the racialized bodies of speakers: "Accents signify more than local/'Canadian' and extra-local/'immigrant'; accents, embodied by racialized subjects, also shape perceptions of language competency. Thus, accents may provide a rationale for (dis)entitlement in employment or full participation in civil society without troubling liberal discourses of equality" (Creese and Kambere 2003, 566). In a multicultural immigrant society such as Canada's, particularly in the large cosmopolitan cities where most recent immigrants live, practices that penalize workers who do not speak with local Canadian accents – like the wholesale dismissal of work experience and post-secondary degrees attained in Africa, Asia, Latin America, and the Caribbean – provide yet more examples of a democratic racism that enhances white privilege in the context of a rapidly changing society.

CONCLUSIONS

Work is a central site that reproduces racial inequality and white privilege in Canada. The gendered-racialization of hiring, differential management practices, the social organization of work, exclusionary workplace cultures, and the social construction of skill, experience, credentials, accents, and language proficiency create systematic advantages for white workers, especially native-born men. A long history of nation-building premised on an imagined white/European nation continues to marginalize Aboriginal people and those of colour. At every occupational level, Aboriginal men and women and people of colour, especially recent immigrants, fail to attain the same economic rewards for their skills and efforts as white workers and are not given the same opportunities to utilize their skills. The result is systemic racial discrimination in the labour market. As economic restructuring creates a more polarized economy, these inequities are exacerbated and the racialization of poverty increases.

Racialization in the labour market is not as straightforward as it was in the first half of the twentieth century, when jobs were clearly segregated by race and gender in ways that preserved almost all jobs considered skilled, professional, and more economically rewarding for white men. Today, women and people of colour are found in every kind of job, although, as we have seen, employment patterns still show most women in traditional women's jobs and Aboriginal people and many groups of colour, especially recent immigrants, under-represented in most higher-paying positions and over-represented in non-standard work and jobs considered less skilled. Patterns of racialization today are most strongly linked to the lack of correspondence between the educational credentials, employment, and income levels of white workers and those of Aboriginal workers, immigrants, and people of colour. The evaluation of human capital is, quite simply, coloured by the race and gender of the worker and the person evaluating them.

Without strong policy initiatives, it seems unlikely that patterns of racialized labour in Canada will change any time soon. Employers' short-term concentration on the corporate bottom line, not to mention the advantages of a cheaper yet highly skilled workforce, suggests little incentive for serious changes in management practices. At the same time, stronger employment equity legislation, with real enforcement sanctions and greater breadth of coverage at federal and provincial levels, could challenge racialized patterns in the workplace. Gaining public support for such measures requires understanding the nature of the systemic inequalities that operate outside of individual motives and prejudices. This broader understanding of processes of gendering and racialization is needed to dispel the prevailing myth that employment equity means granting unfair advantages at work to women, Aboriginal workers, people of colour, and those with disabilities.

Racialization in the Canadian labour market is embedded in a broader social context in which white (male) privilege shapes the terms in which others are incorporated into the social fabric. In the long run, then, a redefinition of the imagined community is essential if racialized patterns of workplace organization are to change. Only then will Aboriginal people, immigrants, and those of colour cease to be subject to various forms of exclusion based on perceptions of somehow inadequate – or inadequately "Canadian" – experience, skills, educational credentials, cultural capital, accents, or bodies. Challenging the racialized nature of the Canadian labour market, therefore, is part of a broader anti-racist strategy to challenge racialized inequalities in all aspects of Canadian life.

NOTES

Author's Note: I would like to thank Wallace Clement, Vivian Shalla, and the external reviewers for comments on a earlier version of this chapter.

1 Post-colonial scholarship is concerned with exploring the complex ways that colonial relations of oppression between North and South, and within former colonial and colonizing territories, continue to structure social relations long after formal decolonization occurred. In addition, feminist scholars have pointed to the gendered and sexualized nature of colonial and post-colonial relations, and many have developed intersectional forms of analysis to explicate the connections between relations of gender, sexuality, race, and class inequalities in Canada and elsewhere.

2 I follow Benedict Anderson (1991) in conceptualizing "imagined communities" or "imagined nations" as common-sense constructions of who belongs (and who does not) within a nation-state.

3 For example, see Henry et al. 1995 and Henry and Tator 2002 for overviews of institutional racism in Canada.

4 The terms Aboriginal and visible minority used in the Canadian Census are based on self-reporting categories. *Aboriginal* includes people who identify as Indian, Inuit, Metis, or other Aboriginal. *Visible minority* is defined as anyone who is not of Aboriginal origin and is "non-Caucasian in race or non-white in colour" (Statistics Canada 2003a, 10). In this chapter, I use census terms interchangeably with the colloquial terms common in public discourse: Aboriginal or First Nations (Aboriginal peoples), people of colour (visible minorities), and white (European origin).

5 For example, in 1996 82 per cent of immigrant women were citizens (Statistics Canada 2000:192–3). In 2001, 84 per cent of those eligible to apply for Canadian citizenship – that is, those who had been landed immigrants for at least 3 years – were Canadian citizens (Tran, Krustec and Chui, 2005).

6 There is no note on what "other" means in this table. Given other tables on occupation in the same text (Statistics Canada 2000), however, it is most likely that "other" includes occupations in the primary industries, trade and transportation.

7 It should be noted that the figures for Aboriginal incomes represent income from all sources, not only employment income. Statistics Canada noted that a smaller share of Aboriginal income comes from employment: 64 per cent for Aboriginal women (compared to 70 per cent for other women), and 75 per cent for Aboriginal men (compared to 79 per cent for other men) (Statistics Canada 2000, 267).

8 Average employment income for Inuit was nearly $18,000, and for Metis it was nearly $20,000. This data is not broken down by gender (Maxim et al. 2001).

9 Of the 1.8 million immigrants who arrived between 1991 and 2001, 73 per cent are people of colour (1.3 million), constituting 33 per cent of the total

number of visible minorities in Canada (4 million) (Statistics Canada 2003a, 10, 39).

10 Not surprisingly, given their occupational distributions, Filipina, Southeast Asian, and Latin American women have lower incomes than Chinese or black women. However, Korean women have lower employment incomes than Filipinas and Southeast Asian women in spite of high numbers employed as managers and professionals. This puzzling finding may reflect the more bifurcated occupational distribution of Korean-origin women, with close to half (43 per cent) employed in sales and service, typically a lower-wage sector of employment than clerical work and administration (where few Korean women are employed). Latin American women, the only group to have a lower income than women of Korean origin, are also heavily employed in the service sector (46 per cent), but they are more likely than Korean women to be in manual and clerical jobs and much less likely to be in managerial or professional jobs. See Table 7.8.

11 In this study, *niche sectors* are defined as manufacturing, construction, truck and taxi transportation, wholesale and retail, restaurants, lodging, and personal service. This sector has high rates of self-employment, employs large numbers of immigrants, and is poorly paid. It is most associated with immigrant workers and entrepreneurs (Hiebert and Pendakur 2003, 11).

12 Unionization dropped from 80 to 20 per cent between 1985 and 1992 (Ng 2000, 228).

13 Galabuzi (2001) employed the term *racialized* only for people of colour, thus failing to recognize that white folks are also racialized even if in a privileged form.

14 As Reitz (2004) pointed out, the overall educational advantage of immigrants disappears when compared only with native-born Canadians in larger urban centres such as Toronto and Vancouver, which are the context in which most immigrants are competing for jobs. Even when education is held constant, however, immigrants are at a disadvantage in large urban labour markets.

15 Tran noted that shifting sources of immigration may be linked to lower labour force participation rates for women. Women born in countries in western Asia and the Middle East tend to have lower participation rates than those born in Europe, the United States, or Southeast Asia (2004, 11).

16 The wage gap varied in different cities, with larger wage gaps in Montreal than elsewhere, and men experience greater disadvantages than women (Pendakur and Pendakur 1998).

17 There was also diversity among ethnic communities within these broad categories; for example, in 1996 women with the largest negative earnings differentials included Jewish and Greek along with South Asian, black, and Aboriginal women; men with negative earnings differentials included Greek and Spanish along with Arab, South Asian, black, and Aboriginal men (Pendakur and Pendakur 2004, 29–30).

220 Gillian Creese

18 It should be noted that the finding of weaker official language abilities among recent immigrants is not corroborated in other research. For example, Badets and Howatson-Leo (1999) and Chui and Zietsma (2003) document stronger English/French language abilities for immigrants who arrived in 1996 than for those who arrived in 1981.

19 Seven provinces subsequently developed employment equity policies. In 1993 the Ontario New Democratic government passed the most far-reaching employment equity legislation, which was repealed in 1995 by the newly elected Conservative government (Bakan and Koybayashi 2000; Abu-Laban and Gabriel 2002).

20 Using 1991 census data, K.G. Basavarajappa and Frank Jones (1999) make the similar point that even visible minorities who graduated from Canadian post-secondary institutions experience income inequality vis-à-vis their white counterparts (256).

21 See note 9.

22 Immigrant women of colour with low levels of official language proficiency fare the worst in the labour market (Boyd 1999).

REFERENCES

Abele, Francis, and Daiva Stasiulis. 1989. Canada as a "white settler colony": What about Natives and immigrants? In *The new Canadian political economy*, edited by Wallace Clement and Glen Williams, 240–77. Montreal and Kingston: McGill-Queen's University Press

Abu-Laban, Yasmeen. 1998a. Keeping 'em out: Gender, race and class biases in Canadian immigration policy. In *Painting the maple: Essays on race, gender and the construction of Canada*, edited by Veronica Strong Boag, Sherrill Grace, Avigail Eisenberg, and Joan Anderson, 69–82. Vancouver: University of British Columbia Press

– 1998b. Welcome/STAY OUT: The contradiction of Canadian integration and immigration policies in the millennium *Canadian Ethnic Studies* 30 (3): 190–211

Abu-Laban, Yasmeen, and Christina Gabriel. 2002. *Selling diversity: Immigration, multiculturalism, employment equity, and globalization.* Peterborough: Broadview Press

Agocs, Carol, and Harish Jain. 2001. *Systemic racism in employment in Canada: Diagnosing systemic racism in organizational culture.* Toronto: Canadian Race Relations Foundation

Anderson, Benedict. 1991. *Imagined communities.* London: Verso

Anthias, Floya, and Nira Yuval-Davis. 1992. *Racialized boundaries: Race, nation, gender, colour and class and the anti-racist struggle.* London: Routledge

Arat-Koc, Sedef. 1997. From "mothers of the nation" to migrant workers. In Bakan and Stasiulis 1997, 53–79

Armstrong, Pat, and Hugh Armstrong. 2001. *The double ghetto: Canadian women and their segregated work.* Toronto: Oxford University Press

Aydemir, Abdurrahman, and Mikal Skuterud. 2004. Explaining the deteriorating entry earnings of Canada's immigrant cohorts: 1966–2000. Statistics Canada, Analytical Studies Branch Research Paper Series. Catalogue no. 11F0019MIE, no. 225 (May)

Badets, Jane, and Linda Howatson-Leo. 1999. Recent immigrants in the workforce. *Canadian Social Trends,* no. 52 (Spring): 16–22

Bakan, Abigail, and Audrey Kobayashi. 2000. *Employment equity policy in Canada: An interprovincial comparison.* Ottawa: Status of Women Canada

Bakan, Abigail, and Daiva Stasiulis, eds. 1997. *Not one of the family: Foreign domestic workers in Canada.* Toronto: University of Toronto Press

Bannerji, Himani. 2000. *The dark side of the nation: Essays on multiculturalism, nationalism and gender.* Toronto: Canadian Scholars' Press

Basavarajappa, K.G., and Frank Jones. 1999. Visible minority income differences. In *Immigration Canada: Demographic, economic, and social challenges,* edited by Shiva Halli and Leo Driedger, 230–57. Toronto: University of Toronto Press

Basran, Gurcharn, and Li Zong. 1998. Devaluation of foreign credentials as perceived by visible minority professional immigrants. *Canadian Ethnic Studies* 30 (3): 6–23

Bauder, Harold, and Emille Cameron. 2002. Cultural barriers to labour market integration: Immigrants from South Asia and the former Yugoslavia. Vancouver Centre of Excellence Research on Immigration and Integration in the Metropolis, Working Paper Series, no. 02–03

Beagan, Brenda. 2001. Micro inequities and everyday inequalities: "Race," gender, sexuality and class in medical school. *Canadian Journal of Sociology* 26 (4): 583–610

Boyd, Monica. 1999. Integrating gender, language, and race. In *Immigration Canada: Demographic, economic, and social challenges,* edited by Shiva Halli and Leo Driedger, 282–306. Toronto: University of Toronto Press

Calliste, Agnes. 2000. Nurses and porters: Racism, sexism and resistance in segmented labour markets. In *Anti-racist feminism: Critical race and gender studies,* edited by Agnes and George Sefa Dei, 143–64. Halifax: Fernwood Publishing

Calliste, Agnes, and George Sefa Dei, eds. 2000. *Anti-racist feminism: Critical race and gender studies.* Halifax: Fernwood Publishing

Canada, Standing Committee on Citizenship and Immigration. 2003. Settlement and integration: A sense of belonging, "feeling at home." Report (June). Available at www.parl.gc.ca/InfoComDoc/37/2/ CIMM/Studies/Reports/cimmrp05/03-cov2-e.htm

Chui, Tina, and Danielle Zietsma. 2003. Earnings of immigrants in the
    1990s. *Canadian Social Trends*, no. 70 (Autumn): 24–8
Clement, Wallace, and John Myles. 1994. *Relations of ruling: Class and gender in post-
    industrial societies*. Montreal and Kingston: McGill-Queen's University Press
Cockburn, Cynthia. 1985. *Machinery of dominance: Women, men and technical
    know-how*. London: Pluto Press
Cohen, Marjorie Griffin. 1997. From the welfare state to vampire capitalism.
    In *Women and the Canadian welfare state*, edited by Patricia Evans and Gerda
    Wekerle, 28–67. Toronto: University of Toronto Press
Collins, Patricia Hill. 1990. *Black feminist thought*. New York: Routledge
Connell, R.W. 1995. *Masculinities*. Berkeley: University of California Press
Creese, Gillian. 1987. Organizing against racism in the workplace: Chinese
    workers in Vancouver before the Second World War. *Canadian Ethnic
    Studies* 19 (3): 35–46
– 1988. The politics of dependence: Women, work and unemployment in
    the Vancouver labour market before World War II. *Canadian Journal of
    Sociology* 13 (1–2): 121–42
– 1988–89. Exclusion or solidarity? Vancouver workers confront the
    "Oriental problem." *BC Studies*, no. 80 (Winter): 25–41
– 1999. *Contracting masculinity: Gender, class and race in a white collar union
    1944–1994*. Toronto: Oxford University Press
– 2005a. African/Canadian boarder crossings: Migration, exclusion and
    belonging. Paper presented at the Women's Worlds 2005 9th
    International Congress on Women, Seoul, Korea (June)
– 2005b. Negotiating belonging: Bordered spaces and imagined
    communities in Vancouver, Canada. Vancouver Centre of Excellence
    Research on Immigration and Integration in the Metropolis, Working
    Paper Series, no. 05–06
Creese, Gillian, and Edith Ngene Kambere. 2003. "What colour is your
    English?" *Canadian Review of Sociology and Anthropology* 50 (5): 565–73
Das Gupta, Tania. 1996. *Racism and paid work*. Toronto: Garamond Press
Dua, Enakshi, and Angela Robertson, eds. 1999. *Scratching the surface:
    Canadian anti-racist feminist thought*. Toronto: Women's Press
Elabor-Idemudia, Patience. 2000. Challenges confronting African immigrant
    women in the Canadian workforce. In *Anti-racist feminism: Critical race and
    gender studies*, edited by Agnes and George Sefa Dei, 91–110. Halifax:
    Fernwood Publishing
Essed, Philomena. 1991. *Understanding everyday racism: An interdisciplinary
    theory*. New York: Sage
Frenette, Marc, and Rene Morissette. 2003. Will they ever converge?
    Earnings of immigrant and Canadian-born workers over the last two
    decades. Statistics Canada, Analytical Studies Branch Research Paper
    Series, Catalogue no. 11F0019MIE, no. 215 (October)

Fudge, Judy, and Leah Vosko. 2003. Gender paradoxes and the rise of
contingent work: Towards a transformative political economy of the
labour market. In *Changing Canada: Political economy as transformation*,
edited by Wallace Clement and Leah Vosko, 183–209. Montreal and
Kingston: McGill-Queen's University Press

Gabriel, Christina. 1999. Restructuring at the margins: Women of colour and
the changing economy. In Dua and Robertson 1999, 127–64

Galabuzi, Grace-Edward. 2001. *Canada's creeping economic apartheid: The
economic segregation and social marginalization of racialized groups*. Toronto:
CSJ Foundation for Research and Education

Geddie, Kate. 2002. Licence to labour: Obstacles facing Vancouver's foreign-
trained engineers. Vancouver Centre of Excellence Research on Immigration and Integration in the Metropolis, Working Paper Series, no. 02–21

Giles, Wenona. 2002. *Portuguese women in Toronto: Gender, immigration and
nationalism*. Toronto: University of Toronto Press

Green, Joyce. 2003. Decolonization and recolonization in Canada. In
Changing Canada: Political economy as transformation, edited by Wallace
Clement and Leah Vosko, 51–77. Montreal and Kingston: McGill-Queen's
University Press

Hamilton, Roberta.1996. *Gendering the vertical mosaic: Feminist perspectives on
Canadian society*. Toronto: Copp Clark

Henin, Bernard, and Michelle Bennett. 2002. Immigration to Canada's
mid-sized cities: A study of Latin Americans and Africans in Victoria, B.C.
Vancouver Centre of Excellence Research on Immigration and
Integration in the Metropolis, Working Paper Series, no. 02–22

Henry, Frances. 1999. Two studies of racial discrimination in employment.
In *Social inequality in Canada*, edited by James Curtis, Edward Grab, and
Neil Guppy, 226–35. 3rd ed. Scarborough: Prentice Hall Allyn and Bacon
Canada

Henry, Frances, and Effie Ginzberg. 1985. *Who gets the work? A test of racial
discrimination in employment*. Toronto: Urban Alliance on Race Relations
and the Social Planning Council of Toronto

Henry, Frances, and Carol Tator. 2002. *Discourses of domination: Racial bias in
the Canadian English-language press*. Toronto: University of Toronto Press

Henry, Frances, Carol Tator, Winston Mattis, and Tim Rees. 1995. *The colour
of democracy: Racism in Canadian society*. Toronto: Harcourt, Brace and
Company Canada

Hiebert, Daniel. 1999. Local geographies of labour market segmentation:
Montreal, Toronto and Vancouver, 1991. *Economic Geography* 75 (3): 339–69

Hiebert, Daniel, and Ravi Pendakur. 2003. Who's cooking? The changing
ethnic division of labour in Canada, 1971–1996. Vancouver Centre of
Excellence Research on Immigration and Integration in the Metropolis,
Working Paper Series, no. 03–09 (March)

Hooks, Bell. 1984. *Feminist theory from margin to center.* Boston: South End Press

Jacobson, Mathew Frye. 1998. *Whiteness of a different colour: European immigrants and the alchemy of race.* Cambridge: Harvard University Press

Kazemipur, Abdolmohammad, and Shiva Halli. 2000. *The new poverty in Canada: Ethnic groups and ghetto neighbourhoods.* Toronto: Thompson Educational Publishing

– 2001. The changing colour of poverty in Canada. *Canadian Review of Sociology and Anthropology* 38 (2): 217–38

Krahn, Harvey, and Graham Lowe. 1998. *Work, industry, and Canadian society.* 3rd ed. Scarborough: ITP Nelson

Lautard, Hugh, and Neil Guppy. 1990. The vertical mosaic revisited: Occupational differentials among Canadian ethnic groups. In *Race and ethnic relations in Canada*, edited by Peter Li, 189–208. Toronto: Oxford University Press

Li, Peter. 1998. The market value and social value of race. In *Racism and social inequality in Canada*, edited by Vic Satzewich, 115–30. Toronto: Thompson Educational Publishing

– 2000. Earning disparities between immigrants and native-born Canadians. *Canadian Review of Sociology and Anthropology* 37 (3): 289–311

– 2003. *Destination Canada: Immigration debates and issues.* Don Mills: Oxford University Press

– 2004. The place of immigrants: Politics of difference in territorial and social space. *Canadian Diversity* 3 (2): 23–8

Lian, Jason, and David Ralph Matthews. 1998. Does the vertical mosaic still exist? Ethnicity and income in Canada, 1991. *Canadian Review of Sociology and Anthropology* 35 (4): 461–81

Luxton, Meg, and June Corman. 1991. Getting to work: The challenge of the women back into Stelco campaign. *Labour/ Le Travail* 28 (Fall): 149–85

– 2001. *Getting by in hard times: Gendered labour at home and on the job.* Toronto: University of Toronto

Mackey, Eva. 2002. *The house of difference: Cultural politics and national identity in Canada.* Toronto: University of Toronto Press

McLaren, Arlene Tigar, and Isabel Dyck. 2004. Mothering, human capital, and the "ideal immigrant." *Women's Studies International Forum* 27: 41–53

Maxim, Paul, Jerry White, Dan Beavon, and Paul Whitehead. 2001. Dispersion and polarization of income among Aboriginal and non-Aboriginal Canadians. *Canadian Review of Sociology and Anthropology* 38 (4): 465–75

Miedema, Baukje, and Nancy Nason-Clark. 1989. Second class status: An analysis of the lived experiences of immigrant women in Fredericton. *Canadian Ethnic Studies* 21 (2): 63–73

Miles, Robert. 1989. *Racism.* London: Routledge

Ng, Roxana. 1990. Immigrant women: The construction of a labour market category. *Canadian Journal of Women and the Law* 4 (1): 96–112

– 2000. Restructuring gender, race, and class relations: The case of garment workers and labour adjustment. In *Restructuring Caring Labour,* edited by Sheila Neysmith, 226–45. Don Mills: Oxford University Press

Pendakur, Krishna, and Ravi Pendakur. 1998. The colour of money: Earnings differentials among ethnic groups in Canada. *Canadian Journal of Economics* 31 (3): 518–48

– 2004. Colour my world: Has the majority-minority earnings gap changed over time? Vancouver Centre of Excellence Research on Immigration and Integration in the Metropolis, Working Paper Series, no. 04–11 (May)

Perry, Adele. 2001. *On the edge of empire: Gender, race and the making of British Columbia, 1849–1871.* Toronto: University of Toronto Press

Picot, Garnett, and Feng Hou. 2003. The rise of low-income rates among immigrants in Canada. Statistics Canada, Analytical Studies Branch Research Paper Series. Catalogue no. 11F0019MIE, no. 198 (June)

Porter, John. 1965. *The vertical mosaic: An analysis of social class and power in Canada.* Toronto: University of Toronto Press

Pratt, Geraldine. 2004. *Working feminism.* Philadelphia: Temple University Press

Preston, Valerie, and Wenona Giles. 1997. Ethnicity, gender and labour markets in Canada: A case study of immigrant women in Toronto. *Canadian Journal of Urban Research* 6 (2): 135–59

Pringle, Rosemary. 1988. *Secretaries talk: Sexuality, power and work.* London: Verso

Razack, Sherene. 1998. *Looking white people in the eye.* Toronto: University of Toronto Press

– ed. 2002. *Race, space and the law: Unmapping a white settler society.* Toronto: Between the Lines

Reitz, Jeffrey. 2003. Occupational dimensions of immigrant credential assessment: Trends in professional, managerial, and other occupations, 1970–1996. Paper presented at the Conference on Canadian Immigration Policy for the 21st Century (February): 39 pages. Available at www.utoronto.ca/ethnicstudies/research.htm

– 2004. Immigration and Canadian nation-building in the transition to a knowledge economy. In *Controlling immigration: A global perspective,* edited by Wayne Cornelius, Philip Martin, and James Hollifield, 79–113. 2nd ed. Stanford: Stanford University Press

Satzewich, Vic, and Lloyd Wong. 2003. Immigration, ethnicity and race: The transformation of transnationalism, localism, and identities. In *Changing Canada: Political economy as transformation,* edited by Wallace Clement and Leah Vosko, 363–90. Montreal and Kingston: McGill-Queen's University Press

Scassa, Teresa. 1994. Language, standards, ethnicity and discrimination. *Canadian Ethnic Studies* 26 (3): 105–21

Stasiulis, Daiva, and Radha Jhappan. 1995. The fractious politics of a settler society: Canada. In *Unsettling settler societies: Articulations of gender, race, ethnicity and class,* edited by Daiva Stasiulis and Nira Yuval-Davis, 95–131. London: Sage Publications

Stasiulis, Daiva, and Nira Yuval-Davis, eds. 1995. *Unsettling settler societies: Articulations of gender, race, ethnicity and class.* London: Sage Publications

Statistics Canada. 2000. *Women in Canada 2000: A gender-based statistical report.* Ottawa: Ministry of Industry

– 2003a. *2001 Census Analysis Series: Canada's Ethnocultural Portrait: The Changing Mosaic,* January 21. Catalogue no. 96F0030XIE2001008

– 2003b. *2001 Census Analysis Series: The Changing Profile of Canada's Labour Force,* February 11. Catalogue no. 96F0030XIE2001009

Tran, Kelly. 2004. Visible minorities in the labour force: 20 years of change. *Canadian Social Trends,* no. 73 (Summer): 7–11

Tran, Kelly, Stan Kustec, and Tina Chui. 2005. Becoming Canadian: Intent, process and outcome. *Canadian Social Trends,* Spring, 8–13

Vallas, Steven. 2003. Rediscovering the color line within work organizations: The "knitting of racial groups" revisited. *Work and Occupations* 30 (4): 379–400 (November)

Zeytinoğlu, Isik U., and Jacinta K. Muteshi. 1999–2000. A critical review of flexible labour: Gender, race and class dimensions of economic restructuring. *Resources for Feminist Research* 27 (3/4): 21 pages (Fall-Winter). Downloaded from ProQuest

8

Shifting Temporalities: Economic Restructuring and the Politics of Working Time

VIVIAN SHALLA

During the past few decades, economic and political restructuring on a global scale, which has been deeply couched in neo-liberal ideology, has had significant implications for workers' overall life conditions. Key on the agenda of nations, transnational corporations, and small and medium enterprises has been a concerted push to intensify the profit imperative. The strategies to achieve this goal have focused on increasing productivity, efficiency, and competitiveness both nationally and internationally. Enhanced flexibility, which has become the mantra of corporate executives, managers, governments, and public policy-makers, has been promoted with fever pitch since the early 1980s as the handmaiden of profitability and capitalist expansion. The quest for flexibility has taken shape through transformed workplaces and labour markets. Working time, which is central to the pay-effort bargain, has been one of the main features of the flexibilization of workplaces and labour markets as well as of employment-related policy reforms. Workers and their families, whose lives are shaped by the ebb and flow of transformations in workplaces and labour markets, have felt the deep impact of changing working times. Different groups of workers have experienced these changes in a variety of ways and have struggled to retain some level of control over their working time. Most have also felt the stranglehold of the new working-time regime on their ability to balance the demands of paid work with responsibilities and commitments to their families, households, and larger communities.

This chapter explores the shifting temporalities of the post-industrial economy by focusing on the changing working times of front-line service workers in the Canadian airline industry, a major sector of activity that has been in a constant state of restructuring for close to three decades. More specifically, I examine key working-time issues affecting customer sales and service agents and flight attendants at Air Canada in order to pinpoint some of the major temporal realities that confront service sector workers under economic restructuring. I also highlight the contradictions that these workers face in trying to ensure a livelihood for their families and care for their children under a temporal order that places little value on well-being and caring. I show that the specific shape that post-industrial work temporalities have been taking is generating a crisis in care that has profound implications for social reproduction.

I begin by delving more generally into the structure and nature of the new post-industrial temporal order, addressing both its class and gendered dimensions to help locate the dynamics of working time in air transportation over the past few decades. The analytical framework for this chapter is founded on a political-economy-of-work approach in which material experiences and human agency are understood within broader economic and political structures and ideological discourses.

The chapter features two studies that I have conducted on working time in the Canadian airline industry. The first case study examines customer sales and service agents' experience of and struggle against an increase in part-time work in the mid-1980s, when Air Canada and the airline industry worldwide had begun the slide towards economic liberalization. The second case study investigates flight attendants' experience of lengthening working time in the mid-2000s following Air Canada's brush with bankruptcy. I use tools of comparative analysis to tease out some of the similarities and differences in the working-time mutations of front-line service workers in an industry under transformation. The goal is to unveil how distinct historical moments in ongoing political-economic restructuring have had different yet similar impacts on the employment conditions of separate groups of front-line service workers within the same organization, and how these fundamental, albeit different, changes in employment conditions not only affect workers' public-sphere realities, but also deeply impinge on their life conditions in the private sphere. The study also explores the potential for worker resistance to worsening conditions against the backdrop of the particular political-economic context of each historical moment of airline industry transformation.

The final section of the chapter draws comparative conclusions on how customer sales and service agents and flight attendants at Air

Canada have been experiencing changing temporalities under airline industry restructuring. I reflect on the implications for service sector workers, especially women, of the new working-time regime, the result of employers' attempts to survive and remain profitable in the face of increasing competition on a global scale. The conclusion also highlights the centrality of working-time issues to class and gender relations, as well as the social and changeable nature of work temporalities. Finally, I propose directions that might be taken to address the problematic nature of the capitalist-driven post-industrial temporal order for workers and their families.

POST-INDUSTRIAL WORKING-TIME REGIME

Over the past few decades, the reorganization of working-time arrangements has been a central dimension of economic restructuring in advanced industrial countries. One of the distinguishing features of the new temporal order is the great degree of heterogeneity in working times. Indeed, a wealth of research points to the growing importance and increased variety of non-standard work arrangements. These configurations, which include part-time, temporary, contract work, and multiple-job holding, represent a significantly new pattern in labour markets (Bosch 1999; Boulin, Cette, and Taddéi 1993; Broad 2000; de Terssac and Tremblay 2000; Shalla 2002, 2003; Zeytinoğlu 1999). Because these work arrangements are either inscribed with non-standard working times or more explicitly circumscribed by the time-money exchange, they are deeply implicated in the changing nature of workplaces and in the way work is experienced temporally by a growing number of labour force participants.

Studies have also shown that, alongside the shift in work arrangements, atypical working times have been on the rise. Shift work, evening and night work, weekend work, early morning work, rotating and split shifts, variable schedules, reduced workweek, paid and unpaid overtime, compressed workweeks, and flex time dot the temporal landscape of advanced industrial economies (Bosch, Dawkins, and Michon 1994; Desrochers 2000; Human Resources Development Canada 1994; Robinson, Chenu, and Alvarez 2002; Shalla 2004; Statistics Canada 1998). These types of work schedules have muscled their way in on more standard work schedules, thereby drastically altering daily, weekly, monthly, and yearly work temporalities. While these transformations point to a broader reordering of the structure of working time, they also highlight the centrality of time to the employment relationship. Finally, empirical evidence reveals that overlying the changing structure of working time is an unquestionable trend towards a polarization in hours of work, with a large number of people working long hours and a significant proportion of the population working short hours (Harkness 1999; Human Resources Development Canada 1994). This polarization in working time is rooted in the broader social division of labour in society.

The structure and nature of the post-industrial working-time regime stand in sharp contrast to those of the Fordist or industrial regime. Indeed, analyses of the temporal order that gradually took hold during the Industrial Revolution and became firmly ensconced in the social, economic, and political fabric of capitalist societies following World War II reveal that the industrial model of organizing time was built around a high degree of homogeneity. Standardized work temporalities became ingrained in, and defined by, Fordist methods of production and the structures of work organizations of the industrial era of capitalism. These workplace systems relied heavily on Taylorist or scientific management principles of time discipline (Bosch, Dawkins, and Michon 1994; Guedj and Vindt 1997; Thoemmes 2000). This particular temporal norm was a central dimension of the standard employment relationship that provided more stability and certainty to a large number of mostly male workers. The reduction and standardization of working time were not part of a natural progression of capitalist development. Rather, as historical research has unveiled, the postwar normative model was the outcome of decades of struggle by workers to improve their conditions of employment and secure a greater amount of time outside of paid work (Cross 1988; Guedj and Vindt 1997; Marx 1967; Murphy 1988; Palmer 1983; Thompson 1967). In the class struggle over the nature and control of working time, women, immigrants, visible minorities as well as groups of unskilled men all too often found themselves relegated to the margins of the standard working-time regime, where inferior non-standard working times usually took hold. The standard working-time regime also helped shape, and was sustained by, the male breadwinner/ female caregiver model of gender relations that prevailed during the postwar years (Crompton 1999; Lewis 1997; Mutari and Figart 2001; O'Connor, Orloff, and Shaver 1999; Walby 1997). While the industrial working-time norm did not govern all employment relationships, it remained dominant and tended to obscure other work arrangements throughout the postwar period. It only began to unravel in the 1970s.

As had been the case with the temporal norm of the industrial era, the working-time regime of the post-industrial period has been shaped by a revolution in the forces of production. Research conducted on different types of workplaces has demonstrated how work schedules are being diversified with the introduction of highly flexible methods of production, often referred to as lean production (Anderson-Connolly et al. 2002; Elger and Smith 1994; Harrison 1994; Ikuko 2002; Kalleberg 2001; Veltz 2000). These methods of work organization are deeply imbued with the principles of just-in-time, which aim, as did the Taylorist system of production, to intensify work by reducing the porosity of the workday, thereby squeezing as much output as possible from workers in a given unit of time. Studies have also revealed that the introduction of information technology is an important factor in the establishment of new work temporalities (Armstrong 1999; Huws, Korte, and Robinson 1990; Mirchandani 1999; Shalla 1997). Constant improvements in computer software and hardware and advances in telecommunications technologies have been instrumental in reducing the space and time limitations of earlier technologies, thus blurring the boundaries between work and non-work and creating opportunities for new working-time configurations. While the significant role played by changes in the methods and forces of production in altering working-time patterns has received much attention, social scientists have also identified the shift to the service or post-industrial economy as an underlying factor in the transformation of work temporalities (Bosch 1999; Fagan and Lallement 2000; Hinrichs, Roche, and Sirianni 1991a). Many have argued that the flexibilization and diversification of working time are fundamental to the service economy because demand for and delivery of services occur around the clock and are more variable than in manufacturing.

Despite the importance of the reorganization of workplaces and the shift to an economy increasingly dependent on the service sector, these transformations cannot explain, in themselves, the temporal order in the closing decades of the twentieth century. These explanations of current work temporalities fall into the reductionist trap of viewing structural changes in working time as an inevitable outcome of the nature of work in post-industrial settings, and thus they fail to account for variations between countries. Indeed, despite the general trend towards diversification and de-standardization of work arrangements and working times, research has demonstrated that important cross-national variations overlie the heterogeneity of the new temporal order (Boulin 2001; O'Reilly, Cebrián, and Lallement 2000; Felstead and Jewson 1999; Hinrichs, Roche, and Sirianni 1991b; Houseman and Nakamura 2001; Rubery, Smith, and Fagan 1998; Wong and Picot 2001). These differences have gender and class dimensions that reflect the broader social relations of inequality that permeate and give shape to specific countries. For example, while women in all Western countries are more likely than men to work part time, women in

Sweden have tended to enter the paid labour force on a part-time basis at a higher rate than their counterparts in France (Fagan 2001a; Anxo and O'Reilly 2000). And, while the annual working time of full-time employees had decreased or stabilized in most industrialized nations over the twentieth century, it began to rise in certain countries in the 1980s, more particularly in the United States, the United Kingdom, and New Zealand (Bosch 1999; Fagan 2001a, 2001b; Rones, Gardner, and Ilg 2001; Rutherford 2001). In countries where a polarization in working time is being witnessed, long hours tend to be associated with highly qualified, often professional, employees as well as workers at the bottom of the occupational hierarchy.

Comparative studies have also shown that social and institutional arrangements play a not inconsequential role in giving shape to working-time regimes. In particular, state policies and practices pertaining to labour regulation, which are inscribed by class and gender relations, have been key in mediating the transformation of work temporalities. Research carried out by industrial relations specialists and other social scientists concerned with the transformation of work has revealed that the rise in power of neo-liberal governments in several Western countries since the late 1970s has been a key factor in the re-regulation of work and employment. While outcomes have varied across countries depending on the particular configuration of institutional and social relations, regulatory reforms, which provide employers with state-sanctioned power and legitimacy, have directly contributed to the weakening of the standard employment relationship in general and of standard working times in particular. Reforms in the realm of industrial relations have also played a role in the re-regulation of employment conditions. Indeed, new rules governing unions and industrial relations have shifted the balance of power decidedly towards management (Anxo and O'Reilly 2000; Felstead and Jewson 1999; Freyssinet 1997; Mutari and Figart 2001; O'Reilly, Cebrián, and Lallement 2000; Scheuer 1999; Supiot 2001). Unions' ability to negotiate improvements in working time, or at least maintain the status quo, has been hampered by the neo-liberal policy agenda. In addition, the attack on the welfare state over the past few decades has had an impact on the shape and direction of the working-time regime. Similar to employment and industrial relations policies, the provision of state programs and services has influenced the gendered supply of labour. For example, the availability or non-availability of childcare has had a strong bearing on women's working-time arrangements (Jenson and Sineau 2001; Michel and Mahon 2002). Couching their private capital demands in the language of global competitiveness, trickle-down benefits, and inevitability, corporations and employers have been successful, to varying degrees, in prodding governments in all countries to adopt and support employment, industrial relations, and social policy platforms geared towards increasing workplace and labour market flexibility. The plethora and hyperflexibility of working times with which workers have had to contend in the past few decades could only be sustained through active state support.

A growing body of scholarship has highlighted that the new temporal order has not only affected workers in their relationship to the labour market and the workplace, it has also had a tremendous impact on their lives outside of paid work. The male breadwinner/female caregiver model of gender relations has been undermined over the course of the past several decades by the massive entrance of women, especially women with dependent children, into the labour force. The difficulties men face in earning sufficient income to support a family owing to falling real wages have also chipped away at this traditional model. Analyses of changing gender relations and employment patterns indicate that the decline of the male breadwinner gender regime, together with the de-standardization, flexibilization, and diversification of working time as the new employment norm for both women and men, has exacerbated the contradictions between labour force work and care work in the home (Crompton 1999, 2001; Fagan, O'Reilly, and Rubery 2000; Jacobs and Gerson 2004; Perrons 2000). These societal transformations have provoked a crisis in care and exposed the difficulties in ensuring social reproduction under the current phase of capitalism. Scholarly and policy literature on the work-family balance has mushroomed in the past decade, a clear sign of the growing pressures felt by workers as they attempt to synchronize paid work with unpaid household and family obligations (Desrochers 2000; Dex and Scheibl 2001; Duxbury and Higgins 2001; Evan Edwards 2001; Evans 2002; Fenwick and Tausig 2001; Hardy and Adnett 2002; Hill et al. 2001; Lewis 1997; Martin 2001; Tausig and Fenwick 2001; Tietze and Musson 2002; Tyrkkö 2002).

Gender analyses of the articulation of the public and private temporal orders have shown that, despite their commitment to paid work, women continue to shoulder the major responsibility for housework and childcare (Daly 2002; Drew, Emerek, and Mahon 1998; Luxton and Corman 2001; Windebank 2001). Women's move into the labour market, and especially into deteriorating working times and employment conditions, has made it difficult for them to adequately provide for their families and coordinate the needs of their families with their paid work schedules and hours of work. One of the contradictions faced by women who are in the labour force while caring for children and other family members is that they are caught between a public temporal order built around linear, quantifiable, divisible, measurable, and rationalized clock time and a private temporal order where time rhythms do not follow these same rigidities. While one must be cautious not to essentialize or naturalize caring activities in the home, it seems clear that the open-endedness, fluidity, and messiness of biological and social reproduction cannot be easily circumscribed by systematic time scheduling and precise deadlines, notwithstanding years of attempts by domestic sciences and childcare experts to devise rigid routines and timetables for these activities. Historical and cultural ideologies and practices pertaining to child rearing and household maintenance also influence domestic and care temporalities. While households do not function according to capitalist economic principles, research continues to show that activities governed by commodified clock time tend to be highly privileged and take precedence over non-commodified activities. Commodified time also determines the organization of, and time commitments to, these non-commodified activities. Feminist analyses of the link between the public and private spheres have demonstrated that these two domains of activity overlap and intersect and that the lines separating them, while never clearly drawn, are becoming more and more blurred (Boyd 1997). By making unpredictable and often excessive time and scheduling demands on workers, the new temporal order has greatly facilitated the seeping of paid work into the private space in capricious ways that leave the work-family interface destabilized and make social reproduction even more problematic.

CHANGING TEMPORALITIES IN THE CANADIAN AIRLINE INDUSTRY

Since the early 1980s, airline industry workers in Canada and worldwide have experienced a forceful attack on their employment conditions. The entire period since neo-liberalism's introduction into the airline industry, nationally and on a global scale, has been very trying for civil aviation workers. The twenty-five-year neo-liberal takeover of air transportation has left deep scars, with specific historical moments presenting particularly daunting challenges for workers and their unions. As part of this tumultuous process, Air Canada, like other air carriers, has systematically sought to cut labour costs. Employment conditions revolving around working time are inextricably tied to the pay packet and have been central to the company's strategy to render its workforce more flexible and maximize the utilization of its workers.

This section analyses findings from two separate research projects on the working-time changes experienced by two groups of front-line service workers at Air Canada. The first case study, conducted from the mid- to late 1980s, focused on the historical transformation of the labour process and employment relationship of customer sales and service agents. One of the key issues under investigation was part-time labour. The second case study, carried out from the late 1990s to the mid-2000s, examined the dynamics of flight attendants' working time and their strategies to juggle paid work and family responsibilities. Women comprise a large majority of both groups of workers. In the mid-1980s, close to 75 per cent of customer sales and service agents were women, and today, in the mid-2000s, close to 90 per cent of flight attendants are women. Extensive documentary research and in-depth open-ended interviews were the main methodologies used for both projects.

Implementing Neo-liberalism in Civil Aviation:
Working-Time Changes for Customer Sales and Service Agents
at Air Canada

When the government of the United States embarked on a very deliberate path to deregulate its air transportation sector in the late 1970s, the neo-liberal agenda was set to infiltrate civil aviation on a global scale. This policy initiative had major repercussions throughout the world as other countries began liberalizing their own airline industry. What is more, nation-states began signing less restrictive bilateral air agreements, effectively sanctioning enhanced international competition in air travel (Dobson 1995; Doganis 1991a; Williams 1993).

In Canada, the federal government, which has regulatory authority over civil aviation, proceeded at a slower pace than its counterpart south of the border. In the late 1970s and early 1980s, it removed some of the long-established restrictions on competition in the industry that favoured Air Canada, which at the time was a crown corporation. These regulatory changes facilitated the expansion of CP Air (the second Canadian mainline carrier), Wardair (Canada's major charter carrier), and the five regional carriers (Pacific Western Airlines, Eastern Provincial Airways, Nordair, Québecair, and Transair) into territory traditionally safeguarded for Air Canada. Competition also intensified on international routes because foreign air carriers were granted access to certain markets under the aegis of bilateral air agreements (McArthur 2004; Sinha 2001; Stevenson 1987). During this time, the deregulation of air tariffs resulted in the deep discounting of fares and cutthroat price wars, practices that were to become quite commonplace in the industry (Duffy and Berlinguette 1983). The late 1970s and early 1980s proved to be particularly difficult years for air carriers because of the increasing cost of doing business, partly owing to the rise in the price of jet fuel and the implementation of much-needed fleet renewal programs. These added costs were borne at a time when national and international economies were faring poorly, a reality that kept business and leisure air travellers at bay. Air carriers had to contend with overcapacity, damaging price initiatives, disappearing markets, and shrinking profits. In this inauspicious climate, Air Canada, like other air carriers around the world, began to take a very close look at labour costs.

In the mid-1980s, Air Canada entered into negotiations with most of its unions to renew collective agreements that had been extended as a result of the enactment in 1982 of the Public Sector Compensation Restraint Act (Bill C-124), the legislation that put in place the federal government's "6 & 5" wage-restraint program.[1] Customer sales and service agents had failed to make many gains during the previous round of contract talks, and the regressive federal legislation not only imposed a significant wage cutback, but also halted any opportunity to discuss major issues that had not been resolved since the late 1970s.[2]

When contract talks began in the summer of 1984 between the Canadian Air Line Employees' Association (CALEA), the union representing customer sales and service agents, and Air Canada, the company was adamant that it needed to cut costs drastically and increase productivity so that it could be in a more favourable position to compete nationally and globally. The company informed all groups of workers that it was seeking enhanced labour flexibility in order to succeed in the newly deregulated environment. Air Canada identified high labour costs, bloated staff levels, generous benefits, inefficient work schedules, and outdated work rules as key dimensions of the employment relationship that were hampering its ability to compete.[3]

From the outset, Air Canada made it clear that a significant increase in the utilization of part-time labour was central to its flexibility strategy.[4] The company felt strongly that the levels of part-time workers as well as rules governing how and when it could make use of part-time workers impeded its ability to staff according to workload and handle the variable daily staffing requirements that flowed from the new reality in the airline industry. This round of negotiations was more difficult by far than any in the past, and various issues remained on the table during the many months of negotiations. However, the biggest obstacle was part-time work. Contract talks had begun in the summer of 1984 and in the spring of 1985, with no resolution in sight, especially on the utilization of part-time labour, customer sales and service agents went on a three-week strike. This action was unprecedented for these front-line service workers.

While customer sales and service agents managed to stave off some of Air Canada's demands, the company nonetheless secured greater labour flexibility through an increase in both the proportion of part-time jobs and the utilization of part-time labour. When the parties entered into collective bargaining, the number of part-time agents that Air Canada could hire stood at 20 per cent of the total number of full-time agents.[5] The company insisted, however, that this level of utilization was not sufficient to handle its variable daily and weekly staffing requirements. Air Canada argued that any cap on the number of part-time workers was an impediment to its competitive position, but it settled for an immediate increase from 20 to 30 per cent of the total number of employees at the base (instead of the total number of full-time employees at the base, as was previously the case). In early April 1986, management would also be able to increase this proportion to 35 per cent.[6] Specific practices also allowed the company to increase its utilization of part-time labour. For example, part-time agents could now be recalled for up to four consecutive hours at time-and-a-half pay rates and be asked to work overtime at straight time for up to two hours beyond their regular shift. Continuous coverage of part-time shifts could be extended from four and a half to five hours.[7] These concessions were significant because they opened the door to the substitution of part-time for full-time jobs, allowing the company to make use of various combinations of part-time hours rather than hire full-time workers. This concession weighed heavily on union negotiators, as shown by the comments of one bargaining team member:

It's hard to describe the sense of loss with that let. The company wouldn't budge on wanting flexibility with more part-time work. They definitely wanted to be able to hire more and more part-timers. We, as a union movement, have always resisted casual labour. It's not good for workers. I know we've got to figure out our strategy on part-time labour, we have got to protect all workers, and we tried to build that into our policy before going into bargaining. But, you still have a sense that more part-time is not the best route to go, well, for workers anyway. (Interview CALEA-5)

While the union had been under a tremendous amount of pressure to concede to company demands regarding part-time labour, it nonetheless succeeded in bargaining important gains for part-time agents. Contract amendments included a guarantee of fifteen hours of work a week, the removal of restrictions on shift trades between part-time and full-time agents, and the right to perform relief duties and fill temporary full-time positions.[8] Other benefits, such as dental and pension plans, important wage improvements, and stronger job security and seniority rights, were registered for part-time agents.[9] These gains, which represented major improvements to the working conditions of part-time agents, were consistent with the new direction taken by the CALEA around part-time labour. Indeed, at its general meeting in 1983, the CALEA had adopted a policy that called for the reduction of inequities between part-time and full-time agents, seeing these inequities as only serving to facilitate the exploitation of part-time workers as cheap labour.[10]

During the turbulent years in the airline industry immediately following the strike, the issue of part-time labour continued to be central to Air Canada's flexibility agenda. Ongoing liberalization in civil aviation on a global scale resulted in the privatization of crown carriers, including Air Canada, the relaxation of route and fare regulations, new bilateral agreements, intense competition, and concentration. Prior to the strike, the CALEA, fearing the effects of emerging liberalization in the airline industry, had entered into discussions to merge with the Canadian Auto Workers union (CAW), which it did immediately after the strike.[11] This reorganization put customer sales and service agents in a stronger position to resist some of the concessions that Air Canada demanded during subsequent rounds of collective bargaining. Despite the difficult context of the late 1980s, improvements to the working conditions of part-time agents were won, including a guarantee of twenty hours of work a week and better seniority and pay provisions.[12] Moreover, the union was able to fend off many, though not all, of the company's demands for the removal of additional restrictions on the use of part-time labour.

The union also sought, unsuccessfully, to bring about more full-time employment. Some of the new work practices did result, however, in an increase in the number of hours available to part-time agents. In addition, the company showed a preference for calling upon part-time workers to fill overtime requirements because of the lower cost of such labour. While an arbitration award in 1986 confirmed the union's position that priority for overtime assignments was to be given to full-time employees regardless of inconvenience or greater cost to the company,[13] the union eventually agreed to allow the company to retain part-time workers before using full-time workers on recall.[14] This practice gave part-time workers access to more hours of work. The following statement by one part-time agent reflects the feelings expressed by many agents about the overtime issue for part-time workers: "I like knowing I might get more than just the four-hour guarantee, 'cause I really need the money. On the other hand, I absolutely resent, absolutely absolutely, that we don't get overtime pay like the full-timers. We do the same work, we've got the same skills, the same commitment to the company, so why won't they give us the same overtime pay. They really get us for cheap, that's why they keep us after our regular shifts on overtime" (Interview CSSA-23).

Some part-time customer sales and service agents who wanted more hours of work were not able to accept the offer of overtime work at the end of their shift. While they needed the money to ensure the well-being of their families, they could not always find someone reliable to care for their children on such short notice. One agent talked about the difficulties with, and worries about, her daughter's care when she accepted overtime work:

My daughter is in daycare part-time, but the place closes at five. If my regular shifts are not at the same time as her daycare, I can sometimes get my mom or my sister to take her in. Other times, I rely on the neighbour's teenager if it's after her school hours. But, I need to go into high gear when I'm asked to stay on after my shift to find someone to mind my daughter. We really need the money, but sometimes when I think of all the hassles we go through, I'm not sure it's worth it. There were a few times when I really freaked out because I wasn't sure where my daughter was. One time, she was supposed to be at Mom's, another time at our house with the sitter, and both times, we could not find her. She was safe and sound, but the feeling of absolute fear and dread is something you don't forget. One of us always double-checks when I do overtime now, because you don't want to live with regret. (Interview CSSA-17)

A few of the part-time agents who were interviewed had relatives living close by who could be counted on to pick up their children from school or from childcare providers. However, not all agents had access to such resources, and this caused them great stress.

Despite the availability of more hours, part-time workers were none-theless still not guaranteed full-time hours with full-time status. While some agents preferred part-time status and others wanted part-time work at some point in their lives, a significant number of part-time agents sought full-time employment, as evidenced by the numerous requests submitted for change to full-time status. Indeed, in May 1987, the union counted over 380 applications from part-time agents seeking a change of status.[15] In early 1987, Air Canada employed close to seven hundred part-time agents,[16] which meant that about half of the part-time workers held that status involuntarily. Others may have wanted full-time employment but had not submitted a formal request to change status.

Because most of the job openings at Air Canada following the strike were part-time positions, the proportion of part-time labour increased. Throughout the 1970s and early 1980s, the proportion of part-time agents had fluctuated but had generally accounted for less than 15 per cent of the total customer sales and service agent workforce.[17] By the end of the 1980s, the proportion of part-time agents hovered around 24 per cent.[18] While this proportion was less than that allowed by the collective agreement, it was nonetheless higher than the proportion of part-time workers in the Canadian labour force, which stood at around 15 per cent in 1988 (Duffy and Pupo 1992, 46).

Earning sufficient income with a part-time position was difficult for customer sales and service agents, a situation that was worsened by the lower starting pay rates that had been introduced during collective bargaining in 1985. Agents who found themselves in this predicament often had to resort to taking on two jobs to make ends meet. One part-time agent who was patiently awaiting a change of status spoke of the difficulties she encountered juggling two part-time jobs and a family:

I'd expected to get on full-time here a few months ago, but when my application to change status was not coming through, I just had to find another job.
Both of my jobs are part-time, yes. It's difficult. With Air Canada, I generally
know my schedule in advance, and that's good. I can plan around Kate's [pseu-
donym for agent's child] school and after-school activities much better. So,
when I had only the one part-time job with Air Canada, it was much easier. But,
with the second part-time job, they don't treat part-timers too well, and our
schedules are very iffy. Since then, my life really is out of control a lot. At home,
we need me to have a full-time job or two part-time jobs, 'cause we can't afford
not to. The cost of living is high in Toronto, you know, and one part-time job
just doesn't cut it. If I had more seniority with Air Canada, even as a part-timer, I
could quit the other part-time job. I would like to get more hours with Air Canada. I've done overtime and I do get extra hours by trading shifts with full-timers. That's a great thing we won, but it's not enough. (Interview CSSA-45)

During interviews, part-time customer sales and service agents expressed frustration that Air Canada could not see the importance of its providing workers with decent hours and income so that they could raise healthy families. Many felt stressed with their job situation, but the hope of attaining full-time status and thus better working condi-tions kept them from quitting a job that offered relatively good condi-tions and benefits despite its part-time status.

Consolidating Neo-liberalism in Civil Aviation: Working-Time Changes for Flight Attendants at Air Canada

In the early months of 2003, Air Canada was facing serious threats to its survival, not unlike its counterparts in other countries. On 1 April

2003, the flag carrier filed for protection against its creditors with the Commercial Division of the Ontario Superior Court under the Companies' Creditors Arrangement Act.[19] The years prior to Air Canada obtaining insolvency protection had been particularly challenging for the carrier, partly because of factors inherent in the state of the airline industry in Canada and globally, but also because of economic and political factors external to the industry that had a rather significant impact on air transportation domestically and internationally.

The difficult circumstances in which Air Canada found itself stemmed largely from the outcomes of the neo-liberal political-economic agenda that had begun infiltrating the airline industry in the United States in the late 1970s and had become deeply entrenched in civil aviation on a worldwide scale by the closing years of the twentieth century. State policies favouring national and international liberalization and intense competition have placed international as well as national and regional carriers in a constant state of uncertainty (Button 1996; Button, Haynes, and Stough 1998; Doganis 2001a; Hanlon 1999; Williams 2002). In Canada, the cutthroat competition in the mid- to late 1990s between Air Canada and Canadian Airlines International Ltd (CAIL), especially in the context of an economic downturn, threatened the viability of both airline companies. In early December 1999, Air Canada emerged the victor when its rival accepted a takeover offer.[20] When Air Canada gained control of CAIL in July 2000, it was confronted with the high costs and major difficulties associated with acquiring an insolvent company and integrating two major carriers and workforces, both with long histories. In the early 2000s, Air Canada was also forced to operate under the clouds of economic slowdowns and the inevitable weakening of passenger traffic. The merger victory was also tempered by the challenge posed by highly aggressive low-cost carriers that were springing up in the scheduled air-travel market in Canada as well as in other countries, a development encouraged by state policies aimed at enhancing competition in air transportation (Doganis 2001b; Ito and Lee 2003; Mentzer 2000). In late March 2003, Air Canada's restructuring plans also suffered a significant blow when, out of concern that the carrier was close to bankruptcy, the Office of the Superintendent of Financial Institutions – the federal body responsible for the administration of the Pension Benefits Standards Act, 1985, to which Air Canada's registered pension plans are subject – demanded that the company remit $135 million towards the payment of outstanding contributions for 2002 and 2003.[21]

In the early years of the new millennium, three calamities that did not originate with the airline industry nonetheless severely afflicted air transportation globally and had deep repercussions for Air Canada.

First, the 11 September 2001 terrorist attacks against the United States led to the demise of some long-established air carriers and threw several others into crisis. Second, the threat and eventual outbreak of war in Iraq in mid-March 2003 resulted in higher fuel prices and lower passenger volumes, making it difficult for air carriers to post profits. Finally, the severe acute respiratory syndrome (SARS) outbreak and the World Health Organization's subsequent issuing of an emergency global travel advisory in mid-March 2003 frightened passengers away from some international routes, including Air Canada's profitable Asian routes, and from the carrier's main hub in Toronto. During these years, the federal government, which has jurisdiction over civil aviation, did not provide meaningful financial assistance to help the mainline carrier weather the crisis, preferring instead to allow market forces, albeit ones that were aided and abetted by its own liberalization policies, to steer the course for the Canadian airline industry.

When Air Canada filed for protection against its creditors on 1 April 2003, workers and their unions, who had borne the brunt of two decades of upheaval in the industry, braced themselves for further attacks on their working conditions and livelihoods. Documents filed by the carrier left no doubt that it viewed high labour costs, low productivity, inflexible work rules, and restrictive collective agreements as the main reasons for its crisis situation. The company's strategy to emerge from bankruptcy protection focused heavily on issues pertaining to labour.[22] Unions representing various groups of workers at Air Canada were under tremendous pressure to grant concessions to the company. When the carrier emerged from bankruptcy protection, workers had lost some of their job protection, wages, and other benefits. A major outcome of court-enforced collective bargaining was a significant dilution of employment conditions revolving around working time. The new contract effectively led to enhanced maximization and flexibilization of airline labour.

Because of the nature of air transportation, flight attendants have always worked non-standard hours. The temporalities that govern the paid work life of these in-flight workers had become more difficult in the years preceding Air Canada's brush with bankruptcy because the company had been strongly pressuring its employees to work more intensely and to extend their workday. Flight attendants had succeeded in warding off some of these demands, partly because, in 1985, they had merged their small, independent union, the Canadian Airline Flight Attendants Association (CALFAA), with the larger Canadian Union of Public Employees (CUPE). Like customer sales and service agents, flight attendants had recognized the need to join a more powerful union to fight to maintain their working conditions under nascent deregulation in the airline industry. Despite CUPE's greater bargaining strength, flight attendants experienced significant losses on issues pertaining to working time when a new collective agreement was signed in late spring 2003. Indeed, their monthly and yearly working time was lengthened as a result of both an increase in monthly flight-time limitations and a reduction in vacation entitlement. In addition, family-care days were eliminated, the result being a loss of flexibility for workers needing to deal with family responsibilities.

Air Canada was able to wring a significant number of extra hours of work from the cabin crew through an increase in the mandatory monthly flight-time limitation. Prior to June 2003, the monthly limitation was 75 hours during the entire year. This number was increased to 80 hours per month for a minimum of eight months and to 85 hours per month for a maximum of four months to cover busy periods of the year. In addition, flight attendants could now voluntarily exceed the monthly flight-time limitations by up to 20 hours instead of 10.[23] While these numbers may give the impression that flight attendants work relatively few hours in a month compared to the standard full-time workweek of 35 to 40 hours, one needs to examine the peculiarities of how cabin crew working time is calculated to better grasp the magnitude of the new time demands placed on these workers. The typical workday and work month of in-flight workers is comprised of flying hours and on-duty hours. The pay scheme for time worked is built around actual flight hours and flight-credit hours. If a flight attendant's record of employment indicates that the monthly earnings are based on 80 flight-credit hours, this worker may actually be on duty for up to 160 hours during that month. On the basis of this formula for counting working time, a mandatory increase of 5 to 10 hours in monthly flight-time requirements means that flight attendants are possibly putting in an extra 10 hours of work each month for eight months of the year and an extra 20 hours of work each month for the remaining four months. When these hours are added up, flight attendants are potentially on the job for up to 160 hours more a year. The same type of formula applies to the calculation of the extra total monthly and yearly work hours when flight attendants volunteer to exceed the monthly limitations. One flight attendant shared her feelings about the new flight-time limitations:

I was not happy about the changes, but I was not too concerned because it didn't seem like that many more hours. But the hours add up and, after a few months, it does start getting to you. I feel more tired by month's end, I'm crankier, and I don't always feel like doing things with hubby and the kids. I'm not always that willing to do the voluntary extension. I mean, how many more hours is that in a month … If I put in five or ten mandatory and ten voluntary, well you understand how they calculate our pay credits. We figured it out, and I could be a working stiff for about twenty to forty hours more each month. That's equivalent to a whole week's work each month. I enjoy my job, but with all the other stuff that is happening with our scheds [schedules], it's just too much. It might help pay off the mortgage faster, but I'm too tired to enjoy the house, so what's the point. (Interview FA-B10)

Another flight attendant, who considered the longer-term implications of increased hours of work, pointed out:

I may be young, healthy and full of energy, and have not had problems working the extra hours. But the new MML [maximum monthly limitation] they bargained out of us seems like a lot of extra time to be spending on the job when you add it up over the years. Our job is physically demanding, something the flying public doesn't always see. When I'm doing my pairings [sequence of flights], we do talk about this stuff a lot. Some don't seem to mind the added hours, but most of my friends, we have families, and we're not happy about the extra hours. (Interview FA-B3)

The increase in voluntary monthly hours of work was also a significant loss because, in the past, the union had resisted such a change to the contract in part because the company seemed to interpret the concept of "voluntary" to its benefit. During interviews, flight attendants decried the pressures that crew schedulers increasingly put on them to work extra hours each month voluntarily. One flight attendant stated emphatically: "Crew schedulers can make your life miserable. I've generally been agreeable to working the extra hours, but when you can't change your life to meet 'the requirements of the operation,' as they like to call it, the crew schedulers can become really, really nasty. It's getting worse. There are more pressure tactics to get you to put in the extra time. Like I said, they can make our life miserable" (Interview FA-B1).

The additional monthly hours of work also mean that flight attendants are less available for family responsibilities or have less time for leisure and other activities. Because in-flight schedules are generally made up of two or three chunks of long hours each month during which workers could be far away from their home base, it is difficult for them to develop regular family routines. Flight attendants often compensate for these irregular work schedules by devoting many hours to children and family when they are off duty. However, working up to an additional fifty hours per month means they need extra time to prepare for work and drive to and from work. With less and less time each month to fulfil child-rearing responsibilities and carry out domestic duties, they find the job increasingly demanding. One flight attendant expressed her concerns about how the added work hours have stolen time she could otherwise have spent with her two elementary school-age children:

My kids are still young, and I want to make the best of my time with them. I try to make as much fun time with them as I could on days off or rest periods. And, that has worked out well in the past, because we do get several days in a sequence when we're home. But, when you look at these extra hours we now work, it doesn't seem like a lot, I know that, but it really does make a big difference when you have young children to care for. I seem to be rushing more when I'm with them, our fun time feels rushed. Even dinner and homework have become more tense, because I feel more pressure to get everything done. We keep hearing that it's more efficient to make us work more hours instead of hiring more people, but efficiency doesn't square with building a strong and loving family. I hope my kids don't feel I'm not there for them enough. Their father has a more regular workweek, and he's there for them, and we do have a network of mostly relatives for emergencies. But, I am there less, and the guilt does get to you, and I think I'm more snippy. I have thought of changing careers, but that's hard with the seniority I've built up. (Interview FA-B12)

Clearly, the raising of monthly flight-time limitations represents an important union concession that has reduced flight attendants' time off work and eaten into family time.

During negotiations in late spring 2003, the union was also compelled to concede to a reduction in vacation entitlement, which resulted in another increase in the cabin crew's yearly work hours.[24] Flight attendants must now work a greater number of years for Air Canada before obtaining extra vacation days. For example, to be eligible for twenty-one annual vacation days, a flight attendant is required to work for five years instead of three. To obtain twenty-eight days of vacation, a flight attendant must work for fifteen years instead of ten. To have the luxury of thirty-five days of vacation, a flight attendant must commit twenty-five years of service to the company instead of eighteen. Before the new contract came into effect, cabin crew could expect to earn eventually up to forty-two annual vacation days. Under the new rules, the maximum the most senior worker can ever achieve is thirty-five days.

While flight attendants' annual vacation entitlement remains higher than that of non-unionized and many unionized workers, the real outcome of this reduction in days off is that they are putting in more hours of work over their lifetime. For some, this extra work time is occurring during their child-bearing and child-rearing years, thus leaving them with fewer hours to spend with their children. One flight attendant, furious with the changes, stated:

I'm incensed with the vacation change. I don't have much seniority, and it is practically impossible to get the best times off when you're more junior. I have eight years of service. Now I have to work seven more years instead of two to get twenty-eight days. I was so looking forward to those extra days to spend more time with my daughter. She is still young, and I want to devote my vacation to my daughter and my husband. The young years are so important, and seven more days does make a world of difference. Even if you're just hanging out with them. Even if I only get vacation rights during the school year, I could be there for the after-school stuff. It's so unfair. (Interview FA-B7)

This concession had not been made easily by the union during bargaining, especially given that it had been able to negotiate improvements to vacation entitlement in the previous contract.

Another clause on working time that Air Canada succeeded in eliminating from the collective agreement during court-enforced bargaining was primary-care leave, or what was commonly referred to as family-care days.[25] This clause gave flight attendants the right to use up to three days annually of their own sick leave entitlement to deal with medical emergencies involving a spouse, parent, or child for whom they were legally responsible, or to deal with unexpected childcare responsibilities. Flight attendants had benefited from this clause, as it helped them balance their paid work with family emergencies. Having to care for family members who either are ill or have a disability is difficult for most workers, but for those with non-standard schedules, such responsibilities can be even more onerous. What is more, the vagaries of air transportation can wreak havoc with flight attendants' already scattered work schedules. Under such circumstances, dealing with unforeseen family illness or childcare problems can be extremely trying. The contractual guarantee of family-care days meant that flight attendants did not have to call in sick when they were dealing with a sick child or parent, or when their carefully planned childcare arrangements broke down. While a review of grievances filed by the union reveals that Air Canada sometimes tried to limit the use of this clause, the company had nonetheless agreed, in December 2002, to strengthen primary-care leave by allowing workers to make use of these days even when the family-care situation that presented itself was not an emergency.[26] This change had removed the obligation for flight attendants to prove that their need to use family-care days was due to an emergency and to have to justify their understanding of what an emergency meant. One flight attendant's story provides a sense of the impact that the deletion of this clause has on workers' ability to balance paid work and family responsibilities: "I didn't use family-care days often, only for real emergencies, but I liked to know that cushion was there. You always felt like you were taking something from the company though. But my youngest was ill recently, and I'd decided that if I really needed to, I would use my own sick days, even if we're not allowed to any more. I didn't have to resort to lying, but I don't think I would've given a shoot. Had there been an emergency, that was that" (Interview FA-B11).

The company's goal in eliminating family-care days was to reduce the level of absenteeism and minimize the number of times that replacement flight attendants had to be called in to cover flight schedules. However, it is not clear that by restricting the use of sick leave entitlement, management could achieve this goal, as highlighted by a senior flight attendant:

I don't think too many people abused the system, so I don't know why management wanted it out of the contract. I guess they felt they had to nickel-and-dime workers to prove to all the hotshot lawyers and accountants they had working for them, and all those investors, that they were serious about clamping down on labour costs. I think that's what it was all about. Managers know that we will use sick days for family emergencies if we really have to. Workers all over the place do that because they have no other choice. So, at the end of the day, you will use up the same number of days, it's just that now you have to lie about it. That's what used to happen. How is that progress when you're forced to be deceitful? (Interview FA-B7)

During interviews, flight attendants expressed a strong sense that workers and their families were being let down by Air Canada. They argued that it was extremely difficult to raise children and develop strong family bonds with the type of schedules and long working hours demanded of in-flight workers. They also felt that eliminating the privilege and security of three family-care days seemed unusually harsh and unnecessary.

CONCLUSIONS

The two case studies discussed in this chapter on the changing work temporalities of front-line service workers in the Canadian airline industry are clear examples of the managerial strategy to increase labour flexibility and reduce labour costs. During two highly significant junctures in the twenty-five-year history of the massive restructuring in the Canadian airline industry, Air Canada has made considerable demands on its employees for concessions on issues pertaining to working time. While these studies involve two different time periods, two moments in the political-economic transformation of air transportation, two distinct groups of front-line, predominantly women, workers, two types of working-time mutations, and two somewhat divergent sets of outcomes, some comparative conclusions can be drawn that can help us understand the new post-industrial temporal order and that highlight how the nature and structure of work temporalities reflect the state of social relations under contemporary Canadian capitalism. Conclusions can also be drawn about how the working-time regime that is becoming firmly entrenched in many Western societies is taking a toll on social reproduction.

In the early to mid-1980s, the Canadian airline industry was beginning to feel the winds of liberalization and deregulation that had started blowing in the United States a few years earlier, whereas in the early to mid-2000s, air transportation in Canada was swathed in the neo-liberal policy agenda that dominated civil aviation and the broader political economy on a global scale. Both periods were extremely difficult for Air Canada. In the first period, the flag carrier was searching for its bearings under the initial wave of liberalization in the industry, whereas in the latter period, it was struggling amidst the cutthroat competition and reorganization that were the reality of deregulation in air transportation globally. These two time periods in Air Canada's history are part of the ongoing process of restructuring that has transformed the airline industry in a relatively short time span. During both moments of restructuring, Air Canada made various demands for concessions from its workers, with some of the most significant revolving around working time. In both instances, the deepening of temporal flexibility was presented by the company as a cornerstone of its strategy to reorganize and survive the particular crisis it was facing.

In the mid-1980s, Air Canada insisted that it needed to increase its utilization of part-time customer sales and service agents to make better use of its labour force under nascent industry deregulation. The growing incidence of part-time labour was one of the key employment issues of that specific period in the broader economy, and unions had only begun to come to terms with the need to develop stronger policies to fend off the casualization of labour while fighting for better conditions and protection for this group of workers. The union representing customer sales and service agents had begun devising strategies to prepare itself for the onslaught of company demands on part-time labour, partly because the carrier had gradually been attempting to relax the rules on the use of such labour. Following a full-scale strike fought mostly around the issue of part-time work, union concessions facilitated casualization and created a two-tier working-time employment norm for customer sales and service agents. However, another outcome of the strike was significant improvements for part-time agents that placed them in an enviable position compared to most part-time workers in other workplaces and industries. The Canadian Air Line Employees' Association was able to resist certain concessions and make gains for all workers partly because it had become more progressive and militant during the decade preceding the strike. Moreover, during negotiations with Air Canada, the independent union had begun merger talks with the more powerful Canadian Auto Workers, which helped strengthen its bargaining power vis-à-vis the company. CALEA's policy and strategy decisions on part-time labour made immediately prior to, and during, negotiations, were a clear indication of the union's more progressive stance on this issue.

At the turn of the millennium, Air Canada was pressuring its flight attendants to work more hours on a monthly and annual basis so that it could deploy with greater ease its labour force to face the competitive environment produced by close to two decades of liberalization in civil aviation domestically and internationally. While part-time labour had been a key issue in the world of work during the 1980s, longer work hours had become a dominant theme in the late 1990s and early 2000s. For the past decade, following almost a century of reduction in annual working hours, different groups of workers throughout the industrial world have had to spend more hours in the formal economy to meet employer demands or ensure their own survival. During rounds of collective bargaining prior to Air Canada's filing for court protection against its creditors, the union representing flight attendants had successfully warded off company demands that workers be obliged to be on duty for more hours each month. Flight attendants had been in a relatively strong position to resist demands for concessions because, like their front-line counterparts on the ground, they had merged their independent union, the Canadian Airline Flight Attendants Association, with the more powerful Canadian Union of Public Employees in the mid-1980s in the midst of early airline industry deregulation. However, the strength of the union did not prove sufficient in protecting flight attendants from having to make concessions under the weight of court-ordered bargaining and looming bankruptcy for Air Canada. The outcome for the cabin crew was a tangible increase in hours of work and a loss of other time-related benefits, although the union was able to resist some company demands.

The temporal flexibility strategies that Air Canada employed to navigate the turbulence of two important phases in the process of airline

industry liberalization created different pressures for both groups of
front-line service workers. For customer sales and service agents, the
outcome of the initial stage of restructuring and subsequent strike
action was increased casualization but a vastly improved quality of
employment for part-time labour. For individual agents, the increase
in part-time work resulted in an insufficient number of hours to ensure
their survival and the well-being of their families. In effect, the shift to
casualization created a situation of time insufficiency for these ground
service workers, which translated into income insufficiency. The only
solution for part-time agents was to take on more than one job in order
to generate adequate income to sustain themselves and their families.
Multiple-job holding engendered further time demands that resulted
in some agents putting in more than full-time hours each week, thereby giving rise to more stress and worries. The time constraints faced by
these workers meant that they could not spend the same amount of
time with their children or, if they chose to retain only one part-time
job, they could not offer their families the same standard of living. Trying to coordinate the time demands of two or more part-time jobs and
arrange childcare for younger children also became extremely difficult. For flight attendants, the outcome of the more recent phase of
restructuring, and more specifically the bankruptcy protection for Air
Canada, entailed more hours of work. For individual flight attendants,
taking on more hours of work was similar to always working overtime.
Monthly working-time overload thus became the temporal experience
of flight attendants. Given the particularities of in-flight workers'
schedules and long periods away from home, the additional hours
committed to the company meant that they found it even more difficult to make time for their children on a regular basis. For some flight
attendants, childcare arrangements had to be reorganized to meet the
new working-time requirements, compounding the stress and pressure
they already experienced in arranging care for their children. Customer sales and service agents and flight attendants faced difficulties
finding adequate childcare partly because of their service sector–type
work schedules. However, the new work temporalities at Air Canada
amplified the care dilemmas for both groups of workers. The working-
time concessions made by each group at key moments in the process of
airline industry restructuring worsened the already stressful task of
finding safe, affordable, and reliable care where their children could
flourish.

This analysis of the transformation of working time in the airline
industry shows that the new temporal order, which is grounded in the
flexibility needs of employers, has diminished workers' control over
their lives in and out of paid work. Work organizations are given priority

in capitalist societies, and they can lay claim to employees' time commitments in terms of duration, scheduling, and intensity largely because most people's sustenance is dependent on their own or someone else's labour force earnings. The inequality of the relationship between free wage labour and private property capital creates an imbalance where workers are structurally compelled to accommodate the time demands of the job. When, in any given conjuncture, the balance of power shifts decidedly in favour of corporations and employers, the reproduction of labour power becomes more tenuous because, in what is obviously a deep contradiction of capitalism, the powerful force of profit accumulation is blinded to the societal need for the reproduction of labour power.

Concretely, social reproduction is ensured, and takes a variety of forms, in individual families and households where people's activities and practices are not consciously put in motion to reproduce workers for capitalist enterprises or to ensure societal reproduction. Workers and their families develop aspirations for a decent and fulfilling livelihood, and they define and redefine the conditions of that livelihood within the context of evolving circumstances, potentialities, and limitations. The new temporal order that has been confronting scores of workers, many of whom have been eking out a living in the growing service sector, has played a not inconsequential role in circumscribing the conditions of social reproduction by creating what can best be described as temporal flexibilities for employers and temporal rigidities for workers. These exacting temporalities cannot be seen as favourable or desirable for human development, which has at its core the nurturing of children, families, communities, and the self. What is more, post-industrial work temporalities have taken hold within a somewhat modified male breadwinner/female caregiver gender model. Despite women's entrance into paid employment, they continue to shoulder much of the caregiving responsibilities in the home. Notwithstanding men's increasing desire and commitment to provide caring in the home, they continue to work longer hours in the public sphere and undertake less of the unpaid care work in the private sphere. The new temporal order is at odds with the postwar gender model, albeit in different ways cross-nationally, yet it continues to bolster inequitable gendered divisions and relations.

The study of the working-time mutations of front-line service workers in the airline industry and the impact of these time shifts on their caring responsibilities is useful for highlighting the underlying social dimension of work temporalities. Indeed, my analysis shows that working times are shaped through relations of domination and contestation. Work temporalities are thus social and mutable. The history of

class struggle over working time has centred on the duration, scheduling, and intensity of commodified time. The labour movement's main
agenda has revolved around expanding workers' time away from paid
work, improving the conditions of paid working time, and giving workers more control over time. These struggles have been, for the most
part, about men's standard working time and have not tended to focus
on creating more equitable gendered temporalities. Women's entry
into paid labour, the nature of their labour force participation, and
the gender dynamics of the past few decades, in conjunction with neo-
liberal economic restructuring and welfare state erosion, have helped
bring to the fore the work-family conflict and the gendered imbalance
built into the work-family interface. This issue has been key in remind-
ing us that not all social times have been treated equally by capitalist
corporations or by labour organizations and that commodified time
has, historically, been given pre-eminence over other social times.
Both these institutional forces have perpetuated the view that time
spent caring for others outside the formal economy, like the caring
activities themselves, is less important than time spent producing commodities or delivering services for profit.

Calls for a different type of temporal regime have surfaced throughout the history of capitalism. Over the past few decades, renewed
demands by progressive movements for re-visioning work and other
temporalities have become more urgent. Rising levels of unemployment following the golden years of the postwar boom have been at the
root of cries in many advanced industrialized nations for a reduction
in, and more equitable distribution of, working time (Boulin and
Hoffman 1999b; Gonäs 2002; Taddéi 1998; Went 2000). Women have
also insisted on a more equitable division of labour in the household,
and they have succeeded in getting the work-family imbalance on the
collective bargaining agenda, as well as on the policy agenda of the
labour movement, governments, and private businesses.

These calls for action have had tangible results. Studies have shown
that family-friendly policies and programs have been implemented by
unions, companies, and governments. Some of the better-known
examples of these policies and programs include extended maternity
and parental leave, paid leaves of absence, flexible working schedules,
job sharing, and other opportunities for reduced work time
(Desrochers 2000; Dex and Scheibl 2001; Duxbury and Higgins 2001;
Evan Edwards 2001; Evans 2002; Fenwick and Tausig 2001; Gerstel
and Clawson 2001; Hardy and Adnett 2002; Hill et al. 2001; Lewis
1997; Martin 2001; Tausig and Fenwick 2001; Tietze and Musson
2002; Tyrkkö 2002). These policies have, to a certain extent, given
workers a greater ability to care for their families while retaining

employment security, benefits, and more favourable working conditions. While they have somewhat alleviated the conflict between the public and private spheres for some workers, family-responsive policies and programs have not challenged the dominance of commodified time, gendered patterns of paid working time, or the gendered boundary between family and paid work. These policies and programs, however, do provide the basis for contesting the gendered and class-based temporal order. Demands by the women's movement, the labour movement, and child-development advocates for significant improvements to state-sponsored childcare programs have led to positive outcomes in some countries (Jenson and Sineau 2001; Michel and Mahon 2002). However, these demands, which contain the seeds for a more fundamental challenge to the contemporary working-time regime, have received either lukewarm support or resistance from governments in most Western nations.

The many changes, while piecemeal, are important foundational elements for an alternative temporal order where commodified time loses its place of prominence and other equally important life-nurturing and life-sustaining social times are valued. Such a temporal order would provide workers and their families with greater time sovereignty so that they could redirect their time commitments, if they so choose, to caring activities. Creating the possibility for workers to have real control over the number of hours they commit to paid work and over the timing of those hours could lay the basis for a deep-seated challenge to the male breadwinner/female caregiver gender model of social organization. A temporal regime built on workers having more time autonomy would also give women and men the opportunity to temporarily exit the labour market to pursue further education and training. Caring and learning activities that are life-sustaining and lead to self-fulfilment give meaning and texture to individuals' lives, but they are also a public good. Time spent on these activities should thus be a key component in policy frameworks developed to forge a new working-time regime.

Alternative approaches to working time, while only beginning to pierce the policy agenda in Canada and barely visible in many Western countries (which have embarked on a decidedly neo-liberal path), have been taking hold in some European countries over the past few years and have been a central feature of the social organization of Nordic countries for some time (Appelbaum et al. 2002; Boulin and Hoffman 1999b; Supiot 2001). These models, which partly derive from the movement to reduce working time, are based on the need to develop better ways of facilitating, reconciling, and sharing paid labour market work, unpaid care work, learning, and volunteer activities over the entire life cycle. This rethinking of the dynamics among paid work, caring, learning, and volunteering over one's lifetime is driven by the progressive social agenda of the European Union and the social democratic principles of Nordic countries.

In most Western countries, patterns of working time have become increasingly diverse and flexible over people's lifetime. This diversity and flexibility could form the basis for the development of a more integrated regulatory framework for a new temporal order, one that would allow movement among the social temporalities of working, caring, learning, and volunteering over a lifetime. This more dynamic approach to temporality cannot be designed, of course, without a sound regulatory framework to ensure social protection during transitions among the different social times and therefore over the whole life cycle (Boulin and Hoffman 1999a, 1999b; Fagan 1999; Freyssinet 2000; Supiot 2001). Without entitlement to social protection, workers and their families could not exercise any real control over their various time commitments. Clearly, given the current structure of the labour market and the neo-liberal dismantling of the welfare state, and also as a consequence of dominant discourses on definitions of work and non-work, Canadian workers and their families face the monumental, but not impossible, task of trying to shift temporalities to create better times.

NOTES

Author's Note: The research for this chapter was supported by grants from the Social Sciences and Humanities Research Council of Canada. I am grateful to union officials representing workers at Air Canada and to Air Canada officials for granting me access to archival documents and agreeing to be interviewed. I am especially indebted to the many airline industry workers who welcomed me so warmly into their homes and shared their lives with me. Finally, I would like to thank Wallace Clement for his comments on an earlier version of this chapter.

1 Bill C-124 overrode all collective agreements between unions and the government of Canada or its crown corporations.
2 CALEA, *Skyways*, September/October 1982, 3–4.
3 Air Canada, "The Future Is in Our Hands" (summation of message from Pierre Jeanniot, President and Chief Executive Officer, Air Canada, circa August 1984); Air Canada, Conciliation Brief, circa late 1984.
4 CALEA, Minutes of Negotiations, 12 July 1984; CALEA, *Skyways*, November/December 1984, 7; Air Canada, Field Management Update, CALEA Negotiations, 31 October 1984.

5 Air Canada-CALEA Agreement, 1 October 1973–30 September 1976, L1.05.11, p. 75; Air Canada-CALEA Agreement, 1 October 1976–30 September 1978, L1.05.11, p. 81.

6 Air Canada-CALEA Agreement, 26 September 1984–21 September 1986, L1.04.08, p. 77.

7 Ibid., L1.04.05, p. 76; L1.04.07, p. 77.

8 Air Canada-CALEA Agreement, 26 September 1984–21 September 1986, article 6.06, p. 14, article 7.06, p. 16, article 8, p. 18, article 12.10.06, p. 44, L1.04.03, p. 76, L4.06, p. 80.

9 Ibid., article 19.10, p. 72, L4.11, p. 81; L4.01, p. 80; L1.04.01, p. 76.

10 CALEA, Report of the Committee on Part-Time Work, September 1983; CALEA, *Policies*, Biennial General Meeting, 18–20 September 1983.

11 CALEA, Minutes of a Special General Meeting, 23–24 April 1985; CALEA and UAW, Merger Proposal, May 1985; CALEA, *Skyways*, July/August 1985, 4.

12 Air Canada-CAW Local 2213 Agreement, 19 September 1988–30 September 1990, L4.01, p. 86; L1.04.03, p. 82, MOU, pp. 121–2.

13 H. Frumkin, Arbitration Award, 29 September 1986.

14 Agreement between Air Canada and CAW Local 2213, Contract no. 26, Effective: 1 October 1990 to 30 September 1992, L1.04.07, p. 88.

15 Letter from T. Freeman, Chairperson, Bargaining Committee, CAW Local 2213, to District Chairpersons, CAW Local 2213, 22 May 1987.

16 CAW Local 2213 and Air Canada, Minutes of a Union-Management Headquarters Meeting, February 1987.

17 CALEA, "Part-Time Work in Air Canada Customer Service" (report of the Part-Time Ad Hoc Committee, January 1978), Table 3; CALEA and Air Canada, Minutes of a Union-Management Headquarters Meeting, May 1979; CALEA, negotiations material, 12 April 1981.

18 CAW Local 2213 and Air Canada, Minutes of a Union-Management Headquarters Meeting, Item 266-AT, February 1988, Item 266-AW, February 1989.

19 Stikeman Elliot LLP (solicitors representing Air Canada and affiliates), Notice of Initial Application, Ontario Superior Court of Justice (Commercial List), 1 April 2003.

20 Air Canada, Revised Renewal Annual Information Form, 14 May 2002, 7, 19–21; Robert Peterson, affidavit, Ontario Superior Court of Justice, 1 April 2003, 6–9.

21 Karen Badgerow-Croteau, Manager of the Financial Institutions Group and Private Pension Plans Division of the Office of the Supervisor of Financial Institutions, *Affidavit*, Ontario Superior Court of Justice, 22 May 2003, 3–7.

22 Robert Peterson, *Affidavit*, Ontario Superior Court of Justice, 1 April 2003, 2; Air Canada, "Air Canada to Restructure under CCAA," *News Release*, 1 April 2003, 1.

23 Memorandum of Agreement between Air Canada and CUPE, Airline Division, 29 May 2003.
24 Ibid.
25 Memorandum of Agreement between Air Canada and CUPE, Airline Division, 29 May 2003.
26 Agreement between Air Canada and the CUPE, Airline Division, 1 November 2001–31 August 2005, article 10.13.

REFERENCES

Anderson-Connolly, R., L. Grunberg, E.S. Greenberg, and S. Moore. 2002. Is lean mean? Workplace transformation and employee well-being. *Work, Employment and Society* 16 (3): 389–413
Anxo, D., and J. O'Reilly. 2000. Working-time regimes and transitions in comparative perspective. In O'Reilly, Cebrián, and Lallement 2000, 61–90
Applebaum, E., T. Bailey, P. Berg, and A.L. Kalleberg. 2002. Shared work – valued care: New norms for organizing market work and unpaid care work. *Economic and Industrial Democracy* 23:125–31
Armstrong, N.J. 1999. Flexible work in the virtual workplace: Discourses and implications of teleworking. In Felstead and Jewson 1999, 43–61
Bosch, G. 1999. Working time: Tendencies and emerging issues. *International Labour Review* 138 (2): 131–49
Bosch, G., P. Dawkins, and F. Michon, eds. 1994. *Times are changing: Working time in 14 industrialised countries.* Geneva: International Institute for Labour Studies
Boulin, J.-Y., 2001. Working time in the new social and economic context. *European Review of Labour and Research* 7 (2): 197–210
Boulin, J.-Y., G. Cette, and D. Taddéi. 1993. *Le temps de travail.* Paris: Syros
Boulin, J.-Y., and R. Hoffman. 1999a. The conceptualisation of working time over the whole life cycle. In Boulin and Hoffman 1999b, 11–48
– eds. 1999b. *New paths in working time policy.* Brussels: European Trade Union Institute
Boyd, S., ed. 1997. *Challenging the public/private divide: Feminism, law, and public policy.* Toronto: University of Toronto Press
Broad, D. 2000. *Hollow work, hollow society? Globalization and the casual labour problem in Canada.* Halifax: Fernwood Publishing
Button, K. 1996. Liberalizing European aviation: Is there an empty core problem? *Journal of Transport Economics and Policy,* September
Button, K., K. Haynes, and R. Stough. 1998. *Flying into the future: Air transport policy in the European Union.* Cheltenham: Edward Elgar

Crompton, R. 1999. *Restructuring gender relations and employment: The decline of the male breadwinner.* Oxford: Oxford University Press

– 2001. Gender restructuring, employment, and caring. *Social Politics*, Fall, 266–91

Cross, G., ed. 1988. *Worktime and industrialization: An international history.* Philadelphia: Temple University Press

Daly, K. 2002. Time, gender and the negotiation of family schedules. *Symbolic Interaction* 25 (3): 323–42

Desrochers, L. 2000. *Travailler autrement: Pour le meilleur ou pour le pire? – Les femmes et le travail atypique.* Gouvernement du Québec: Conseil du statut de la femme

de Terssac, G., and D.-G. Tremblay, eds. 2000. *Où va le temps de travail?* Toulouse: OCTARÈS Éditions

Dex, S., and F. Scheibl. 2001. Flexible and family-friendly working arrangements in UK-based SMEs: Business cases. *British Journal of Industrial Relations* 39 (3): 411–31 (September)

Dobson, A.P. 1995. *Flying in the face of competition.* Brookfield, Vt: Ashgate

Doganis, R. 1991. Deregulation and its impact on the industry. In *Flying off course: The economics of international airlines,* 46–78. 2nd ed. London: HarperCollins Academic

– 2001a. *The airline business in the 21st century.* New York: Routledge

– 2001b. The low-cost revolution. In Doganis 2001a, 126–62

Drew, E., R. Emerek, and E. Mahon, eds. 1998. *Women, work and the family in Europe.* New York: Routledge

Duffy, A., and N. Pupo. 1992. *Part-time paradox: Connecting gender, work and family.* Toronto: McClelland and Stewart

Duffy, T.E., and P.R. Berlinguette. 1983. *The low-priced air fare review: The first five years.* Ottawa: Supply and Services

Duxbury, L., and C. Higgins. 2001. *Work-life balance in the new millennium: Where are we? Where do we need to go?* Ottawa: Canadian Policy Research Networks

Elger, T., and C. Smith, eds. 1994. *Global Japanization? The transnational transformation of the labour process.* London: Routledge

Evan Edwards, M. 2001. Uncertainty and the rise of the work–family dilemma. *Journal of Marriage and Family* 63 (1): 183–96 (February)

Evans, J.M. 2002. Work/family reconciliation, gender wage equity and occupational segregation: The role of firms and public policy. *Canadian Public Policy – Analyse de politiques* 28, supplement 1: S187–S216

Fagan, C. 1999. Developing the concept of lifetime working hours: The potential role of part-time work. In Boulin and Hoffman 1999b, 51–74

– 2001a. The temporal reorganization of employment and the household rhythm of work schedules. *American Behavioral Scientist* 44 (7): 1199–212 (March)

– 2001b. Time, money and the gender order: Work orientations and working time preferences in Britain. *Gender, Work and Organization* 8 (3): 239–66 (July)

Fagan, C., and M. Lallement. 2000. Working time, social integration and transitional labour markets. In O'Reilly, Cebrián, and Lallement 2000, 25–60

Fagan, C., J. O'Reilly, and J. Rubery. 2000. Part-time work: Challenging the "breadwinner" gender contract. In *The gendering of inequalities: Women, men and work,* edited by J. Jenson, J. Laufer, and M. Maruani, 174–86. Aldershot: Ashgate

Felstead, A., and N. Jewson, eds. 1999. *Global trends in flexible labour.* London: Macmillan

Fenwick, R., and M. Tausig. 2001. Scheduling stress: Family and health outcomes of shift work and schedule control. *American Behavioral Scientist* 44 (7) : 1179–98 (March)

Freyssinet, J. 1997. *Le temps de travail en miettes: Vingt ans de politique de l'emploi et de négociation collective.* Paris: Les Éditions de l'Atelier/Éditions Ouvrières

– 2000. Les négociations sur les temps de travail en Europe. In *Où va le temps de travail?* edited by G. de Terssac and D.-G. Tremblay, 235–46. Toulouse: OCTARÈS Éditions

Gerstel, N., and D. Clawson. 2001. Unions' response to family concerns. *Social Problems* 48 (2): 277–98

Golden, L. 2001. Flexible work schedules: Which workers get them? *American Behavioral Scientist* 44 (7): 1157–78

Golden, L., and D.M. Figart, eds. 2000. *Working time: International trends, theory and policy perspectives.* London: Routledge

Gonäs, L. 2002. Balancing family and work to create a new social order. *Economic and Industrial Democracy* 23 (1): 59–66

Guedj, F., and G. Vindt. 1997. *Le temps de travail, une histoire conflictuelle.* Paris: Éditions de La Découverte et Syros

Hanlon, P. 1999. *Global airlines: Competition in a transnational industry.* 2nd ed. Woburn, Mass.: Butterworth-Heinemann

Hardy, S., and N. Adnett. 2002. The parental leave directive: Towards a ' family-friendly' social Europe? *European Journal of Industrial Relations* 8 (2): 157–72

Harkness, S. 1999. Working 9 to 5? In *The State of Working Britain,* edited by Paul Gregg and Jonathan Wadsworth, 90–108. New York: Manchester University Press

Harrison, B. 1994. *Lean and mean: The changing landscape of corporate power in the age of flexibility.* New York: Basic Books

Hill, E.J., A.J. Hawkins, M. Ferris, and M. Weitzman. Finding an extra day a week: The positive influence of perceived job flexibility on work and family life balance. *Family Relations* 50 (1): 49–58

Hinrichs, K., W. Roche, and C. Sirianni. 1991a. From standardization to flexibility: Changes in the political economy of working time. In Hinrichs, Roche, and Sirianni 1991b, 3–25

– eds. 1991b. *Working time in transition: The political economy of working hours in industrial nations*. Philadelphia: Temple University Press

Houseman, S., and A. Nakamura, eds. 2001. *Working time in comparative perspective*. Vol. 2: *Life-cycle working time and nonstandard work*. Kalamazoo: W.E. Upjohn Institute for Employment Research

Human Resources Development Canada. 1994. *Report of the Advisory Group on Working Time and the Distribution of Work*. Hull: Minister of Supply and Services Canada

Huws, U., W.B. Korte, and S. Robinson. 1990. *Telework: Towards the elusive office*. Toronto: John Wiley and Sons

Ikuko, N. 2002. Cooperation engineered: Efficiency in the 'just-in-time' system. In *Making time: Time and management in modern organizations*, edited by R. Whipp, B. Adam, and I. Sabelis, 104–14. New York: Oxford University Press

Ito, H., and D. Lee. 2003. *Low cost carrier growth in the U.S. airline industry: Past, present, and future*. Providence, R.I.: Brown University

Jacobs, J.A., and K. Gerson. 2004. *The time divide: Work, family, and gender inequality*. Cambridge, Mass.: Harvard University Press

Jenson, J., and M. Sineau. 2001. *Who cares? Women's work, childcare, and welfare state redesign*. Toronto: University of Toronto Press

Kalleberg, A.L. 2001. Organizing flexibility: The flexible firm in the new century. *British Journal of Industrial Relations* 39 (4): 479–504

Kalleberg, A.L., and C. Fuchs Epstein. 2001. Introduction: Temporal dimensions of employment relations. *American Behaviorial Scientist* 44 (7): 1064–75 (March)

Lewis, S. 1997. "Family friendly" employment policies: A route to changing organizational culture or playing about at the margins. *Gender, Work and Organization* 4 (1): 13–23 (January)

Luxton, M., and J. Corman. 2001. *Getting by in hard times: Gendered labour at home and on the job*. Toronto: University of Toronto Press

Martin, J.A. 2001. A Canadian province highlights work/family issues: The Saskatchewan Balancing Work and Family Initiative – process, outcomes, limitations. *Community, Work and Family* 4 (1): 109–20

Marx, K. 1967. *Capital*. Vol. 1: *A critical analysis of capitalist production*. 1867. Reprint, New York: International Publisher Co.

McArthur, K. 2004. *Air monopoly: How Robert Milton's Air Canada won – and lost – control of Canada's skies*. Toronto: McClelland and Stewart

Mentzer, M.S. 2000. The impact of discount airlines on domestic fares in Canada. *Transportation Journal* 39 (4): 35–42

Michel, S., and R. Mahon. 2002. *Child care policy at the crossroads: Gender and welfare state restructuring*. New York: Routledge

Mirchandani, K. 1999. Legitimizing work: Telework and the gendered reification of the work-nonwork dichotomy. *Canadian Review of Sociology and Anthropology* 36 (1): 87–107

Murphy, T. 1988. Work, leisure, and moral reform: The ten-hour movement in New England, 1830–1850. In Cross 1988, 59–76

Mutari, E., and D.M. Figart. 2001. Europe at a crossroads: Harmonization, liberalization, and the gender of work time. *Social Politics*, Spring, 36–64

O'Connor, J.S., A.S. Orloff, and S. Shaver. 1999. *States, markets, families: Gender, liberalism and social policy in Australia, Canada, Great Britain and the United States*. Cambridge: Cambridge University Press

O'Reilly, J., I. Cebrián, and M. Lallement, eds. 2000. *Working-time changes: Social integration through transitional labour markets*. Northampton: Edward Elgar

O'Reilly, J., and C. Fagan, eds. 1998. *Part-time prospects: An international comparison of part-time work in Europe, North America and the Pacific Rim*. New York: Routledge

Palmer, B.D. 1983. *Working class experience: The rise and reconstitution of Canadian labour, 1800–1980*. Toronto: Butterworth and Co.

Perrons, D. 2000. Living with risk: Labour market transformation, employment policies and social reproduction in the UK. *Economic and Industrial Democracy* 21:283–310

Robinson, J.P., A. Chenu, and A.S. Alvarez. 2002. Measuring the complexity of hours at work: The weekly work grid. *Monthly Labor Review*, April, 44–54

Rones, P.L., J.M. Gardner, and R.E. Ilg. 2001. Trends in hours of work in the United States. In Wong and Picot 2001, 45–70

Rubery, J., M. Smith, and C. Fagan. 1998. National working-time regimes and equal opportunities. *Feminist Economics* 4 (1): 71–100

Rutherford, S. 2001. "Are you going home already?" The long hours culture, women managers and patriarchal closure. *Time and Society* 10 (2/3): 259–76

Scheuer, S. 1999. The impact of collective agreements on working time in Denmark. *British Journal of Industrial Relations* 37 (3): 465–81

Shalla, V. 1997. Technology and the deskilling of work: The case of passenger agents at Air Canada. In *Good jobs, bad jobs, no jobs: The transformation of work in the 21ˢᵗ century*, edited by A. Duffy, D. Glenday, and N. Pupo, 76–96. Toronto: Harcourt Brace and Co.

– 2002. Jettisoned by design? The truncated employment relationship of customer sales and service agents under airline restructuring. *Canadian Journal of Sociology* 27 (1): 1–32

– 2003. Part-time shift: The struggle over the casualization of airline customer sales and service agent work. *Canadian Review of Sociology and Anthropology* 40 (1): 93–109

– 2004. Time warped: The flexibilization and maximization of flight attendant working time. *Canadian Review of Sociology and Anthropology* 41 (3): 345–68

Sinha, D. 2001. *Deregulation and liberalisation of the airline industry: Asia, Europe, North America and Oceania.* Burlington, Vt: Ashgate

Statistics Canada. 1998. *Work arrangements in the 1990s.* Analytic report no. 8. Ottawa: Minister of Industry

Stevenson, G. 1987. *The politics of Canada's airlines from Diefenbaker to Mulroney.* Toronto: University of Toronto Press

Supiot, A. 2001. *Beyond employment: Changes in work and the future of labour law in Europe.* New York: Oxford University Press

Taddéi, D. 1998. *Reduction in working time (a literature review).* Dublin: European Foundation for the Improvement of Living and Working Conditions

Tausig, M., and R. Fenwick. 2001. Unbinding time: Alternate work schedules and work-life balance. *Journal of Family and Economic Issues* 22 (2): 101–19

Thoemmes, J. 2000. *Vers la fin du temps de travail?* Paris: Presses universitaires de France

Thompson, E.P. 1967. Time, work-discipline and industrial capitalism. *Past and Present*, no. 38: 86–97

Tietze, S., and G. Musson. 2002. When "work" meets "home": Temporal flexibility as lived experience. *Time and Society* 11 (2/3): 315–34

Tyrkkö, A. 2002. The intersection between working life and parenthood: A literature review. *Economic and Industrial Democracy* 23 (1) : 107–23

Veltz, P. 2000. Temps et efficacité du travail: Un lien à repenser. In de Terssac and Tremblay 2000, 105–18

Walby, S. 1997. *Gender transformations.* London: Routledge

Went, R. 2000. Making Europe work – The struggle to cut the workweek. *Capital and Class*, no. 71 (Summer): 1–10

Williams, G. 1993. *The airline industry and the impact of deregulation.* Brookfield, Vt: Ashgate

– 2002. *Airline competition: Deregulation's mixed legacy.* Aldershot: Ashgate

Windebank, J. 2001. Dual-earner couples in Britain and France: Gender divisions of domestic labour and parenting work in different welfare states. *Work, Employment & Society* 15 (2): 269–90

Wong, G., and G. Picot, eds. 2001. *Working time in comparative perspective.* Vol. 1: *Patterns, trends, and the policy implications of earnings inequality and unemployment.* Kalamazoo: W.E. Upjohn Institute for Employment Research

Zeytinoğlu, I.U. 1999. *Changing work relationships in industrialized economies.* Amsterdam: John Benjamins

9

Social Reproduction and the Changing Dynamics of Unpaid Household and Caregiving Work

JUNE CORMAN AND MEG LUXTON

INTRODUCTION

One of the exciting changes in contemporary understandings of work has been the reconceptualization of unpaid household and caregiving labour. An important acquisition of the women's movement is its insistence that the unpaid activities that women (and men) engage in when looking after their homes contribute to the social reproduction of the population and the economic productivity and well-being of society. Feminists have argued that this socially necessary work should be recognized, valued, and included in economic measures of productivity. While individual women and men have struggled over domestic labour and the sexual division of labour in their families, political debates have raged about how domestic labour should be organized, who should do it, who should pay for it, and what its implications are for its recipients, for those who do it, and for the larger society.

Since the late 1970s, these debates have been complicated by transformations in the global economy and in international and state policies that have changed the way most people in Canada live their lives. These transformations (identified as globalization and restructuring, informed by neo-liberal economic and political orientations) undermined many of the gains that movements for equality and social justice had won in the earlier period, eroding standards of living for most working people. In this context, struggles to increase the social responsibility for caregiving confront a contradiction. Neo-liberal policies implement cuts in benefits and social services without regard to the availability of other sources of caregiving. At the same time, current economic conditions compel most people to spend more time on income-generating work even when, in some cases, their actual incomes are reduced. Both changes leave most people with less time and fewer resources for unpaid caregiving. The tensions produced by these competing demands have generated, at a national level, a crisis in social reproduction. This crisis is most clearly indicated by a dramatic decline in fertility; in 2002 the birth rate was the lowest it had ever been – an average of just 1.5 births per woman (Statistics Canada 2003a, Table 5.1).[1]

In this chapter, we begin by exploring how the politics of domestic labour have prompted extensive research on domestic divisions of labour, particularly caregiving; have stimulated new ways of measuring and valuing unpaid work as part of the larger economy; and have inspired new theoretical formulations, particularly of social reproduction. We then examine the changing dynamics of unpaid care work to show how the crisis in social reproduction is affecting people's lives in Canada. Most research on this topic has concentrated on nuclear family households that depend on paid labour for their income. We expand on that scholarship by examining two different situations – farm families in Saskatchewan and households in Toronto where adult children and parents are cohabiting because at least one of them cannot generate sufficient income to support an independent home. We do so by focusing on two central dynamics of social reproduction – the ways in which families negotiate changing gendered divisions of labour in both their income-generating work and their domestic labour and the ways in which parents and adult children negotiate intergenerational material support and caregiving. We investigate three themes that relate to household and caregiving work: the changing political economy of income-generating work; prevailing gender and familial divisions of labour, ideologies, and power relations; and family demographics, stages in the life course, and intergenerational relations. We show how people manage to provide care for each other in a context where the pressures of making a living make it difficult to do so.

THE POLITICS OF DOMESTIC LABOUR

The development of capitalism in the eighteenth century into the dominant economic system in western Europe and North America coincided with the consolidation of a heterosexual nuclear family form based on a strict sexual division of labour (Seccombe 1992,

1993). Men, as husbands and fathers, were expected to be income earners; women, as wives and mothers, were expected to bear and raise children, take care of other family members, and maintain their homes. Such families were deemed to be the main and often only appropriate source of caregiving for most people. The problems posed for women by such expectations, and by the demands imposed on them by that labour, have shaped all women's lives, although they played out differently depending on women's class, race, ethnicity, religion, and other social locations (Davis 1981; Bourgeault 1983). The most overwhelming problem has been the dominance of the idea that the heterosexual nuclear family with its strict sexual division of labour is the only, or at least the best, way for people to live. Anyone who could not, or did not, conform found other ways of living difficult. Any complaints women had about the way life was organized, any dreams they held about doing things differently, were typically dismissed as personal problems or inappropriate aspirations (Friedan 1963). The social and political circumstances of women's lives that resulted from such divisions of labour, such as discrimination in the labour force, were naturalized; those who protested and called for changes were either dismissed as naive or demonized as dangerous (Luxton 1983).

Eighteenth- and early nineteenth-century advocates of women's equality documented the inequality that resulted from the dominant perspective and analysed the social and political nature of such family forms and divisions of labour. Liberal arguments led to demands for recognition of women's domestic contributions (Mill and Taylor Mill [1851, 1869] 1983). Socialists and other left-wing activists called for an end to marriage, for socialized domestic labour, including childcare, and for an end to competitive private property (Thompson [1825] 1983). A wide variety of other political views and social practices attempted to organize personal life in ways that challenged hegemonic practices (Hayden 1981), and feminists fought for an array of changes to relieve some of the oppression women faced (Taylor 1983). The problems resulting from women's domestic responsibilities as wives and mothers continued, although public attention waxed and waned with the fluctuating strength of the women's, labour, and socialist movements (Rowbotham 1972). Even in socialist societies and the most developed welfare states, family caregiving, and particularly women's unpaid labour, was a taken-for-granted part of welfare provision (Urdang 1989; Heitlinger 1979). State policies have assumed that families have always been the main provider of welfare; family members are left to work out their own solutions to the problems of combining paid employment and unpaid domestic labour, and women have typically had the primary responsibility for implementing those solutions (Ursel 1992).

The conjuncture of women's growing participation in the paid labour force and the explosion of the women's liberation movement in the mid-twentieth century produced renewed demands for changes designed to relieve women of the oppressive aspects of their domestic responsibilities and ease the conflicting demands of their "double day" of paid employment and domestic labour (Armstrong and Armstrong 1994). Women working in family businesses, on farms, or as fishers argued that as their labour was indispensable, they were entitled to recognition and to services such as childcare and financial recompense on divorce (Davis 1988). In particular, feminists asked why so much caregiving was done by women who received no pay or social recognition for doing it. For a brief period in the 1970s, left-wing activists revived and built on earlier socialist demands, calling for the elimination of private property and profit (Cunningham 1994) as well as private, nuclear families (Barrett and McIntosh 1982). Instead they proposed shared access to wealth and resources and collective living arrangements in which domestic labour would be shared by all. They argued that everyone should be entitled to quality care regardless of their family situation and that its provision should be a social responsibility. Other feminists argued that women should be paid "wages for housework," a proposal intended to offset the loss of income housewives endured. More social democratic demands gained greater support, such as calls for men to take up a greater share of domestic labour, for a variety of government- and workplace-funded programs to help women (and men) combine income-generating and domestic work, such as paid maternity, parental, and personal leaves (de Wolff 2003), and for initiatives that would recognize a limited social responsibility for caregiving, such as a national system of high-quality, non-profit childcare centres (Friendly and Lero 2002).

Since the 1970s, the women's movement, the labour movement, and the left have developed such positions, articulating well worked-out demands, many of which were realized in European countries and some of which have been implemented in certain locations in Canada, for example, in specific union contracts (de Wolff 2003). These demands include making changes in the workplace that recognize and accommodate workers' personal lives, such as improved pay and benefits, shorter working hours, and more paid and unpaid leaves. A range of proposals aimed at changing government policies include legislation to extend workplace benefits and protections to all, including to those in rural areas and those running family businesses. These provisions include income support (e.g., unemployment insurance and welfare), especially for single parents and low-income people; good-quality, affordable housing; health care, including home care and drug plans; education; and childcare. As more and more women, and especially those with young children, were in the paid labour force, there was increasing pressure for the implementation of policies that would either help women meet their caregiving responsibilities or provide alternative sources of care. Some of these demands have been met to a limited extent at various times.

However, the implementation of neo-liberal policies in the 1980s and 1990s represented a direct challenge to feminist, labour, and left-wing demands for greater social responsibility for care (Luxton 1997). Committed to the unfettered investment of capital, to private profit making, and to a growing reliance on markets, neo-liberalism advocates that states have a reduced role in providing services and protections for the population as a whole, but a stronger role in support of business interests and private profit making (Gill and Bakker 2003). Central to this position is the claim that individuals and their families should take more responsibility for their own care, that government provision of services is inefficient and costly, that reliance on state services weakens individual initiative and undermines family and community ties, and that caregiving is best arranged through voluntary familial and community networks (Cohen 1997). The success of neo-liberalism rests on the widespread acceptance that households must absorb more of the work necessary to ensure the livelihoods of their members. As various levels of government have implemented specific neo-liberal policies, people in Canada have typically had fewer supports and resources available to them, making personal caregiving more difficult. In a context where oppositional movements such as feminism, the left, and the labour movement are weak, efforts to mobilize support for greater social investments in caregiving face complex challenges in Canada and internationally.

The complexity of struggles over domestic labour was revealed at the United Nations' major conferences on women. The first two, in 1975 and 1985, resulted in member governments signing agreements to improve the status of women in their countries and specifically to redress the problems produced by the failure to recognize and value women's unpaid family work. However, despite the formal recognition of women's oppression and despite explicit commitments to promote equality, with special emphasis on the centrality of domestic labour and unpaid caregiving, by the third conference in 1995, women from all 185 participating countries reported a decline in the position of women in their countries. They noted that women's unpaid contributions had increased while, in almost all countries, the policies and services designed to support women had been reduced or eliminated. Participants at the 1995 Beijing NGO (non-governmental organization) conference noted that the widespread international acceptance of neo-liberalism as the economic framework for governments and international monetary organizations was a key factor in the deterioration of women's status (NAC 1995). They affirmed their commitment to fighting neo-liberalism as a central strategy in the struggle to improve women's situation and identified unpaid caregiving as one of the most important sites of that struggle (Luxton 2004).

The politics of domestic labour has produced an extensive body of research revolving around several key questions: What does unpaid domestic labour involve? How does it contribute to the economy and the larger society in general? Why is it overwhelmingly women's work and what impact does it have on women's social, economic, and political status? Given the significant changes over the past thirty years in the organization of work, in gender relations and in families, what changes have occurred in domestic labour and what impact have such changes had on those who do the work and those who are the recipients of it?

ACADEMIC RESEARCH ON DOMESTIC LABOUR

Until the remobilization of the women's movement in the 1960s, women's domestic labour attracted little scholarly attention. Indeed, the social sciences for the most part took for granted prevailing European and North American middle-class family forms and sexual divisions of labour and had little to say about woman (Coward 1987). The earlier writings of activists for women's equality were largely ignored by the academy, and the few scholars who did focus on women's domestic work were marginalized (Folbre 1991). Most scholarship reflected and reinforced popular conceptions of gender relations, consolidating a theoretical and political framework that made domestic labour virtually invisible.

In the 1880s, a new economic theory emerged that would have a powerful effect on how domestic labour was understood. This theory, which eventually came to be known as "neo-classical economics," replaced the older political economy as the dominant paradigm. Based on theories of supply and demand, it limited the concept of labour to those activities that generated income directly, effectively denying that unpaid domestic activities could be considered work (Marshall [1890] 1959; Pigou 1929). Reflecting common-sense notions that women's activities in the home as wives and mothers reflected natural feminine proclivities, economics confirmed the irrelevance of domestic labour to the economy. The 1890–91 census did not record those whose chief work was "the charge of their homes" (Census of Canada 1893), and by 1911 women working in their homes were deemed to have "no occupation" (Census and Statistics Office 1915).

The women's movement of the mid-twentieth century challenged prevailing analyses of the economy and developed a sophisticated analytical framework that was well supported by numerous case studies. Captured politically in the slogan "Every mother is a working mother," this perspective began from the recognition that what women (and some men) do in looking after their homes and the people they live with is work that contributes not just to the survival of their own households, but to the daily and generational maintenance of the population and to the formal economy. As such, domestic labour is socially necessary, producing workers to sustain the economy, freeing others to devote their time to income-producing activities, reducing household dependency on purchased goods, and providing an important market for consumer goods. While domestic labour includes a range of housekeeping activities, such as cooking, cleaning, laundry, and household repair, its most important aspect is caregiving, all the activities involved in looking after and providing for a range of emotional, physical, and social needs (Oakley 1974; Luxton 1980). For minority populations subject to subordination and oppression, such as First Nations, Afro-Canadians, francophones, and immigrants, domestic labour can be crucial to preparing children to cope with and fight racism and resist imperial domination (Caulfield Davis 1974; Mandell 2005, 207–13). While children and partners or spouses are the most immediate recipients of care, other household members or kin, friends, and community members are often part of the caregiving network. Caregiving is profoundly gendered and privatized work, and women remain its primary providers, even though this means that they have less leisure time than men and that, over their lifetime, they earn less and are more likely to live in poverty.

Such research provoked further studies. Some studies have documented what unpaid labour involves for those who do it, for its recipients, and for the larger society and economy; others have analysed why this labour remains so privatized, unrecognized, and unvalued. In particular, researchers have noted that unpaid care work is a site of conflict in at least three different, though related, situations. In many private households, there are ongoing struggles over who does, or should do, domestic labour and over whose standards should prevail. Few studies have examined the division of labour in the homes of lesbian, gay, or trans couples or in communal arrangements. The main focus is on the households of heterosexual couples, where, typically, women try to get their husbands and children to do more, while men and children often resist (McMahon 1999). In the larger society, the women's movement has waged a struggle since the nineteenth century for women's work in the home to be recognized, valued, and relieved (Hayden 1981; Ghorayshi 1989; Luxton and Vosko 1998). There have been ongoing struggles over the extent to which domestic labour and especially caregiving should be a private responsibility of individuals or should be shared by the population as a whole through state-provided services such as childcare, health care, and education (Weibe 1995; Grant et al. 2004).

An extensive body of literature is preoccupied with the question of why men do so little domestic labour. Large international and national surveys and smaller case studies repeatedly document that, regardless of women's labour force participation, they continue to bear more responsibility for and spend more time doing domestic labour than their male partners (Bittman 2002; Kubik 2004). For example, in 2000 Statistics Canada showed that, since the 1960s, women have done about two-thirds of all unpaid work in Canada and did more domestic labour than men, even as teenagers (Statistics Canada 2000, 97). Women who were employed did more domestic labour than their male partners; in fact, men living with employed women did less than men whose wives were not employed (Statistics Canada 2000, 111). The 2001 census reported that women were 2.5 times more likely than men to spend more than thirty hours a week looking after children without pay, 2.9 times more likely to spend more than thirty hours a week on unpaid housework, and 2 times more likely to spend ten or more hours on unpaid caregiving to seniors (Statistics Canada 2003b).

A variety of factors affect the extent to which men living with women are able and willing to increase their share of domestic labour. Prevailing social norms and cultural values still assume that domestic labour is women's work; men who do it are regarded as anomalous. It is usually easier for women to take time off paid work to stay home; men are more likely to be criticized as not serious about their careers and to be viewed with some suspicion if they forgo paid employment for domestic responsibilities (Fox 2001). Women are more likely than men to have learned how to do domestic labour as they were growing up. They are often more confident about the work. Some women resist men's involvement. Many are reluctant to put pressure on their male partners for fear of putting their relationships at risk (Dempsey 1997, 1999). If someone needs to take time away from the labour force to provide caregiving, it makes economic sense for the lower earner to do so. Since, in the majority of families, men earn more than women or

are more involved in income-generating activities, economic rational-
ity supports prevailing cultural norms. However, studies from many
countries repeatedly show that the main reason that men are less
involved in domestic labour than women is that men resist becoming
more involved and continue to believe that caregiving in particular is
women's work (Maushart 2002, 204).

Different forces affect the extent to which domestic labour remains
the private responsibility of individuals and their families and friends
or the degree to which it is socialized through the provision of state
and community social services. At stake is the outcome of class struggle
in any particular time and place, and people's practices reflect the specific constraints and possibilities available to them (Clement and Myles
1994). Individual employers and employees struggle over the level of
wages and benefits. Employers' associations, the labour movement,
competing levels of government, and other political actors contest the
regulations shaping working conditions. Various sectors of the population lobby governments about levels of taxation, the types of government services available, and regulations that affect standards of living.
At the heart of the arguments presented in defence of the various positions lies questions about whether caregiving is a private or a social
responsibility, whether or not women can and will continue to provide
unremunerated caregiving, and the extent to which individuals should
be able to get care if they need it, regardless of their personal ties and
economic resources.

As feminist scholarship revealed the importance of women's unpaid
work and its negative consequences for women, it focused particularly
on developing a critique of neo-classical economics, showing how its
gendered assumptions produce and sustain women's subordination
(Picchio 1992; Gardiner 1997). As feminists developed their claim
that women's domestic labour was socially necessary – and not just an
expression of women's innate emotional devotion to their families –
they advanced the contention that prevailing economic theory and the
policies informed by it were fundamentally flawed. One of the most
serious feminist challenges to prevailing economic theory was articulated as a critique of the United Nations System of National Accounts
(UNSNA).

Since 1953 UNSNA has been widely implemented as the international standard for the production of national accounts and labour
force statistics. Membership in the United Nations became contingent
on adopting this system. UNSNA establishes a "production boundary"
that differentiates between those activities that have a market value or
are paid for and those that are not paid for and thus, in this system, are
not considered to be economic activities. Marilyn Waring (1988)

offered a detailed critique of UNSNA, showing how it both ignores women's work and creates incomplete and misleading assessments of economic growth. Critiques such as Waring's prompted a range of activists to call for a revision of not only the UNSNA but also the underlying economic theories that informed it. While they have managed to win a few concessions, such as the inclusion of unpaid work in satellite accounts, they have not succeeded in displacing either the theory or its major policy expression, the UNSNA.

In the 1980s and early 1990s, responding to demands that women's work be recognized, international and national agencies took up the task of developing ways of measuring and valuing unpaid work, using the same tools employed to measure market activities. Their findings confirmed feminist claims that women's unpaid work contributes extensively to the global economy. The United Nations reported that, internationally, in 1995 the monetary value of unpaid labour was $16 trillion, $11 trillion of which was produced by women (UNDP 1995, chap. 4). In 1992 Statistics Canada assessed the value of unpaid household work at $285 billion, equal to 41 per cent of the gross domestic product (GDP) and 60 per cent of personal disposable income (Chandler 1994). Unfortunately, few international or national agencies continued or updated this work, largely because of the strength of neoliberal opposition to such enquiries.

As research deepened the understanding of the contribution of domestic labour to the global economy, feminist theorists mobilized the concept of social reproduction. Where domestic labour refers to the unpaid activities carried out in the home that ensure the day-to-day and generational maintenance and reproduction of the labouring population, social reproduction refers to the production and reproduction of the population as a whole on a day-to-day and generational basis. This larger concept includes not only the biological reproduction and subsistence of people, but also the knowledge, cultural values, and individual and collective identities of specific groups and of the society as a whole. Social reproduction occurs in many places, but three major sites are households, states, and markets. Through domestic labour, households produce and sustain their members. They try to ensure as high a standard of living as possible within the constraints imposed by income-generating activities and the options available from state services and in consumer markets. The higher their standard of living from income and available services, the easier it is for households to reduce their domestic labour. People with high disposable incomes can purchase a wide range of services and comforts, such as childcare or personal nursing care. Developed welfare states often provide such services and comforts to the population as a whole through national childcare and health-care systems. When such services are not available, household members have to increase their domestic labour to try to ensure a satisfactory standard of living.

According to Statistics Canada, the vast majority of people in Canada, at some point in their lives, live in a nuclear family, in what Statistics Canada calls a "census family" (i.e., a couple, a couple with their unmarried children, or a lone parent with her or his unmarried children). The great majority combine income-generating work and unpaid domestic labour to maintain themselves and their households. At the level of the household, social reproduction involves two interdependent labour processes of production and consumption. People who rely on paid employment sell their labour power, or their capacity to work, to an employer. At work, their labour power is consumed, or used up, and in exchange, they receive their pay. In their homes and in the consumer market, people use that pay and their unpaid domestic labour to produce the means of subsistence for themselves and their family members. From this perspective, women subsidize the costs of labour power to capital. Other people generate an income by labouring to produce commodities for sale – for example, by farming or fishing or by operating a small business. For them, tension exists concerning the proportion of income that is reinvested in the enterprise or used to buy goods and services for household use. However their income is generated, households prepare and consume the means of subsistence, ensuring that the capacity to work again is produced. While sexual divisions of labour are contested in paid employment and in the home, women and men typically have had different responsibilities for income-generating work and domestic labour.

Our study of working-class families that relied on jobs in the steel industry in Hamilton from 1980 to 1996 (Luxton and Corman 2001) documents how these households managed the competing demands of income-generating work and domestic labour. It shows how they negotiated the changing sexual divisions of labour as women's labour force participation increased in the context of neo-liberal cuts to state services, growing labour market insecurity for most workers, and changing market conditions in the context of globalization. Stelco, the Steel Company of Canada, had 13,000 employees in 1980, but by 1996 there were only 5,200. Permanent job loss for some workers, including almost all the newly hired women, a protracted cycle of lay-offs and recalls for many, and continued uncertainty for those who retained their jobs undermined steelworkers' long-standing practice of providing a stable income for their families. This job insecurity coincided with the movement of married women into the workforce in the 1980s, prompted by a complex set of individual, social, and economic circumstances. Families struggled to fill the vacuum created by the absence of someone at home full-time to do the household and caring work. Some employed women simply did less and more frequently purchased ready-made meals and conveniences. Families with young children prevailed on relatives to look after them or purchased childcare. Men, used to their wife's care and attention, were under pressure to do more housework and childcare. Some responded willingly; others resisted.

When the permanency of the job losses at Stelco became apparent, even those who still had jobs at the plant realized that their children would not have access to these high-paying jobs. Many steelworkers had gained their jobs through relatives, but they could not provide the same opportunities for their children. People had to develop new strategies to help young adults achieve financial self-sufficiency. The lack of other high-paying jobs with benefits in Hamilton during this period exacerbated this situation. Some young adults continued to live with their parents; others returned home after attempting to live independently. Studies such as ours show that more and more people in Canada are under pressure to provide more caregiving for themselves and those close to them at a time when they are also working harder in less secure circumstances.

Here we present two new case studies that demonstrate how the caregiving crisis has developed. The first explores changing patterns of social reproduction among farm families. The second shows what happens to people whose livelihood is based on paid employment but whose income is no longer sufficient to support their households.

The Farm Family Study (1940–2005)

Changes in the global economy with respect to the production, marketing, and consumption of food have directly affected how farm families in Saskatchewan organize their lives (Diaz, Jaffe, and Sterling 2003; Epp and Whitson 2001). Research on farm families shows the indispensable nature of women's work to family survival (Shaver 1990). While men do most of the field work and women do most of the domestic labour (Silver 2001), there is a growing reliance on waged or salaried incomes for both women and men (Haymes 1999; Kubik 2004). June Corman's longitudinal study (1940 to 2005), based on archival data, participant observation, and in-depth interviews conducted in 2004 and 2005, involves neighbouring farms within a bounded area of southern Saskatchewan and illuminates the complicated relationship between income-generating work and domestic labour. In response to the complex and changing economics of

agriculture, these contemporary farm families employed diverse strategies to take up and stay in farming, to make a living, and to provide
care for each other.

The vast majority of the people who took these homesteads between
1900 and 1910 were Protestants from England and Scotland, some via
Ontario, because homestead recruitment strategies guaranteed that
central and northern Europeans were given preference. Over the next
three generations, the farm men married women of similar backgrounds. The generation of farm operators who established their
farms during the 1940s and 1950s were sons of farmers. Moving
directly from the care of their mothers to the care of their wives, these
men never lived on their own. At marriage, a man and his wife either
lived with the man's parents or moved into a small house within sight
of his parents on their land. Women were well prepared for the specific labours associated with farm living because the majority of them
had apprenticed as children by growing up in farm families.

Even as late as the 1960s, all the households in the study were
remarkably homogenous ethnically and in social-class terms. These
families were involved in grain or mixed grain and livestock operations
and lived in farm yards, and all the land was owner operated with the
exception of one farm, rented to a tenant. None of the women had
paid help, and the men tried to avoid paying for farm labour because
it depleted their cash reserves. All the men and women worked
full-time on the farm; none had paid employment. The neighbouring
families formed a strong community, institutionally supported by the
neighbourhood-run rural United Church, socials at the country
school (converted into a community centre in 1960), a collectively
maintained curling rink, and a community-owned well (Corman
2003). The children all rode on the same bus to attend school in the
local town.

A clearly gendered division of labour characterized each of the
neighbouring farm families. The importance of generating an income
and the assignment of men to this priority labour meant that women
actively tried to free their husbands and sons for field work by doing
barnyard chores, running errands, doing housework, gardening, and
caring for family members. Despite women's obligations in the field or
at the barn, their husbands rarely assisted with shopping, housework,
or food preparation. Women grew and preserved as much food as possible and, through this self-provisioning, reduced costs and thereby
facilitated the reinvestment of farm profits into land payments and
machinery. Farm women and girls also served as a reserve labour
force, participating directly in the production of agricultural commodities when needed, especially when their husbands and fathers farmed

without the assistance of other male kin. In all these ways, women's labour on the farm contributed to its sustainability in the context of low returns on investment. It also contributed to low grocery prices, which were advantageous to consumers. Cheap food also reduced labour costs for employers. Thus, while domestic labour by urban women reproduced labour power on a daily and intergenerational basis, labour by farm women indirectly subsidized the costs of that reproduction.

Children fit into the rhythm of the farm in gendered ways, and sexual divisions of labour were set by example. Girls' participation in cleaning, gardening, and meal preparation often resulted in a pointed compliment when they baked a favourite dessert: "You'll make some young farmer a good wife." Instead of learning domestic skills, boys worked alongside their fathers in the workshop, barn, pastures, and fields. Boys were never expected to do the dishes by their mothers, fathers, or sisters. Even in families without daughters, boys did not do "mother's work." Although there were rarely exceptions to the gendered pattern of work for the boys, girls were involved in select types of "father's work" even if they had brothers. At a young age, most boys and girls learned to clear stones from the fields, scour the old grain out of wooden granaries, and build stacks of over a thousand bales. Parents imparted the knowledge necessary so that children could assist them, their daughters would make good farmwives, and their sons could farm. Of the eighty children born into these families between 1940 and 1965, twenty-three (four females and nineteen males) attempted to farm; sixteen survived. The majority of these had established themselves on land within the community, although some men had bought other land because of a shortage near their parents' land and some women had married men with land elsewhere.

This third generation, who started farming in this community between 1962 and 1982, relied on support from their parents because of the huge investment in capital required to buy land and equipment. For five young operators, however, parental assistance was not enough to overcome poor crops, low grain prices, health issues, and management problems, and they failed to establish viable farms.

By 2005, only twelve farm families still lived in the area, all but one descended from the earlier generation. Eight third-generation resident farm operators were under the age of sixty, and the four second-generation farm operators were over sixty-five. One farm operator lived on a farm out of the district, and another five farm operators lived in urban centres and commuted to farm. The twelve resident farm families represent a precipitous drop from the thirty-four farm families in the 1950s and seventy-eight homesteads in 1913. The decline in the number of farm operators in this area mirrored provincial trends, the numbers dropping from a high of 140,000 in 1936 to 94,000 in 1961 and then to 50,500 in 2001 (Warnock 2004, 141). Fewer families farming more land is the direct consequence of the harsh market conditions facing prairie food producers. Because the price of grain does not rise proportionately with the costs of production, the main way to increase revenue was to produce more grain, either by planting more fields, increasing the application of fertilizer, or switching to a more rewarding crop.

Given the fragile position of Saskatchewan farmers in the global grain market by the late twentieth century, households had to find other sources of income to support themselves and to keep the farm in operation. In the 1950s, 1960s, and 1970s, their parents had responded to low returns by diversifying into livestock and intensifying domestic labour (e.g., doing more self-provisioning), but such a response was no longer sufficient. For this third generation, the family farm strategy, where both women and men lived and worked on the farm, was not financially viable. In 2004 a farmer in his forties expressed regret: "I want to farm the way my parents did. They only planted wheat and sold it through the Wheat Board. They hardly used fertilizer. Wild oats, wild mustard, and grasshoppers were the main problems. And best of all, my father got a reasonable price for his wheat. Neither he nor my mother had to scramble around working off the farm."

By 2005, people with economic ties to the land developed many diverse strategies to make a living. Some men owned a farm but lived in the city and rented it to others; others lived in urban centres with their families and drove out to farm. Where families lived on the farm, the women often drove to town to work at paid jobs. While these were farm-based families, the women's lack of participation in farm-related work, either directly in the fields or indirectly through self-provisioning, decreased the relevancy of the family farm label. Another group of families lived on their farm land but rented out their fields. In addition to all these various types of farm-related families, there were other families who owned and lived in farmhouses but did not own farm land, relying for their income on waged employment. The diversity of the material circumstances of the people living in close proximity was striking in comparison to the similar circumstances of the people who lived in these farm yards from the 1940s through the 1960s.

The ways that women contributed to these cash-hungry farms had changed remarkably for women married to the generation of farmers who had entered farming between 1962 and 1982. Earning an income by taking paid employment replaced self-provisioning and assisting the men with agricultural production. Commenting on his situation, a forty-year-old man with three children lamented, "I can't support my family on my farm's income. My wife has to earn money." In addition to the economic benefits of employment, this generation of women also enjoyed social and personal advantages. Earning an income positioned women to have more autonomy over personal and household purchases. They did not have to negotiate with their husbands about how much farm income was available for new furniture or clothing. The shift in women's energy from self-provisioning to paid employment moved farm families into the consumer marketplace.

The activities of children living on farms after the late 1970s has also changed. The highly mechanized nature of farm work means that young children now have fewer responsibilities and are less likely to be involved in farm work. Moreover, families are having few children. The reduced number of families had a total of only eighteen children – fourteen girls and four boys – a sharp contrast to the eighty children raised by the previous generation. Although girls were called upon to assist their fathers if other male kin were not available, none of these families expected their daughters to take over the farm. Two of the four young men had established themselves in other forms of employment. Only one young man was farming with his father, and the remaining potential male farmer was only three years old. If this pattern is typical throughout the province and fewer children are gaining the knowledge to farm, a potential crisis for the reproduction of farm operators and farm labour lies ahead.

The strategies that these farm families adopted to earn an income had direct consequences for the possibilities afforded family members to divide the tasks associated with domestic labour and caring for each other. When both women and men earned money, the prerogatives associated with the traditional male responsibility for generating the income were somewhat disrupted, and, in turn, there was an increased possibility of the blurring of the boundaries that associate women with domestic labour. Women with paid employment were not home to prepare lunch for their husbands, run household errands, or care for young children. Rather than adapting to the needs of the agricultural enterprise, their employment scheduled their lives.

Caregiving became a problematic and charged issue. Some husbands tentatively, and in some cases with resistance, began to fill the vacuum left by their wives as they left for their jobs. Men's participation increased during the winter months, when some took over meal preparation and childcare. This shift was more likely if they had lived alone prior to marriage and if their wives had moved into a home that they had previously maintained. By 2004, some of the elderly farm men of the second generation had also made an effort to assist their wives or to care for grandchildren, but other men of this generation never made the adaptation to domestic work. Their reluctance was jokingly referred to as "man power."

By 2005, the forms of caregiving between generations had become complicated and were often tied to the economic arrangements that bound families together. During the 1950s and 1960s, the elder generation of farm women lived in close proximity to their sons and their families and were thus available to tend young children. In turn, the younger farm women could provide services to aged parents-in-law. As the homesteaders aged and the population of young people declined, a community group responded by building an inexpensive and excellent seniors' complex with three levels of care. The elder generation of homesteaders eventually moved to this facility or other urban centres, vacating their farmhouses for the use of one of their children but not necessarily selling the land.

Maintaining ownership of the land was an attractive option for the second generation who began farming in the 1940s and 1950s. Ownership structured relevancy into their senior years, keeping them actively interested in the prosperity of their farm and the agricultural sector. They enjoyed their identity as farmers. When asked why an eighty-five-year-old man who now lived two hundred kilometres from his land and had not farmed it in years still retained ownership, his friend, shocked at the question, replied, "He is not ready to die yet." In addition, a structured interaction with sons, wives, and grandchildren was guaranteed through the cooperative economic arrangements that would be entailed in the farmers retaining ownership. Economic relationships did not lead to co-residential arrangements. None of the elder generation of farm women or men lived with their adult children, and they did not foresee this circumstance. Many second-generation farm men and women had moved into the local town, close to the people they had known all their lives, and those remaining on the farm envisioned a similar future.

By 2005, the previously clear-cut distinction between farmers and their families and urban wage-reliant households was not so sharp. In the earlier period, farms were family farms and only farm families lived in farm yards, planted the seeds, and harvested the grain. Living in the country, having title to land, growing commodities for sale, and not participating in the paid labour force differentiated farm families from urban families, who relied on wages or salaries to make a living.

Farming in the age of neo-liberal government and corporate policies had propelled many farm-based people into the paid workforce, forcing them to develop new routines for doing domestic labour and especially for caregiving. Women who had full-time employment organized their lives around the obligations of their employment and to a much lesser extent around the seasonally based farm labours of their husbands. The rhythms of their children's lives were also orchestrated according to these employment patterns. Having developed a reliance on paid employment, these families were now exposed not only to the vulnerabilities of farming, but also to job uncertainties associated with economic downturns and decreased profits.

The Intergenerational Family Support Study (1999–2002)

Between 1999 and 2002, Meg Luxton interviewed forty-eight people from twenty-one households in Toronto in which adult children and parents were cohabiting because at least one of them lacked enough money to sustain their own household.[2] All of them agreed that parents and children should take care of each other, providing material and emotional support. However, most of them also firmly believed that adult children and parents should live separately, in their own homes, if at all possible. As they struggled to reconcile their various and sometimes contradictory beliefs and to negotiate their cohabiting relationships, most of them found that their domestic labour and especially their caregiving practices were challenging and often strained. Their experiences offer insight into the ways in which family relationships can be mobilized to help people in crisis, while also revealing some of the deeply entrenched dynamics of household work and caregiving that often undermine people's capacities to provide care for each other.

The vast majority of people in Canada live either in nuclear families or alone. Between 1971 and 1991, only 3 per cent of the population living in private households lived with other relatives (Ghalam 1996, 20). In the 1990s, in response to both economic restructuring and cuts to social services, the number of people cohabiting with other relatives increased. While the percentage of young people between the ages of 25 and 29 who still live in their parents' home more than doubled, from 15 per cent of men and 8.3 per cent of women in 1981 to 29 per cent of men and 19 per cent of women in 2001, the prevailing practice continues to be that young adults form their own households sometime in their late twenties or early thirties, either with a partner or on their own (Statistics Canada 2003c, 7). Independent household formation is an important marker of the transition to adulthood.

For parents, the "empty nest" signals the end of active parenting and typically implies that parents no longer have regular financial obligations to their children, although, of course, many parents remain actively involved in their children's lives and continue to provide financial support, which culminates in an inheritance. However, as parents age, they may become less able to maintain their own home; one of their options is to move in with their children. Older men without a partner have been more likely to move in with their children than older women without partners, who were more likely to live on their own. Between 1981 and 2001, 13 per cent of men aged 65 or older lived with their children; women's patterns of residing with their children increased from 8.9 per cent in 1981 to 12 per cent in 2001. However, the majority of people over 65 live either with a spouse or partner or on their own (Statistics Canada 2003c, 6). Clearly, the dominant and preferred pattern of household formation continues to be either the nuclear family or living alone.

The ability to form and maintain an independent household depends primarily on access to an income, sufficient to meet household expenses, through one's own labour, from a relationship with a partner who is willing and able to provide financial support, or from a combination of both. In the 1990s, changes in the labour market and the impact of neo-liberal policies undercut standards of living for many working people, making it harder for them to maintain independent households. This was most obvious among young people. In 1991, 33 per cent of people between 20 and 29 lived with their parents, increasing to 39 per cent in 1996 and to 41 per cent in 2001 (Statistics Canada 2003b, 6). However, the decline in standards of living affected older people as well. Many workers either lost their jobs or were forced to take jobs that paid less and had fewer benefits. The numbers of homeless people increased dramatically in this period, and they included many families with children. As many individuals found themselves unable to maintain their households in a context where state supports were reduced or unavailable, they turned to relatives for support and care.

In each of the households in this study, financial need on the part of at least one person was the primary motivation. These financially strapped people said that they were facing dire straits and would be close to living on the street or seeking welfare services were family cohabiting not an option. Their financial difficulties were caused by layoffs (11), by job loss due to illness (2), by the long-term impact of low-income jobs (4), by the end of a marriage and the resulting loss of the spouse's income (9), by the loss of resources following a divorce settlement (5), or by some combination thereof. In some cases, there were other factors in addition to financial need. Four women who had young children asked their mothers to move in to help with childcare.

Cohabitation was more likely when people were single; in 16 of the 21 households, both parties were single at the time, although most had previously lived with a partner.

The circumstances that produced each household were unique, but the following example shows how several factors interacted. A woman widowed for many years was forced to retire at 65 from her minimum-wage job as an office cleaner. While her house was paid for, she did not have enough income to pay the monthly expenses. She tried getting another job, but after five months she was discouraged and running out of money, having exhausted her savings. She applied for welfare but believed she would have to sell her house to get it. Her son, aged 42, had recently ended a twelve-year marriage. He was employed by a temporary agency as a mechanic, not making very much money and paying support to his wife. He was living in a rented apartment, but threatened rent increases would mean he would have to either go back to court to get his payments lowered or find a cheaper apartment. His mother asked him to move in with her and pay her a lower rent each month. The arrangement was financially beneficial for both of them.

Family members also chose to live together in part because they thought they could make a comfortable home together. They all expected to provide and receive material and emotional support. As one man said, "I imagined something like the good times from my childhood and my marriage, a friendly, happy home where I would enjoy nice meals, good conversation. There'd be someone to look after me if I was sick or feeling miserable. I imagined me cooking nice meals for the both of us" (H5). A mother expressed similar dreams and her despair at the outcome: "I thought it would be wonderful. We could take care of each other. I wouldn't be so lonely, there would be someone there who loves me and I feel so good caring for him. But it doesn't work like that. Him and me are always … well, let's just say it's a disaster and now we are both trapped" (H2).

Household and caring labour are one of the measures by which people assess the quality of their relationship and express their love for each other. A mother who lived with her daughter explained: "It isn't easy but I think we have worked it out well. We have a little friendly competition going, you see, about who can make the nicest dinner. We take turns and it's, like, a way of saying, "I love you" to make the table look pretty and the food taste good. She trumped me last week when she made my favourite cake for dessert! We never eat dessert but last week, when she brought it out, she was so pleased and I felt so good" (H15).

While most insisted that they could live together because they loved each other, they also expressed surprise and dismay that cohabiting proved to be more difficult and more threatening than any of them had imagined. Already vulnerable because of the circumstances that forced them to live together, many were shocked by the damage that cohabiting imposed on their relationships. As one woman observed, "I find myself being careful instead of caring. I think living together is destroying our relations" (H9). While the family members' interpersonal dynamics were central, several social factors undermined their caring impulses, particularly the hegemony of gender and familial ideologies that shape both expectations and material circumstances and their lack of alternatives when family responsibilities became unduly strained.

Most of the people interviewed identified problems with how household labour was divided between or among household members, whose standards apply, and how to handle disputes. While these issues confront any people who live together, parents and children found themselves entangled both by old patterns established when the children were young and by their sense that the only models available were couples. A mother living with her son described the tensions: "It's so weird. We lived together all his growing up, and I just assumed it would be easy to pick up where we left off, so to speak. And anyway, he and his wife shared housework. He's a man who knows how to do housework and cooking and all that. Why wouldn't it be easy? But it isn't. I'm in a constant state of rage and have no idea what to do. It feels like such a man/woman thing, you know like men just don't get it – but he's my son" (H1). Her son offered his perspective: "I really like my mom; we've always got along. And you know, my wife and I, we didn't fight over the house stuff – not after the first year or so. But it seems Mom and I – we don't know how to do it. You know what I think? I think it's like people do housework and cooking and shopping and that with their wife or husband and it's all tied up in their marriage and we don't know how to do it differently" (H1).

This mother's sense of how gendered such negotiations are and her son's claim that household divisions of labour are intimately associated with marriage and less easily negotiated in other relationships were both affirmed by others. Unlike relations between spouses or between parents and young children, which are recognized as important and complex, are widely discussed in popular culture, and are supported by a range of legal and social structures, adult intergenerational relations are largely ignored. The tensions and conflicts inherent in household and caring work are intensified for people living in unconventional households because there is so little support. Several people shared this woman's view: "I got way more support when I talked about how things were with my husband. When I talk about [how things are] with my kids, my friends laugh. They insist that it's easy to get along with kids. My neighbour even said I should quit complaining because every mother longs to have her kids with her. No one takes me seriously when I say this is killing me" (H23).

Some people interviewed pointed out how even architecture is predicated on the assumption of a couple and children. Most housing offers a "master bedroom," often with an en suite bathroom, and smaller bedrooms with a shared bathroom providing little privacy. One man noted: "I never thought, but it's made me celibate. I can't have a woman here when my mother can hear everything through the walls" (H1). A daughter, in describing why she could share with her mother, confirmed his point: "I have this cool apartment with room. She was struggling so I thought, 'Why not?' When I think of how much she sacrificed for me and my brother, it's the least I can do, and besides, the guy I'm seeing has a great place so I can always go there" (H11).

Perhaps the most damaging factor was that these people had no other choices. Even when cohabiting became strained, their sense of kin-based obligation and responsibility forced them to remain in situations far longer than the relationships could sustain. A mother explained: "It's easier to break up a bad marriage. Children are for life and so we are stuck, hating it but what choices have we?" (H14). A father agreed: "We don't like it but what can you do? You can't let your kids live on the streets" (H23). However, six months later, he explained that relations had deteriorated so badly that he had "turfed them out" one night and hadn't spoken to them since. His experience, repeated in several other households, suggests that people are often well disposed to help out their kin, but there are limits to how much strain even parent-child relations can sustain.

CONCLUSION

The feminist analysis of the centrality of domestic labour to social reproduction offers new ways of understanding work and labour, revealing the ways in which the operations of capitalist economies rely on women's unpaid and unrecognized domestic labour. In particular, advocates of neo-liberalism, which has dominated international business and government agendas for the last several decades, favour a relatively unregulated market economy that puts many people at risk, arguing that it is up to individuals and their families to cope. The unstated assumption of neo-liberalism is that families, meaning women, will intensify their own labour and reduce their standards of living to get by in hard times. Feminist research shows both the extent to which women and men do struggle to provide for themselves and their families and the negative costs such individualized struggles impose on those families and on the society as a whole. Current global economic trends and the lack of effective government policies to mediate their effects have led to crises for various sectors of the population that are widespread enough to disrupt patterns of social reproduction. The challenge posed by such an analysis is to determine what alternative forms of social organization could encourage respect for and give value to unpaid household and caregiving work and create conditions that would foster people's willingness and ability both to help each other and to support state responsibility for the well-being of the population.

NOTES

Authors' Note: We acknowledge the contributions of Vivian Shalla, Wally Clement, and the anonymous reviewers, as well as those of Kate Bezanson, Judith Blackwell, and Ana Isla.

1 The birth rate, as measured in 2002, dropped to 10.5 live births for every 1,000 population, the lowest since vital statistics began to be produced nationally in 1921. The rate represents a drop of 25.4 per cent in the last ten years alone (see www.lifesite.net/ldn/2002/mar/020306.html).

2 This study is part of a project funded by SSHRC grant #410-94-1502. The people interviewed included 22 parents (20 women and 2 men); 22 adult children (13 men and 9 women); and 4 people who were spouses of children (3 women and 1 man). The parents ranged in age from 52 to 83; the median age was 62.5. The children and their spouses ranged in age from 22 to 59; the median age was 41.5. They came from a variety of ethnic and racial backgrounds: Canadian 8, American 12, Caribbean 8, British/Irish 3, southern Europe 4, eastern Europe 7, East Africa 4, and Chinese 2. All were working class or lower middle class.

REFERENCES

Armstrong, Pat, and Hugh Armstrong. 1994. *The double ghetto: Canadian women and their segregated work.* 3rd ed. Toronto: McClelland and Stewart

Barrett, Michele, and Mary McIntosh. 1982. *The anti-social family.* London: Verso

Bittman, Michael. 2002. The visible and the hidden: States, markets and non-market activity. Unpublished PhD thesis, School of Social Science and Planning, Faculty of the Constructed Environment, RMIT University, Melbourne, Australia

Bourgeault, Ron. 1983. The development of capitalism and the subjugation of native women in northern Canada. *Alternate Routes* 6:109–40

Caulfield Davis, Mina. 1974. Imperialism, the family and cultures of resistance. *Socialist Revolution* 20 (October): 67–85

Census and Statistics Office. 1915. *Fifth census of Canada, 1911.* Vol. 6: *Occupations of the people.* Ottawa: J. de L. Tache, Printer to the King's Most Excellent Majesty

Census of Canada. 1893. *1890–91.* Vol. 2. Ottawa: E. Dawson, Printer to the Queen's Most Excellent Majesty

Chandler, William. 1994. The value of household work in Canada, 1992. In *Canadian economic observer.* Catalogue no. 11-010 (April): 3.1–3.9. Ottawa: Statistics Canada

Clement, Wallace, and John Myles. 1994. *Relations of ruling: Class and gender in postindustrial societies.* Montreal: McGill-Queen's University Press

Cohen, Marjorie. 1997. What women should know about economic fundamentalism. *Atlantis: A Women's Studies Journal* 21 (2) (Spring/Summer)

Corman, June. 2003. From rural municipality to school district to community: Transitions in rural Saskatchewan. In *The trajectories of rural life: New perspectives on rural Canada,* edited by R. Blake and A. Nurse, 111–21. Regina: Canadian Plains Research Centre, University of Regina

Coward, Rosalind. 1987. *Beyond patriarchy.* Oxford: Oxford University Press

Cunningham, Frank. 1994. *The real world of democracy revisited and other essays on democracy and socialism.* Atlantis Highlands, N.J.: Humanities Press

Davis, Angela. 1981. *Women, race and class.* New York: Random House

Davis, F. 1988. *The social, economic and legal equality of Saskatchewan farm women.* Saskatoon: Women's Legal Education and Action Fund

Dempsey, Ken. 1997. Women's perception of fairness and the persistence of an unequal division of housework. *Family Matters,* Spring–Summer, 15

– 1999. Attempting to explain women's perceptions of their fairness of the division of housework. *Journal of Family Studies,* April, 3–24

de Wolff, Alice. 2003. *Bargaining for work and life.* Toronto: Ontario Federation of Labour

Diaz, Harry P., Joann Jaffe, and Robert Sterling, eds. 2003. *Farm communities at the crossroads: Challenge and resistance.* Regina: Canadian Plains Research Centre

Epp, Roger, and Dave Whitson, eds. 2001. *Writing off the rural West: Globalization, governments, and the transformations of rural communities.* Edmonton: University of Alberta Press

Folbre, Nancy. 1991. The unproductive housewife: Her evolution in nineteenth century thought. *Signs* 16 (3): 463–84 (Spring)

Fox, Bonnie. 2001. The formative years: How parenthood creates gender. *Canadian Review of Sociology and Anthropology* 38 (4): 373–91

Friedan, Betty. 1963. *The feminine mystique.* New York: W.W. Norton and Co.

Friendly, Martha, and Donna Lero. 2002. *Social inclusion through early childhood education and care.* Perspectives on Social Inclusion Working Papers Series. Toronto: Laidlaw Foundation

Gardiner, Jean. 1997. *Gender, care and economics.* London: Macmillan Press

Ghalam, Nancy Zukewich. 1996. Living with relatives. In *Canadian social trends.* Catalogue no. 11-008-XPE (Autumn): 20–4. Ottawa: Statistics Canada

Ghorayshi, Parvin. 1989. The indispensable nature of wives' work for the farm family enterprise. *Canadian Review of Sociology and Anthropology* 26 (4): 571–95

Gill, Stephen, and Isabella Bakker, eds. 2003. *Power, production and social reproduction: Human in/security in the global political economy.* London: Palgrave Macmillan

Grant, Karen, Carol Amaratunga, Pat Armstrong, Madeline Boscoe, Ann Pederson, and Kay Willson, eds. 2004. *Caring for/Caring about women, home care, and unpaid caregiving.* Aurora, Ont.: Garamond Press

Hayden, Delores. 1981. *The grand domestic revolution: A history of feminist designs for American homes, neighborhoods, and cities.* Cambridge, Mass.: MIT Press

Haymes, Greg. 1999. Farm women head to work off the farm – more or less. In *Canadian agriculture at a glance.* Catalogue no. 96-325-XPB: 271–5. Ottawa: Statistics Canada

Heitlinger, Alena. 1979. *Women and state socialism: Sex inequality in the Soviet Union and Czechoslovakia.* Montreal and Kingston: McGill-Queen's University Press

Kubik, Wendee. 2004. The changing roles of farm women and the consequences for their health, well-being, and quality of life. Doctoral thesis, University of Regina

Luxton, Meg. 1980. *More than a labour of love: Three generations of women's work in the home.* Toronto: Women's Press

– 1983. Conceptualizing "women" in anthropology and sociology. In *Knowledge reconsidered: A feminist overview.* Canadian Research Institute for the Advancement of Women papers. Ottawa

– 1997. Feminism and families. In *Feminism and families: Critical policies and changing practices,* edited by Meg Luxton, 10–26. Halifax: Fernwood Publishing

– 2004. Family responsibilities: The politics of love and care. In *Globalization, gender, economics and work,* edited by Linda Lucas. Kampala: Fountain Press

Luxton, Meg, and June Corman. 2001. *Getting by in hard times: Gendered labour at home and on the job.* Toronto: University of Toronto Press

Luxton, Meg, and Leah Vosko. 1998. Where women's efforts count: The 1996 census campaign and family politics in Canada. *Studies in Political Economy* 56 (Summer): 49–81

McMahon, Anthony. 1999. *Taking care of men: Sexual politics in the public mind.* Cambridge: Cambridge University Press

Mandell, Nancy. 2005. Making families: Gender, economics, sexuality, and race. In *Feminist issues race, class, and sexuality*, edited by Nancy Mandell, 188–225. 4th ed. Toronto: Pearson, Prentice Hall

Marshall, Alfred. [1890] 1959. *Principles of economics* London: Macmillan

Maushart, Susan. 2002. *Wifework: What marriage really means for women.* London: Bloomsbury Publishing

Mill, John Stuart, and Harriet Taylor Mill. 1983. *The subjection of women* (1869) and *The enfranchisement of women* (1851). London: Virago

NAC (National Action Committee on the Status of Women). 1995. *A decade of deterioration in the status of women in Canada.* Toronto: NAC

Oakley, Ann. 1974. *The sociology of housework.* New York: Pantheon

Picchio, Antonella. 1992. *Social reproduction: The political economy of the labour market.* Cambridge: Cambridge University Press

Pigou, A.C. 1929. *The economics of welfare.* London: Macmillan

Rowbotham, Sheila. 1972. *Women, resistance and revolution.* London: Penguin

Seccombe, Wally. 1992. *A millennium of family change: Feudalism to capitalism in northwestern Europe.* London: Verso

– 1993. *Weathering the storm: Working-class families from the Industrial Revolution to the fertility decline.* London: Verso

Shaver, F.M. 1990. Women, work and transformations in agricultural production. *Canadian Review of Sociology and Anthropology* 27 (3): 341–56

Silver, Cynthia. 2001. From sun-up to sundown: Work patterns of farming couples. *Canadian Social Trends,* Summer, 12–15

Statistics Canada. 2000. *Women in Canada 2000: A gender-based statistical report.* Ottawa: Industry Canada

– 2003a. *Annual demographic statistics, 2003.* Catalogue no. 91-213. Ottawa

– 2003b. *Census of Canada 2001.* Ottawa: Ministry of Industry, Science and Technology. Available at www12.statcan.ca/english/census01/products/analytic/companion/paid/canada.cfm.

– 2003c. *Profile of Canadian families and households: Diversification continues, 2001 Census.* Catalogue no. 96F0030XIE2001003: Ottawa: Statistics Canada

Taylor, Barbara. 1983. *Eve and the new Jerusalem: Socialism and feminism in the nineteenth century.* London: Virago

Thompson, William. [1825] 1983. *Appeal of one half of the human race, women, against the pretensions of the other half, men, to retain them in political and thence in civil and domestic slavery.* London: Virago

UNDP (United Nations Development Programme). 1995. *Human development report.* New York and Oxford: Oxford University Press

Urdang, Stephanie. 1989. *And still they dance: Women, war, and the struggle for change in Mozambique.* New York: Monthly Review Press

Ursel, Jane. 1992. *Private lives, public policy: 100 years of state intervention in the family.* Toronto: Women's Press

Waring, Marilyn. 1988. *If women counted: A new feminist economics.* San Francisco: Harper Collins

Warnock, John. 2004. *Saskatchewan: The roots of discontent and protest.* Montreal: Black Rose Books

Wiebe Nettie. 1995. Farm women: Cultivating hope and sowing change. In *Changing Methods: Feminists Transforming Practice,* edited by Sandra Burt and Lorraine Code. Peterborough: Broadview Press

10

Blurring the Distinction between Public and Private Spheres: The Commodification of Household Work – Gender, Class, Community, and Global Dimensions

NORENE PUPO AND ANN DUFFY

With the rapid transformations in the paid labour force and market economy over the past fifty years, Canadian households[1] have been revolutionized. In the process, the notion of "home" as a haven where mothers worked privately to meet their families' personal, social, and emotional needs while breadwinner fathers provided them with the means to do so has increasingly faded into rhetoric. In the best of instances, the 1950s family household was indeed a sanctuary – safe and comforting – where personal lives were played out in privacy and where the surrounding neighbourhood provided opportunities to socialize and relax among friends, relatives, and co-workers and, in many instances, to exchange goods and services. Without romanticizing the support and camaraderie experienced within postwar households or neighbourhoods, we clearly must acknowledge that communities have changed both structurally and socially. Profound upheavals in the globalizing labour market now demand that many Canadians yield daily to numerous work-related pressures, with the result that they spend little time in their communities or getting to know their neighbours. Today, many undertake long hours of work, multiple jobs, and irregular schedules, spend extra time commuting to work, juggle family responsibilities with work-related roles, and often live great distances from extended family and friends. Under these circumstances, households have been reorganized, communities have been reshaped, and, necessarily, not only has the interpenetration of public and private spheres[2] been intensified, but the notion of a private, non-monetarized, non-work space in our lives has been further eroded.

Over the last thirty years, major shifts within the economy – the demise of manufacturing and primary industry, the parallel growth in the service sector, the process of globalization, and the consequent reshaping of the state and social programs – have coalesced with major social trends – the increased labour force participation of women, particularly married women with children, the growth in the number of dual-earner families, and transformations in urban processes, family structures, and community life. Taken together these historical shifts have contributed to the repositioning of the household within the market economy. In many respects, this reshaping of the family and household reflects and reinforces structures of work within the new economy. These developments since the "happy days" of the 1950s have contributed not only to the now public recognition of the work of the household, blurring the distinction between public and private spheres, but also to alterations in the cultural understanding of community life, the transformation of family work, and the commodification or formalization of a growing number of spheres of private life. Moreover, these contextual developments have become integral to the negotiations within the household between partners over the division of labour, just as they are embedded in public concerns over the restructuring of social programs, the fraying of the social safety net, and the formal and informal privatization of caring and other social processes. Finally, these changes in the relationship between public and private and between home and work have reflected and reinforced the growing social inequalities that characterize Canada along with other industrialized countries.

In this chapter, we examine transformations in the nature and structure of household task arrangements[3] and the complex interrelationships among Canadian households, the marketplace, and the community. In particular, we consider the tendency for Canadian households to interface with the formal market economy more directly, more frequently, and in more complex ways for matters that previous generations identified as personal and outside the realm of the market. We examine factors affecting households' interconnection with the broader community and marketplace, review trends in paid work affecting family and household work, and consider ways in which structural change within the economy has affected the household, particularly with respect to gender. We also discuss the expansion of family work and the commercialization of many areas of family life, particularly those areas involving children. We argue that in the changing context of community, now characterized by disconnections to the extended family and the neighbourhood, individual households may be viewed as pillars with weakened local links and increasingly strong connections to a corporatized world. While access to a market-place for household services has modestly eased the burden of domestic responsibility and labour, especially for women, it has contributed to financial, social, and competitive pressures within the household. Buying household services often is neither time- nor labour-saving.

THE COMMODIFICATION OF HOUSEHOLD WORK: CONTRADICTIONS

Commodification refers to the process by which capitalists buy labour power in exchange for wages or salaries, and *commodification of household work* refers to the process of compartmentalizing or packaging particular aspects of domestic work and buying suitable labour to do this work.[4] Various forms of household work are commodified, but we refer here mainly to housework (for example, cleaning, repair, and food preparation) and carework (for example, childcare, elder care, care of persons with disabilities, and teaching children). Service may be purchased directly from the individual provider, as is often the case in hiring a nanny, or from a company, such as Molly Maid. In these sit-uations, the service providers come into the home to perform work that is otherwise unwaged. Householders may also purchase labour that is embedded within the products they buy, as, for example, in take-away meals (purchased and prepared at restaurants by service workers) or in fully cooked frozen meals (prepared in factories and purchased at grocery stores). In other situations, services such as laun-dering and dry cleaning may be purchased or companies may be retained to run errands or perform such services as house-sitting or caring for pets. In many respects, commodification of the household represents a commodified life in which cultural commodities (for example, food, clothing, home decoration and arrangement) are reconstructed but without any genuine cultural meaning or sense of the past (Teeple 2000, 165; Hochschild 2003). Rather, individual households become an intrinsic part of a homogenized and commodi-fied global culture.

Given the diversity of products and processes that can be marketed to the household, it is not surprising to discover an ongoing and relentless search for new product ideas. Virtually every major appli-ance has been "improved" in recent decades – frost-free refrigerators, high-efficiency washing and drying machines, refrigerators with a built-in ice-maker, convection ovens that save time like microwaves but crispen food like conventional ovens, cordless irons, and so on. In addition, new lines of products have become essential home appliances – the leaf blower, snow blower, coffee maker, cappuccino maker, and so on. At the same time, various tasks (especially those that are particularly onerous or time-consuming) are commodified as services – childcare,[5] snow removal, lawn-care services, child-proofing the home, carpet and upholstery cleaning, de-cluttering (organizing) the home, housecleaning after catastrophic floods, and so on. Given the time-consuming and continuous demands of meal preparation, it is understandable that numerous lines of time-saving products have been introduced; most major supermarkets, for example, provide the elements of a hot and ready cooked meal on a daily basis. Similarly, as noted above, meal options are available in ever-increasing variety in the frozen food section. There is also a growing diversity of fresh meal options that are partially or completely prepared for the consumer. Of course, restaurants and fast-food chains are providing an increasingly popular alternative to home food preparation while also constituting a location for formal or informal socializing. In the process, not only the meal preparation but also the cleaning and maintenance work can be reduced or eliminated.

The dramatic growth in various supercentres provides the consumer with ever more diverse optional on-site services. Grocery shopping can be combined with dropping off the dry cleaning, picking up a prescription, buying flowers at the florist, or purchasing any kind of household or clothing product. Many centres offer drop-off childcare services, workout gyms for women, or community meeting spaces.[6] In addition, many supercentres are in close proximity to big box stores so that the consumer is able to conveniently combine a myriad of routine household purchases and activities with economic purchasing options. In this manner, going shopping entails an increasingly complex array of activities, and shopping centres occupy a more and more significant space (geographic and temporal) in personal and community lives.

While this ongoing commodification of domestic labour has a long history, it is the postwar period that we focus on here. With the emphasis on getting women back into the home in the post–World War II period, the role of the middle-class housewife as manager of the domestic sphere was glorified (the domestic goddess), as apparent in numerous articles in *Chatelaine, Good Housekeeping, Family Circle,* and other popular "women's" magazines. The housewife was typically the manager through whom most day-to-day decisions regarding domestic work, child raising, and home decoration (including the keeping up of appearances) were made. In the increasingly affluent 1950s and 1960s, the list of household activities grew. Even with the development of new so-called labour-saving appliances, there was always "more work for mother" (Cowan 1983). Through women's reproductive roles and the expansion of unwaged domestic work, capitalism flourished, "commodifying almost every aspect of life within the nation state" (Teeple 2000, 81), with newly developing service industries contributing to a new set of social relationships surrounding the "private" domestic sphere.

Since the 1970s, women's (especially, wives' and mothers') increased labour force participation, together with the shift towards a service economy, established new market relationships for household-related commodities and in the process negotiated new relationships between public and private spheres. In the course of the last several decades, many aspects of household work have been commodified and many householders have adopted an employment or contractual relationship with numerous service providers in and about the home. With considerable domestic work to do and less time available to do it, householders predictably looked to the marketplace for goods and services to substitute for household work. For example, contemporary families are spending more on restaurant meals (including drive-ins, canteens, cafeterias, and take-outs), a household expenditure that increased by about 10 per cent between 2000 and 2001 (*The Daily* [Statistics Canada], 11 December 2002). Similarly, more families are purchasing domestic help, with one in ten husband-wife families (especially affluent families, families with larger dwellings, families with children under age five, and families with employed wives or wives aged 60 or over) securing these services (*The Daily*, 26 August 2003).

Although there is considerable evidence of the commodification of household labour, it is important to note that there are converse pressures working simultaneously towards the decommodification of household work. The net result is felt particularly by women in the home, especially those in low-income households. Reductions in social services – notably education and health care – have meant that many women have been expected or required to take on tasks "formerly done by women for pay in the market" (Armstrong and Armstrong 2002, 49). Nona Glazer (1993, 6) uses the term *work transfer* to refer to this phenomenon – that is, when the labour of paid service workers, primarily women, is redistributed to unpaid women family members. Women, for example, increasingly find themselves responsible for care of elderly, sick, hospitalized, or family members with disabilities. The pressure of these responsibilities is, of course, much worse for those women whose households lack the financial resources to provide some respite (occasional paid support workers) from their work.

While the postwar period has seen a general escalation in consumerism and in households' specific involvement with the marketplace, it is important to note that the trend towards commodification is closely associated with the pressure towards decommodification; these two seemingly conflicting patterns are intricately related and both relate in large part to structural differences between the public and private sectors. Considering the Swedish experience, Anita Nyberg (2002) argues that from the 1970s to the 1990s, women gained greater economic independence from men, primarily because they became more self-reliant with respect to forming and maintaining households. Nyberg attributes women's autonomy to higher transfers, or decommodification, rather than to higher earnings in the labour market. If we take into account the decommodification or transferral of services, households' greater access to relatively cheap consumer goods, and the commodification of the domestic sphere, then we may suggest that when women (or men) engage in paid work, they may be able to maintain a level of self-sufficiency with respect to their household and family without the support of a partner/spouse and at arm's length from the state.[7] Barbara Ehrenreich (1983) made a very similar argument with regard to the commodification of domestic labour and men's new-found opportunities in the 1960s and 1970s to establish and maintain single-person/single-parent households through the purchasing of labour-saving products along with household services.

Recognizing the complexity of the interrelationships between the commodified and non-commodified spheres, Williams (2003) supports the notion that commodification is profoundly uneven, that in advanced economies there are non-profit-oriented monetarized exchanges, non-monetarized exchanges, and non-exchanged work – in other words, significant alternative spaces where the logic of commodification is missing. For example, it is interesting to note that the 1988 National Child Care Survey reported that almost one-third of the child sitters surveyed said that they provided their services for free and about two in five children were looked after by a relative, frequently a grandparent (*The Daily*, 26 April 2002). Williams points to Denmark, Finland, France, the United Kingdom, and the United States, for example, where unpaid work is occupying an increasing proportion of people's total working time. Marianna Pavlovskaya's (2004) examination of contemporary Moscow households (victims of considerable decommodification of household services) identifies the complex role played by non-cash-based and cashed-based activities in the formal and informal economies in piecing together the means of survival. In many Third World countries, non-monetarized economies (reciprocity networks and family and kinship strategies) may play an important (though often unrecognized) role in sustaining the household. Similarly, Guida Man (2004) reports similar use of agency among Chinese immigrant women in Canada who utilized family networks, formed their own professional organizations, and worked with grassroots advocacy services to respond to the decommodification of services that previously eased their integration into the community and into paid employment.

What is clear from these examples is that the dual and simultaneous processes of commodification and decommodification expose the contradictions inherent in an economy characterized by service work, high technology, vast differences between good and bad jobs, and wide variations in the scheduling and structures of work. Fiscal restraints and measures to reduce social costs, thrusting care and support work back into the home, allow economies to compete globally. Within this context, many households may operate outside the system, conducting non-exchanged work, non-monetarized exchanges, and non-profit-motivated monetary exchanges more often than the less well-to-do. Affluent populations may also participate in alternative economic activities, including do-it-yourself work and care work, as an act of resistance against the logic of commodification. For the well-to-do these activities are taken up on a "non-commodified basis more out of choice rather than economic necessity" (Williams 2003, 865).

Not only has commodification of household labour been countered by tendencies towards decommodification, but commodification itself has not resulted in less work time in the home or in more equitable gender relations within the family. As convincingly documented in the research literature, time-saving appliances in the household have not resulted in reduced unpaid household work or more equal gender relations (Bittman, Rice, and Wajcman 2004, 412).[8] Similarly, buying household services is often neither time-saving nor labour-saving. Overall, the availability of household services as commodities (for example, appliances) or as marketed services (for example, house cleaning) has contributed only marginally to Canadian households having more free time (see, for example, Silver and Crompton 2002). In many families, the commodification of household work has significantly reshaped men's and women's roles in the division of household work, but it has not changed how much time individuals spend on it or how much they do.

While there are diverse explanations for the failure of commodification to reduce the time obligations of households significantly, several important considerations should be noted. First, as some analysts have argued, time-savings result in labour being redeployed to meet higher standards of cleanliness, greater output, and new tasks (transporting children to after-school activities) (Cowan 1983). Second, increased consumption – larger homes, more clothing, special soaps – results in increased time burdens (Bittman, Rice, and Wajcman 2004). Finally, it must be acknowledged that household labour complexly intersects with important issues of identity. Being a "good" mother or father or being a "good" housekeeper may translate into a resistance (personal and/or cultural) to spending less time on home-related activities. In the prewar period, for example, there was considerable resistance to the introduction of instant coffee. The prevailing view, apparently, was that a good housekeeper would provide brewed coffee, while only a lazy individual would want to save time with the instant alternative. In short, despite the apparent market for goods and services that promise to reduce the time burden of household tasks and provide increased free time, there are countervailing cultural forces that resist any attempt to provide speedier, easier alternatives.

In short, commodification of household services may jeopardize important linkages between domestic labour and personal identities. In general terms, for example, the interest and time spent in shopping, and most importantly in the selections made, have been an intricate part of identity formation, particularly for women. This starts during the teenage years, with girls striking out on their own to select clothing or makeup, sometimes in reaction to their parents' preferences. Shopping is a determinant of identity not only for shoppers but also for their families (Communication Studies 1999). There are obvious difficulties in commodifying such tasks. Personal shoppers (individuals who purchase clothing for clients or gifts for clients and their friends and family) cannot carry out the job in the same way as consumers themselves, since they are not involved in the friendships or family relationships in the same way. Not surprisingly, the commodification of the shopping process has tended more towards alternatives to traditional shopping, such as Internet shopping, since identity formation and confirmation can still be envisioned within the process. The employment of home decorators occupies an interesting middle ground in that the selection of the appropriate home decorator and personal consultations with the decorator may still satisfy any identity-related concerns. Purchasing the services of personal shoppers has tended to remain within the spheres of the very affluent, for whom, presumably, issues of identity are less likely to be connected to the purchase of specific goods.

This contradiction between identity and the commodification of household tasks may be particularly marked in terms of gender and social class. A woman's identity as a mother is a kind of master identity that is presumed to take precedence over all aspects of her life, including her participation in the paid labour force. A good mother is someone who is "expected to be always there for her children," while a good father (unless he lays claim to being the primary caregiver) is not (Ridgeway and Correll 2004, 690, 695). Simply living up to her status as good mother compels a woman to respond clearly to household time demands, not try to elude them. While this identity may not be inconsistent with participation in the paid labour force (and, indeed, the stay-at-home mother may be negatively portrayed as confused, overwhelmed, and interested only in superficial topics), it does imply an ongoing availability for domestic labour demands (Johnston and Swanson 2003).

Further, to the degree to which social class defines the parameters of mother, father, or housekeeper, there may be intersecting pressures that provide intensified time commitments. The pressure is not simply to ensure that tasks are completed – for example, that the children are bathed, fed, and sent to school – rather there has long been an intertwining obligation to ensure that these tasks are completed in a class-appropriate fashion, a fashion that changes in response to the availability of time and income. For example, professional and upper-class mothers may rely on nannies, private schools, and tutors to provide much of their childcare, since these forms are deemed to be of such high quality (cost) and so similar to what the stay-at-home mother could provide that they are generally acceptable. Conversely, working-class women/men may feel that their children need additional parental support after school and so may assume a greater time commitment in this regard.

A number of other factors, of course, will have an impact upon both the availability of commodification to a particular household and the possibilities of time-saving. Throughout the life course and across the diversity of household forms, the need to engage with the market varies. Families with children, particularly those with two earners, are likely to be involved in commodified relationships. Class, gender, age, ability, and cultural differences among Canadian households contribute to a complex and multi-layered approach to understanding work transfers and commodification/decommodification processes. Families with a child with a disability, for example, may find that there are few affordable commodified services available and that decommodification (as a result of government cutbacks) results in increasing time pressures. Women and men, alone or with partners, may negotiate and renegotiate this dynamic to adjust to changing circumstances – as babies are born, caregivers move on, young adults leave home for college, mothers re-enter the paid labour force, and so on.

REPOSITIONING THE HOUSEHOLD WITHIN THE
EMPLOYMENT AND COMMODITIES MARKET

The commodification of household work is not a new phenomenon. However, historically, the practice of hiring help was confined to the wealthy, a rite of privilege (Katz 1975). From the late nineteenth century to the 1950s, contrary to the notion of a clear private/public divide, poor and working-class women did reproductive labour not only in their own homes, taking in boarders for example (Kessler-Harris and Sacks 1987; Duffy and Pupo 1992), but also for middle-class families. During the latter half of the nineteenth century, the growing "cult of motherhood" and a new emphasis on childhood and the mother's nurturing role, along with higher standards of cleanliness and larger homes requiring more attention, gave rapid rise to a demand for servants (Glenn 2001, 73–4). Middle-class women turned to working-class women and women of colour for housework, allowing them some free time to pursue social, leisure, and cultural activities. Their domestic roles were primarily supervisory. Servants and domestic helpers were hired by women and reported to them, often with little or no interaction with the male heads of households.

Through the early twentieth century, rapid industrialization in urban centres soon depleted the ranks of household servants. Young men and women opted for the better-paying factory jobs, which, whatever their drawbacks, allowed for some personal, private time away from work. Increasingly well-to-do households sought out alternative sources of domestic help. In the prewar era, a new range of household appliances and time-saving services were appearing in the marketplace. This process was given a dramatic boost with the expansion of capital in the post–World War II period, placing a new set of demands on families and on women's time. It was during this period that households began in earnest to exchange commodified goods and services for women's household labour (for example, the automatic washer was first marketed in 1949, the automatic dryer in 1955, and wash-and-wear clothing in 1964) (Bittman, Rice, and Wajcman 2004, 403). Over the course of the next several decades, sales of pre-packaged convenience foods (TV dinners, cake mixes) and labour-saving products (no-iron shirts) skyrocketed. At the same time, however, rapid suburban development,[9] the dislocation of communities, and the loss of extended-family support (as family members dispersed) meant that women faced new forms of household work and time pressure.

The volume of household work, with new standards for household cleanliness and maintenance, escalated with the size of typical family homes. At the turn of the century, towns and cities were small and compact, with few high-rise buildings and radial patterns to maximize the number of people who could easily reach the centre. Gradually cities and towns adopted a grid-like structure. Increased mobility with the rapid growth of car ownership in the late 1950s and 1960s encouraged suburban development, and with these suburbs came larger and larger homes, culminating in the contentious "monster homes" appearing in many contemporary suburban communities (Kremarik 2000b, 18–20). Between 1941 and 1996, the rate of home ownership grew from 57 to 64 per cent and the number of rooms per owned dwelling increased from 5.5 to 7.1 (20).[10] Not only were there more rooms to clean and decorate indoors, but yards were also larger and required more maintenance. The expansion of outdoor work contributed to the gendered division of domestic labour, as males took up yard maintenance, leaving women to care for the larger living spaces inside the home. This indoor/outdoor pattern was also supported by the trend to more reliable motor vehicles and more contemporary family homes. Car maintenance and home repairs were also increasingly purchased in the market economy. Men, as a result, were free to assume increasing responsibility for yardwork, landscaping, and home renovations.

Emerging from the postwar period, Canadian society saw a dramatic shift towards non-standard employment. Beginning in 1953, Statistics Canada tracked the growth of part-time employment, and since that time, the part-time workforce has grown at least fivefold and other non-standard work forms (contract, self-employment, homeworking) have become significantly more prominent among Canadians' employment experiences. In the early twenty-first century, these two seemingly disparate trends – increases in part-time work as well as growth in other non-standard forms of work – appear likely to intertwine, with significant implications for patterns of employment, quality of personal life, domestic and generational interconnections, and workplace relationships.

Interwoven with these changes in the structure of employment were important changes in the composition of the labour force. Throughout the 1970s and 1980s, women's labour force participation rates, in both full- and part-time work, increased rapidly, exceeding growth rates among males and establishing women as an integral part of the Canadian labour force. In particular, the participation rates of married women, including those with young children, rose exponentially. Since the late 1960s, the traditional male breadwinner arrangement has been steadily replaced by the dual-earner couple. By 1997, approximately 61 per cent of two-spouse Canadian families were dual earners compared with 33 per cent in 1967 (Drolet 2002, 1). Married women, aged 24 to 44, increased their labour force participation rates from 50 per cent in 1976 to 78 per cent in 1998 (Drolet 2003, 19). This new household configuration, with both partners heading for work, changed the ways in which domestic work was done and managed.

A variety of intersecting factors combined to pull women into the paid labour force: families needed to respond to financial pressures as average family incomes stagnated or declined in the 1980s and early 1990s; women struggled for some measure of economic self-reliance as rates of separation and divorce dramatically increased and the number of mother-headed single-parent families grew; the women's movement and attendant changes in cultural values encouraged women's desire for greater economic independence; and improvements in women's educational qualifications spurred women to explore employment options (Duffy and Pupo 1992, 26–9). A number of other factors and social processes pushed women into the labour force and facilitated their employment decisions (Duffy and Pupo 1992, 29–36). These included later marriages; birth control; family planning and smaller family sizes; liberated attitudes towards working wives and mothers; increased availability of childcare; technological developments and labour- or time-saving household appliances, products, and services; more equitable divisions of domestic labour and childcare; state legislation, such as extended maternity leave; changing employment practices; and a greater willingness among employers to hire women.

By 1996, the average age of a woman at first marriage had increased significantly to 27.3, up from 22.1 years in 1979 (Drolet 2002, 1). In the latter part of the twentieth century, women became more highly educated, and today their enrolment in higher education programs typically outstrips that of men.[11] Because women have more educational credentials, their numbers in professional and managerial positions have steadily increased. This has had an effect on women's pattern of work interruptions (Drolet 2002, 11). More women are delaying motherhood, often not having their first child until they have completed their education, their career paths are established, they are well placed on an upward trajectory, and they have some measure of economic security and labour market stability. Further, they have dramatically reduced the amount of "time-out" when children are born. In 1998 the average hourly earnings of women who made the decision to delay childbearing were 17 per cent higher than those of women who had their children earlier (Drolet 2003, 20). Decisions about the timing and length of labour force interruptions associated with having children have lifelong consequences for women because "a significant portion of real lifetime earnings growth occurs during the first years after graduation" (Drolet 2003, 20). Older mothers' higher incomes allow them to buy more household and childcare services. Educated women who worked hard to achieve professional recognition and their desired labour market position appear to be reluctant to trade these for full-time unpaid domestic work or for shortened hours of paid work, and they therefore buy household services more readily.

As women's numbers in the paid labour force swelled from the 1970s through the 1990s, the fastest-growing occupations were in the service sector, where lower-level jobs in health care within the public sector and in food, business, and personal services within the private sector were growing rapidly. While the expansion of the service sector meant that there were more jobs available for women, most of these jobs could be described as "McJobs" with classic bad job characteristics – poor pay, few benefits or opportunities to advance and learn, and low rates of unionization (Duffy, Glenday, and Pupo 1997). Among these service sector employers were some that provided help to households and family members, from standard housekeeping to more specialized services such as pet sitting. The availability of these services contributed to the commodification of household work in that it allowed women and men the means by which they could meet some of their domestic responsibilities, provided they could afford them. This process often involved shifting work out of middle-class households onto the shoulders of working-class women and youth, who, in turn, engaged in parallel processes of work transfer.

Within the public sector, and in health care specifically, work was restructured so that its costs could be lowered. For example, many of the tasks usually assigned to the more highly educated registered nurses were reassigned to registered practical nurses or assistants, and then, at the earliest time possible, all this work was transferred back to unpaid family members (Armstrong and Armstrong 1996; White 1997). More affluent families were often able to contract out some portion of this caregiving to private agencies. This form of commodification, the direct result of retrenchment within the public sector and the process of decommodification, triggers emotional pain in the many family members who prefer to avoid the piecemeal care and segmented relationships in the service economy approach to caregiving for their loved ones. However, in an increasingly mobile society, with neighbourhoods changing shape, becoming less reliable as a source of informal support and exchange, families have few options available to them. While middle-class professional women are reluctant to trade their relatively high pay and coveted labour market positions to take on more unpaid work, working-class women may be unwilling to trade the security of employment, however meagre, for unpaid responsibilities. Ultimately, the determination of whether or not to assume the burden of giving care to family members hinges on the availability and affordability of private sector alternatives as well as on the perceived responsibilities of individual family members.

Certainly, at this point in our economic development, paid employment provides little leeway in terms of combining private caregiving with paid employment activities. Indeed, the overall trends suggest a movement towards longer working hours, not shorter. For example, evidence indicates that Canadians are generally working longer hours today than they did two decades ago, despite the slower rate of economic growth. Between 1979 and 2000, the number of hours per worker in Canada grew by 2.2 per cent per year, from 1,669 to 1,706 hours, and this increase in the number of hours worked primarily reflects a rise in hours worked by women (Statistics Canada 2003d, 6).[12] Between 1979 and 1989, Canadian women increased their hours of work by 25.5 per cent,[13] and for the period between 1979 and 2000, the increase for women aged 25 to 54 was 39.7 per cent (6). This period of deindustrialization saw heavy losses in manufacturing and primary industry, strongholds of male employment, and, to some degree, women's increased hours of work compensated for men's losses. Rates of unemployment among Canadian men skyrocketed during the 1980s and early 1990s. As a result, from 1989 to 1993, work hours per person fell by 7.8 per cent (7). Overall, there was a narrowing of the difference in hours worked between Canadian men and women between 1979 and 2000. In 1979, among those aged 25 to 54, Canadian women worked 48 per cent as many hours as their male counterparts, whereas by 2000 they worked 71 per cent as many hours as men (7). As a whole, households became busier, and this has far-reaching consequences for all family members as well as for the running of Canadian households.

The busyness of Canadian households prompts questions regarding the commodification of time and leads researchers to conclude that time has become the scarcest resource in many homes (Williams 2002). Most employed Canadians aged 25 to 54, both high- and low-income earners, spend the largest portion of their day doing paid work. The well-to-do have experienced a dramatic intensification of their compulsory paid-work time. The General Social Survey (1998) reported that those in high-income households[14] spend an average of 15 per cent more time on their paid job, 46 hours compared with 40 hours spent by those with low income (Williams 2002, 8). However, more high-income as compared to low-income earners were satisfied with their situations. Among high-income households, 56 per cent were satisfied with their paid work hours, while 20 per cent would prefer to work fewer hours for less pay and only 8 per cent were willing to work more hours. Among those with low incomes, nearly one-third stated that they would be willing to work more hours for more pay, while only 6 per cent said they wanted to work less time for less pay (8). Although instructive on some of the class differences regarding work-time pressure, these data do not include gender differences. Yet studies continue to conclude that women have less free time than men and that their free time is different from men's. In particular, the combination of young children and paid employment results in less free time for women (Mattingly and Bianchi 2003), as does the combination of having unmarried children in the home while also caring for a senior (Williams 2004). As a result, many women may be under greater pressure than men to accommodate the need to balance paid and unpaid hours of work by purchasing products or services to ease the time strain.

A study of women in management positions in Belgium, where there are many family-supportive policies, found few women at the higher ranks in leadership positions (Lyon and Woodward 2004). Those who do achieve high-level positions succeed in striking a balance in organizing their time, whether the time issues are large, such as when to have children, or just day-to-day matters involving the commodification of household labour. One of the interviewees who did not have children, for example, accommodated the career-home conflict by making deliberate decisions to ease the tensions: "'[A]t the beginning of my career, I invested a lot of money in household appliances, in comfort at home, in a cleaning lady and all those kinds of things'" (quoted in Lyon and Woodward 2004, 215). Mothers' choices revolve around being there for the children "'for the essentials,'" and this means condensing their time with their children (quality time over quantity), reducing leisure time, and not taking time for one's own pleasures. Yet the researchers conclude that even for those at the top who can afford all types of homemaking services, "the state and the market together are still not sufficient to totally replace a homemaker" (17). While those in high-income brackets can buy the flexibility, public or private market services operate under a different "logic of commitment" and are incapable of providing the same "'person-specificity'" of care (17).

The pressures on low-income households are more intense. Low-income Canadians spend significantly more time per day – almost an hour more – on unpaid work, including housework, meal preparation, and childcare, than their high-income counterparts (Lyon and Woodward 2004, 10).[15] In the course of a seven-day week, the difference between high- and low-income earners in the time spent on housework and meal preparation alone is almost 4 hours (3.7). The

well-to-do accomplish this by, for example, purchasing cleaning services and eating at restaurants. On an average day in 1998, about one
in four high-income Canadians but only one in eight low-income earners ate at least one restaurant meal. Well-to-do Canadians are also able
to reduce their shopping time, spending only 48 minutes a day on this
activity compared with the 51 minutes a day spent by low-income earners. Presumably, less concern with budgeting and comparison shopping can free up time for other activities (10). Interestingly, while
both the high- and low-income groups do other activities, such as
cleaning, cooking, or watching television, when they are with their
children and spend very little time actually reading or talking to them
or playing with them, low-income parents spend more time teaching
or helping their children than high-income parents do (10).

This class-distinct deployment of parental time in educational support activities is consistent with patterns of private school enrolment[16]
and the emerging supply of private agencies (Boyle 2004; Choi 2004).
By purchasing private schooling for their children or placing them in
public schools located in affluent neighbourhoods, well-to-do parents
are able to reduce the need for school-supportive activities while
ensuring academic success.[17] Superior private schools provide after-
school programs that allow students to complete their homework with
the assistance of teachers and mentors prior to going home. Public
schools in affluent neighbourhoods not only are likely to have their
pick of prospective teachers, but are also much more successful in
parent-run fundraising efforts. As a result, problems at school related
to inadequate instruction or insufficient teaching resources are less
likely to occur. Recent years have seen the emergence of a number of
private national tutoring services that provide more affluent parents
with another way to supplement and support their children's educational efforts without their having to give up their own time. In contrast, working-class and poor parents, whose children are more likely
to attend deprived schools and who, perhaps as immigrants, may be in
particular need of educational assistance, may have to provide the service themselves (McLaren and Dyck 2004).

Of course, the provision of childcare extends beyond babysitting,
daycare centres, nannies, and educational facilities. Particularly among
well-to-do families, parenting implies considerable attention to extracurricular activities. Working-class households often lack the free time
to devote to such activities and the money to pay for the commodities
and services that would ease the time pressures. In a study for the Australian Council of Trade Unions, Barbara Pocock argues that long
work hours mean that workers cannot devote time to care work and to
activities involving the extended family or the community and this

undermines the social fabric and relations in the household (ACTU 2004). The interaction of three forces – the patriarchal family structure, the (new) economy, and state social policies – undermines the family's ability to perform the unpaid work that forms the basis of community, work that includes the production of social capital and caregiving. Long hours subsidize the economy and labour markets at the expense of households and families, which become subject to the tensions among their members. For mothers in particular, extended hours of work give rise to the "time crunch," and this means they must constantly juggle too many commitments and obligations at once. In these stressful situations, it becomes impossible for them to maintain close relationships with their extended family and reasonable ties to the broader social community.

The financial and time pressures experienced by lower-income households may result in market positions that exacerbate problems. For example, working-class women may seek part-time evening or weekend work so that when they are at work, their husbands can assume childcare responsibilities. In this way, costly and cumbersome childcare can be circumvented. However, the low income resulting from such practices may, in turn, prompt these mothers to combine multiple part-time jobs, further intensifying the pressures of both time and employment. Reflecting poor labour market conditions (the proliferation of part-time work in the absence of significant gains in full-time employment), many Canadians – especially women – engage in multiple job-holding. Between 1978 and 1998, the number of multiple job-holders more than tripled and the gender mix among Canada's moonlighters changed remarkably. By 1997, women slightly outnumbered men as moonlighters; yet, twenty years earlier, 77 per cent of multiple job-holders were men (Sussman 1998, 24). Along with the new gender ratios among moonlighters, interestingly, by 1997 people with or without children undertook a second job at the same rate, whereas earlier it was primarily those without children who did so (26). Multiple job-holding not only requires workers to juggle schedules and meet different employers' demands, but also costs them in time travelling to and from the various jobs, leaving them little free time for themselves.

Persistent high rates of unemployment and increasing numbers of insecure jobs have meant that many Canadian workers, not just those holding multiple jobs, have little choice but to devote a considerable portion of each day simply getting to and from their workplace. In 1998 General Social Survey data revealed that on an average weekday almost half (47 per cent) of the adult population commuted to and from work, spending about 62 minutes on the road. These Canadians

spent about 6 more minutes travelling by car or 12 minutes more by
public transit than they did in 1986 on an average weekday (Clark
2000, 18–19). Given the high cost of housing in many urban centres,
the problematic nature of much employment, and the continuing suburban sprawl, it is not surprising that many workers find themselves
working at a great distance from their household. Not only does commuting elongate the working day, but it also means spending more
time alone, since most commuters travel by car and are increasingly
likely to travel alone.[18]

In short, the contemporary Canadian household is at the fulcrum of
powerful market and societal forces. Individuals, particularly those in
low-income families, may be particularly pressured by time impover-
ishment and the absence of alternatives – in or out of the commodities
market. Certainly, work transfers from the home to the marketplace
and vice versa are indicative of the difficult and complicated balancing
of public and private roles required of many Canadian households.
The meanings attached to such work transfers are not transparent.
Seeking paid services to substitute for unpaid household work may be
an important strategy for keeping private and public obligations in balance, but undertaking unpaid caregiving work for family members –
work that formerly belonged in the public sector in schools, hospitals,
nursing homes, and social agencies – may signal more than a capitula-
tion to harsh economic realities. In some instances, it may be indicative of agency, a keen desire for more control over intimate matters.
Below we consider two specific forms of family and household work –
first, domestic service, and second, caregiving and teaching children.
We then look at the ways in which Canadian households interact with
the market to satisfy these responsibilities.

THE GLOBAL COMMODIFICATION OF HOUSEHOLD LABOUR

Domestic Service

As indicated above, over the last forty years, the labour market has
made significant inroads into family life. The economically and socially
generated mobilization of wives and teens into paid employment has
had a direct impact on the family on both a daily and a life-course
basis. One of the most dramatic effects has been the marketplace's
penetration into domestic lives. More and more of the activities previously undertaken within the home have become either commodities
or commodified services to be purchased in the consumer market. In
many respects, particularly for women, this has meant that more of the

time that people spend on household work is spent on managing everything. A major preoccupation of many mothers is keeping the family's schedules. With hockey practice and numerous other schedules held by magnets to the fridge door, many families literally run short of space (not to mention time). This process of commodification, however, is by no means evenly distributed among Canadian families and globally, but among higher-wage earners and dual-income couples, being able to buy, or "contract in," household help has effectively reduced the gender gap in housework (Presser 2003, 134). Middle-class, dual-income households tend to consume more services than working-class households, and the most affluent are able to make use of a globalized labour force of nannies, housekeepers, servants, or other home helpers.

The extreme social inequality that typically accompanies industrializing economies of the South usually means access to cheap domestic labour. In some instances, this labour is available through import (Filipina domestic workers into Saudi Arabia), while in other cases segments of the population (children of poor families in China, Hong Kong, and Haiti) are employed to undertake extensive domestic labour obligations in the local homes of the more well-to-do (Blagbrough and Glynn 1999). In Western countries, children and youth are often deployed to perform household tasks to make up for shifts in their own family's time structures. In both dual-career and female-headed families, children's participation in household work has risen significantly, often including such tasks as starting the evening meal, tidying up, and looking after younger siblings (Lee, Schneider, and Waite 2003).

A study that examined work-family arrangements in the United States, with a particular focus on gender, class, and race/ethnicity, provides rich evidence that differences may be viewed in relation to local political economies and that, rather than there being sharp distinctions among families on the basis of race, class, marital status, or other characteristics, the work-family strategies are overall more nuanced (Lamphere et al. 1993, 295–6). Converging and diverging strategies are shaped as the life course unfolds, as women marry, migrate, have children, take jobs, quit, change jobs, and retire. In Canada, vast regional differences among households prevail, with different strategies employed, for example, in fishing communities, where (male) fishers may be absent for extended periods of time, or in farming households, where both partners may be working indoors in close quarters for the winter months. Still other strategies are necessary when one or both of the parents work on call (medical and emergency services, for example), and contingency plans may be needed in situations where fathers (or mothers) have a variable schedule entailing extended absences (long-distance truckers, for example).

Families at the lower end of the economic scale are more likely to be the creators and providers of commodified services for middle- and upper-income families, working as nannies, babysitters, daycare workers, home cleaners, personal trainers, and so on, than to be the consumers of commodified services. A globalized division of domestic labour and the poor's worldwide role as service providers are evident, for example, in the commodification of reproductive activities. For immigrant domestic workers, the meaning of motherhood becomes skewed, as they are sometimes faced with dramatic separations, spatially and temporally, from their own families (Hondagneu-Sotelo 2001, 51). They become "mothers" to well-to-do children, most often within cultural contexts different from their own. Although the new transnational arrangements allow for the migration of an increased number of non-white domestic workers, the system through which they are allowed entry and work is coercive and does not recognize these workers' family rights. Rather, international labour migration and the job characteristics of paid domestic work, "virtually impose transnational motherhood on many ... women who have children of their own" (51).

In recent years, housecleaning has become increasingly situated in the service economy. In the United States in 1999, between 14 and 18 per cent of households employed outsiders as cleaners, and the number has been rising dramatically (Ehrenreich 2004, 90). One report found a 53 per cent increase between 1995 and 1999 in the number who hired a cleaner or service once a month or more, and 30 per cent of people who hired help in 1999 did so for the first time. The affluent home has become a Taylorized workplace, where workers are kept on task and exploited, with low wages, difficult working conditions, and tiring, fast-paced work. International cleaning services such as Merry Maids, Molly Maid, and Maids International have been created since the 1970s and now control 20 to 25 per cent of the $1.4-billion housecleaning business (93–4). With the corporatization of cleaning services, householders hire a service, not a particular person. The company sends in a team of two to four uniformed people who perform a routine cleaning according to the company's rules. In many cases, the individual cleaners and homeowners never meet face to face, nor do they even know each other's names. The customer's contract is with the company, to which complaints or compliments are to be directed. Usually only one team member is appointed as team leader, and only this person is allowed to interact directly with the householder. With large multinational firms establishing themselves in this industry ("McDonaldization"), mobile transnational professionals (Sassen 2002) will be able to find the same branded and standardized services or products wherever they locate/relocate (Ehrenreich 2004, 99).

The globalization of clothing and household furnishing production has also influenced the burden of domestic labour in the North. Where in past generations the high cost of clothing and household furnishing meant that many families had to maintain and repair these commodities, globalization has resulted in the production of low-cost alternatives. In the time-pressured household, it has become increasingly more sensible to buy new clothes or furnishings than to engage in repair work. Home shoe repair, for example, and the darning of socks, once commonplace in working-class homes, are almost unheard of in the contemporary family.

Deborah Barndt's (2002) comprehensive examination of the globalized labour involved in the production of greenhouse and field tomatoes in Mexico for export to Canada and the United States speaks to another important aspect of the commodification of domestic labour. The fruits and vegetables produced by foreign and migrant labour – a labour force that is highly gendered, raced, and divided by social class – are products that eliminate the domestic labour that would be required in Canadian households to cultivate and process the same foods. Indeed, in many postwar households, the maintenance of a family garden for the provision of fresh vegetables and fruits and the canning of much of this produce were significant elements of household production (Luxton 1976). Today, many families rely on their local supermarket for fresh produce. Fresh produce, by its nature, is often amenable to low-labour food preparation, since it can be simply sliced, chopped, or peeled in advance of consumption. The globalization of this food production process – using produce from low-wage southern countries (tomatoes from Mexico, apples from Chile) or from the United States, which uses low-wage migrant (often foreign) workers (oranges from Florida, avocados from California) – has meant that many households can reduce domestic labour by turning to these quick, low-skill, and purportedly nutritious food alternatives. However, access to these commodities varies considerably by household income level, and consequently some commodities are primarily marketed in well-to-do urban areas.

The globalization of household food production is also evident in the growing role of international corporations in fast-food and snack-food production. The corporate giants in these industries are direct beneficiaries of families' need to turn to the market for quick and easily accessible meals. McDonald's has more than 30,000 restaurants in 119 countries, and Subway has 21,528 restaurants in 75 countries. Indeed, in 2003 Subway overtook McDonald's in terms of numbers of outlets in the United States (Mokhiber and Weissman 2004b). Subway markets "homelike" sandwiches and emphasizes nutrition in its advertising. In some ways, these businesses capitalize on the commodification of household work, especially food production, by describing their products as homestyle cooking or comfort food. In 2001 Americans spent $110 billion on fast food, more than on higher education, personal computers, computer software, or new cars (Schlosser 2002, 3).

Fast-food industries launch massive campaigns that appeal to children and young adults, who are among their biggest consumers. For children, their appeal is wide-ranging. They offer toys with "kids' meals," restaurants often include play areas, and the decor features bold primary colours. Moreover, these corporations have adopted a community-minded identity, often sponsoring sporting events (Tim Horton's "Timbits" hockey days, for example) or providing beverages or other snacks (McDonald's) at charitable or fundraising events. Recently, *National Geographic Kids*, a publication with a long-standing reputation for education, began to carry advertisements. While only three years ago, this magazine was ad free, now it is filled with ads, particularly for fast food, candy, sugary cereals, snacks, and other junk foods. Thirty to 40 per cent of revenues for the magazine comes from junk-food companies, and it has a circulation of 1.2 million (Mokhiber and Weissman 2004a).

However, as with other aspects of the commodification of household labour, the emergence of global fast-food enterprises has a distinct social-class element. Although McDonald's and Burger King are seen to be available to all but the poorest North Americans, fast foods and convenience foods are often the domain of the more affluent classes in emerging economies such as China and Southeast Asia. Here, convenience food may be as important for its social panache as for its ability to replace household labour. While the difference in consumption is less extreme in more industrialized economies, the well-to-do are more likely than the average household to adopt convenience or fast food as a strategy. A recent survey of households in Spain, for example, found that convenience meat products were more likely to be consumed by large, high-income families in which both the man and woman work (Manrique and Jensen 1997).

Caregiving and Educating

The provision of personal care in the context of familial relationships has long been considered one of the mainstays of the private sphere.

However, as detailed below, the provision of care has increasingly been commodified, and an international as well as national labour force is being called upon to meet the needs of the household. If, as has been suggested by Pat Armstrong and Hugh Armstrong (1994), sexual relations may be conceptualized as part of the care provisions of the family household, then it is noteworthy, not only that sexuality has been exported into the public domain (in terms of products, notably pornography), but also that the sex industry increasingly draws upon an international labour force for its workers (Malarek 2003). Among other intensely personal services that are now in the process of commodification is the business of surrogacy. Surrogate mothers are typically drawn from the less well off, and it is the poorest among Third World women who provide children for international adoption.[19] The end result is an attenuation, both nationally and internationally, of class differences in experiences of caregiving and care receiving (Banks 1983; De Graffe, Wann, and Naylor 2001). In sum, the commodification of domestic labour activities and products is an important factor in the intensification of national and global inequalities.

Given the intensity of the time demands of childcare, it is not surprising that the commodification of this activity has been a significant phenomenon in recent decades. As families became increasingly dependent on multiple incomes, a demand was created for various childcare services. This commodification has occurred in the international labour force, in the creation of state-funded and/or state-regulated services, such as childcare centres, and in the emergence of unregulated services, such as local babysitters. Predictably, the more costly alternatives – live-in nannies, for example – are also the services that provide the most complete reduction in childcare responsibilities. The live-in nanny may be available throughout the day and night, on holidays, when children are sick, and when parents or families travel. In contrast, formal childcare centres frequently entail some restrictions in terms of the age at which children are admitted, the hours of service provided (although some childcare centres provide twenty-four-hour service where shift work is a significant factor in the community), and the availability of service during holidays or when children are ill. Further, parents must provide transportation to and from the childcare centre, which adds additional tasks to the domestic labour list and entails further expenses. The use of informal childcare providers and babysitters may mean reduced costs and somewhat enhanced flexibility, but it raises concerns about reliability. What happens, for example, if the service provider becomes ill or obtains another form of employment. Predictably, high-income Canadians are able to reduce the time they spent on their childcare responsibilities (68 minutes per average day) more significantly than their low-income counterparts (82 minutes per average day). The net result over the course of a seven-day week is almost two hours of additional child-free time for high-income Canadians (Williams 2002, 10).

Providing care for the ill, persons with disabilities, and, most notably, seniors has been commodified for many years. Long-term care facilities, old age homes, and other care facilities have long been available for the care of elderly household members. While many of these services are publicly funded, some are not. Once again, it is the affluent who are in a better position to secure reliable, high-quality assistance. However, with the dramatic increase in the numbers of seniors in the population and dissatisfaction in the ranks of care providers, many facilities for seniors have come to rely heavily on immigrant and visible minority workers. Like the nannies who provide childcare, many of the long-term care providers who look after seniors emigrated to Canada in search of better economic and social opportunities. While the percentage of health-care providers in Canada who have emigrated from a foreign country is currently low (7 per cent) (Pyper 2004), there is certainly evidence that Third World nations are playing an increasingly important role as exporters of nurses. It is estimated, for example, that 250,000 Filipina nurses are employed around the world, and according to the World Health Organization, the Philippines is the largest global exporter of registered nurses. In this way, the commodification of household tasks in Western countries can be directly linked to a globalized labour market that is both racialized and gendered (Ball 2004).

For the workers involved in caregiving, whether immigrants or native, there is a disjuncture between the provision of care and the logic of commodification. The need for profit and decent wages and the uncommodifiable interest in the well-being of others are often at odds (Jones 2003, 282). It is possible that paid care workers develop a class consciousness because their job, caring for others, contradicts management's goals, and this causes them a great deal of stress (284). Some of the difficulty of caring work is that it does not lend itself easily to commodification within the context of the marketplace (Himmelweit 1999). Caring involves sustained relationships between caregivers and care receivers, but corporate and other pressures work to prevent the possibility of such relationships.

Changes in social programs and in forms of paid care work have contributed to the commodification of care. Informal care for persons with disabilities, for example, is being commodified in many countries in Europe and North America. Clare Ungerson (2000, 71) argues that welfare states are seeking to find ways to underwrite the provision of care, particularly for persons with disabilities, within households and kin networks through cash subvention both to caregivers and to care recipients. This is done by means of caregivers' allowances paid directly to caregivers through social security and taxes; wages to caregivers (who may be relatives of care users), based on the prevailing wage rates of state-employed home helpers; symbolic payments paid directly by care users out of pocket or out of money coming from various types of benefits they may be receiving; and paid volunteering (Britain), which is a contractual arrangement with a social organization that ensures regularity and reliability in volunteering. The consequence is the marketization of intimacy and the commodification of care (Ungerson 2000, 69). Furthermore, according to John Eriksen (2003), this solution to the care of persons with disabilities tends to entrench a gendered role pattern, since the care wage is typically paid to the mother of the child/ren with disabilities.[20]

Even when household members assume responsibility for care work, there may be significant class as well as gendered differences in the nature and execution of that work. Jennifer Johnson (2002, 154) describes class differences as manual as opposed to managerial. In discussing the way that daughters give care, she suggests that since working-class women cannot afford help with their own household and family work, they do the work of shopping, cleaning, bathing, dressing, and driving, and also provide many other types of physical and emotional care for their parents. Their help is hands-on. When middle-class women are called on to attend to their aging parents' needs, they adopt a managerial role, taking on the task of case managers, connecting their parents with appropriate medical specialists, and finding home-care providers. With an aging population and high levels of labour force participation by women, caring work is expanding, offering work opportunities for thousands of women. However, most caring work is devalued, especially the work available to working-class and poorly educated women (Theobald 2003). Not only is most of this work poorly paid and lacking in status as well as opportunities to advance, but most of it is done in the privacy of people's homes, where work conditions may be oppressive and below standard and relations with the people therein abusive.

LOCATING THE HOUSEHOLD AND ITS WORK IN THE COMMUNITY

While household work can be meaningfully located in a maze of national and international relationships, it should also be recognized that local communities have a significant role in contextualizing this work, particularly as it occurs in working-class households. For low-wage workers, the consumption of services often takes place primarily through informal networks, with exchange and bartering as tender. This informal exchange facilitates the labour market involvement of lower-skilled, lower-wage workers (Henly 2002). Saskia Sassen (2002, 76) argues that the expansion of low-wage jobs implies a "reorganization of the employment relation" and that one of the results is the casualization of the employment relation. In some communities, this means a shift of labour market functions to the household, as is the case in immigrant communities (Sassen 2002, 83). This may have many hidden (non-monetary) costs for workers and their families.

Low-wage women, particularly those who are sole-support parents, are likely to use bartering as a way of expanding their resources (Hertz and Ferguson 1998, 26–7). This is especially the case with respect to space, as they will often rent out rooms in their homes, turning space into exchange value. Working-class women in these circumstances are very resourceful, sometimes drawing on a huge network of friends and family members to create a "patchwork" of interchangeable arrangements. On occasion they combine their unpaid caring roles with paid work; they may, for example, take their children along to an odd job, like housecleaning, selling cosmetics, or babysitting. This practice may be more acceptable in less formal working-class neighbourhoods, where bartering and exchange are more commonly employed. However, in more formal exchanges within the labour market, this form of balancing would not be permitted.

There are many different skills and talents hidden in the household. One mother may care for her neighbour's children while her friend goes shopping, and in return, the neighbour, a former hairstylist, may trim the children's hair. In some circumstances, services such as hair-styling, catering, tailoring, and editing are businesses that are run out of people's homes and are often unregulated. Sometimes these home services are operated like a restaurant, the front rooms serving as the area where familiar "customers" or "clients" are greeted and served and the back region being the place where the family resides. Advertising is strictly through word of mouth, and each business operates primarily through a network of connections. While unregulated, informal, and irregular, these businesses bring traffic and other services (delivery, courier, etc.) through the neighbourhood, and in leaving their imprint upon the community, they help create a familiar and safe environment.

In large cities, the needs and habits of relatively sizable groups of well-to-do and upwardly mobile professionals have changed household consumption patterns to the extent that there is now a demand for a different organization of work. According to Sassen (2002, 88), high-income gentrification generates a demand for goods and services that are not mass produced or sold in the broader marketplace; rather they entail customized production (such as tailoring, hand-made draperies), small runs (cards, business gifts), specialty items (artwork, crafts), and fine-food catering for dinner parties. Firms often subcontract this work out to low-cost operations, including sweatshops and households. In these situations, two distinct processes confront one another: first, the formal requirement to meet the contractual obligations and deliver the product or service as specified, even if this entails violations of reasonable labour practices and codes (employing children to help out, working excessively long hours to complete tasks); and second, the process of informalization, which relates to the demand for specialized services or one-of-a-kind items. Lower-wage workers readily accept this home-based work, however, and may come to rely on it, as it meets their need for flexibility and offers some extra income.

THE INCREASING PENETRATION OF THE CONSUMER ECONOMY

Over the past twenty years, Canadians' entertainment choices have changed tremendously. Although this reflects the availability of many electronic devices for home consumption at affordable prices, it may also be indicative of the long hours many spend working outside their homes and thus their desire to relax at home. Not surprisingly, families with children spent more on home entertainment equipment in 1999 than in 1982, with increases of 31 per cent among two-parent families and 68 per cent in lone-parent households (Kremarik 2002, 18). On average, household expenditure on home entertainment equipment rose 19 per cent between 1982 and 1999, despite the drop in real prices. Most of this increase was due to more households buying these goods over this time period rather than to some households spending more on them.[21] Average household spending on cablevision grew by 253 per cent from 1982 to 1999 (Kremarik 2002, 15). During this period, cable programming and services improved remarkably, providing access to greater numbers of channels and expanding into smaller urban and rural areas (18).

Another source of home entertainment is the computer. In 2001, 60 per cent of Canadian households owned a computer, up from 50 per cent in 1999 (*The Daily*, 11 December 2002). While home computers are primarily used for work-related and academic purposes, they are also increasingly used for entertainment purposes, allowing users to download and record music and videos, for example. A growing number of Canadians also use their computer to shop from home. According to the 1999 Household Internet Use Survey, 1.8 million households, or 15 per cent of all Canadian households, shopped from home on the Internet (Ellison and Clark 2001). In 2003 an estimated 3.2 million Canadian households participated in e-commerce, placing 21.1 million orders (worth $3 billion, up from $2.4 billion in 2002) (*The Daily*, 23 September 2004). Based on the penetration of high-speed Internet into homes and the growing interest in e-Bay and other marketing sites, many analysts project continued significant growth in home computer–based shopping over the next few years as consumers gain confidence over the security issues. These trends speak dramatically to the growing interpenetration of public and private spaces.

Children, Sports, and Recreation

The increasing urbanization and suburbanization of Canadian society, with attendant problems of crime, violence, and gang-related activities, have reduced the possibilities for informal sports activities for children. It is interesting that even though families have become smaller, the time spent in and around children's activities has not necessarily diminished. Instead, parents have accepted, created, and maintained a much more formal system of extracurricular activities for their children.

It is revealing, for example, that about twice as many high-income Canadians (49 per cent) as low-income Canadians (24 per cent) indicated that they engaged in a sports activity (Williams 2002, 10). Among children, in 1998 about 54 per cent of Canadian children aged five to fourteen living in two or one-parent households regularly took part in an organized-sport activity and almost 48 per cent of these active children participated in more than one sport (Kremarik 2000a, 21). Once again, it is the well-to-do families who are more likely to have the resources to engage in these domestic activities. Rates of participation reflect income differences: 49 per cent of children in households with incomes under $40,000 were active in sports, while 73 per cent of those in households with incomes over $80,000 were active. Income also affects kids' choice of sports. While relatively equal numbers of children from lower- and higher-income households were involved in hockey (one in five), Canada's "national" game, those with household incomes of less than $40,000 were more likely to be involved in less expensive sports like baseball and basketball, and high-income kids were more likely to be involved in downhill skiing and swimming (Kremarik 2000a, 22).

The reduction in or elimination of school-based sports and recreation programs as a result of neo-liberal social policies has produced intensified demands for private (club-based) sports and recreation programs for children. Child and youth care has been extended to include parental involvement in after-school and weekend sports and recreation activities. Parents are responsible for "shopping" for appropriate programs, purchasing and providing transportation to the programs, and supporting the programs through fundraising events or volunteer coaching. For many parents, their children's sports and activities, especially those involving weekend trips to tournaments or other events, have become the family's leisure pursuits and thus deplete the entertainment budget. Predictably, well-to-do families can afford to purchase these activities and participate fully. Soccer, basketball, hockey, figure skating, gymnastics, and numerous other commodified activities have become hallmarks of middle- and upper-class childhood and provide an important elaboration on these children's education.

THE COMMODIFICATION OF HOUSEHOLD WORK

The transfer of work from the home to the public domain or from the market back to the home is a complicated and multi-levelled process. While past analyses have tended to draw attention to the gender inequalities in the division of domestic labour and commodification was often envisioned as a solution to such inequities, contemporary realities are, in fact, much more complex. The commodification of services and goods for the family has not dramatically eased the burden of domestic work, particularly from the shoulders of women. Indeed, as argued here, the commodification process may have exacerbated class differences between women and their households, resulting in working-class women becoming increasingly stressed and pressed for time. The reasons behind this failure to create more leisure time are complex and speak, in part, to the noted contradictions embedded in household labour. In addition, trends towards decommodification (resulting from cutbacks to medical services and social programs and compounded by the aging population) have tended to run counter to any prospects of increasing "free" time. However, decommodification as a process is not inherently objectionable, since it may speak to the growing, or at least persistent, possibilities for non-monetarized, non-exchange-based social relations. Finally, increasing commodification of household labour must be approached as an international phenomenon and located in terms of a global labour market. Many household consumer goods are the products of low-wage, insecure work in Third World countries. Further, many of the workers being imported to provide replacements for family-provided caregivers are coming to Canada to escape politically and economically oppressive home regimes. In this sense, the commodification of household labour in Canada must be understood as firmly located in gender, class, and international inequalities.

NOTES

Authors' Note: This chapter is based on research funded by a Social Sciences and Humanities Research Council of Canada Initiatives on the New Economy (INE) grant entitled "Restructuring Work and Labour in the New Economy." The authors shared equally in the preparation of this chapter.

1 "Household" here is used to refer to the diverse ways in which families and individuals situate themselves in society. While it encompasses families, with or without children, it also includes individuals living alone and non-familial arrangements of individuals living together. Excluded from this conception of household are those people living in retirement homes, workers' hostels, hospitals, and prisons (Ogden and Hall 2004, 102 n). As noted by Ogden and Hall, the household, compared to the individual, is often a more relevant unit to the understanding of societal trends and phenomena (88).

2 While the distinction between private (personal) and public spheres is useful, analysts have long pointed out that the notion of a barrier between public and private lives is both inaccurate and misleading. Clearly, any boundary between the two is permeable and flexible. See Pavlovskaya 2004 for an excellent demonstration of the complex relationships between households and various elements of the formal/informal state sector and formal/informal private sector in contemporary Moscow.

3 While household arrangements have long been diverse, recent social trends reveal increasing complexity. In particular, since the 1950s, the growth of single-person households, single-parent households, households with adult children present, same-sex households, and post-retirement households speak to the multiplicity of forms now subsumed by the term "household." By the turn of the century, in Canada and throughout much of the industrialized West, households composed of a male-female couple and their biological children were a relatively small minority of household arrangements (Carson 2002, 25). For the purposes of this discussion, the authors emphasize the multiplicity of forms assumed by modern households and the diversity of relationships between the household and market economy that may result.

4 The *commodification of household work* refers to the broad range of processes involved in the movement of household tasks into the monetarized public

domain. These processes include the creation of labour-saving appliances, the mobilization of various services in the market economy to the performance of household tasks (ranging from household cleaning to childcare), and, more generally, shifts in the market economy that seek to draw the household more firmly into an ongoing relationship with the monetarized economy.

5 By 1999, the domestic market for childcare services in Canada surpassed $3.5 billion and about 13 per cent of households paid for childcare services at some point during the year (*The Daily*, 26 April 2002).

6 The provision of gyms for women speaks interestingly to the domestic labour entailed in presenting and maintaining an appropriate "personal front."

7 Needless to say, given women's occupational segregation, lower wage rates and so on, women who maintain single-parent households are more likely to be economically disadvantaged than their male counterparts.

8 The research in Bittman, Rice, and Wajcman 2004 is particularly significant, since it is based on an examination of the direct impact of the presence of specific appliances in specific households, rather than (as in past research) matching the historical deployment of new appliances to changes in domestic labour activities.

9 The rapid suburbanization was triggered, for example, by government-sponsored veterans' housing. In many contemporary Canadian cities, the legacy of this period is still evident in the low-cost communities constructed on the then agricultural perimeter of urban areas. These suburbs helped to rapidly transform Canadian households and their relationships to the surrounding community.

10 Along with an increase in the number of rooms within individual homes, we might also consider changes in the square footage of living spaces as contributing to additional household labour.

11 Recently released figures from Statistics Canada indicate that 57 per cent of full-time university students in Canada were women in 2003–4. At many Ontario universities, including McMaster, Brock, and Guelph, women hold between 62 and 63 per cent of undergraduate seats. This trend is not new. Among undergraduates, females have outnumbered males for twenty years. Nevertheless, clearly marked gendered strongholds remain within some academic programs. In the humanities, for example, women far outnumber men, in some cases holding 70 per cent or more of the seats, whereas they are distinctly the minority in traditional male strongholds, such as engineering, technology, business, and computer sciences (Cox 2004, G5).

12 Throughout the 1990s, Americans worked more hours than Canadians, and this gap may be attributed to the healthier economic growth in the United States. Between 1979 and 2000, the number of hours worked by Americans grew by 9.6 per cent (Statistics Canada 2003d, 6).

13 Comparatively, between 1979 and 1989, American women worked 20.1 per cent more hours. Considering women aged 25 to 54, American women

increased their hours of work by 33.7 per cent between 1979 and 2000. However, Canadian prime-aged women on average worked fewer hours than American women in the same age group.

14 The 1998 General Social Survey classifies high income as individuals whose total household income is equal to or greater than $80,000 and low income those whose total household income is $30,000 or less. Following from these definitions, 2.4 million Canadians are high income and 1.9 million are low income (Williams 2002, 7).

15 Low-income Canadians spend 50 minutes a day on housework, while high-income Canadians spend 30 minutes, and they spend 52 minutes on meal preparation while those with high incomes spend 40 (Williams 2002, 8). Low-income earners spend more time on childcare, 82 minutes a day, than do their high-income counterparts, who spend 68 minutes (10).

16 There is, of course, a significant distinction between private schools that provide a religious curriculum and do not necessarily seek to distinguish themselves in terms of academic performance and those private schools that have long marketed themselves as providing a superior, if costly, education for the well-to-do.

17 In modern China, private schools are enjoying a rebirth as affluent parents seek to ensure their children's future (Liying 2003).

18 In 1998, on a typical weekday, about 75 per cent of the adult population used cars to commute, up from 70 per cent in 1986, and those who travelled by car were increasingly likely to drive alone. According to the 1998 General Social Survey, 77 per cent of commuters were alone, up from 69 per cent in 1986 (Clark 2000, 19).

19 In one of their earlier analyses of household work, Armstrong and Armstrong (1994) made the argument that in some respects sexual relations could be approached as an aspect of domestic labour. Extending this line of analysis, one could argue that sex work has always been amenable to commodification, as prostitutes, pornography, and other elements of the sex industry provided a consumer alternative to domestic sexual relations. Clearly, this commodification of sex work was highly gendered, since almost all of the workers were female and their clients male. In recent years, there has been a marked trend towards the globalization of this commodity market. Increasing numbers of Third World women are migrating to Canada to provide sexual and reproductive services as well as domestic services (Lepp 2002, 94).

20 In 2001 in Canada an estimated 155,000 children between five and fourteen had some form of an activity limitation. Parents in these households reported that they received inadequate support from external agencies. Predictably, they reported that their situation affected the family's employment situation, resulting in their working fewer hours or having to change their work hours to a different time of day. Once again, it was mothers who were most likely to be affected (*The Daily*, 29 July 2003).

21 Increased spending accounted for only about one-quarter of this growth, while two-thirds was due to more households buying these goods in 1999 than in 1982 (Kremarik 2002, 15).

REFERENCES

ACTU (Australian Council of Trade Unions). 2004. The effect on social and human capital: The externality effects of households' longer hours of (paid and unpaid) work. Posted 27 October 2003 at www.actu.asn.au/public/papers/pococklit/index-The-6.html

Anderson, Bridget. 2004. Just another job: The commodification of domestic labor. In *Global woman: Nannies, maids, and sex workers in the new economy*, edited by Barbara Ehrenreich and Arlie Russell Hochschild, 104–14. New York: Owl Books

Armstrong, Pat, and Hugh Armstrong. 1994. *The double ghetto: Canadian women and their segregated work*. 3rd ed. Toronto: McClelland and Stewart

– 1996. *Wasting away: The undermining of Canadian health care*. Toronto: Oxford University Press

– 2002. Thinking it through: Women, work and caring in the new millennium. *Canadian Woman Studies* 21/22 (4/1): 44–50 (Spring/Summer)

Ball, Rochelle E. 2004. Divergent development, racialised rights: Globalised labour markets and the trade of nurses – The case of the Philippines. *Women's International Forum* 27:119–33

Banks, R. 1983. *The tyranny of time – When 24 hours is not enough*. Downers Grove, Ill.: InterVarsity Press

Barndt, Deborah. 2002. Fruits of injustice: Women in the post-NAFTA food system. *Canadian Woman Studies* 21/22 (4/1): 82–8 (Spring/Summer)

Bittman, Michael, James Mahmud Rice, and Judy Wajcman. 2004. Appliances and their impact: The ownership of domestic technology and time spent on household work. *British Journal of Sociology* 55 (3): 401–23

Blagbrough, Jonathan, and Edmund Glynn. 1999. Child domestic workers: Characteristics of the modern slave and approaches to ending such exploitation. *Childhood* 6 (1): 51–6 (February)

Boyle, Theresa. 2004. Rise of new class system. *Toronto Star*, 3 October, A3

Carson, Jamie. 2002. Family spending power. *Perspectives on Labour and Income* 14 (4): 24–32 (Winter). Statistics Canada, Catalogue no. 75-001-XPE

Choi, Paul. 2004. William Li. *Toronto Star*, 6 September, B3

Clark, Warren. 2000. Traffic report: Weekday commuting patterns. *Canadian Social Trends*, no. 56 (Spring): 18–22. Statistics Canada, Catalogue no. 11-008

Communications Studies. 1999. Shopping for family. *Qualitative Inquiry* 5 (2): 147–80

Cowan, Ruth Swartz. 1983. *More work for mother.* New York: Basic Books

Cox, Christine. 2004. Outnumbered. *Hamilton Spectator,* 17 November, G5

De Graffe, J., D. Wann, and T.H. Naylor. 2001. *Affluenza: The all-consuming epidemic.* San Francisco: Brett-Koehler Publisher

Drolet, Marie. 2002. Wives, mothers and wages: Does timing matter? Research Paper Series, 11F0019, no. 186, 1 May 2002. Ottawa: Statistics Canada

– 2003. Motherhood and paycheques. *Canadian Social Trends,* no. 68 (Spring): 19–25. Statistics Canada, Catalogue no. 11-008

Duffy, Ann, Daniel Glenday, and Norene Pupo. 1997. *Good jobs, bad jobs, no jobs: The transformation of work in the 21st century.* Toronto: Harcourt, Brace

Duffy, Ann, and Norene Pupo. 1992. *Part-time paradox: Connecting gender, work and family.* Toronto: McClelland and Stewart

Ehrenreich, Barbara. 1983. *The hearts of men.* Garden City, N.Y.: Anchor Press

– 2004. Maid to order. In *Global woman: Nannies, maids, and sex workers in the new economy,* edited by Barbara Ehrenreich and Arlie Russell Hochschild, 85–103. New York: Owl Books

Ellison, Jonathan, and Warren Clark. 2001. Net shopping. *Canadian Social Trends,* no. 60 (Spring): 6–9. Statistics Canada, Catalogue no. 11-008

Eriksen, John. 2003. Public payment for informal care of disabled children: Some dilemmas of the Norwegian welfare state. *European Societies* 5 (4): 445–63

Glazer, Nona Y. 1993. *Women's paid and unpaid labor: The work transfer in health care and retailing.* Philadelphia: Temple University Press

Glenn, Evelyn Nakano. 2001. Gender, race, and the organization of reproductive labor. In *The critical study of work: Labor, technology, and global production,* edited by Rick Baldoz, Charles Koeber, and Philip Kraft, 71–82. Philadelphia: Temple University Press

Henly, Julia R. 2002. Informal support networks and the maintenance of low-wage jobs. In *Laboring below the line: The new ethnography of poverty, low-wage work, and survival in the global economy,* edited by Frank Munger, 179–203. New York: Russell Sage Foundation

Hertz, Rosanna, and Faith I. Ferguson. 1998. Only one pair of hands: Ways that single mothers stretch work and family resources. *Community, Work & Family* 1 (1): 13–37

Himmelweit, Susan. 1999. Caring labor. *Annals of the American Academy of Political and Social Science* 561 (January): 27–38

Hochschild, Arlie Russell. 2003. *The commercialization of intimate life: Notes from home and work.* Berkeley: University of California Press

Hondagneu-Sotelo, Pierette. 2001. *Domestica: Immigrant workers cleaning and caring in the shadows of affluence.* Berkeley: University of California Press

Johnson, Jennifer. 2002. *Getting by on the minimum: The lives of working-class women.* New York and London: Routledge

Johnston, Deirdre D., and Debra H. Swanson. 2003. Invisible mothers: A content analysis of motherhood ideologies and myths in magazines. *Sex Roles* 49 (1/2): 21–33 (July)

Jones, Andrew W. 2003. Caring labor and class consciousness: The class dynamics of gendered work. *Sociological Forum* 16 (2): 281–99

Katz, Michael B. 1975. *The people of Hamilton, Canada West: Family and class in a mid-nineteenth-century city.* Cambridge, Mass.: Harvard University Press

Kessler-Harris, Alice, and Karen Brodkin Sacks. 1987. The demise of domesticity in America. In *Women, households, and the economy,* edited by Lourdes Beneria and Catharine R. Stimpson, 65–84. New Brunswick: Rutgers University Press

Kremarik, Frances. 2000a. A family affair: Children's participation in sports. *Canadian Social Trends,* no. 58 (Autumn): 20–4. Statistics Canada, Catalogue no. 11-008

– 2000b. 100 years of urban development. *Canadian Social Trends,* no. 59 (Winter): 18–22. Statistics Canada, Catalogue no. 11-008

– 2002. The changing recreational spending patterns of Canadian families. *Canadian Social Trends,* no. 64 (Spring): 13–18. Statistics Canada, Catalogue no. 11-008

Lamphere, Louise, Patricia Zavella, Felipe Gonzales, with Peter B. Evans. 1993. *Sunbelt working mothers: Reconciling family and factory.* Ithaca: Cornell University Press

Lee, Yun-Suk, Barbara Schneider, and Linda J. Waite. 2003. Children and housework: Some unanswered questions. *Sociological Studies of Children and Youth* 9:105–25

Lepp, Annalee. 2002. Trafficking in women and the feminization of migration: The Canadian context. *Canadian Woman Studies* 21/22 (4/1): 90–9 (Spring/Summer)

Liying, Kang. 2003. Chinese children's changing family and school environments. *Journal of Family and Economic Issues* 24 (4): 381–95 (Winter)

Luxton, Meg. 1976. *More than a labour of love.* Toronto: Women's Press

Lyon, Dawn, and Alison E. Woodward. 2004. Gender and time at the top: Cultural constructions of time in high-level careers and homes. *European Journal of Women's Studies* 11 (2): 205–21

McLaren, Arlene Tigar, and Isabel Dyck. 2004. Mothering, human capital, and the "ideal immigrant." *Women's Studies International Forum* 27:41–53

Malarek, Victor. 2003. *The Natashas: The new global sex trade.* Toronto: Viking Canada

Man, Guida. 2004. Gender, work and migration: Deskilling Chinese immigrant women in Canada. *Women's Studies International Forum* 27:135–48

Manrique, Justo, and Helen H. Jensen. 1997. Spanish household demand for convenience meat products. *Agribusiness* 13 (5): 579–86

Mattingly, Marybeth J., and Suzanne M. Bianchi. 2003. Gender differences in the quantity and quality of free time: The U.S. experience. *Social Forces* 81 (3): 999–1030

Mokhiber, Russell, and Robert Weissman. 2004a. National Geographic kids under the corporate thumb. *Focus on the Corporation Web Column.* Posted 5 August 2004 at http://lists.essential.org/pipermail/corp-focus/2004/000182.html

– 2004b. Subway: Junk food, junk economy. *Focus on the Corporation Web Column.* Posted 13 July 2004 at http://lists.essential.org/pipermail/corp-focus/2004/000181.html

Nyberg, Anita. 2002. Gender, (de)commodification, economic (in)dependence and autonomous households: The case of Sweden. *New Divisions of Labour: Alternatives for Caring and Working* 22 (1): 72–95

Ogden, Philip E., and Ray Hall. 2004. The second demographic transition, new household forms and the urban population of France during the 1990s. *Transactions of the Institute for British Geographers* 29:88–105

Pavlovskaya, Marianna. 2004. Other transitions: Multiple economies of Moscow households in the 1990s. *Annals of the Association of American Geographers* 94 (2): 329–51

Presser, Harriet B. 2003. *Working in a 24/7 economy: Challenges for American families.* New York: Russell Sage Foundation

Pyper, Wendy. 2004. Employment trends in nursing. *Perspectives on Labour and Income* 5 (11): 5–13 (November)

Ridgeway, Cecelia, and Shelley J. Correll. 2004. Motherhood as a status characteristic. *Journal of Social Issues* 60 (4): 683–700

Sassen, Saskia. 2002. Deconstructing labour demand in today's advanced economies: Implications for low-wage employment. In *Laboring below the line: The new ethnography of poverty, low-wage work, and survival in the global economy,* edited by Frank Munger, 73–94. New York: Russell Sage Foundation

Schlosser, Eric. 2002. *Fast-food nation: The dark side of the all-American meal.* New York: Perennial Books

Schor, Juliet B. 1992. *The overworked American: The unexpected decline of leisure.* New York: Basic Books

Silver, Cynthia, and Susan Compton. 2002. No time to relax? How full-time workers spend the weekend. *Canadian Social Trends* 65 (Summer): 20–5. Statistics Canada, Catalogue no. 11-008

Statistics Canada. 2002a. Child care services industry 1999. *The Daily,* 26 April

– 2002b. Household spending. *The Daily,* 11 December

– 2003a. Household spending on domestic help. *The Daily,* 26 August

– 2003b. Survey of Household Spending 2002. *The Daily,* 17 December

– 2003c. Participation and Activity Limitation Survey: Children with disabilities. *The Daily,* 29 July
– 2003d. Working hours in Canada and the United States: 1979 to 2000. *The Daily,* 11 September
– 2004. E-commerce: Household shopping on the Internet. *The Daily,* 23 September
Sussman, Deborah. 1998. Moonlighting: A growing way of life. *Perspectives on Labour and Income* 10 (2): 24–31 (Summer). Statistics Canada, Catalogue no. 75-001-XPE
Teeple, Gary. 2000. *Globalization and the decline of social reform.* Aurora: Garamond Press
Theobald, Hildegard. 2003. Care for the elderly: Welfare system, professionalisation and the question of inequality. *International Journal of Sociology and Social Policy* 23 (4–5): 159–85
Ungerson, Clare. 2000. Cash in care. In *Care work: Gender, labor and the welfare state,* edited by Madonna Harrington Meyer, 68–88. New York: Routledge
White, Jerry. 1997. Health care, hospitals, and re-engineering: The nightingales sing the blues. In Duffy et al. 1997, 117–42
Williams, C.C. 2003. Evaluating the penetration of the commodity economy. *Futures* 35:857–68
Williams, Cara. 2002. Time or money? How high and low income Canadians spend their time. *Canadian Social Trends,* no. 65 (Summer): 7–11. Statistics Canada, Catalogue no. 11-008
– 2004. The sandwich generation. *Perspectives on Labour and Income* 5 (9): 5–12. Statistics Canada, Catalogue no. 75-001-XIE

11

Doubtful Data: Why Paradigms Matter in Counting the Health-Care Labour Force

PAT ARMSTRONG, HUGH ARMSTRONG, AND KATE LAXER

INTRODUCTION

Health care is labour intensive and female dominated. According to the Canadian Institute for Health Information (CIHI 2001, ix), "over 1.5 million people across the country worked in health and social services in 2000," accounting for "about one in 10 employed Canadians." Four out of five are women, although the report does not explore this gender dominance. It does go on to say that the "largest groups of unregulated health care providers are family members, friends and community volunteers." And most of these providers are also women. Their numbers, however, are not included in the 1.5 million.

As impressive as these numbers are, they tell only one kind of story about health-care work. They reflect a particular definition of, or way of understanding, this work, one that excludes many of those people whom an alternative definition would include as providers. This way of counting health-care work is consistent with a move towards defining care in narrow medical terms. Such a definition leaves out much of traditional women's work.

This chapter is about the relationships among paradigms, data, and policy. Using Canadian data published at the federal level, we begin by looking at the medical model that dominates in health care and at the ways this model is evident in data collection. The emerging definitions of health-care work that accompany current reforms build on a medical model, emphasizing and reinforcing intervention and cure. The second section of the chapter sets out a social determinants of health approach to health-care work. This alternative approach leads to a different way of counting this work, one that considerably expands the numbers of health-care workers and includes much more of traditional women's work in health-care labour.

A MEDICAL MODEL FOR CARE PROVIDERS

Allopathic medicine is at the core of Canadian health care. What we think of simply as medicine is a particular approach that emphasizes the penetration of the body physically by surgery and chemically by drugs (Willis 1983, 2). It is based on a set of assumptions that are often implicit or even unrecognized but are nonetheless powerful (Armstrong and Armstrong 2003, 18–46). For allopaths, illness is understood as being determined primarily by biology and the focus is on fixing or curing particular body parts. Diagnosis and cure are directed by a physician whose expertise and authority are based on a command of scientific research that has established the causes and corrective treatments. Thus, the physician is at the centre, directing the treatment that is understood as the central purpose of health care. It is not surprising then that doctors and nurses are the ones who are the subjects of research on health-care work, given that the dominance of allopathic medicine puts them at the centre of diagnosis and cure.

Indeed, for the first half of the last century, the overwhelming majority of those working for pay in recognized hospitals were doctors and nurses. However, at the beginning of the twentieth century, doctors outnumbered nurses, and most care was provided at home by unpaid women relatives and low-paid servants, who either worked under the direction of doctors or simply followed what they had learned from other women. Women in religious orders, supported by paid women who undertook a range of tasks, did much of the institutional care.

Nursing first appeared in the Canadian census in 1901, even though a successful training school for nurses had been established in 1874 (Coburn 1987:447). In 1901 the census reported 5,000 physicians but only 208 student and graduate nurses. Thirty years later, there were over 30,000 nurses, and according to the census, they outnumbered doctors three to one (Coburn 1987, Table 2). Nurses in training were included in these counts because they learned mainly by apprenticing in hospitals and thus provided much of the labour. By 1961, there were 85,000 nurses (graduate or in training) compared to 21,000 physicians and surgeons (Dominion Bureau of Statistics 1966, Table 8B). Ninety-seven per cent of the nurses were women, while 93 per cent of the doctors were men.

The increase represented both a growing shift to institutional care and the increasing numbers of women formally trained for the work. It indicated as well the increasingly complex nature of medical intervention and the growing use of technology in care. Nurses did most of the work on the wards, combining a wide variety of tasks and skills in providing care. With public health insurance covering hospital care available across Canada by 1961, the demand for nurses grew significantly. The 1986 census recorded 277,000 nurses, including in this definition only nurse supervisors, graduates, and those in training (Statistics Canada 1988, Table 2). Although only 4 per cent of these nurses were male, men accounted for 9 per cent of the nurse supervisors.

There are still a large number of nurses providing care in Canada, 300,000 of them according to CIHI (2001, 9). And most of them work in general duty, performing a range of care work in hospitals. However, two significant developments have altered what nurses do. First, registered nurses (RNs) successfully organized both to limit entry into their profession through registration and to demand better pay and conditions of work. The overwhelming majority are now unionized. Second, care became increasingly complicated and the numbers receiving care grew significantly. Both developments contributed to the narrowing of nursing work and to the move to hand over some of what nurses had been doing to workers with less formal training.

Employers looked for ways to reduce their reliance on these increasingly expensive employees, and nurses looked for ways to hand over parts of their work. Other kinds of nurses, with fewer years of education, were brought in to do some of this nursing work at lower pay and often under the direction of the RNs. This change is reflected in the census. The 1961 census lists only two categories of nurses – namely, graduate nurses and nurses in training (Dominion Bureau of Statistics 1966: Table 8B) – but the 1971 census lists seven categories in the nursing, therapy, and related assisting occupations: nurse supervisors, graduate nurses, nurses in training, nursing assistants, nursing aides and orderlies, therapists, and assisting occupations in nursing (Statistics Canada 1988, xxxi). In 1986 the supervisors, graduate nurses, and nurses in training accounted for just 68 per cent of this broad nursing category, even though everyone in the category was doing work once done by those defined as nurses.

The combined number of nursing assistants and aides grew from 98,000 in 1971 to 117,000 in 1986. More than four out of five were women. But these non-RN nurses, too, successfully fought for registration and for better pay and conditions. As the licensed practical nurses (LPNs)[1] became more expensive, their work was also handed over to others, such as to personal care workers with little formal education.

The numbers in these "assisting occupations" grew from 10,000 to 27,000 during the same period (Statistics Canada 1988, Table 2). Meanwhile, clerical, housekeeping, laundry, and dietary workers also took on more of the work once done by nurses.

There were similar developments in doctors' work. The introduction of public insurance for doctors' care a decade after hospital insurance's introduction contributed to a significant increase in the number of doctors, from 21,000 in 1961 to 47,000 in 1986 (Statistics Canada 1988, Table 2). The number of female doctors grew over this period, but women still accounted for only 20 per cent of the profession in 1986. According to CIHI (2001, 10), there were 58,000 physicians in Canada in 2000, and by this date, 30 per cent of them were women. Women's share will continue to grow, given that now just over half of medical students are women (Hawley 2004, 9). As was the case with nurses, some of the work done by doctors was carved out to be done by others. Doctors' work has become increasingly complemented by the work of a range of technicians, who take specimens and do tests often previously done by doctors. The number of medical and dental technicians nearly tripled between 1951 and 1961 (Dominion Bureau of Statistics 1966, Table 8B), and there were 48,000 radiological and laboratory technologists and technicians by 1986. Almost 80 per cent of them were women. These lower-paid workers have also organized and sought regulation to protect their interests. And they too are being replaced by others with less training.

The data on health-care occupations have been revised to reflect this process of carving out tasks formerly done by doctors and nurses. A much broader range of nurses, technologists, and technicians are now included. But the new categories not only reflect changes in the division of labour; they also reflect a particular way of understanding care. The focus on doctors and nurses, as well as on some of those who have taken on parts of their work, leaves out many of those who work for pay in care. And it leaves out all of those who provide unpaid care.

The nature of this understanding of health care can be seen in the way work is organized and in the way providers are counted. Take, for example, the Canadian Institute for Health Information's report entitled *Canada's Health Care Providers*. This report is "intended to serve as a consolidated reference about what we know and don't know about Canada's health care providers" (CIHI 2001, 1), and says it "covers a broad range of health care providers, including regulated and unregulated providers, as well as family and volunteer caregivers" (9). However, the chapter "Who's Who in Health Care" has only four categories: nursing, physicians, other health professionals, and "other members of the team." Included in the nursing category are registered nurses

(RNs), licensed practical nurses (LPNs) and registered psychiatric nurses (RPNs), although nursing aides are listed in a chart on providers. The "other team members" are the family, friends, and community volunteers. These others are described as helping around the house, assisting with personal care, and providing emotional support if they are women and with providing home maintenance and repairs if they are men (12). These unpaid providers are not included in the later chapters, even though estimates indicate they provide up to 90 per cent of care (Denton 1997).

The most detailed data in the CIHI report focus on doctors and RNs. These two groups account for the largest occupational categories within the data if we leave out the unpaid ones. While the report has a broad definition of nursing that includes licensed practical nurses, it says that the information on LPNs "is more limited" (CIHI 2001, 9), as is that on other health professionals – hence the more expansive discussion of RNs. Yet the absence of data on these other nurses itself raises the issue of who is central to care and worthy of further investigation. It is clear that the health-care labour force is defined primarily in terms of doctors and RNs, with some informal help from friends, relatives, and neighbours.

The assumptions of a system based on diagnosis and cure is more obvious in Statistics Canada data. In Statistics Canada's journal *Perspectives on Labour and Income*, Diane Galarneau (2004, 16) reports that there are three categories of health-care workers: "professionals, technical personnel, and support personnel." Professionals are those who "are primarily concerned with diagnosing and treating health problems in humans and animals and with providing related services." This group includes doctors and nurses, as well as therapists. The other two groups are defined in relation to these professionals. "Technical personnel are primarily concerned with providing technical services to professionals," while support personnel are "primarily concerned with providing technical support to professionals" (17). In short, the core work force is defined as those who diagnose and cure, with others understood as assisting them in their work.

More recently, Health Canada dedicated a special issue of its *Health Policy Research Bulletin* to health human resources. The article "Canada's Health Care Workers: A Snapshot" begins by saying that "health care providers include physicians, nurses and other health professionals regulated by provincial legislation, as well as unregulated health care providers" (Hawley 2004, 8). Unregulated health-care providers are further defined to include workers "such as nursing aides and orderlies." Complementary and alternative providers are also mentioned, as are the informal and formal volunteers. This article then goes on to say, in an interesting equation of family care with female care, that "[h]istorically, the family has been key in providing care. Today, however, most women participate in the paid labour force and have less time to meet the needs of family members who are ill, especially when they care for their own children as well" (9). The article then proceeds to focus almost exclusively on doctors and nurses, although in addition to the brief comments on complementary, alternative, and unpaid providers, there is a small paragraph on the lack of data on other health professionals and another paragraph on interdisciplinary teams.

All three of these publications – from CIHI, Statistics Canada, and Health Canada – rely on occupational categories to determine who are to be defined as health-care workers. People are grouped into occupations on the basis of the kind of work they do. Only the kinds of work defined by Statistics Canada or CIHI as health care will thus be included in their analyses. Although both of these statistical agencies mention some other paid and unpaid providers, their detailed analyses focus on those defined as involved in diagnosis and cure. This narrow clinical definition of care leaves out many people who define themselves as care providers. It also fits neatly with reform efforts to restrict access to public services by more narrowly defining care to include only those aspects that involve clinical intervention, thereby opening up many other aspects of care work to delivery by the for-profit sector.

Figure 11.1 presents a breakdown of the paid health-care labour force, as viewed according to the medical model. Physicians and surgeons form the largest single group within the "professional occupations in health" category, but at something under 60,000 individuals they make up less than half of this category.

A SOCIAL DETERMINANTS OF HEALTH MODEL FOR PROVIDERS

Although the medical model increasingly dominates formal health-care practices and data collection, policy literature talks more and more about the determinants of health (Evans, Barer, and Marmor 1994; National Forum on Health 1997; Wilkinson and Marmot 2003; Raphael 2004). The focus in this approach is on a range of factors that influence people's health, with health rather than illness the central concern. From this "upstream" perspective, health is primarily the result of favourable economic, social, and physical conditions, as distinct from the "downstream" effects of most health-care interventions, which are undertaken to treat individuals who have become diseased

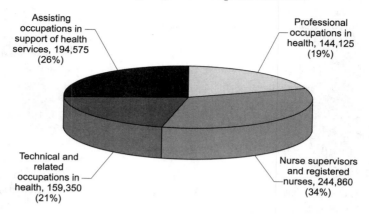

Figure 11.1 Composition of health-care labour force according to medical model, count, and percentage, Census 2001

or injured. This is not to ignore the biological realities of genetic pre-dispositions, infectious diseases, and so on. Nor is it to ignore those health-care interventions that prevent disease (such as vaccinations against polio), that detect disease (such as mammograms for breast cancer), and that cure or control disease (such as prescription drugs and surgical operations). Rather, this approach locates biology and health care in a broader context, one that focuses on the root causes of health and ill-health.

Health Canada recognizes twelve determinants of health. Its list, which has changed somewhat over time, includes biology and health care, but also contains gender, culture, income, employment, education, healthy child development, physical environments, social environments, social support networks, and personal health practices. Diagnosis and cure, at the core of the medical model, constitute components, albeit the dominant components, of health care, itself but one of twelve determinants on Health Canada's list.

The determinants are neither mutually exclusive nor independent variables. They overlap and interpenetrate one another. Income, education, and employment, for example, interact to help form social classes as well as health outcomes. Both the classes and the outcomes are highly gendered and racialized. Although the social determinants are at times deployed rhetorically as a justification for cutbacks in public spending on health care, the focus of this chapter is on the central role of the other determinants in health-care services.

Years ago, political economists such as Ivan Illich (1976) and Vincente Navarro (1976) pointed to the critical role these determinants play within health-care delivery. Health care cannot be treated simply as a discrete variable determining health. Income, working conditions, and employment security matter profoundly to those working in care. Equally important, the income, education, and employment of care providers have an impact on the quality of care they deliver (Rogers et al. 2004). People are even more vulnerable to their physical environments, especially in terms of standards of cleanliness, when they are ill or disabled. So, too, are those who provide the ill with care. The need for social support is strong, for both those receiving care and those providing it. The personal practices of providers and patients are also critical, as the enforcement of handwashing at hospital doors during the SARS (severe acute respiratory syndrome) crisis taught us all.

Such an approach, then, leads to a broader vision of health care than one confined to the medical model. Adopting this broader vision means including all those who work in care, because physical, economic, and social environments, as well as diagnosis and cure, contribute to health care. Cleaners and chaplains, laundry workers and cooks all contribute to health care, and thus they should all be counted in the sector. This would expand our numbers well beyond the data provided by CIHI or Statistics Canada because it means including everyone who works in care. What would matter is their contribution to care, with care broadly defined to include such critical aspects as clean rooms and laundry, record keeping, and food preparation. Moreover, such workers would be counted as health-care workers rather than as cleaning, clerical, laundry, or cooking workers, as if they were employed in a hotel or an office building.

A social determinants of health approach would also include those who work in social services. People in these jobs provide not only social support, but also income support, childcare, and education for both parenting and employment. Quebec local health centres (CLSCs) recognize social services as integral to care by including social workers in their staff, as do the community health and social service centres in several other provinces. Equally important, this approach to health would acknowledge the contribution of unpaid care. In short, it produces a much larger number of people paid (or not paid) to work in health and social services than is the case with an approach that focuses on doctor-centred health services alone.

The extent of the effect of this broader vision is evident in Figure 11.2. In this figure, all those included in Figure 11.1 are present again, but together they constitute only 46 per cent of the paid health-care labour force as viewed according to the social determinants model.

Looking at the totality of the paid health-care workplace, as opposed to looking only at those jobs defined as health-care work, allows us to

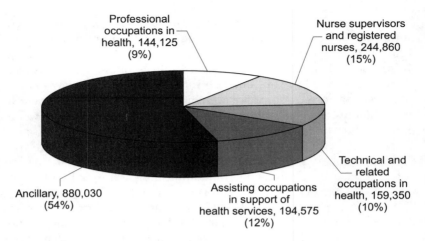

Figure 11.2 Composition of health-care labour force according to the social determinants of health model, count, and percentage, Census 2001

get some idea of the numbers missing from the occupational data on health-care providers. Statistics Canada does produce data that count those employed in the health and social service industries, allowing a somewhat broader approach to care. Because these data are based on the nature of the organization rather than on the type of work, the health and social service category includes more people than the category of those defined above as health-care workers.

A Statistics Canada report indicated that in 1941 health professionals (physicians and surgeons, dentists, graduate nurses and nurses in training, osteopaths and chiropractors, medical and dental technicians)[2] did not include all the paid workers in health services. Almost 25,000 other people worked in health care, accounting for 28 per cent of the health-care labour force. By 1961, these other workers made up 51 per cent of those counted as working in health services (Dominion Bureau of Statistics 1966, Table 8B and Table 12). There are, in other words, an enormous number of people missing from the data when the focus is exclusively on professionals, technical personnel, and support personnel – that is, on those the medical model guides us to see as the health-care workers.

MISSING PAID CARE PROVIDERS

Who are these missing people and what do they do? These data leave out people who have taken over some of the health-care workload. Increasingly called ancillary workers, they cook, clean, do laundry,

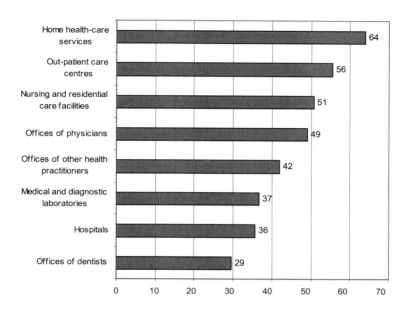

Figure 11.3 Percentage of ancillary workers within various health services, Census 2001

keep records, deliver food and patients, and ensure security as well as the maintenance of facilities. A growing number are managers. Most are women.

As Figure 11.3 indicates, these ancillary workers can be found in every health service. They account for just over a third of all hospital and laboratory workers. They make up nearly half of the people who work in doctors' offices and 42 per cent of the people who work in the offices of other health professionals. And they are the majority in long-term care facilities, outpatient centres, and homecare services. Because hospitals employ the bulk of the labour force, the number of ancillary workers in hospitals is actually larger than the number in other settings. Moreover, care is shifting to those areas where ancillary workers make up the majority of the labour force. In other words, their numbers are large and are growing along with health-care reforms. At the same time, however, they are becoming increasingly invisible in the data on health-care workers.

Equally important, even these data now underestimate the number of people working for pay in health services. Under the North American Industrial Classification System (NAICS), people are classified according to who their employer is rather than according to where they work. As a consequence of this classification method, work that has been contracted out is often not recorded as health services work. So, for example, people who were once counted as health services housekeepers could disappear from the data on health services if they continue to do the same job in the same hospital but their work has been contracted out to a private firm. Their absence from the data is not simply a definitional issue of interest only to a few academics immersed in numbers, however. Their absence both reflects and reinforces developments in managerial practices and government policy, as well as in gendered strategies for reform and a medical model for care. Fewer and fewer of those who are not engaged directly in intervention and cure are included in the definition of care.

The Ontario minister of health and long-term care suggested recently that one way hospitals could save money would be to lower wages for jobs such as sweeping to match the private sector (Urquhart 2004). Here he was following the lead of British Columbia, where such reform strategies targeting these ancillary workers are well underway (Cohen and Cohen 2004b). Indeed, the B.C. government has made it policy to override collective agreements that prohibit the contracting-out of these services. Quebec has introduced a similar policy that "covers all unionized workers, overrides job security provisions, removes successorship rights and eliminates provisions requiring new employers to retain the terms of existing agreements for a minimum of one year" (Cohen and Cohen 2004a, 76).

These non-clinical jobs are done primarily by women, and it is primarily women who will suffer the consequences of the kind of privatization strategies that the Ontario minister suggests and British Columbia practises. In British Columbia, thousands of women lost their jobs and those who remained saw their wages and benefits plummet. Cleaners, for example, who continued to do the same jobs in the same workplaces had their wages cut in half (Stinson 2004, 20). Pay equity gains were lost, and these workers went from being among the highest paid for their unionized job category to the lowest paid. The employers with the contracts are also less likely than public sector employers to have policies that are vital for women, such as strategies to prevent sexual harassment. Investigations by consulting firms indicate that laundry, food, and cleaning contracts have resulted in few cost savings and poor working conditions. More importantly, contracting-out may not improve quality of care and may even undermine it (Cohen and Cohen 2004b; Cohen 2001; CUPE 2003). In more than one case, contracting-out has been reversed in favour of old forms of direct employment in the public sector because costs and quality had suffered.

Research in other countries suggests that contracting out services makes work more precarious. Case studies in the United Kingdom and Northern Ireland "found that exposure to tendering led to the, often dramatic, erosion of terms and conditions of employment ... Estimates state that some 40 per cent of the NHS ancillary jobs were lost" (Sachdev 2001, 5). Moreover, the impact on women is more extensive, resulting in a widening of the gender gap. According to the Equal Opportunities Commission of Northern Ireland (1996), most of the work that was contracted out was female dominated. The rate of female job loss was more than double that of men. While both women and men experienced wage reductions, the proportionate reduction was larger for women. Some benefits disappeared, along with some entitlements.

Contracting-out not only has an impact on those working in the firms with the contracts; it also has an impact on those who remain in the public sector. In order to maintain their positions, the public sector workers who remain are increasingly pressured to act like the contractors. The British research shows how the same practices that the for-profit firms applied were introduced in the public sector. Manual staff, which includes cleaners and caterers among others, "in particular, has borne the brunt of the changes that have been made in working methods, pay and conditions" (Walsh and Davis 1993, 163).

Defining these jobs as ancillary and non-health care contributes to these processes. So does the fact that most of the workers are women and most of the work is associated with women. Figure 11.4 shows the very gendered nature of work in health care. Four out of five people counted as part of the health and social service industry are women. This figure also shows that women make up the overwhelming majority of those employed in ancillary services. Ninety-three per cent of secretaries and clerical workers, 95 per cent of childcare and homecare workers, and over two-thirds of the cleaning and food service workers are women. Just over one in ten are identified as visible minorities. Compared with other health-care workers, ancillary workers are also less likely to have union coverage. While 71 per cent of those whom CIHI and Statistics Canada count as health-care providers have union coverage, this is the case for only 43 per cent of the ancillary workers currently counted as working in the health industry (Figure 11.5).

The strategy of contracting out these ancillary jobs is based on two assumptions, both of which have been challenged. The first assumption is that housekeeping, clerical work, food preparation, and other non-clinical jobs in health care are the equivalent of similarly titled jobs in the private sector. We need go no further than the reports out of Quebec hospitals on C. difficile to see that cleaning hospitals is not

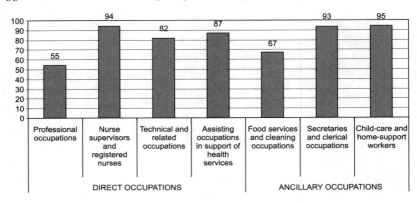

Figure 11.4 Percentage of women in various health occupations, Census 2001

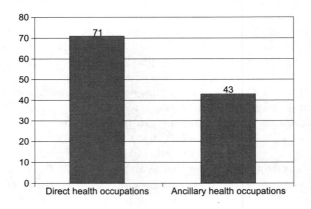

Figure 11.5 Percentage of union coverage, direct and ancillary occupations, Survey of Labour and Income Dynamics, 2001

the same as cleaning empty office buildings at night. Indeed, Quebec health-care experts are talking about the importance of clean surfaces in preventing the spread of the disease (Branswell 2004, A4). Similarly, SARS is a hospital-transmitted disease. During the crisis in Toronto, prevention strategies focused on cleaning and on recognizing that health care places special demands on all staff, from physicians to housekeepers. Such strategies were particularly important given the concern that SARS could be spread by providers moving among different workplaces. More than half (55 per cent) of ancillary workers are employed in multiple job sites, making them the most likely to be transmitting germs from place to place. Clerical work, too, is quite specialized in health care, and so are the demands. Mistakes in records or in filing can easily costs lives.

Everyone who works in health care is essential to the teamwork approach so recently promoted by the current Ontario government. They are all health-care workers. Separating out these workers and targeting them for lower pay could undermine the entire team. The British House of Commons Health Select Committee warned that "[t]he often spurious division of staff into clinical or non-clinical groups can create an institutional apartheid which might be detrimental to staff morale and to patients" (NHS Estates 2003).

The second assumption around contracting-out is that housekeeping, dietary, and clerical work is unskilled and thus appropriately low paid in the private sector. Indeed, the article in Statistics Canada's *Perspectives on Labour and Income* speaks of "support occupations requiring few skills" in reference to "dental assistants, nurses aides, orderlies, and patients service associates" (Galarneau 2004, 17). If these jobs are assumed to require few skills, it is unlikely that those who work in ancillary jobs will have any of their skills recognized. Yet research has demonstrated that this work is undervalued and the skills required to perform it rendered invisible primarily because it is women who do the work. The skills and responsibilities of women are invisible in part because many of them are learned outside the formal education system, do not result in differentiated credentials, and are often learned from other women on the job (see Armstrong and Armstrong 2003, 96–102; Cohen 2001). They are skills we too often think any woman has simply because she is a woman and because the skills are innate, deserving little financial reward. The high numbers of immigrant and visible minority workers employed in these jobs further contribute to the undervaluing. As a self-described hospital support worker explained in a *Toronto Star* article, "to clean a room for a SARS patient, hospital cleaners have to 'terminally' clean the room twice. Each cleaning takes 85 minutes. The cleaner must put on and take off masks, gowns, and gloves in a specific order. Failure to do this correctly will mean infection and possibly death" (Wilson 2004). By reducing the job to sweeping, the Ontario minister of health demonstrates a profound ignorance of the nature of cleaning work in health care.

When women clean, cook, do laundry, and do clerical work in the private sector, the work is low paid and often precarious in other ways as well. The food and accommodation sector is characterized by low pay and job insecurity (Maxwell 2002). Service and clerical work constitute two of the four lowest-wage occupational categories, and women account for two-thirds of low-wage earners. Employees in food and accommodation services are among those whose job quality is lowest.

And these are the standards the minister seems to be promoting. Private sector jobs with the same titles as jobs in the public sector are even less likely to have union coverage, benefits, or full-time employment (Armstrong and Laxer 2006). In other words, making bad jobs in the private sector the model for hospital work not only is bad practice but is also discriminatory against women and other equity-seeking groups.

The new industrial classification system used by Statistics Canada, then, does reflect a new policy of defining some workers out of health care and contracting out their work to for-profit firms. However, this is a policy that contradicts the Canada Health Act, which at least defined everyone working in hospitals as part of the health-care system. It also contradicts what we know about recovery, cure, and health maintenance. Both the full range of workers and their conditions of work contribute to the quality of care. The ways in which CIHI and Statistics Canada count health-care workers may fit with the new corporate strategies in care, but they do not fit with what we know about the factors involved in health care or with how the workers themselves define their work. As a result, large numbers are missing from their count of health-care workers and most of those missing are women.

MISSING UNPAID CARE PROVIDERS

It is not only the majority of paid workers that CIHI and Statistics Canada leave out of their count; they also leave out the unpaid care providers, most of whom are also women. CIHI (2001, 12) does provide a section on "other members of the team," by which they mean people who care for friends and family either informally or formally through voluntary organizations. These unpaid care providers remain invisible in the rest of the report, however, just as they are in the other two publications based on Statistics Canada data.

Statistics Canada has developed a way to count this unpaid labour, although there remains no internationally recognized definition of unpaid work (McCredie and Sewell 1999). Several surveys collect relevant data, but the most detailed are those produced by the time-use diaries that are the basis for the General Social Survey (GSS). Participants in the GSS record the start and end time for each of their daily activities; they are also interviewed over a twelve-month period. However, there are significant problems with the data that result.

One of the problems is the invisibility of work in households and the traditional division of labour there. This invisibility is linked to the privacy of homes and the unpaid nature of domestic work, as well as to the work's association with women. Women have long taken the major responsibility for cooking, cleaning, laundry, shopping, and caring.

When people become ill, disabled, or frail, the workload in the house-hold increases, but the ongoing labour, along with the additional work, frequently seems to be just part of what women do. As a result, when women are asked to calculate the time spent on care, much of it may be invisible to them and thus unrecorded in surveys. A Canada-Australia study of time-diaries found a significant discrepancy between the time women record they spent on care work in particular and the time they talk about in interviews. "Most of the additional domestic work seems to take the form of cooking and cleaning, as well as laun-dry for women, and home repairs and maintenance for men" (Bittman et al. 2004, 85). In contrast to the women, men were found to be more likely to record their care workloads precisely, likely because it is non-traditional work for them. In other words, the same work that is increasingly missing from the counts of paid health-care providers is also missing from the counts of unpaid providers.

Although the data are far from precise, they do reveal some obvious patterns. As daughters, mothers, partners, friends, or volunteers, women make up the overwhelming majority of unpaid primary care-givers and spend more time than men in providing care. A national survey by Decima Research Inc. (2002, 1) reported that nearly 80 per cent of family caregivers are women. They also make up the over-whelming majority of the volunteers who provide unpaid personal care to non-family members.

Apart from putting in more hours than men, women are also much more likely than men to provide personal care and offer emotional support. According to the data from the General Social Survey, 21 per cent of women compared with 11 per cent of men are involved in the physical care of children. Women also provide 120 of the 190 million hours per year devoted to personal and other care for adults. And they provide twice as much care for the ill or disabled as men do and more than three times as much unpaid babysitting (Zukewich 2003, 17). Men's contributions are more likely to be concentrated in care management or household maintenance, shopping, or transpor-tation (Campbell and Martin-Matthews 2000; Rosenthal and Martin-Matthews 1999). In other words, women are more likely to provide the care that is daily and inflexible, while men provide care that can be more easily planned and organized around paid work (Gignac, Kelloway, and Gottlieb 1996). Men are also more likely than women to get formal support when they do provide care, on the assumption that they must have paid jobs and that they lack the skills necessary to pro-vide care (Aronson and Neysmith 1997; Morris et al. 1999; Keefe and Fancey 1997). Women provide personal care even when they have paid jobs, although higher-income women may be better positioned to become care managers rather than care providers (Rosenthal and Martin-Matthews 1999).

Some men have to, and continue to, provide care in a variety of forms. Like women, they care for their spouses. However, fewer men are called on for such care because their wives usually outlive them, given women's greater longevity and the general pattern of men marrying women younger than themselves. Men care for their parents, too, providing up to a quarter of this care (Campbell and Martin-Matthews 2000). Men also care for their same sex partners, and they serve as community volunteers in a number of capacities, managing care, providing transport and support, delivering meals, and doing household chores. And like women, they may provide care to siblings, in-laws, or other relatives (Buchignani and Armstrong-Esther 1999).

Friends – male and female – also provide considerable caregiving, although we know less about them than we do about the spouses, parents, and children who are caregivers. A Statistics Canada study found that nearly one in five of the people who had moved in order to provide care were friends of the person needing care, rather than relatives, suggesting that friends do much more than offer the occasional visit (Cranswick 1999, 12).

In addition to the family and friends who provide care, there are volunteers who offer various kinds of support. Statistics Canada does record volunteering, distinguishing formal volunteers who work through organizations from those informal volunteers who simply offer their time or money on their own. As with unpaid caregiving, it is important to assess what kind of volunteering is being recorded and what kinds of hours are spent volunteering. Statistics Canada counts a very wide range of activities as volunteering, many of which are quite remote from care work broadly defined.

Volunteers are most commonly found in the arts, culture, and recreation industry. The social services industry comes second, with volunteers' services including visiting to offer social support and undertaking other health-promoting activities. The health industry comes fifth, accounting for only 13 per cent of volunteers and 9 per cent of volunteer hours (Hall, McKeown, and Roberts 2001). In other words, volunteering is not primarily about providing care, but a significant number of people do volunteer as caregivers. Women are more concentrated than men in volunteer work that is time-consuming and/or involves direct care.

The kind of care provided by the unpaid workers involves much more than the "helping" that CIHI suggests (2001, 12). Very little research has been done on the skill level of such care providers, and there is very little evidence that providers are tested for skills. It is assumed that women in particular have the skills and the desire to do the work, along with the moral obligation. This remains the case in spite of the shift towards quite sophisticated forms and technologies of care in the household. Some short training is sometimes provided to family and friends by nurses and others. Nurses find themselves teaching women family members in minutes how to do tasks that took them entire courses to learn. This process makes the skills of all those involved – many of whom are from racialized or immigrant groups – less visible and, ultimately, less valued.

Thus, in looking for the missing health-care providers, we need to go beyond large categories such as volunteering to look at the nature of the work. This closer examination tells us that it is mainly women who are missing from the data on unpaid providers. Equally important, we need to ask which women are missing from the data. The research suggests that income and education matter at least as much as culture and racialized categories in terms of the kinds and amounts of care provided and thus in the choices women have (Chubachi 1999; Decima Research 2002; Dorazio-Migliore 1999; Guberman 1999). Women with money are more likely to purchase care and have the means to do so, regardless of their cultural background or immigration status. And the poorer women are, regardless of their culture, the more likely they are to have little choice about providing care (Morris et al.1999). Therefore, leaving out the data on unpaid care means leaving out the women with the fewest resources.

On the one hand, Statistics Canada counts unpaid care workers, and on the other, it leaves them out of the overall count of providers. As is the case with CIHI's way of counting who works in the health-care industry, Statistics Canada's inclusion/absence method is consistent with current policy. More and more care is being shifted to the household and community, and it is important for government to know something about the care provided there. At the same time, those providing care receive few formal supports from employers or government.

The federal government has made a small move to support some unpaid care providers who have paid employment. Employment Insurance (EI) now provides for up to six weeks compassionate leave to care for a dying relative. However, this is very limited support, and many women may be ineligible for the benefit if they lack the required hours of paid work to qualify for EI. Some unions have negotiated leave arrangements that can be used to care for ill relatives. And there is some small support in the form of tax relief. But in general unpaid providers are missing from both data and policy as they take up more of the work left undone by paid providers of care (Grant et al. 2004).

Measuring the extent of unpaid care work and including the people who perform it in the data on providers not only makes visible women's unpaid work, but also offers a more accurate account of economic production. If women did not do this work without pay, it would in many instances have to be done by someone with pay. Indeed, some of the current care work done in the home was previously done by paid female providers.

In sum, both a medical model and current policy are evident in who are counted as health-care providers. The focus is on those paid to provide diagnosis and treatment. The farther care providers work from this core, the less likely they are to be counted as part of care work. As institutional care becomes more and more restricted to those with needs that fit the medical model, more and more care workers are excluded from the count. Most of those thus excluded are women, especially those women who do the traditional women's work of cleaning, cooking, and laundry. These exclusions fit with current government policies for contracting out ancillary work and for shifting care to the community and household. And they contribute to the shift of care work to low-paid, insecure jobs and to unpaid providers.

In short, the broader definition of care that flows from a determinants of health approach counts many more people as care providers. Even though policy-makers increasingly talk about the need for such an approach, it is not evident in the practices or the data.

CONCLUSIONS

Paradigms matter. The way health-care providers are counted reflects the medical model that is dominant in health care. Statistics Canada defines health-care providers in ways that place doctors and nurses – those who diagnose, treat, and cure – at the core. Others are counted as health providers if they directly assist these doctors and nurses in their work. Their jobs are described as support occupations because they assist this medical core, not because they support those in need of care. Missing from the data are those who would be included under a determinants of health approach, one that appreciates how health is influenced by physical and social environments. Some of these invisible providers are paid and even more are unpaid for their work. As more care is moved out of health services into communities and households, more people who provide care are left out of the count and the focus is even more on providers who fit in the medical model. Statistics Canada does provide data by industry, and many of the missing paid workers can be found in the occupation and industry data. However, Statistics Canada has begun, with NAICS, to reflect new managerial and government practices. In an effort to save money and control the workforce in care, health managers have contracted out much of the ancillary work. Once this happens, these workers may be defined out of health care in spite of their demonstrated contribution to care. Most of those contracted out and defined out of care are women, the women who are already the lowest-paid workers with the fewest benefits and the least security.

The issue is not simply one of counting. Making these mainly female workers invisible in health care reinforces strategies that allow those with pay to have their labour conditions undermined and those without pay to be conscripted into care.

NOTES

Authors' Note: The authors would like to thank the Canadian Health Services Research Foundation, the Canadian Institute for Health Research, and the Canadian Foundation for Innovation for providing funding that contributed to the development of this chapter.

1 The title "registered practical nurse" is used in several provinces instead of "licensed practical nurse." Because some other provinces employ the title "registered psychiatric nurse" the acronym RPN can be confusing. We are thus using licensed practical nurse and LPN to refer to registered practical nurses as well as licensed practical nurses, and RPN to refer solely to registered psychiatric nurses.
2 Note that there is no listing of pharmacists in the published data from the Dominion Bureau of Statistics for 1961.

REFERENCES

Armstrong, Pat, and Hugh Armstrong. 2003. *Wasting away: The undermining of Canadian health care.* Toronto: Oxford University Press

Armstrong, Pat, and Kate Laxer. 2006. Precarious work, privatization, and the health-care industry: The case of ancillary workers. In *Precarious employment: Understanding labour market insecurity in Canada*, edited by Leah F. Vosko. Montreal and Kingston: McGill-Queen's University Press

Aronson, Jane, and Sheila M. Neysmith. 1997. The retreat of the state and long-term provision: Implementations for frail elderly people, unpaid family carers and paid home care workers. *Studies in Political Economy* 53 (Summer): 37–66

Bittman, Michael, Janet E. Fast, Kimberley Fisher, and Cathy Thompson. 2004. Making the invisible visible: The life and time(s) of informal caregivers. In *Family time: The social organization of care*, edited by Nancy Folbre and Michael Bittman. London: Routledge

Branswell, Helen. 2004. Epidemic linked to one bug strain. *Toronto Star*, 2
    October, A4
Buchignani, N., and C. Armstrong-Esther. 1999. Informal care and older
    native Canadians. *Ageing and Society* 19 (1): 3–32
Campbell, L.D., and A. Martin-Matthews. 2000. Caring sons: Exploring
    men's involvement in filial care. *Canadian Journal on Aging/La Revue
    Canadienne du Vieillissement,* Spring, 57–79
Chubachi, N. 1999. Geographies of Nisei Japanese Canadians and their
    attitudes towards elderly long-term care. MA thesis, Queen's University
CIHI (Canadian Institute for Health Information). 2001. *Canada's health care
    providers.* Ottawa: CIHI
Coburn, Judi. 1987. "I see and I am silent": A short history of nursing in
    Ontario 1850–1930. In *Health and Canadian Society,* edited by David
    Coburn et al. 2nd ed. Toronto: Fitzhenry and Whiteside
Cohen, Marjorie Griffin. 2001. Do comparisons between hospital support
    workers and hospitality workers make sense? Report prepared for the
    Hospital Employees Union (CUPE), Burnaby, B.C.
Cohen, Marjorie Griffin, and Marcy Cohen. 2004a. The politics of pay equity
    in B.C.'s health care system. *Canadian Woman Studies* 23 (3–4): 72–6
– 2004b. *A return to wage discrimination: Pay equity losses through privatization in
    health care.* Vancouver: Canadian Centre for Policy Alternatives
Cranswick, K. 1999. Help close at hand: Relocating to give or receive care.
    Canadian Social Trends 55 (Winter)
CUPE (Canadian Union of Public Employees). 2003. *Annual report on
    privatization 2003.* Ottawa: CUPE
Decima Research Inc. 2002. *National profile of family caregivers in Canada 2002.*
    Ottawa: Health Canada
Denton, Margaret. 1997. The linkages between informal and formal care of
    the elderly. *Canadian Journal on Aging/La Revue Canadienne du Vieillissement*
    16 (1): 18–36
Dominion Bureau of Statistics. 1966. *1961 Census of Canada. Labour Force.
    Occupation and Industry Trends.* Ottawa: Minister of Trade and Commerce
Dorazio-Migliore, M. 1999. Eldercare in context: narrative, gender, and
    ethnicity. PHD dissertation, University of British Columbia
Equal Opportunities Commission of Northern Ireland. 1996. *Report on the
    formal investigation into competitive tendering in health and education services in
    Northern Ireland.* Belfast: Equal Opportunities Commission of Northern
    Ireland
Evans, R.G., M.L. Barer, and T.R. Marmor, eds. 1994. *Why are some people
    healthy and others not? The determinants of health of populations.* New York:
    Aldine De Gruyter
Galarneau, Diane. 2004. Health care professionals. *Perspectives on Labour and
    Income* 16 (1): 16–29 (Spring). Statistics Canada, Catalogue no. 75-991-XPE

Gignac, M.A.M., E.K. Kelloway, and B.H. Gottlieb. 1996. Impact of caregiving on employment: A mediational model of work-family conflict. *Canadian Journal on Aging/La Revue Canadienne du Vieillissement* 15 (4): 525–42

Grant, Karen, et al., eds. 2004. *Caring for/Caring about: Women and unpaid caregiving in Canada.* Aurora: Garamond Press

Guberman, Nancy. 1999. *Caregivers and caregiving: New trends and their implications for policy.* Ottawa: Health Canada

Hall, Robert, Larry McKeown, and Karen Roberts. 2001. *Caring Canadians, involved Canadians: Highlights from the 2000 National Survey of Giving, Volunteering and Participation.* Ottawa: Ministry of Industry for Statistics Canada

Hawley, Gordon. 2004. Canada's health care workers: A snapshot. *Health Policy Research Bulletin* 8 (May): 8–11

Illich, Ivan. 1976. *Limits of medicine.* London: Penguin

Karasek, R. 1979. Job demands, job decision latitude, and mental strain: Implications for job redesign. *Administrative Science Quarterly* 24 (2): 285–307

Keefe, J.M., and P. Fancey. 1997. Financial compensation or home help services: Examining differences among program recipients. *Canadian Journal on Aging/La Revue Canadienne du Vieillissement* 16 (2): 254–78

MacBride-King, J.L. 1999. *Caring about caregiving: The eldercare responsibilities of Canadian workers and the impact on employers.* Ottawa: Conference Board of Canada

McCredie, I., and D. Sewell. 1999. Statistics Canada's measurement and valuation of unpaid work. Ministry of Industry, Ottawa

Marmot, Michael G., et al. 1991. Health inequalities among British civil servants: The Whitehall II study. *Lancet* 337:1387–93

Maxwell, Judith. 2002. Working for low pay. Canadian Policy Research Network presentation to Alberta Human Resources and Employment, 4 December

Morris, J.M., et al. 1999. The changing nature of home care and its impact on women's vulnerability to poverty. Status of Women Canada, Ottawa

National Forum on Health. 1997. *Canada health action: Building on the legacy.* Vol. 1, *Final report,* and vol. 2, *Synthesis reports and issues papers* (determinants of health working group synthesis report). Ottawa: Minister of Public Works and Government Services

Navarro, Vincente. 1976. *Medicine under capitalism.* New York: Prodist

NHS Estates. 2003. Available at http://patientexperience.nhsestates.gov.uk/ ward_housekeeping/wh_content/home/hom...28/02/2003b

Poland, Blake, et al. 1998. Wealth, equity and health care: A critique of a "population health" perspective on the determinants of health. *Social Science and Medicine* 46 (7): 785–98

Raphael, Dennis, ed. 2004. *Social determinants of health: Canadian perspectives.* Toronto: Canadian Scholars Press

Rogers, A.E., W.T. Hwang, L.D. Scott, L.H. Aiken, and D.F. Dinges. 2004. The working hours of hospital staff nurses and patient safety. *Health Affairs* 23 (4): 202–12 (July–August)

Rosenthal, C.J., and A. Martin-Matthews. 1999. Families as care-providers versus care-managers? Gender and type of care in a sample of employed Canadians. (SEDAP) Research Paper no. 4. McMaster University

Sachdev, S. 2001. Contracting culture: From CCT to PPPs. *The private provision of public services and its impact on employment relations.* London: UNISON

Statistics Canada. 1988. *Census Canada. Occupational trends, 1961–1986.* Ottawa: Minister of Supply and Services

Stinson, Jane. 2004. Why privatization is a women's issue. *Canadian Woman Studies* 23 (3–4): 18–22

Urquhart, Ian. 2004. Hospitals wary of cuts. *Toronto Star,* 22 September, A1, A8

Walsh, J., and H. Davis. 1993. *Competition and service: The impact of the Local Government Act 1988.* London: HMSO

Wilkinson, Richard G. 1992. Income distribution and life expectancy. *British Medical Journal* 304:165–8

Wilkinson, Richard G., and Michael Marmot. 2003. *Social determinants of health: The solid facts.* Copenhagen: World Health Organization, European Office

Willis, Evan. 1983. *Medical dominance.* Sydney: George Allen and Unwin

Wilson, Joanne. 2004. Don't target hospital cleaners. *Toronto Star,* 29 October, A27

Witz, Anne. 1992. *Professions and patriarchy.* New York: Routledge.

Zukewich, Nancy. 2003. Unpaid informal caregiving. *Canadian Social Trends* 70 (Autumn): 14–18

12

Social Citizenship and the Transformation of Paid Work: Reflections on Possibilities for Progressive Change

JANET SILTANEN

In the current literature on the place of equality in the development of social policy in Canada, many contrasts are drawn between the achievements of the past and the limitations of the present. For those with hopes for progressive change, a dominant theme is one of loss, of a shift away from a commitment to equality as a social policy goal towards more minimal, and less morally worthy, policy ambitions. Many summarize this shift in the objectives of Canadian social policy as a move away from the social rights of citizenship, rights that enable all citizens to participate fully in the resources and duties of their communities. Taking the place of the social rights–bearing citizen, it is suggested, is one who is re-familialized, individualized, and marketized. This transition in the identity of citizen is seen to be located within larger institutional and political shifts away from a Keynesian policy regime with an active welfare state towards the lean state of a neo-liberal policy regime. That there was a post–World War II golden age in welfare state development in Canada is widely reported. There is an equally general sense, in both political and academic discussion, that this age is now passed and we have moved on to something very different.

Transformations in the structure and content of paid work feature largely in this sense of a movement away from a governance regime committed to enhancing the social rights of citizens. Indeed, a shift from secure employment with benefits and decent wages to precarious jobs that are short term, unprotected, and poorly compensated has become a strong symbol of the general trend towards a marketized citizen. Many of these transformations in paid work are extensively documented and undeniable (Jackson and Robinson 2000; Saunders 2005; Vosko 2000; Winson and Leach 2002). What they mean for the well-being of individuals and their communities is, however, an intensely contested question. Whether these transformations are appropriate targets for intervention is a central political issue that speaks directly to two fundamental concerns: (1) whether, or to what extent, inequality should be considered unjust; and (2) whether, or to what degree, this injustice should be tolerated. This chapter speaks to this central issue and examines the possibilities for using social citizenship claims to challenge the injustice of inequalities in paid work.

As Rice and Prince have observed, "a new social policy world is in the making, and as yet it is not entirely clear what this new world will look like" (2000, 12). While forces are lining up against the introduction of "third way" strategies in Canada, alternatives are awaiting formulation.[1] Policy advocates and others are posing significant questions about how to conceptualize new agendas for progressive policy development in Canada. The aim of this chapter is to contribute to this process. I argue that thinking about how to challenge the injustice of inequalities resulting from transformations in paid work is hampered by the idea that we have experienced *a shift away* from a governance regime based on social citizenship. By reassessing how social citizenship has featured in Canadian social policy in the past, we may get a clearer picture of how claims for social citizenship may help to formulate equality-enhancing policy developments in the future.

This chapter draws on interview material from a project funded by the SSHRC (Social Sciences and Humanities Research Council of Canada) entitled "Social Citizenship and the Transformation of Work." The overall objective of this project was to investigate how individuals negotiate change in their work profiles, with work understood as including paid, unpaid domestic, volunteer, and training activities. The project was set in Ottawa, a city that has been experiencing tremendous flux in the fortunes of private and public sector employment. A few years before the study got underway, the federal government announced the largest-ever downsizing of government jobs, most of them located in the city of Ottawa itself. Local newspapers presented a roller coaster of boom and bust headlines regarding the fortunes of the high-tech sector. There was continual speculation about exactly when Ottawa would cease to be a city dominated by government jobs and fully take on the mantle of Silicon Valley North.[2] Over one hundred qualitative interviews were conducted between 2001 and 2003. To be eligible for interview, individuals had to have experienced change in their work profile at some point since 1995 (when the news of the significant reductions in federal government jobs was announced). The personal characteristics of the people interviewed reflect significant features of the Ottawa population in terms of gender, age, first language, ethnic background, domestic arrangements, work circumstances, industrial sectors, and occupational groups.

The chapter has two parts. In part one, I suggest that there has been a tendency to overstate the achievement of the social rights of citizenship in Canada's past and that this affects our current sense of how useful social citizenship might be as grounds for challenging inequalities now and in the future. In part two, I set out the character and potential of "equality-enhancing" social citizenship claims. By looking at two issues, the working poor and the capacity to negotiate work change, I illustrate how claims of social citizenship could be mobilized to present a direct challenge to the inequality generated by the neo-liberal hold on employment relations and conditions.

SOCIAL RIGHTS AND SOCIAL CITIZENSHIP

A point of departure for this discussion is that in order to answer questions about the future we need to re-visit our vision of the past. To begin, we need to briefly review how social citizenship has been understood and positioned in relation to the policy developments in Canada in the last half of the twentieth century.

Social Policy in Canada – Was the Past So Much Better Than the Present?

In his 1995 budget speech, Canada's minister of finance, Paul Martin, committed the Liberal government to "the largest set of actions in any Canadian budget since de-mobilization after the Second World War." He pledged to act on "a new vision of the role of government in the economy" and trumpeted the main achievement of the budget as "the very redefinition of government itself."[3] Many date the consolidation of neo-liberalism at the national level from that moment. It was not, in reality, a very sharp turning point, for national governments had been chopping away at public service employment levels, social programs, and income-support commitments for at least the two previous decades.[4] Indeed, the literature on the historical trajectory of the welfare state in Canada identifies the early 1970s as the high-water mark. Nevertheless, contemporary commentators on the nature of change in the 1990s welfare state in Canada draw a picture of a movement away from an older, established welfare state paradigm based on the social rights of citizenship (Broadbent 1999, 35; Jensen and Philips 1996, 113–15). For example, Burke, Mooers, and Shields (2000, 11) observe that, in Canada, the "severe regime of neoliberalism has swept away Keynesian understandings by fundamentally reconfiguring the roles and responsibilities of states, markets, individuals, families and groups." Included in the reconfiguration is a shift from a Keynesian to a neo-liberal policy regime involving "a movement from the idea of social citizenship to that of 'lean citizenship'" (Burke, Mooers, and Shields 2000, 13). Broad and Antony (1999, 11) argue that "[c]ut-backs in education, health care, anti-poverty programs, unemploy-ment, women's shelters and so on ... represent a retreat from social welfare and security as social rights." Brodie is equally definitive in her summary of where we've been and where we're going when she states: "Social citizenship is being eclipsed by market citizenship" (Brodie 1997, 223).

While it is clear that national governments of the 1980s and 1990s have diluted rather than developed progressive elements of social poli-cies in Canada, the question is whether these changes have involved a paradigm shift away from social citizenship as claimed above. Was there *ever* a commitment to the social rights of citizenship in the social policy of the Canadian welfare state?

Welfare State Development in Canada and the Social Rights of Citizenship

There appear to be two points of consensus in the Canadian literature on welfare state development. One, there was at some point a golden era, and two, it has always been a complex, messy, fragmented, and frustrating business. While the latter observation seems to withstand scrutiny, the lustre of the former statement starts to fade upon closer inspection. Discussions of the golden era in Canada refer to this period as one in which a Keynesian welfare state was put into place. This is said to have involved commitments to full employment, univer-sal social programs, and the redistributive role of the state. Yet evi-dence of government practice and social policy implementation over this period shows very minimal, if any, adherence to these founda-tional activities. Mishra (1990), Guest (1985), and others (Broadbent 1999; O'Connor 1989) have argued that the federal state has never shown a commitment to full employment, and Cohen describes the attention to the possibility as "more rhetorical than practical" (1997, 63 n. 18). Entitlements to income security have not been based consis-tently on universality. At the federal level, the universal family allow-ance (now eliminated) and old age pension are the exceptions in an otherwise means-tested, or insurance-based, orientation. While access to education and health (both provincially administered with the assistance of federal funding) has universal elements, these have always been accompanied by stratifying, income-related components (access to medication, to dental care, and to higher education, for example). And as Banting's analysis (1987) shows, evidence of the redistributive impact of the federal tax system reveals only a very modest, though positive, effect. Banting concludes that the postwar Canadian welfare state is "a relatively limited response to the social tensions inherent in a capitalist economy. Nor has it proven to be a powerful engine of egalitarianism" (315). In keeping with this overall assessment, Bakker and Scott (1997) summarize the character of the "Keynesian Welfare State" in Canada as including a "weak commitment to redistribution and full employment" and a "modest network of income security programs and social services' (300–1).

If we are to judge by these criteria and this evidence, the Canadian welfare state would seem to have been spectacularly unsuccessful in realizing any alleged commitments to the social rights of citizenship.[5] But was the realization of the social rights of citizenship ever an ambition of social policy in Canada?

Seeing the positive developments of the welfare state in Canada as the result of a commitment to the social rights of citizenship overstates the clarity, coherence, and comprehensiveness of the historical development of Canadian social policy. Although Canada is typically identified as a liberal welfare regime (Esping-Andersen 1990; Janoski 1998), analysts within Canada usually highlight the more mixed character of policy and programs. Valverde (1995, 36–7) makes the very important point that Canada has always had a hybrid approach to welfare based on a "mixed social economy," and as many commentators have concluded, such circumstances are unlikely to produce outcomes with a consistent or comprehensive vision. Responses to the identification of Canada as a "liberal" regime type have pointed to the more complex and varied character of the welfare effort (O'Connor 1989, 1998). Some, for example Tuohy (1993), identify two welfare forms in Canada – a social democratic form (largely represented by health care) nested within a more dominant liberal form. Olsen (1994) agrees that Canada would look more social democratic if social services such as health care were taken into account. However, even health care, the area of policy and service that is regarded as the *most* social democratic, is varied in its profile of entitlement and organization. Olsen (1994, 15) presents a much more complex picture of health care in terms of the "social citizenship" involved, with some dimensions liberal, some social democratic, and others a mixture of both.

Viewing social policy achievements of the past as evidence of the realization of social rights also overstates the extent to which particular social programs associated with the welfare state project were achieved as a matter of principle. Several writers have argued convincingly that the prime motive for the development of the Canadian welfare state was a nation-building strategy on the part of the federal government, in terms of the regional redistribution of resources (Smardon 1995) and a legitimation of federalism (Jensen 1989). Indeed, in this earlier work, Jensen (1989, 81) endorses the observation that the Canadian welfare state was the product of "state-initiated policies" rather than the proclamation of "new citizenship rights."

Reflecting on the role of principle in social policy development in Canada, two contemporary observers of the high-water days paint a rather unflattering picture. Porter (1965) argued in *The Vertical Mosaic* that "[i]n Canada, as in other industrial societies, there has been some extension of social rights, although, because generally they fall within the sphere of the provinces, they are by no means uniform throughout the country. Their haphazard development has come about more by the 'demonstration effect' of their existence in other countries, than because they have formed the social philosophy of either of the two parties which have been in power at the federal level" (370). In his review of Porter's work, Marshall (1965) himself highlights the significance of this point and the negative consequences for policy of a national politics dominated by opportunism rather than a contest of principles.[6]

Echoes of these conclusions can be found in more recent work that aims to uncover the intention and effect of Canada's welfare effort. Moscovitch's (1991) historical review of a broad range of federal and provincial social welfare programs has the specific purpose of assessing the extent to which these were introduced and developed in a manner consistent with Marshall's social rights of citizenship. Two related principles are the focus of Moscovitch's assessment: the first is that entitlement is solely on a non-market basis (citizenship), and the second is that all citizens are entitled (universality). Of the programs he considers,[7] Moscovitch concludes that only family allowances came close to Marshall's criteria and that the bulk of social programs are "conditional programs that define a range of non-market services that are in this sense democratic and equalizing. They are, however, benefits and not rights of citizenship" (41).

Responding to innovations and developments in the analysis of welfare state development, O'Connor (1989) uses a broader set of criteria for evaluating the character of Canada's welfare effort: decommodification, solidarity, redistribution, and full employment. She canvasses a range of social transfer payment and civil consumption expenditure initiatives between 1960 and 1983. As she laments, the weakness of Canada's commitment to social justice through government action can be discerned even in the midst of the so-called golden age. She identifies Canada's best efforts as in the area of civil consumption, with universal entitlements to education and health. However, she concludes that both areas of effort are marked by a disinclination to move beyond equality of opportunity to equality of outcome, as well as by increasing pressure to lessen universal entitlements.[8] O'Connor's later consideration of the same issues (1998) concludes that the Canadian welfare state continued to function throughout the 1990s in that, for example, a system of social transfers was moderately successful in addressing the increasing inequality in earning and investment incomes. However, there was an overall decline in the quality of social support (she refers to this as a decline in the quality of social citizenship) traceable to a continuing weakness of political commitment to a broader program of social justice that did little to stem the intensification of inequality overall.

Bradford (2000) makes a very significant contribution to the question of whether the present character of the Canadian state is so different from the recent past. He develops the interesting notion that there was a contest between the different interpretations of Keynesianism involved in the move towards a more active federal state in Canada. He presents a very detailed and persuasive argument that the golden era in Canada was a period of technocratic Keynesianism and not social Keynesianism. Bradford uses the contrast between social and technocratic Keynesianism to cast the policy and political struggles during the 1930s and 1940s in Canada as including a struggle of ideas. Essentially, the contrast is between a political and a bureaucratic project. Social Keynesianism promotes a more socially progressive and proactive form of state involvement in shaping the social foundations of the economy, including "institutional change to provide full employment and universal social security" (57). This contrasts with technocratic Keynesianism, which promotes a more limited and administrative form of state–economy relations, with the role of the state focused on generating and disseminating relevant information about economic performance in order to assist economic adjustment in times of cyclical instability. Bradford's important point is that proponents of social Keynesianism lost the struggle between these two paradigms, and technocratic Keynesianism became the dominant governing paradigm after the World War II, emphasizing "policies of pump priming, not investment control, and actuarially sound, contributory social insurance programs, not labour-market planning" (61).

Given the success of the more limited interpretation of Keynesian possibilities, Bradford maintains that the "embedding of technocratic
Keynesianism in the 1940s made it highly likely that neoliberalism
would triumph in the 1990s" (76). In other words, there has been a
great deal *of continuity* in government-economy relations in the post–
World War II period in Canada.[9]

Two aspects of Bradford's argument are especially useful in helping
us understand how current circumstances relate to the recent past.
First, the important distinction between social and technocratic
Keynesianism helps to explain why, in the postwar period, the Canadian
state was relatively slow to live up to any wartime rhetorical commitments to security and justice.[10] While there was much *talk* about equality
and social progress, *action* towards this end was laboured and limited in
scope. It helps to locate a historical trajectory for the *liberalness* of the
Canadian welfare state. In looking back, we might see a different path to
the present if where we have been is technocratic and not social
Keynesianism. Second, as crucial as national–provincial relations are in
tracing the vagaries of social policy development in Canada, there has
also been an important struggle between policy paradigms – a struggle
of ideas – in which the more progressive ideas, in the sense of being
more overtly committed to using government policy to enhance equality, have yet to win out. Bradford suggests that the struggle between the
social and technocratic paradigms included efforts to realize ideas
within institutional and organizational configurations. The success of
the technocratic interpretation of Keynesianism can be traced to the
leverage gained by the greater strategic ability of its supporters to
embed its set of ideas in bureaucratic implementation strategies.

While I recognize that there has been a profound deterioration in
the range and level of social support and services available to Canadian citizens, I do question whether it is correct to see this deterioration as also a shift away from social citizenship. The question is
whether these services and supports ever rested on accepted claims of
the social rights of citizenship. Talk of equality and rights may have
been more tolerated, even welcomed, in the golden age, but the proof
of principle, especially on the part of governments, must be in actions
and results. On these latter criteria, there do seem sufficient grounds
to question whether the establishment of the social rights of citizenship ever grounded the welfare policy regime of the immediate post–
World War II period.

It is instructive to turn for a moment to earlier contributions regarding the possible foundations of welfare states. The development that
Marshall (1963) observed in Britain over the twentieth century is of
"incorporating social rights into the status of citizenship" (100), where

"social rights imply an absolute right to a certain standard of civilization which is conditional only on the discharge of the general duties of citizenship. Their content does not depend on the economic value of the individual claimant" (98). Regarding variations in welfare state development, Marshall comments that some welfare states can form in the absence of the social rights of citizenship or some may institute a form of social rights that undermines citizenship. In his discussions of the potential conflict between civil and social rights, Marshall clearly acknowledges that governments can address welfare issues with highly oppressive forms of intervention. Similarly, Titmuss (1987, 122) is adamant that "welfare statism," like rights themselves, can serve many masters: "What matters then, what indeed is fundamental to the health of welfare, [is] the objective toward which its face is set. To universalize humanistic ethics and the social rights of citizens, or to divide, discriminate and compete?" In a more recent context, it is precisely the inequality-maintaining aspects of gendered forms of welfare states that have motivated feminist critiques. O'Connor, Orloff, and Shaver (1999) have emphasized the need to identify the balance of and struggle between civil and social rights in addressing demands for equality. Social policy in a context of civil rights emphasizes equality of opportunity, whereas social policy based on social rights has greater potential to address equality of outcome.

It may be useful, in the interests of conceptual clarity and strategic possibilities, to examine trajectories of social rights of citizenship and of social policy as though they were potentially independent of one another. Thus, looking back on policy development in Canada, we could move away from a regime-change perspective to one that can identify the specific configuration of circumstances in which social rights and social policy have come together. This would entail identifying circumstances favourable to *equality-enhancing*, rights-based policy development, as will be discussed later in this chapter.

Given a more complex picture of ideological and practical forces shaping the direction and content of social policy, it does not serve the purpose of assessing the nature of change to see it in terms of a shift from one ideologically homogeneous paradigm to another. For example, regarding the analytical use of the concept of the welfare state itself, Valverde (1997, 45) advises against "talking about the *rise of the welfare state* and then about the present-day process of *privatization*, ways of talking that assume there is an irreconcilable opposition between *realms* and that there is only one dynamic going on at any one time."

A more productive analytical strategy may be to keep in mind that there are many trajectories flowing from the past through the present, and the dominance of one does not mean the disappearance of the

others. Rather than positioning social rights of citizenship as the success of the past and the market as the success of the present, it would
be helpful to see the ideological and practical struggle between social
rights and the market as an ongoing feature of how Canadians are governed. We might get further by asking what it is that has impeded the
introduction of social citizenship rights in Canada and in what circumstances and contexts progress has been made. A central issue is the
long-standing dominance, and recent resurgence, of other historical
projects that have been aligned against the implementation of social
citizenship rights. In this sense, there may be greater continuity
between present and past struggles to realize a more just Canadian
society than many current discussions present.[11] Challenges to the effi-
cacy of the nation-state, including the eroding influences of deficit
reduction strategies, free trade agreements, and the activity and rhetoric of globalization, are significant factors in the current dispute about
the appropriate role of the Canadian government. There has been
nevertheless a long-standing contestation about the rationale of social
policy in which forces of progressive change have rarely, and only
briefly, had the upper hand. Rather than a regime change, we may be
witnessing a regime clarification and intensification – where the lean
and mean impulses of past social policy have been released from the
pressure of contrary tendencies to become leaner and meaner.

SOCIAL RIGHTS OF CITIZENSHIP – EXPANDING AND STRENGTHENING THE POSSIBILITIES

While I have taken issue with interpretations that see the recent past in
Canada as the rise and fall of the social rights of citizenship, I support
strongly current efforts to consider whether the ideas and claims of citizenship have any value in the push for progressive change.[12] The successful insinuation of neo-liberal thinking into the prioritization of
issues and the boundaries of solutions means these efforts must
address the intellectual and political capacity of citizenship claims to
disrupt and dislodge neo-liberal thinking.

If we want to aim for more than a new form of liberal welfare state
(Myles and Pierson 1997), we need to give the current framework for
understanding political choices and possibilities a strenuous assessment and overhaul. Old formulations of social rights of citizenship
cannot serve the present needs of a new progressive agenda because of
the recognition that their relation to equality is conditional. A key
insight in the work on social rights is that they can be inequality maintaining.[13] They are not inherently equality enhancing. Social rights
linked to citizenship have greater equality-enhancing potential, because

all citizens are included. However, as analysts interested in inequalities of gender and race have established, this position is only as inclusive as the definition of citizen allows (Bannerji 1995; Brodie 1997; O'Connor, Orloff, and Shaver 1999; Stasiulis and Bakan 2003). But even with a maximally inclusive definition of citizen, more than universality is required to bring social rights of citizenship into the service of promoting equality. Again the feminist critique of gendered forms of social citizenship is instructive in showing us there can be differentiated forms of social citizenship that are inequality maintaining.

To promote an equality-enhancing agenda, we need to develop arguments exposing the weakness of neo-liberal claims. Times may have changed, but the descriptions of change and the interpretation of its consequences are matters for challenge and debate. For the idea of the social rights of citizenship to be currently useful in this task, significant elements of the conceptual foundation need to be reformulated. One way to strengthen the contemporary formulation of the social rights of citizenship is to give it a stronger position against one of the central claims of neo-liberalism – that is, the distinctness and primacy of the market.[14] The significance of this challenge is emphasized in Slater and Tonkiss's (2001) analysis of market society. They comment that the "expanding reach of market structures and values makes them an urgent site of contest, not only as economic solutions to be embraced or rejected, but as social and political forms whose effects and purposes are open to question" (203). To give social citizenship claims equality-enhancing potential, I suggest they must come from a position that opposes the idea that we live in a market society and claims the market as a social arena.

In assessing the equality-enhancing capacity of new understandings of social citizenship, it is important for us to consider what understanding of the social is offered. More specifically, we would want to know how the social is positioned vis-à-vis market activity. In some contemporary reworkings of social citizenship, too much intellectual room and political space are conceded to a separate realm of the economic generally and of the market in particular. For example, Esping-Andersen's (1990, 1999) operationalization of social citizenship rights as decommodification and, more recently, as defamilialization does not challenge sufficiently the idea of a separate economic realm organized as a market system.[15] Further, some recent policy innovations and suggestions, such as basic income programs or negative income tax (Myles and Pierson 1997), also maintain a considerable distance from market intervention.

A way to strengthen current social citizenship claims is to challenge the claims for, and of, the market more directly. As many have noted, government efforts to address inequality through constitutional, legislative, or policy means have been limited by the attitude that the *primary* distribution of resources is off-limits (O'Connor 1989; Bakan 1997; Jhappan 2002a). Social citizenship rights must move beyond redistribution and challenge primary distribution. To do so, they must be seen as an issue *within* the market, not just outside of it.[16] If we see the market as a proposed set of social relationships, then it is open to claims about the social and claims about social citizenship. This implies that responsibility for the delivery of social citizenship is broader than a state-individual relationship. This is not to let governments, at any level, off the hook. It is to insist that our claims for a decent life are as relevant in our relationships with employers, banks, insurance companies, retailers, service providers, family members, and neighbours, for example, as they are in our relationships with national, provincial, and municipal governments.

If we try to use social citizenship as a way of opposing attempts to promote the primacy of the economic in determining the quality of life, we have to work from the starting position that much feminist analysis has brought us to. Lives are lived within and across alleged borders between the economic and the social, and the vision of quality of life needs to be based on a more holistic and integrated understanding of the complex social relationships and obligations that our lives entail. The market does not represent the absence of the social. It has not become disembedded from the social. Rather, market claims promote a particular vision of the social – typically as separate and derivative. They are a claim for a particular kind of social arrangement (Irwin and Bottero 2000), and we could, therefore, work towards formulating equality-enhancing social rights claims that challenge the form of the social projected by market-thinking.

To illustrate aspects of this argument, I would like to briefly review two areas of interest in our research project concerning social citizenship and the transformation of work.[17] The first area of interest – the working poor – is a chronic problem that has been exacerbated by shifts in both the structure of employment (towards retail and service work) and the quality of employment contracts (towards temporary, casual, and "flexible" agreements). The second area of interest – how individuals negotiate change in their work profiles – is an issue that has emerged with particular intensity, and general relevance, in the new economy. Both issues involve contestation over the primacy of the market in structuring processes and outcomes. In both cases, the actions of the market involve social conditions and relations that bring many aspects of an individual's life, and many sets of social relationships, into play. That these issues are fundamentally social in character, and profoundly structured by inequality, makes them candidates for social citizenship claims.

Social Citizenship Claims and the Working Poor

Our current approach to equality in terms of wages involves comparisons within and between groups that say very little about the social adequacy of the wages compared. Equal pay for work of equal value, whatever its other merits, says nothing about the social capacities made possible by particular pay levels. Social citizenship claims that challenge the primacy of the market-based understandings of wages could promote an assessment of wages in terms of their social capacities. One way that social citizenship claims *within* the market could be formulated is on the basis of the social adequacy of wages. They would insist, for example, that no person be paid wages that do not provide them with the resources to live the life of an independent adult in the community. Using the concepts of component wages and full wages, I have demonstrated elsewhere (Siltanen 1994; see also Siltanen 2002 and Rubery 1997) that many women, and an increasing number of men, even when employed full-time, do not earn enough to support themselves as independent adults in their community.[18] Among other hardships, this severely compromises the ability of individuals to form an "autonomous household" (Orloff 1993) by providing for themselves and their dependants. This is an issue of social citizenship for women and men, as it concerns the ability to realize adult expectations and responsibilities in one's community.

It might come as a surprise to some that the nation's capital has not escaped the overall trend towards increasing inequalities in employment and standards of living observed elsewhere in the country. However, it has been clear for some time that Ottawa has become a "tale of two cities," with luxury lifestyles escalating at one end and homelessness, joblessness, and poverty at the other (Jackson and Kahn 2005; Klodawsky 2004; Social Planning Council 1999). In our interviews with people experiencing work change in the city of Ottawa, these dramatic contrasts in life experience were very prominent. While some were doing more than very well, others experienced wage insufficiency and extensive insecurity.

Many individuals in our interviews tell of profound instability in the flow and level of employment income. Financial budgeting and forward planning is often limited to a matter of weeks. Planning horizons of two to three months are not uncommon, even for individuals with mortgages and dependent children. This is not a question of deficits in human capital, for most have buckets full of training course certificates, community college diplomas, and university degrees. It is an issue of the quality of employment and the sufficiency of wage levels that are being offered in the community. It is also, in some cases, a matter of the creation of race-based employment ghettos. The situation facing "Nelson" is a case in point. He works in a far from glamorous and highly exploited sector of the high-tech industry in Ottawa – electronic assembly.[19]

NELSON – WORKING THROUGH AN EMPLOYMENT AGENCY IN ELECTRONIC ASSEMBLY, DESPITE HAVING A MASTER'S DEGREE FROM A CANADIAN UNIVERSITY

Nelson, his wife, and their young child came to Canada from Africa more than ten years ago on his student visa. They have since become Canadian citizens, have had two more children, and have taken into their home a nephew recently arrived from Africa. Despite having a master's degree from a Canadian university, Nelson has not been able to secure anything but precarious, low-paying, unskilled work. Between them, he and his wife are currently holding four jobs – two full-time and two part-time – and even so they are barely surviving financially. Nelson's most significant employment is working on the assembly line of a local high-tech company, a job he holds through an agency that supplies the high-tech company with assembly workers employed on a contract basis. He works the night shift so that he can earn an extra dollar per hour for a total of $11.39. He describes his co-workers as "Anglo dropouts" and foreign-born degree holders like himself who he estimates make up a large portion of the work-force. The company is not doing well financially, and Nelson is expecting to be laid off any day. Nelson's wife works a part-time night shift as a cleaner and a full-time day shift as a care assistant, both contracted through agencies. Three of the fours jobs held in this household are subject to the fees that agencies deduct from their employees' paycheques. Nelson calculates that, between them, he and his wife pay out 20 per cent of their earnings in agency fees.

The wages offered in Nelson's primary job, electronic assembly, are not adequate either to support him or to cover the adult responsibilities he has for dependants. The same is the case for the wages of his wife's primary job. Together, he and his wife struggle to make ends meet, needing to work unsocial hours to give a small boost to their hourly wage and to take on extra jobs to add to the overall household income. This is certainly not the type of employment experience Nelson expected as a Canadian citizen with a Canadian graduate degree. The racism that features in Nelson's inability to move up to more decent and appropriate employment is compounded by a public discourse about employment experience that identifies the only active agent in the fortunes of individuals as the individuals themselves.

The insufficiency of wages can add tremendous strain and anxiety to the lives of individuals, and this situation can become more severe when people go through difficult times. When you and your household are working hard just to get by, any additional strain can be devastating. "Denise" is in a not uncommon situation where care responsibilities fall on women's shoulders to the point where they have a hard time bearing the weight. She is a determined but struggling member of the sandwich generation, giving priority to the needs of older and younger family members to the detriment of her own mental and physical health. Her divorce and limited employment prospects make a tough situation even more difficult.

DENISE – STRUGGLING TO DEAL WITH DIVORCE, DEBT, CHILDREN'S NEEDS, ELDER CARE, AND LIMITED EMPLOYMENT PROSPECTS

Denise is in her mid-fifties. She lives with her infirm elderly father and her daughter. She has a high school diploma. She went no further in education because she was drawn to a life in business and has spent most of her career in self-employment. Fifteen years ago, she was running a business with her husband. The business was doing reasonably well, although Denise and her husband had a lot of personal money invested in it (including a second mortgage on their house). Both the business and the marriage came to an abrupt end, and Denise found herself without a job, without a home, and with substantial debts to pay. She has no further contact with her ex-husband and neither does her teenage daughter, who hopes to go to university in two years. Denise and her daughter rented an apartment, and both found jobs – Denise as a full-time retail clerk and her daughter as a part-time waitress after school. It became clear to Denise very quickly that one full-time job in the retail sector, at $9.25 an hour, was not going to help her clear her debt or help her support her daughter through university. She therefore took on a second job in the evening as a cook's assistant in a small private nursing home. She also took in a border to help cover some of the day-to-day running costs of the apartment. Just as things seemed to be picking up, Denise's father became very ill. He had access to some homecare, but it was not enough to cover all of his needs – especially his need for nighttime care – and Denise took on the responsibility of staying with him through the night. After several weeks of working two jobs and taking care of her father at night, she herself became ill. She and her daughter decided to leave their apartment and move in with Denise's father. Denise left her day-time job, as she now had less to pay out in terms of rent and utilities. She and her daughter both kept their part-time jobs. Denise is deter-mined to get her life back on track and to find time to develop her own business interests. In the meantime, she says her only consola-tion in the midst of their very difficult circumstances is that they have become poor enough for her daughter to qualify for a student loan.

A report prepared in 2000 by Social Services of the Ottawa-Carleton Regional Government contains information that helps to put Nelson's and Denise's experiences of low-paying jobs in a larger perspective. The report calculates "livable income" and "livable wage" estimates for the city of Ottawa and provides a sobering indication of the extent to which jobs in the city are paying insufficient wages. The report uses fairly conservative estimates of the gross wage required by adults to support themselves at a standard of living described as "decent" and "self-sufficient." For example, it is estimated that a single adult sup-porting one child would need a gross hourly income of $14.27. The report then uses a survey of median wages by occupation to determine what proportion of jobs in the city offer wages at this level. Comparing the livable wage requirement of $14.27 with the survey of occupational wage rates reveals that only 39 per cent of occupations are offering this level of wages.[20] If this single adult was supporting two children, their livable wage would be a gross hourly rate of $22.02, but only 5 per cent of occupations in Ottawa are offering this rate.

All of the research demonstrating the chronic existence of, and recent increase in, the working poor,[21] aligns with our own research to underscore the need to expand the social-rights claims of citizenship to include the ability to achieve a standard of living *within* the employ-ment relationship. A primary reason why individuals are not able to share in the resources and duties of their communities is that they have to do paid work for too many hours for too little remuneration. This is not simply an issue of work-life balance; it is an issue that con-cerns the very standards of experience we are willing to allow within employment relationships and the degree of inequality in living stan-dards that we are prepared to tolerate in our society. Wage levels are closely tied to social capacities, and all of the parties to wage setting – employees, employers, unions, and government – share responsibility for addressing and realizing social citizenship claims for livable wage levels.

Social Citizenship Claims and the Negotiation of Work Change

A signature feature of the public discourse on the new economy is the claim about the constancy of change. In terms of employment trajectories, the now common wisdom is that we shall all have many jobs, many employers, and many forms of employment relationships over our lifetime. Messages from the federal and provincial governments make it clear that dealing with the demands for and of change in the new economy is primarily an individual responsibility.[22] Building human and social capital, with a specific emphasis on lifelong learning and networking, is the main theme of the individualized, market-focused policy approach being adopted in Canada. The emphasis on these individualized strategies for negotiating work change begs questions about the capacity individuals have to undertake such activities. At the very least, both require substantial amounts of time and money – resources not equally distributed among the population. Our research suggests that the capacity to deal with work change is highly structured by inequality, and the individualized approach to negotiating work change exacerbates these inequalities.

An increase in inequality has been widely observed as one consequence of neo-liberal–influenced policies directed at enhancing the operation of market processes. Material from our interviews with people who have attempted to negotiate work change in the context of neo-liberal conditions points to aspects of the social conditions and processes that result in increased inequality. The two composite biographies presented below represent individuals –"Jane" and "Jeff" – who undertook new learning opportunities and networking strategies to very substantially change their skill set and redirect their employment trajectory. Jane was able to reconfigure her work profile and at least maintain her living standards; Jeff was not. As their circumstances illustrate, the success of relaunching attempts is influenced by the circumstances people are in when they start their transition, the extent and quality of support they get as they go through it, and the extent and quality of the educational and networking resources they are able to access.[23]

The more advantaged relaunch themselves with good personal and social supports in place to manage the time and money costs of the transition. Although income generation is typically suspended during the retraining process and outlays often increase owing to the costs of education and training, these individuals are able to maintain their general standard of living throughout their transition period. Also, this group typically has access to learning and networking opportunities that are of higher quality. They have the resources to take the time for, and spend the money on, more extensive training opportunities, often at more advanced educational levels and always from more reputable educational and training institutions. They also have well-established networks of personal and professional contacts that supply information about appropriate training resources, and they have strategies for moving successfully from training into the new area of employment. "Jane" is such a case.

JANE – RELAUNCHING A WORK PROFILE FROM A POSITION OF ADVANTAGE

Jane is in her late fifties. She is separated and has no dependants. Jane receives emotional support from her extended family but never any financial assistance. She was a full-time employee of the federal government for many years, building up a good local network of colleagues and contacts. She was laid off during the 1990s and decided to change careers. She enrolled in a full-time training program as a chiropractor. This involved moving to another city for the duration of the training, a period of over two years. She sold her townhouse, in part to finance her training. After the training course was completed, Jane returned to Ottawa and set up practice on a self-employed basis. The colleagues and contacts from her previous job helped her establish the beginnings of a client base for her new profession. During Jane's absence from Ottawa, however, the price of housing shot up; for this reason, coupled with the financial demands of setting up a new business, Jane has not been able to get back into the housing market.

The leaving package offered to Jane by the federal government involved a lump sum payment, plus the early start of pension payments at half the full amount. This financial base was sufficient and secure enough for Jane to undertake an entirely new direction in life, involving extensive and intensive retraining. Even so, she decided to sell her townhouse in order to help finance her costs while she was on the training program. The flexibility of Jane's personal circumstances made it possible for her to move to another city in order to participate in the training program she judged to be the best available. The networks she had built up over many years as a resident of Ottawa and an employee of the federal government made self-employment as a chiropractor a feasible option, as it provided an initial source of clients. Jane has worked very hard to establish herself in her new profession and is doing well. Although she lost her housing investment, she feels financially secure and able to plan for the future.

In contrast, those in less-advantaged circumstances are less likely to be successful in reconfiguring their work profile despite intense effort and considerable expense. In the hope of advancing themselves and their households into an improved situation, these individuals also use strategies of networking and lifelong learning. However, the time and money demands of both strategies put extreme stress on their resources. While there are no formal costs, such as tuition fees, involved in developing networks, there are nevertheless time and money costs involved in networking activities such as visiting, meeting, mailing, and calling. Also, networks are reciprocal, requiring those who want something from the other people in their network to be prepared to respond when they themselves are called upon for advice or a favour. Attempts at lifelong learning typically involve reduced income and increased costs, and we learned of many examples where these time and money investments did not move individuals on to more-advantaged circumstances.[24] Often these individuals returned to where they started (metaphorically and in fact), sometimes with heavier burdens than when they started because of the costs of their relaunching attempt. This was the situation for "Jeff."

JEFF – RELAUNCHING A WORK PROFILE FROM A POSITION OF DISADVANTAGE

Jeff is in his late twenties. He is single and supports no dependants. After leaving high school and working in a series of retail jobs, Jeff decided it was time to try building a decent career. Attracted by television advertisements for careers in information technology (IT), he opted to take IT training in the city where his parents live, moving in with them to save on living expenses. He entered a nine-month course and borrowed $15,000 to cover the tuition. After completing the course, Jeff moved to Ottawa and was hired through a local employment agency to work at a computer customer service call centre. The initial pay was $15 an hour. Although he lived simply and tried to keep costs down by boarding, Jeff had difficulty covering his

expenses. As for his loan, he could pay off only the monthly interest
and nothing of the principal. He continued to look for better
IT-related employment and regularly undertook self-directed training
courses. His interest in our interview was to gain experience commu-
nicating with people to help his networking skills. When contacted a
year later, however, Jeff was still in the same job and now concerned
that he would be laid off because there was talk of the call centre
being shipped overseas. His pay had increased by $1.20 an hour to
$16.20.

Jeff's story is a poignant case of hope and effort betrayed. While prepared to be self-motivated, flexible, and proactive in embracing lifelong
learning opportunities and establishing networks, Jeff has ended up far
worse off than when he started his relaunching attempt. Jeff tried to
relaunch himself but did so from a fairly disadvantaged position. With
no leaving package from his previous employer and no other forms of
income to support himself, he was tempted by training opportunities
that promised much in a short time and at a high price. His new IT credentials are not getting him access to the sorts of jobs he had hoped for
– in fact, many of his current workmates have no qualifications at all. He
is $15,000 in debt with no immediate prospect of paying this off. While
he had a strong network of personal support, none of his contacts had
any connections to the IT industry. His initial position of relative disadvantage and his limited capacity to take time out of income earning for
retraining made him vulnerable to those training enterprises prepared
to take advantage of his constrained circumstances.

If negotiating work change is indeed to become a lifelong obligation
of us all, there are social responsibilities to be claimed and acknowledged in facilitating the conditions and processes of change. As our
research has demonstrated, undertaking work change affects and is
affected by many aspects of an individual's life. It takes courage, initiative, and determination. It also takes considerable time and money,
and the inequalities structuring these resources appear to figure
largely in how individuals fare. As a society, we accept that preparing
for adulthood is a social responsibility that must be collectively shared,
and we make social citizenship claims accordingly in terms of, for
example, access to public education. So, too, in the new economy, we
need to consider the lifelong preparations required for one to be
a contributing and productive adult in society as a social responsibility to be collectively shared – and to be subject to claims of social citizenship. Being prepared to undertake work change should not be

politically encouraged, on the one hand, and left, on the other, to the happenstance of personal fortune, predatory market forces, and the consolidation of existing inequalities. The issue here is not only about having access to education resources of sufficient quality and quantity or of being able to cover the costs of, and making available, childcare during retraining. It is also a matter of addressing aspects of inequality *within* employment contracts, such as the dramatic differences between jobs in terms of leaving entitlements and packages, study leave entitlements and provisions, training monies, pension entitlements, and access to services promoting the well-being of employees.

CONCLUSION

The idea and experience of change has captured contemporary imagination and anxiety. Many observers of contemporary change come to the conclusion that change means social disruption and dislocation. In particular, there is a notion that the social and political arrangements that contributed to our orderly life in the past, and possibly to progress towards a more just and equal society, have been profoundly displaced by the successful realization of neo-liberal ambitions. In academic literature and policy reports in Canada, as elsewhere, this change is often described as a shift away from social citizenship towards a more marketized form of personal and collective life. While I do not wish to deny the significance of progressive developments in social policy in Canada in the latter part of the twentieth century, I do think we need to reconsider how we are thinking about changes that have occurred.

Specifically, I question the positioning and conceptualization of social rights of citizenship in discussions about the rise and decline of equality-focused social policy. By equating social policy development in Canada with the realization of social rights of citizenship, we are being encouraged to assign meanings to the past that are not always appropriate. This is a conceptual fusion with potentially important consequences for our visioning of the possibilities for progressive change in the future. With the sense that social citizenship rights have been embedded in past institutional expressions of welfare, there is a "been there, done that" attitude that rules them out as a possible source of future arguments and struggles. They can be mischaracterized as the old paradigm that did not work or is out of date.

I suggest, in contrast, that the equality-enhancing possibilities of claims of social rights of citizenship have never been fully considered or strongly pursued in Canadian society. Even if change in Canada is locked in a pattern of "relentless incrementalism" (Battle 2001), progressive change, of whatever dimensions, requires a rationale for the meaningfulness of equality, including a vision of what it is and what it is for. As we search for new ideas that will provide the foundation of an agenda for progressive change, it is worth considering how an equality-enhancing formulation of the social rights of citizenship might contribute.

The continuing value of the social rights of citizenship lies in the potential to strengthen and promote these rights as a discursive and practical challenge to neo-liberal interpretations of the "good" society as a "market" society. If the idea of the social rights of citizenship is to dislodge neo-liberal thinking, it must contest central claims. A useful formulation of social citizenship needs to challenge the idea that the social and the market are separate spheres of activity and that the constitution of the former is dependent on the level of development of the latter. This would involve contesting the claim that the market is the arbiter of the quality of life and claiming the market itself as a social arena.[25] An expanded claim for the significance and presence of the social would provide a rich grounding for new conceptualizations of equality and a broader sense of where and how equality demands can be made. Insisting, for example, that the employment relationship is fundamentally socially determined opens it up for possibilities and practices that the lens of market-thinking either can not see or does not value.

There is a push in different areas of work to find a way of conceptualizing equality that offers a richer formulation of the purpose of progressive change. The feminist and development literature is especially active in pursuing new visions of equality – for example, ones that break free from considering white male experience as an appropriate norm (Jhappan 2002a), emphasize the need to debate the insufficiency of distributive justice (Fraser 1997; Vosko 2002), embed issues of the role of the state within wider questions about securing the quality of social relationships (Hobson 2000), and promote freedom as a socially produced capability to live the life "one has reason to value" (Sen 1999). As we question and explore the defining criteria of progressive change, we will revision not only what counts as equality, but also our sense of what equality is for.

Setting the social rights of citizenship within a conceptual foundation that promotes the social by challenging the separation and priority of the market will offer a broader scope for the interpretation of equality. How we envision the purpose and substance of equality is as much a part of historical time and place as is the extent of its realization. A particular visioning of equality sets limits on our appreciation of what is possible, or even desired. This is a matter of how the dominant neo-liberal meta-narrative frames and positions the very idea of equality, but it is also about how the dominant meta-narrative is opposed – the extent to which the alternative to "there is no alternative" actually proposes a new and progressive set of understandings and practices. We can find a more expansive and progressive means of conceptualizing equality that challenges its inferior positioning in relation to economic exigencies and speaks to both continuing (such as the working poor) and newly emerging (such as negotiating work change) experiences of inequality.

NOTES

Author's Note: This chapter is a substantially revised version of "Paradise Paved? Reflections on the Fate of Social Citizenship in Canada," in *Citizenship Studies* 6, no. 4 (2002): 395–414, and is published with the permission of Taylor & Francis Ltd (www.tandf.co.uk/journals). Work towards this chapter was supported by the Social Sciences and Humanities Research Council of Canada through a grant in support of a project entitled "Social Citizenship and the Transformation of Work." I would like to express my thanks to Vivian Shalla and Wallace Clement for their advice in preparing this chapter, to Hugh Armstrong and Daiva Stasiulis for suggested changes based on their use of this material for teaching purposes, and to all participants of the "Social Citizenship and the Transformation of Work" project for their continued support and interest.

1 See the discussion forum on the third way in *Studies in Political Economy* 61 (Spring 2002).

2 See Hunt 2001 for a more extensive discussion of these developments up to the year 2000, and Marquardt 2004 and Jackson and Khan 2005 for a more recent picture.

3 The proposed actions included reducing the federal public service by 45,000 and reducing the proportion of spending on social programs to below 1951 levels.

4 Cohen (1997) provides an eleven-page list of deletions and reductions just between 1985 and 1995. O'Connor (1998) gives an excellent account of the history of welfare state development and retrenchment in Canada.

5 At this point in this discussion, I am following the general drift in Canadian work on the social rights of citizenship by referring to T.H. Marshall's (1963, 1965) broad formulation of social rights, including their location in government-sponsored policy. Broadbent (1999) gives a good rendition of how the idea of the social rights of citizenship has been linked to welfare state development in Canada. It is important to recognize that the Canadian Charter of Rights and Freedoms has set parameters for equality seeking in Canada. Charter provisions do have an influence on the formulation of government

policy, but this can be a very "residual" influence (as in doing the minimum required to avoid a Charter challenge). Bakan 1997 and discussions in Jhappan 2002b offer an excellent review and assessment of the Charter's impact on (in)equality.

6 The issue of the uneven development of social rights in Canada, due to, among other factors, the role of provincial and municipal governments, is also discussed by Moscovitch (1991) and, more recently, by Klodawsky (2001).

7 Moscovitch (1991) considers programs for worker's compensation, old age pensions, unemployment insurance, family allowance, and social (unemployment) assistance.

8 Civil consumption expenditure refers to publicly provided goods and services. In this paper, O'Connor does see citizenship entitlements reflected in government programs and forms of civil expenditure, and argues that over this period she can observe class replacing citizenship as the basis for the distribution of benefits. Her more recent work on these issues (O'Connor, Orloff, and Shaver 1999) provides a more complex analysis of citizenship, distinguishing between civil and social rights in the development of the Canadian policy regime.

9 See Gordon 1965 for a fascinating account of the very mixed response to Keynesian ideas at the height of the golden age in Canada. Hall 1998 is an interesting collection of articles that discuss factors that influenced the degree of acceptance of Keynesian ideas in various parts of the world.

10 Canada is not unique in this respect, as O'Connor, Orloff, and Shaver (1999, 58) indicate: "There was considerably more diversity in the measures implemented in [Canada, the United States, Australia, and Britain] than the rhetoric of their formative periods might suggest."

11 Not all discussions emphasize discontinuity – see, for example, Teeple 1995.

12 For a diverse sampling of these discussions, see Broad and Antony 1999, Kaplan 1993, and Maxwell 2001. A special issue of the journal *Citizenship Studies* reveals the breadth of issues considered in current discussions of social citizenship in Canada (Stasiulis 2002), and Donnan 2004 presents an excellent review of contemporary thinking about the progressive possibilities of social citizenship claims.

13 See Lessard 1997 and Jhappan 2002b for a discussion of this point regarding the Charter of Rights and Freedoms, and White 1999 for further discussion in the context of citizenship.

14 Focusing on the contestability of a specific claim identified closely with neo-liberal renditions of the social organization required for capitalism takes up, I think, aspects of the analytical challenges posed in Gibson-Graham 1996, Larner 2000, and Somers 2001.

15 I would argue that the ground Esping-Andersen concedes to the economic over the social is what leads him in his later work (e.g., 1999) to give up on the idea of equality in the here and now.

16 This raises the difficult and important issue of the separation of social and economic rights. There is not the space to consider this issue here, but it is worth noting the relevance of Macpherson's discussion (1987) of how conceptualizations of justice have taken particular forms depending on the positioning of the economic in relation to the social.

17 The study, entitled "Social Citizenship and the Transformation of Work," was supported by a grant from the Social Sciences and Humanities Research Council of Canada and involved collaboration between Carleton University faculty (Janet Siltanen, Wallace Clement, Hugh Armstrong, and Jay Drydyk) and graduate students (Donna Coghill, Ken Fish, Chris Hunt, Richard Marquardt, Karine Pepin, Jennifer Quaile, Carrie Sanders, Willow Scobie, Al Vachon, and Alette Willis). The study was conducted from the Centre for Labour and Community Research, an organized research unit of Carleton University. Further details of the study can be found on our project website: www.carleton.ca/clcr/WorkinOttawa.

18 The distinction between component wages and full wages concerns the social capacities made possible by different wage levels. Component wages are insufficient to support an individual as an independent adult in the community. Full wages do provide this social capacity and could be further differentiated by levels of social responsibility (for example, by the number of dependants). See Siltanen 1994 and 2002 and Rubery 1997 for a discussion of the methodology required to identify component wages and full wages.

19 These profiles are composites from individuals interviewed, and do not represent any one individual's experience. The profiles do present common features and details of individuals in similar situations.

20 The report (authored by Frank Kumapley), "Livable Income Estimates for Ottawa-Carleton," was prepared by the Policy, Planning and Performance Management Services Branch, Strategic and Operational Support Directorate, Social Services, Region of Ottawa-Carleton, in 2000. Estimates of livable income and livable wages are based on a modified version of the "market basket methodology" developed at Human Resources Development Canada (HRDC). The wage survey was conducted in 1999 by Statistics Canada, with HRDC and a community training organization. The survey reviewed wages paid in 219 occupations by over 15,000 businesses in Ontario. Information for Ottawa-Carleton is based on approximately 148 occupations. The principal investigator of the "Social Citizenship and the Transformation of Work" project, Janet Siltanen, participated in a number of workshops and consultations involved in the preparation of this report.

21 See recent Canadian work on the insufficiency of wages in Jackson and Robinson 2000, Myles 2005, and Saunders 2005. See also Stanford and Vosko 2004 for wide-ranging discussions challenging the success of "flexibility" and the market determination of work and income.

22 Municipal governments are also implicated in the individualized drift of employment policy. Marquardt (2004) discusses this in the context of Ottawa, highlighting the significance of policy initiatives at the local level for the overall profile of inequality. See also Hunt 2001 for an account of how the municipality of Ottawa has attempted to position itself as an entrepreneurial city, particularly by marketing itself as "Silicon Valley North." The shift from public sector to private sector employment in the city has had major consequences for, among other things, standards of employment relations and contracts.

23 The research on negotiating work change presented here is from a joint paper, Siltanen, Scobie, and Willis 2005b. Aspects of this research have also been presented at two conference, Siltanen, Scobie, and Willis 2002 and 2004. See also Siltanen, Scobie, and Willis 2005a.

24 See also Swift 1995 for a critique of the "training fix."

25 Angus (2001) explores the idea of sustainability as a way to oppose a market-led determination of value.

REFERENCES

Angus, I. 2001. Subsistence as a social right: A political ideal for socialism? *Studies in Political Economy* 65:117–35

Bakan, J. 1997. *Just words: Constitutional rights and social wrongs.* Toronto: University of Toronto Press

Bakker, I., and Scott, K. 1997. From the post-war to the post-liberal Keynesian Welfare State. In *Understanding Canada,* edited by W. Clement. Montreal and Kingston: McGill-Queen's University Press

Bannerji, H. 1995. *Thinking through: Essays of feminism, Marxism and anti-racism.* Toronto: Women's Press

Banting, K.G. 1987. The welfare state and inequality in the 1980s. *Canadian Review of Sociology and Anthropology* 24:309–38

Battle, K. 2001. Relentless incrementalism: Deconstructing and reconstructing Canadian income security policy, 57 pp. Caledon Institute of Social Policy, Ottawa

Battle, K., S. Torjman, and M. Mendelson. 2000. Social programs: Reconstruction not restoration, 21 pp. Caledon Institute of Social Policy, Ottawa

Bradford, N. 2000.The policy influence of economic ideas: Interests, institutions and innovation in Canada. In *Restructuring and resistance: Canadian public policy in an age of global capitalism,* edited by M. Burke, C. Mooers, and J. Shields. Halifax: Fernwood Publishing

Broad, D., and W. Antony. 1999. Citizenship and social policy: Neo-liberalism and beyond. In *Citizens and consumers? Social policy in a market society,* edited by D. Broad and W. Antony. Halifax: Fernwood Publishing

Broadbent, E. 1999. Citizenship today: Is there a crisis? In *Citizens or consumers? Social policy in a market society*, edited by D. Broad and W. Antony Eds. Halifax: Fernwood Publishing

Brodie, J. 1997. Meso-discourses, state forms and the gendering of liberal-democratic citizenship. *Citizenship Studies* 1:223–42

– 1999. The policy of social policy in the twenty-first century. In *Citizens or consumers? Social policy in a market society*, edited by D. Broad and W. Antony. Halifax: Fernwood Publishing

Burke, M., C. Mooers, and J. Shields. 2000. Introduction: Critical perspective on Canadian public policy. In *Restructuring and resistance: Canadian public policy in an age of global capitalism*, edited by M. Burke, C. Mooers, and J. Shields. Halifax: Fernwood Publishing

Cohen, M.G. 1997. From the welfare state to vampire capitalism. In *Women and the Canadian welfare state: Challenges and change*, edited by P.M. Evans and G.R. Wekerle. Toronto: University of Toronto Press

Crouch, C., K. Eder, and D. Tambini. 2001. Introduction: Dilemma of citizenship. In *Citizenship, markets, and the state*, edited by C. Crouch, K. Eder & D. Tambini. Oxford: Oxford University Press

Donnan, M.E. 2004. The meanings of citizenship. PhD dissertation, Carleton University

Espada, J.C. 1996. *Social citizenship rights: A critique of F.A Hayek and Raymond Plant*. London: Macmillan Press

Esping-Andersen, G. 1990. *The three worlds of welfare capitalism*. Princeton: Princeton University Press

– 1999. *Social foundations of postindustrial economies*. Oxford: Oxford University Press

Fraser, N. 1997. *Justice interruptus – Critical reflections on the "post-socialist" condition*. New York: Routledge

Gibson-Graham, J.K. 1996. *The end of capitalism (as we knew it): A feminist critique of political economy*. Cambridge: Blackwell Publishers

Gordon, H. Scott. 1965. A twenty year perspective: Some reflections on the Keynesian revolution in Canada. In *Canadian economic policy since the war* (a series of six public lectures delivered at Carleton University). Montreal: Canadian Trade Committee

Guest, D. 1985. *The emergence of social security in Canada*. Vancouver: University of British Columbia Press

Hall, P.A. 1998. *The political power of economic ideas: Keynesianism across nations*. Princeton: Princeton University Press

Hobson, B. 2000. *Gender and citizenship in transition*. New York: Routledge

Hunt, C. 2001. Constructing the entrepreneurial city: Silicon Valley North. PhD thesis, Carleton University

Irwin, S., and W. Bottero. 2000. Market returns? Gender and theories of change in employment relations. *British Journal of Sociology* 51:261–80

Jackson, A., and D. Robinson. 2000. *Falling behind – The state of working Canada 2000.* Ottawa: Canadian Centre for Policy Alternatives

Jackson, E.T., and K. Graham, eds. 1999. *Diversification for human well-being: Challenges and opportunities in the National Capital Region.* Ottawa: Carleton University, Centre for the Study of Training, Investment and Economic Restructuring

Jackson, E.T., and R. Kahn. 2005. *Steering on black ice: The continuing search for sustainable livelihoods in the Ottawa tech sector.* Ottawa: Carleton University, Centre for Community Innovation

Janoski, T. 1998. *Citizenship and civil society: A framework of rights and obligations in liberal, traditional, and social democratic regimes.* Cambridge: Cambridge University Press

Jenson, J. 1989. "Different" but not "exceptional": Canada's permeable Fordism. *Canadian Review of Sociology and Anthropology* 26:69–94

– 1997. Fated to live in interesting times: Canada's changing citizenship regimes. *Canadian Journal of Political Science* 30:627–44

Jenson, J., and S.D. Phillips. 1996. Regime shift: New citizenship practices in Canada. *International Journal of Canadian Studies* 14:111–35

– 2001. Redesigning the Canadian citizenship regime: Remaking the institutions of representation. In *Citizenship, Markets, and the State,* edited by C. Crouch, K. Eder, and D. Tambini. Oxford: Oxford University Press

Jhappan, R. 2002a. The equality pit or the rehabilitation of justice? In Jhappan 2002b

– ed. 2002ab. *Women's legal strategies in Canada.* Toronto: University of Toronto Press

Kaplan, W., ed. 1993. *Belonging: The meaning and future of Canadian citizenship.* Montreal and Kingston: McGill-Queen's University Press

Klodawsky, F. 2001. Recognizing social and economic rights in neo-liberal times: Some geographic reflections. *Canadian Geographer* 45:167–72

– 2004. Tolerating homelessness in Canada's capital: Gender, place and human rights. *Hagar: An International Social Science Review* 5 (1): 105–20

Larner, W. 2000. Neo-liberalism: Policy, ideology, governmentality. *Studies in Political Economy* 63:5–25

Lessard, H. 1997. Creation stories: Social rights and Canada's constitution. In *Women and the Canadian welfare state: Challenges and change,* edited by P. Evans and G.R. Wekerle. Toronto: University of Toronto Press

Macpherson, C.B. 1987. *The rise and the fall of economic justice and other essays: The role of state, class and property in the twentieth-century democracy.* Oxford: Oxford University Press

Marquardt, R. 2004. The redesign and rescaling of employment policy in Ottawa. Doctoral paper, Carleton University, Ottawa. Mimeographed

Marshall, T.H. 1963. *Sociology at the crossroads and other essays.* London: Heinemann

- 1965. Class and power in Canada. *Canadian Review of Sociology and Anthropology* 2:215–21

Maxwell, J. 2001. Toward a common citizenship: Canada's social and economic choices. Ottawa: Canadian Policy Research Networks

Mishra, R. 1990. *The welfare state in capitalist society: Policies and maintenance in Europe, North America and Australia.* New York: Harvester Wheatsheaf

- 1996. The welfare of nations. In *States against markets: The limits of globalization,* edited by R. Boyer and D. Drache. London: Routledge

Moscovitch, A. 1991. Citizenship, social rights, and Canadian social welfare. *Canadian Review of Social Policy* 28:28–44

Myles, J. 1989. Understanding Canada: Comparative political economy perspectives. *Canadian Review of Sociology and Anthropology* 26:1–9

- 2005. *Postponed adulthood: Dealing the with new economic inequality.* Ottawa: Canadian Council on Social Development

Myles, J., and P. Pierson. 1997. Friedman's revenge: The reform of "liberal" welfare states in Canada and the United States. *Politics and Society* 25:443–72

Myles, J., and J. Quadagno. 2000. Envisioning a third way: The welfare state in the twenty-first century. *Symposium* 29:156–66

Noel, A., G. Boismenu, and L. Jalbert. 1993. The political foundations of state regulation in Canada. In *Production, state, identity: Political economy faces the 21st century,* edited by J. Jenson, R. Mahon, and M. Bienefeld. Toronto: Canadian Scholar's Press

O'Connor, J.S. 1989. Welfare expenditure and policy orientation in Canada in comparative perspective. *Canadian Review of Sociology and Anthropology* 26:127–50

- 1998. Social justice, social citizenship and the welfare state, 1965–1995. In *The Vertical Mosaic Revisited,* edited by R. Helmes-Hayes and J. Curtis. Toronto: University of Toronto Press

O'Connor, J.S., A.S. Orloff, and S. Shaver. 1999. *States, markets, families: Gender, liberalism and social policy in Australia, Canada, Great Britain and the United States.* Cambridge: Cambridge University Press

Olsen, G. 1994. Locating the Canadian welfare state: Family policy and health care in Canada, Sweden and the United States. *Canadian Journal of Sociology* 19:1–20

Orloff, A.S. 1993. Gender and the social rights of citizenship: The comparative analysis of gender relations and welfare states. *American Sociological Review* 58:303–28

Parker, J. 1998. *Citizenship, work and welfare: Searching for the good society.* London: Macmillan Press

Porter, J. 1965. *The vertical mosaic: An analysis of social class and power in Canada.* Toronto: University of Toronto Press

Rice, J.J., and M.J. Prince. 2000. *Changing politics of Canadian social policy.* Toronto: University of Toronto Press

378 Janet Siltanen

Roche, M. 1992. *Rethinking citizenship: Welfare, ideology and change in modern society.* Cambridge: Polity Press

Rose, N. 1996. The death of the social? *Economy and Society* 27:327–56

Rubery, J. 1997. Wages and the labour market. *British Journal of Industrial Relations* 35 (3): 337–66

Saunders, R. 2005. *Left behind: Low-paid workers in Canada.* CPRN (Canadian Policy Research Networks), Work Network: www.cprn.org/en/doc.cfm?doc=1309

Sen, A. 1999. *Development as freedom.* New York: Anchor Books

Siltanen, J. 1994. *Locating gender: Occupational segregation, wages and domestic responsibilities.* London: UCL Press

– 2002. Full-wages and component-wages. In *Gender – A sociological reader,* edited by S. Jackson and S. Scott. London: Routledge

Siltanen, J., W. Scobie, and A. Willis. 2002. Flows, eddies and whirlpools – Work change in the new economy. Paper presented at Thinking Smart Cities Conference, Carleton University, Ottawa

– 2004. Flexible, networked and going nowhere! Strategic inequalities in negotiating work change. Paper presented at Colloque International du CRISES, Innovation et transformation sociale, Montreal

– 2005a (forthcoming). Flexible, branché et dans un cul-de-sac! Les inégalités stratégiques dans la négociation du changement au travail. In *L'innovation sociale,* edited by Juan-Luis Klein et Denis Harrisson. Quebec City: Presses de l'Université du Québec

– 2005b. Flows, scrambles, eddies and whirlpools: Experiences of work change in the new economy. Paper under review

Slater, D., and F. Tonkiss. 2001. *Market society: Markets and modern social theory.* Cambridge: Polity Press

Smardon, B. 1995. The federal welfare state and the politics of retrenchment in Canada. In *Social welfare policy in Canada: Historical readings,* edited by R.B. Blake and J. Keshen. Toronto: Copp Clark

Social Planning Council of Ottawa-Carleton. 1999. *A tale of two cities: Socio-demographic and economic trends in Ottawa.* Ottawa: Social Planning Council of Ottawa-Carleton

Somers, M. 2001. Romancing the market, reviling the state: Historicizing liberalism, privatization, and the competing claims to civil society. In *Citizenship, markets, and the state.* Oxford: Oxford University Press

Standing, G. 1999. *Seeking distributive justice.* London: Macmillan Press

Stanford, J., and L. Vosko, eds. 2004. *Challenging the market: The struggle to regulate work and income.* Montreal and Kingston: McGill-Queen's University Press

Stasiulis, D., ed. 2002. *Citizenship Studies* (special issue on reconfiguring Canadian citizenship) 6 (4)

Stasiulis, D., and A. Bakan. 2003. *Negotiating citizenship – Migrant women in Canada and the global system*. Hampshire and New York: Palgrave

Swift, J. 1995. *Wheel of fortune – Work and life in the age of falling expectations*. Toronto: Between the Lines

Teeple, G. 1995. *Globalization and the decline of social reform*. Toronto: Garamond Press

Titmuss, K. 1987. *The philosophy of welfare: Selected writings of Richard M. Titmuss*. London: George Allen and Unwin

Tuohy, C. 1993. Social policy: Two worlds. In *Governing Canada: Institutions and public policy*, edited by M.M. Atkinson. Toronto: Harcourt Brace Jovanovitch

Turner, B.S. 2001. The erosion of citizenship. *British Journal of Sociology* 52:189–209

Valverde, M. 1995. The mixed social economy as a social tradition. *Studies in Political Economy* 47:33–60

– 1997. Six dimensions of social governance: Research questions beyond the dichotomy of "public" and "private." *Cahiers d'histoire*, xviii, 40–54

Vosko, L.F. 2000. *Temporary work: The gendered rise of a precarious employment relationship*. Toronto: University of Toronto Press

– 2002. The pasts (and futures) of feminist political economy in Canada: Reviving the debate. *Studies in Political Economy* 68:55–83

White, M. 1999. Neo-liberalism and rise of the citizen as consumer. In *Citizens or consumers: Social policy in a market society*, edited by D. Broad and W. Antony. Halifax: Fernwood Publishing

Winson, A., and B. Leach. 2002. *Contingent work, disrupted lives – Labour and community in the new rural economy*. Toronto: University of Toronto Press

13

Remaking the Canadian Labour Movement: Transformed Work and Transformed Labour Strategies

ROSEMARY WARSKETT

The last twenty to thirty years have witnessed significant changes in paid and unpaid work. This is the case in Canada as well as in other liberal democracies. Corporations and governments have restructured the production of goods and services. Some labour processes of thirty years ago no longer exist, while new ones have been created. There have been significant changes in the labour supply for these restructured processes in terms of the gender and the ethnicity of workers. As for unpaid work in the household, this is still mostly performed by women. However, since the 1980s, there has been a rise in low-paid work in the home, of both a domestic and industrial nature, performed for the most part by immigrant women.

This chapter focuses on Canadian labour unions' organizing strategies and responses to the changes in work and employment relationships arising out of neo-liberal restructuring. The model of industrial relations that was developed in the 1940s still remains in place, but by the mid-1980s it was becoming clear that this model was an obstacle to extending union organization to the workers in the private service sector. This problem is now deepening as a result of the restructured work relations of the last few decades. The model was originally designed to promote collective bargaining in the private industrial sectors. While it was adapted to fit the needs of public sector workers who wanted to participate in collective bargaining, it does not facilitate the organization of certain private service sector workers. In general, these are workers who have little bargaining power and little ability to take

wages and benefits out of the competition of the labour market, particularly when faced with the power of large multinational corporations
(Fudge and Tucker 2000; Warskett 1988). Furthermore, neo-liberal
restructuring of work has led to an increase in non-standard work.
Workers engaged in non-standard working arrangements include
independent contractors, who in many cases are not eligible to be
unionized. The numbers of workers in non-standard work arrangements have grown considerably in the last twenty years, and consequently, the model of union organizing and collective bargaining,
developed in the earlier period, is a poor fit for the restructured work
and employment relationships that developed during the period of
neo-liberalism.

The first section of this chapter briefly explores the changes that
have occurred in paid and unpaid work in Canada. The focus then
shifts to the Canadian labour movement and the effect that the transformation of work has had on union density and membership. The
major part of the chapter examines the responses of Canadian labour
to the restructuring of work and the consequent decline in union density, focusing particularly on the movement's ability to continue to be
an important agent in the workplace, an important benefit to the
household, and a significant force in politics and society generally.
The overall argument is that while the labour movement is responding
to transformed work organization and its detrimental effect on union
density, its response is piecemeal, union by union, with some moves
forward and some backward. This fragmented and uncoordinated
response reflects the structure of the movement and the labour relations system within which it is embedded. Still, there have been some
creative and innovative attempts to organize workers that have run
counter to the current labour relations system. And, indeed, these new
organizing initiatives may point the way towards a new paradigm and
regime of labour relations.

THE RISE OF NON-STANDARD FORMS OF WORK AND NEO-LIBERAL RESTRUCTURING

The transformation of the postwar Keynesian political economy into
neo-liberalism began in Canada in the mid-1970s. By the beginning of
the 1980s, the crisis in capital accumulation and economic growth and
expansion was becoming apparent (Gindin and Stanford 2003). The
rise of neo-liberal forms of political and economic restructuring in the
workplace was underway in the form of cutbacks and wage controls in
the public sector and layoffs in the private sector. The postwar Keynesian political economy had promoted the concept of the standard

employment relationship, which was tied to the goal of relatively full employment and a social safety net to protect those in search of a relatively well-paying standard form of work. For those in a standard employment relationship, this meant job security, a family wage, and benefits, either negotiated by a labour union in collective bargaining or reached through an individual professional contract. Many men achieved this kind of employment. It was an ideal, however, that many male workers did not enjoy, although through to the mid-1970s it seemed achievable given the continued growth and expansion of the economy.

During the Keynesian postwar period, women were regarded and in general were treated as secondary workers. Their participation rate in the paid labour force was considerably lower than men's, and they were crowded into the lowest-paid contingent forms of work. Contingent work "includes those forms of employment involving atypical employment contracts, limited social benefits and statutory entitlements, job insecurity, low job tenure, low wages, and high risks of ill health" (Fudge and Vosko 2003, 181). It was, and still is, work that is non-unionized for the most part.

The imposition of wage controls beginning in 1975 and the search by capital for flexible forms of labour power resulted in the undermining of the standard employment relationship that had been part of work and employment norms during the postwar Keynesian period. Moreover, as Fudge and Vosko (2003) point out, the move away from Keynesian political economics paradoxically came precisely at the moment when women's demands for equality were being written into labour and employment law and policy. This resulted in a contradiction between governments' pay and employment equity policy and women's lower pay and occupation segregation, which continues to this day.

The rise of neo-liberal restructuring of the economy also caused employers to search for flexibility within the workplace, with the aim of lowering labour costs. Part of the solution for some employers was to move away from the standard employment contract and promote an increase in contingent work, including independent contractors. Indeed, by 1995 only 33 per cent of Canadians held standard employment contracts (HRDC 1995). Non-standard forms of work can now be found not only in the rapidly expanded private service sector, but also in all other parts of the economy, resulting in an increase in independent contractors and own-account workers in both the public and private sectors.

An example is the contract work that has developed in clothing manufacturing. The production of clothing used to thrive in city factories in Montreal, Toronto, Winnipeg, and Vancouver. This industry is now, for the most part, closed down, with production outsourced to cheap-labour countries such as China. Whatever sizable clothing manufacturing remains is now found in homework in these same cities, with the workers defined as independent contractors (Ocran 1997). Furthermore, with the deregulation of certain industries, new forms of work are wholly staffed by contract labour. We see this arrangement in the courier industry, where same-day delivery services, using contract workers rather than employees, have proliferated in cities across the country (Courier Research Group 2005). In the public sector, cutbacks have resulted in understaffing and an increased reliance on temporary contract workers or agency staff, who receive lower pay and fewer benefits (England 2000). The contracting-out of public sector services has meant a move away from the standard work norms to contingent, precarious forms of employment in the private sector.

At the same time that neo-liberal workplace restructuring was on the rise, during the 1980s and 1990s, there was a gradual increase in women's labour force participation and a slight decrease in men's (Armstrong 1996). This change contributed significantly to a shift away from the ideal of the male breadwinner family wage model of work towards the new ideal of the universal breadwinner model, within which women and men are equal participants in the economy (Mahon 2002). In one respect, the model has been realized – women and men participate in equal numbers in the paid labour force. In other respects, inequality is still a feature of the neo-liberal economy. Women are still, in general, occupationally segregated into lower-paying contingent forms of work. And women still continue to take most of the responsibility for caring work, whether it is unpaid in the home or poorly paid in the labour force. With their high participation in the paid labour force, there has been an increased need for childcare. This has resulted in an expansion of childcare centres (both for-profit and not-for-profit), staffed by low-paid women workers, along with a substantial increase in private arrangements, with women providing childcare as a form of paid homework (Mahon 2002). This work is sometimes performed by foreign domestic workers, who are not entitled to citizenship rights or any kind of coverage through statutory employment legislation (Stasiulis and Bakan 2002; Arat-Koc 1989).

THE CANADIAN LABOUR MOVEMENT AND THE DECLINE OF STANDARD WORK

Canada's labour relations system was put in place in the 1940s as part of the historic compromise between capital and labour that trans-

formed Canada's liberal political economy into a particular form
of the Keynesian welfare state (Panitch and Swartz 2003; Fudge and
Tucker 2001). The system was propelled into being, in large part,
through industrial and political conflict. The strike rate in 1943 was
nearing that reached in 1919, and the Co-operative Commonwealth
Federation (CCF), as well as the Communist Party, had recently
achieved success in the federal by-elections (Panitch and Swartz
2003). Mackenzie King's federal Liberal government had already
adopted welfare state reforms, such as unemployment insurance, in
the 1930s as a response to the Depression. The government was further compelled in 1944 to introduce Privy Council Order 1003 in an
attempt to gain the consent of the increasingly militant labour movement. After the war was over, this regulation provided the model for
federal and provincial labour laws (Fudge and Tucker 2001).

The labour relations system that emerged out of the conflicts
between capital and labour in the immediate postwar period reflected
both the strengths and weaknesses of the male-dominated Canadian
labour movement of the time. By dint of their industrial leverage in
the goods-producing factories and primary industries of wartime Canada, industrial unions achieved a limited form of industrial democracy. This system was inscribed in labour relations laws that remain in
place in all jurisdictions in Canada. Its main elements consist of the
legal certification, by a state labour board, of a single, exclusive bargaining agent (union) if the union is supported by a majority of
employees in the bargaining unit; legal recognition of the union by
the employer, together with the requirement to collectively bargain;
no right to strike during the life of the collective agreement; and settlement of grievances arising during the life of the agreement by a system
of arbitration administered by state-regulated labour boards. It is a system of limited rights and extensive responsibilities as far as labour
unionists are concerned. The right to free association and collective
bargaining is severely tempered by restrictions on the right to strike.
Grievances during the life of the collective agreement cannot be
legally settled by work stoppages. And in terms of the organizing of
unorganized workers into unions, these same labour boards play a
dominant role in determining the outcome of the contest between
employers and unions for the hearts and minds of workers.

An important outcome of the postwar labour relations system was
the legitimation of trade union activity by the liberal democratic state.
Labour unions became the junior partners in labour relations that
required them to play a responsible role in endorsing and upholding
the entire labour law system. This meant distancing their activities and
discourse from that of illegitimate unions. In the 1950s, during the

Cold War period, irresponsible unionists were defined as Communists and fellow travellers (Fudge and Tucker 2001, 298–301). Later on, in the 1970s, illegitimate actors were feminists as well as socialists and even socially minded unions (Warskett 1987).

By the 1960s, the labour relations system came under pressure from public sector workers wanting to share in the benefits of legal union-ism. The introduction of a more limited but similar form of labour law resulted in large numbers of public sector employees and significant numbers of women becoming unionized and joining the Canadian labour movement. As noted earlier, the labour movement had diffi-culty extending the collective bargaining system into the private ser-vice sector with the same kind of success. We will return to this problem in the next section of the chapter.

As has been the case for other labour movements, neo-liberalism has severely affected the strength of Canadian unions. As many labour researchers have pointed out, however, Canadian labour has fared better than most other movements in that there has been no drop in overall members (Kumar 2004; Murray 2004; Panitch and Swartz 2003). In the United States, Britain, Australia, Japan, and many Euro-pean countries, union density has been declining over the last twenty years. Canada's unions, in contrast, are still growing in absolute num-bers (Kumar 2004, 148). Despite this, since 1985 union density has steadily declined as a percentage of those in the paid labour force. This decline is continuing even though women and various ethnic groups are joining unions at a faster rate than ever before (Yates 2002). The reasons for this steady decline are directly linked to the transformation of work organization in both private and public sec-tors, but it is particularly the change in work in the private sector that has produced a decline in overall union density.

In 2002 slightly fewer than one in three Canadian workers were cov-ered by a collective agreement. Using Statistics Canada data, Jackson and Schetagne found that the union coverage rate was 32.2 per cent of all workers in the paid labour force. This was down from a high in 1984 of 41.8 per cent (Jackson and Schetagne 2003).[1] The one in three figure, however, needs to be considered in light of those who cannot legally unionize. This figure is estimated to be near one million workers and includes professional employees and those at the lower end of the labour market who perform non-standard forms of work and are thereby deemed in law to be ineligible to join a union. If this figure is taken out of the equation, union coverage is "currently closer to 37 %" (Murnighan 2003). While there are not absolutely accurate statistics about the union coverage rate, it does seem clear that the Canadian labour movement has not lost members in absolute terms.

Canadian union membership increased in absolute numbers between 1997 and 2002, while union coverage grew by 350,000 to 4.2 million (Jackson and Schetagne 2003). In fact, the Canadian labour movement, as compared to others, is in the fortunate position of having enough union strength, at present, to stem the downward trend to the kind of low union density found in the United States (Kumar 2004).

It appears that Canadian union density, in percentage terms, has declined more because of strong job growth in non-union workplaces than because of job losses in union workplaces. For example, between 1984 and 2002, job creation in the private business services sector grew from 5.5 to 10.2 per cent of all jobs. This sector has been traditionally non-unionized, and recent union organizing efforts have not changed that fact substantially. Job losses in traditional unionized sectors, however, have affected the overall union coverage rate. For example, there has been a decline in direct public sector jobs (i.e., those public sector jobs within the administration of the federal, provincial, and municipal governments as opposed to the broader public sector, which includes NGOs), from 26.1 per cent to 22.2 per cent of all jobs since1984, and a small loss of manufacturing jobs, from 16.9 per cent to 15.1 per cent (Jackson and Schetagne 2003, 2).

What has this meant in terms of the people filling the jobs? The data reveal that it is men, rather than women, who are now less unionized than in the past. "The coverage rate for men has fallen from almost one-half in the mid-1980s, and has continued to slip since 1997. The rate for women has fallen much less, and has remained steady at 32 per cent since 1997" (Jackson and Schetagne 2003, 2). This means that there is no longer a substantial difference in union coverage rates between women and men, a significant change from the early 1980s, when the union coverage rate for women was 10 per cent less than for men (White 1993). While this change appears at first glance to have a positive aspect to it, in that women are now as unionized as men, we should be careful about the conclusions we draw from this seeming equality.

On examining the statistics more closely, we can see that although there has been a decline in unionized jobs in the direct public sector, there is little change in jobs in the broad public sector. Unionized women are found in both parts of the public sector. Overall, in the private sector, where jobs have increased substantially in number, especially in business services, there has been a decline in union density for men, from 26.1 to 23.3 per cent, and for women, from 16 to 14 per cent (Jackson and Schetagne 2003). In other words, the problem of declining unionization seems in large part to be due to the increase of jobs in the private sector, where there has traditionally been no union presence and where a very aggressive anti-union approach has been adopted by employers (Kumar 2004). Although there have recently been some successful organizing drives among women and equity-seeking groups in the private service sector, overall these groups are far less unionized than white men working in this sector.

There is a need to place these statistics within the context of the significant changes in employment relationships since the 1980s that were discussed in an earlier section. These changes include the substantial rise in women's labour market participation, which is now nearly at the same level as men's. They also include the significant increase in non-standard forms of work that have various dimensions of precariousness. Statistics Canada reports that "34% of men and 41% of women workers were in non-standard types of employment in 2002. This is an increase from 29% of men and 37% of women in 1989" (Vosko, Zukewich, and Cranford 2003). Standard and non-standard types of employment can be reconceptualized in terms of dimensions of precariousness. From this point of view, the workers who are most likely to be found in precarious employment are women of all ages and ethnicities, young men, and men of colour (Vosko, Zukewich, and Cranford 2003). These groups have the lowest rates of unionization in the private sector, and according to a Vector poll conducted on behalf of the Canadian Labour Congress (CLC), these are the groups that most want and need to be organized. Unions are seen by members of these groups, many of whom are the most vulnerable workers, not only as a force that can improve their terms and conditions of employment, but also as a force to help them gain satisfaction and respect in the workplace (Kumar 2004, 149).

Some unions have undertaken to organize women and other equity-seeking groups in the private service sector. In fact, attempts to organize the private service sector "increased by more than 50 per cent between the decade of the eighties and the nineties. In the same periods, organizing in traditional areas of union support, namely manufacturing and construction, declined" (Yates 2002, 32). Interestingly, the evidence from Ontario and British Columbia presented in Yates 2002 reveals that employees in female-predominant workplaces were more likely to vote in favour of union certification. Despite increased organizing efforts and the willingness of marginalized and vulnerable workers to unionize, union density in the private sector continues to decline as compared to that in the public sector. While the public sector continues to be "a bastion of union strength," the private sector sees its union density slipping both as a result of job creation, much of it in contingent forms of work in traditional non-union sectors, and, to a lesser extent, as a result of economic restructuring in traditionally unionized industries (Jackson 2004, 134–40).

TRANSFORMATION OF LABOUR ORGANIZING STRATEGIES

By the 1980s, it was clear that the industrial relations model developed in the 1940s, which had resulted in the successful unionization of the private industrial sectors and the public service sector, was not producing the same success in the private service sector. One of the most important campaigns to try to break the impasse in this sector took place in the mid-1970s – the attempt to organize chartered bank workers. The Service, Office, and Retail Workers Union of Canada (SORWUC) made an important breakthrough in organizing predominantly women bank tellers in British Columbia and Saskatchewan. At the height of the organizing drive, more than a thousand workers were signed up. SORWUC was a small, avowedly feminist union, dedicated to implementing a non-bureaucratic, democratic labour relations process (Warskett 1988).

Prior to SORWUC's bank worker organizing efforts, the CLC had in the early 1970s levied its entire membership to establish a fund dedicated to organizing in the private service sector, targeting clerical workers in particular. Even at this early stage, members of the CLC were concerned that the successful organizing by women in the public sector had not flowed over into clerical jobs in the private sector. In response to SORWUC's campaign, the CLC, using this fund, established the Bank Workers Organizing Committee (BWOC) with the purpose of enlisting all their affiliates to contribute organizers and union support to the committee. Several of the affiliates, however, refused to participate, arguing that bank workers were part of their jurisdiction and that they, not the CLC, should be the ones to organize the banks. This stance on the part of many affiliate unions remains to this day, blocking the possibility of a coordinated approach to organizing the unorganized. It is a discourse of ownership. Unions in a particular jurisdiction perceive that they own the workers and that if the workers join a union it must be their union. The lack of solidarity among unions over how and who should organize bank workers contributed to the failure of the BWOC. The most important reason for the failure, however, was the lack of bargaining power of the workers in the chartered banks' branches. Under the labour relations legislation with respect to the certification of bargaining units, unions had to fight for and win the right to organize workers on a branch by branch basis. This meant that each bank branch could be certified separately as a union.

It is clear that many chartered bank workers, a large majority of them women, did wish to unionize. Between 1977 and 2003, 174 chartered bank units were certified by the Canada Labour Relations Board, but because of decertifications only 22 bargaining units remained as of 2003 (Canada Labour Relations Board 2003). Most of these bank branch bargaining units had less than twenty employees. Decertifications mainly took place because of the branch units' relative lack of bargaining power compared to the power of the multinational Canadian chartered banks. Unions were unable to negotiate substantial improvements in the terms and conditions of employment through collective bargaining, leading to the disaffection of the organized bank workers. Added to this was the very aggressive anti-union campaign conducted and coordinated from the headquarters of the chartered banks.[2]

The failure of the Canadian labour movement to break through and substantially organize the private service sector by the 1980s meant that neo-liberal restructuring proceeded during the late 1980s and 1990s without much hindrance from the labour movement. Given the decline in union density during the 1990s, many Canadian unions, like parts of the American and European labour movements, adopted a more aggressive approach to organizing the unorganized: "The recognition that unions need to organise or die is relatively widespread in the labour movement, even among conservative unions, and the expenditure of resources on organising drives has been significant" (Gindin and Stanford 2003, 432). Some unions, particularly in the United States, expended more than 50 per cent of their annual resources on organizing the unorganized. Moreover, they announced that they had changed their model of unionism from the servicing model to the organizing model. The servicing model of unionism places all its emphasis on representing and supplying services to the current union membership. In contrast, the organizing model gives very high priority to signing up new members, even if this means taking union resources – staff and money – away from servicing the established membership.

During the 1990s, a new organizing model developed out of AFL-CIO (American Federation of Labor and Congress of Industrial Organizations) President John Sweeney's challenge to the American labour movement to build a "new labor movement." As Katherine Sciacchitano (2000) points out, the revitalized AFL-CIO "has set its sights on nothing short of movement building. Inspired by the militancy and industry-wide drives of the 1930s, the federation and its affiliates are pouring millions of dollars into rebuilding organizing capacity in workplaces and communities" (75). The intention seemed revolutionary, coming as it did from a labour movement that seemed to be hitting rock bottom, with organized labour at a low of 12 per cent and less. For a number of reasons, movement building in many cases evolved into the not so new practice of signing up potential members rapidly – that is, getting as many applications for certification as possible (Rooks 2003). In other words, organizing is a strictly quantitative concept. As Sciacchitano (2000, 75) points out, "organizers' primary responsibility runs less to the people they are organizing than to the campaign." It is the requirements of the campaign plan that takes over, with organizing defined in narrow, quantitative card-signing terms.

It is argued, on the other hand, that the servicing model produces passive members who are hierarchically and bureaucratically ordered in unions. Furthermore, this approach does not build an active, democratically inspired membership. It has been linked to the insurance policy mentality, where organizing campaigns appeal to workers' individual self-interest. This approach tends to lead union organizers to make inflated promises about the advantage of unionism in terms of higher wages and benefits and the members' stated needs. In many cases, little account is taken of the strength of the bargaining unit that is being organized and whether advantages achieved by other unionized members can in fact be translated into a collective agreement for the particular unit. The history of the labour movement is replete with examples of first contracts that achieved few increases in terms of wages and benefits and that resulted in decertification in the next round of bargaining, as we saw earlier with bank workers (Warskett 1988). Even more serious for the labour movement is that this kind of organizing neither changes the internal culture of the labour movement nor creates a movement based on democracy, inclusion, and social justice.

A similar kind of logic, however, permeates the organizing model. Daisy Rooks (2003) argues that a "cowboy mentality" often pervades the organizing campaigns of the new labour movement in the AFL-CIO. She points out that the new organizing strategy involves groups of organizers descending *en masse* on a workplace target. This means that the organizers must submit themselves to extensive travel, long hours, and emotionally demanding work. Women with caring responsibilities at home cannot set off on the road in this way. All of this points to a false dichotomy between the two models of servicing and organizing. Both models are predicated on a similar bureaucratic, business union approach to union members and unorganized workers. Both accept the present labour relations system uncritically. While there may be repeated calls to improve and add to its regulation, the system as a whole is not questioned and the problem of workers in non-standard forms of work goes unexamined.

NEW FORMS OF ORGANIZING WITHIN THE CANADIAN LABOUR MOVEMENT

The recent attempts at union renewal have raised crucial questions about what it means to win when organizing new members (Bronfenbrenner and Juravich 1998). Does winning mean successfully applying for certification for a new bargaining unit or does it mean something much broader and more complex than this? Does it mean certifying and building union locals and organizations that are capable of successfully taking on the employer and achieving good collective agreements? Is that enough in terms of building a democratic, participatory union movement that includes women and equity-seeking groups in general? I maintain that winning should be equated with the realization of a labour movement that is open to developing collective worker capacity, establishing a strong, progressive presence in the workplace, and broadening workplace problems by linking them to social and political issues in the community. Included in this is a kind of organizing that allows for learning and development and encourages the self-activism (as opposed to member passivity) of all members. Winning involves creating a culture of inclusion, a movement that "embraces, attracts, and promotes women, people of color, immigrants, and lesbians and gays" (Fletcher and Hurd 2000, 60).

Despite the continuing prevalence of the servicing model in many union locals and the limitations of the organizing model, there have been a number of attempts in Canada to organize workers in non-standard forms of work, including independent contractors. These attempts have sought to avoid the problems associated with the labour relations system developed in the 1940s, and in some cases they have served as an important means of subverting the perception that unionism involves only the legal certification of unions.

One of the earliest examples of an attempt to organize workers in non-standard forms of work was the International Ladies Garment Workers Union's (ILGWU) campaign to organize women homeworkers in Toronto. These women are mainly new immigrants working at home, making clothes. It is estimated that Canada has approximately 100,000 industrial homeworkers, and most of these are garment workers (Ocran 1997, 149). Under the current labour relations system, these workers are ineligible to form certified bargaining units, and they have great difficulty accessing the provisions of employment standards legislation.

The ILGWU had to reconceptualize the space of work and home and devise new ways of acting and thinking about organizing homeworkers (Tufts 1998, 240–4). This form of unionism involved various community initiatives to address the increasing numbers of women engaged in paid work in their homes. In Toronto in the early 1990s, the union began with a research project designed to find out more about immigrant homeworkers. The contacts made during this project led to the formation of the Homeworkers Association and ultimately to the important idea that workers can be members of a union without legal recognition and that, through their association, they can develop and build their collective capacity without entering the legal system. Other initiatives entailed seeking community support through a "Clean Clothes" campaign (designed to make visible the low wages and poor working conditions of women homeworkers) and a community coalition that lobbied the legislature for "fair wages and working conditions for homeworkers" (Tufts 1998, 242–3; Cranford and Ladd 2003, 48).

The form of unionism that developed around immigrant homeworkers had as its initial goal the unionization of these workers. The ILGWU went out into the community both to contact the workers and to build support for their cause, even though these workers could not be legally unionized. In doing this, the union played a crucial role in providing a means for these workers to step into the public arena and begin a learning process of self-activism that gave them the opportunity to achieve dignity, public recognition, and respect, when once they were hidden in the household. Alex Dagg of the Ontario District ILGWU writes: "What has become clear is like organizing work, there is no one magic wand or one magic technique that will work to organize workers in such a sector. A variety of creative techniques must be developed and tried and retried" (quoted in Rowbotham 1993, 73).

It is clear that organizing homeworkers into an effective union will require changes in the law and the traditional labour relations system. The work done by the ILGWU is preliminary in that it has focused on the self-activism of the workers who could become part of "the long-sought explosion of workers organizing themselves into unions" (Gindin and Stanford 2003, 433). The lessons learned by the garment homeworkers are relevant for daycare homeworkers. A campaign to organize these workers was undertaken in the early 2000s by the Confederation of National Trade Unions (CNTU) in Quebec. An amendment in 2005 to Quebec's Labour Relations Act by Jean Charest's Liberal government, however, explicitly removed any possibility that homeworkers might acquire the right to unionize through the courts. This change is one of a number of measures that has led the Quebec labour movement to take an increasingly confrontational stance against a government engaged in neo-liberal measures to re-regulate the economy. The most recent measures, implemented in December 2005, include the removal of the right to strike by public sector employees and the imposition of a collective agreement.

UNION ORGANIZING BY SIDESTEPPING THE LAW

Another important example of unions finding a way to sidestep the law was a recent campaign mounted by the Canadian Union of Postal Workers (CUPW). Well over twenty years ago, CUPW began to realize that if it was to prevent the closing of post offices in rural locations, it would need the support of the community. In 1987 the community organization Rural Dignity was established "to fight the withdrawal of government support from rural areas." The organization gained support from the postal unions and the Canadian Labour Congress (Tufts 1998, 233). The contacts and alliances built during that period developed into another campaign in support of the rural route drivers. Because these workers were deemed by Canada Post to be independent contractors rather than employees, they were not eligible for unionization, despite the fact that their working conditions were similar to those of the unionized parcel carriers. The main differences lay in the very poor remuneration received by the rural route drivers, 66 per cent of whom were women. CUPW embarked on a ten-year campaign and funded the costs of building an association of these workers. The rural route drivers chose their own leaders and developed their own democratic structures. They attempted, without success, to change the law so that they could unionize in their own right. Finally, the rural route drivers joined CUPW, and the union used the bargaining strength of its traditional membership to force Canada Post to recognize the drivers as employees. The outcome was a new collective agreement in January 2004 for both groups of workers (Bourque and Bickerton 2004). This strategy was costly for CUPW and was opposed by some of its traditional membership, however, because the union had to give up certain benefits for its traditional membership to win a settlement for the rural route drivers. Nevertheless, the strategy is an important example of how the union movement is not always constrained and limited by legal unionism. It is also an important example of the altruism of better-off workers who act in solidarity with those living marginally, and in this sense the campaign to unionize the drivers was not just a struggle for redistribution narrowly conceived. Furthermore, through the creation of their new association, rural route workers acquired public-speaking and representation skills, which was less likely to happen had they remained individuals isolated in their communities (Bourque and Bickerton 2004). In other words, the association helped these workers learn to engage in self-activism and democratic decision making.

COMMUNITY ORGANIZING BY SUPPORTING NON-UNIONIZED WORKERS

It is important to draw attention to two other examples of alternative forms of unionism: the Workers' Action Centre (WAC) in Toronto and the Workers' Organizing and Resource Centre (WORC) in Winnipeg. Both of these organizations are committed to supporting non-unionized workers, as well as to helping them defend their rights. Both are engaged in mobilizing the non-unionized, the WAC around issues of fair employment and the WORC around issues involving independent contractors who are denied employment rights. The WORC is funded, at the moment, by CUPW, but it is hoped that other unions will take a role in offering resources.

The WORC has played a significant role, not only in advising non-union employees of their statutory rights, but also in providing an organizing base for couriers in the same-day delivery service. In the business services sector of the economy, the same-day courier industry had its beginnings with the deregulation of Canada Post in 1981. This opened the door to the quick delivery of letters and parcels for those willing to pay at least three times the rate charged by the crown corporation. This change, together with "just in time business strategies and the technology to support those strategies[,] allowed for direct delivery models; and, more recently, the explosion of e-commerce technology allows consumers and businesses the ability to communicate their demand for goods and services immediately" (Courier Research Group 2005, 8).[3]

The core of the courier industry provides overnight or even later shipments of letters, packages, and parcels. This represents 85 per cent of the industry's revenue and 80 per cent of the volume. Workers in this industry in general have a standard employment contract with one of the larger courier companies, such as Canada Post, UPS, Purolator, and Federal Express. This industry is characterized by unionized employment, with relatively good pay and benefits and, as a consequence, with a low turnover of workers. In a few exceptions, owner-operators also work in the overnight courier business according to union-negotiated rules and regulations (Courier Research Group 2005, 10). Research reveals that "[d]ue to the nature of the market, requiring large distribution networks and high levels of technology, the core overnight segment of the market has significant barriers of entry for new business" (9).

A study of the same-day delivery segment of the courier industry operating within the confines of the city of Winnipeg presents a sharp contrast to the industry's core. This part of the industry accounts for only 20 per cent of the industry's volume and an even lower percentage of its revenue, but it has a large oversupply of labour. Because the deliveries are local, there is no need for expensive technology and complicated distribution networks. "Essentially anyone who can walk, has a bike or has access to a vehicle can participate in this segment of the market" (Courier Research Group, 10). Work is non-standard in that it involves owner-operator and independent contractor relationships. The oversupply of this form of labour provides an important revenue stream for the courier companies, leading to increased exploitation of the workers. In general, it was found that "the company deducts regular costs from couriers including monies for insurance, radio rental, company decal rental and uniform purchase" (10). In Winnipeg it was found that there is no incentive for companies to rationalize the industry and make it more efficient, as it is the couriers who bear all the costs while providing revenue to the company through their employment. For the great majority of individual same-day couriers, this means job insecurity, low incomes, no benefits, not even access to employment insurance or maternity leave, all because they are not employees. These are the conditions that the WORC is trying to change by supporting, in various ways, non-unionized workers. The example of courier workers at Dynamex is a case in point.

Dynamex is a large multinational courier company active in the same-day courier business in Winnipeg. Through the advocacy of WORC and CUPW, the independent contractor status of the workers at Dynamex was challenged. Finally, the case of *Dynamex Canada* v. *Mamona* came before the Supreme Court of Canada in 2003.[4] The court affirmed the workers' status as employees and therefore their right to unionize under the Canada Labour Code. This important decision may open the door for other contractors who wish to unionize. Currently, the decision is being used by bicycle couriers in Montreal in their application for union certification.

CONCLUSION

The Canadian labour relations system that was established in the 1940s postwar period gave rise to a form of legal unionism, imposed by the liberal democratic state, based on a compromise between the forces of capital and labour. One of the most important aspects of the system at that time, as far as labour unions were concerned, was that where sufficient numbers of workers warranted it, unwilling employers were compelled to recognize and collectively bargain with unions. It was this intervention by the state that, more than any other aspect of the law, served to legitimize the industrial relations system in the eyes of labour unionists. This aspect remains fully in place in labour relations law, but today it is not sufficient on its own to force large multinational companies such as Canadian chartered banks, McDonald's, and Wal-Mart to accept collective bargaining and unions as a part of their corporate existence. These large companies, as well as many others in the private service sector, have found ways of preventing the law from being applied in their bid to remain union free. Their methods have included unfair labour practices such as firing union activists, closing down stores, and using other aggressive anti-union tactics. In addition, like myriad companies worldwide, these large multinational companies have constantly restructured their labour processes in their unending search for the accumulation of capital, for example, by increasing the numbers of workers engaged in non-standard work.

As a consequence, the model of legal unionism that was constructed in the postwar period is losing its relevance for large numbers of workers in Canada, especially for women, various ethnicities, and youth who work in contingent forms of work. It is clear that a number of Canadian unions are attempting to construct new approaches and rethink the relationship between the world of work and the communities in which services are situated. These attempts, however, are fragmented and uncoordinated with the traditional organizing model adopted by many other unions, which in some cases does not fit with the new realities of work. The examples of new forms of organizing described in this chapter are encouraging, not only in terms of organizing the unorganized, but also in terms of rethinking the traditional labour relations system and the lack of fit with many of the contingent forms of work that have developed during the period of neo-liberal restructuring. They are small beginnings, but they may indicate that the old models of union organizing are beginning to lose their grip on the Canadian labour movement.

NOTES

Author's Note: My thanks to Vivian Shalla and Wallace Clement for helpful comments on an earlier draft of this chapter. I gratefully acknowledge the financial support provided by the Social Sciences and Humanities Research

Council of Canada for the research for this chapter. This support was provided through a grant awarded to the Centre for Research on Work and Society for the project "Restructuring Work and Labour in the New Economy."

1 It should be noted that this comparison is very approximate, as the Statistics Canada, *Labour Force Survey* union data have been available only since 1997. For a useful explanation of the data problems, see Andrew Jackson's recent article in *Studies in Political Economy* (2004, 145).

2 The chartered banks' aggressive anti-unionism was well reported and documented in the unfair labour practice decisions of the Canada Labour Relations Board. See Warskett 1988.

3 This research was funded by an Initiative on the New Economy (INE) Social Sciences and Humanities Research Council (SSHRC) grant through the Centre for Research for Work and Society, initiated by Geoff Bickerton and Rosemary Warskett. As a result, the Courier Research Group included members of the WORC and CUPW in Winnipeg.

4 *Dynamex Canada* v. *Mamona* [2003] S.C.R. 383.

REFERENCES

Arat-Koc, Sedef. 1989. In the privacy of our own home: Foreign domestic workers as a solution to the crisis in the domestic sphere in Canada. *Studies in Political Economy* 28:33–58

Armstrong, Pat. 1996. The feminization of the labour force: Harmonizing down in a global economy. In *Rethinking restructuring: Gender and change in Canada,* edited by Isabella Baker, 29–54. Toronto: University of Toronto Press

Bickerton, Geoff, and Catherine Stearns. 2002. The struggle continues in Winnipeg: The Workers Organizing and Resource Centre. *Just Labour* 1:50–7

Bourque, Deborah, and Geoff Bickerton. 2004. Stepping out of the legal framework: Organizing rural route couriers. Presentation at the Political Economy section of the annual meetings of the Canadian Political Science Association (CPSA), Winnipeg

Briskin, Linda, and Patricia McDermott. 1993. *Women challenging unions: Feminism, democracy and militancy.* Toronto: University of Toronto Press

Bronfenbrenner, Kate, and Tom Juravich. 1998. It takes more than house calls: Organizing to win with a comprehensive strategy. In *Organizing to win: New research on union strategies,* edited by K. Bronfenbrenner et al. Ithaca, N.Y.: Cornell University Press

Canada Labour Relations Board. 2003. Chartered Bank Worker Certifications and Decertifications, 1976–2003, Data issued on the request of David Sauve, Carleton University research assistant

Clement, Wallace, and Leah F. Vosko, eds. 2003. *Changing Canada: Political economy as transformation.* Montreal and Kingston: McGill-Queen's University Press

Courier Research Group. 2005. Straddling the world of traditional and precarious employment: A case study of the courier industry in Winnipeg. Canadian Centre for Policy Alternatives, Manitoba, 23 September

Cranford, Cynthia J., and Deena Ladd. 2003. Community unionism: Organising for fair employment in Canada. *Just Labour* 3 (Fall): 46–59

England, Geoffrey. 2000. *Individual employment law.* Toronto: Irwin Law

Fletcher, Bill, and Richard W. Hurd. 2000. Is organizing enough? Race, gender and union culture. *New Labor Forum* 6:59–69

Fudge, Judy, and Eric Tucker. 2000. A pluralism or fragmentation? The twentieth century employment regime in Canada. *Labour/Le Travail* 46 (Fall): 251–306

– 2001. *Labour before the law: The regulation of workers' collective action in Canada 1900–1948.* Don Mills, Ont.: Oxford University Press

Fudge, Judy, and Leah F. Vosko. 2003. Gender paradoxes and the rise of contingent work. In Clement and Vosko 2003, 183–209

Gindin, Sam, and Jim Stanford. 2003. Canadian labour and the political economy of transformation. In Clement and Vosko 2003, 422–42

HRDC (Human Resources and Development Canada). 1995. *A twentieth century employment system for Canada: Guide to the employment insurance legislation.* Ottawa: Ministry of Supply and Services Canada

Jackson, Andrew. 2004. Forum reorganizing unions: Solidarity forever? Trends in Canadian union density. *Studies in Political Economy* 74 (Fall/Winter): 125–46

Jackson, Andrew, and Sylvain Schetagne. 2003. Solidarity forever? An analysis of changes in union density. Canadian Labour Congress, Research Paper no. 25, Ottawa, July

Katz-Rosene, Ryan. 2003. Union organizing: A look at recent organizing activity through analysis of certification across Canadian jurisdictions. Canadian Labour Congress, Research Paper no. 26, Ottawa, June

Kumar, Pradeep. 2004. Forum reorganizing unions: Diffusing innovations and articulating labour's vision. *Studies in Political Economy* 74 (Fall/Winter): 147–55

Mahon, Rianne. 2002. Introduction: Gender and welfare state restructuring: Through the lens of child care. In Mahon and Michel 2002, 1–27

Mahon, Rianne, and Sonya Michel, eds. 2002. *Child care policy at the crossroads: Gender and welfare state restructuring.* New York: Routledge

Murnighan, Bill. 2003. Organizing at a crossroads: A good news, bad news story. *Our Times,* July

Murray, Gregor. 2004. Union myths, enigmas, and other tales: Five challenges for union renewal. Forum: Reorganizing unions. *Studies in Political Economy* 74 (Fall/Winter): 157–69

Ocran, Amanda Araba. 1997. Across the home/work divide: Homework in garment manufacture and the failure of employment regulation. In *Challenging The Public/Private Divide: Feminism, Law, and Public Policy,* edited by Susan B. Boyd, 144–67. Toronto: University of Toronto Press

Panitch, Leo, and Donald Swartz. 2003. *From consent to coercion: The assault on trade union freedoms.* 3rd ed. Aurora, Ont.: Garamond Press

Rooks, Daisy. 2003. The cowboy mentality: Organizers and occupational commitment in the new labor movement. *Labor Studies Journal* 28 (3): 33–62 (Fall)

Rowbotham, Sheila. 1993. *Homeworkers worldwide.* London: Merlin Press

Schenk, Chris. 2004. Union organizing: An Ontario labour perspective. Forum: Reorganizing unions. *Studies in Political Economy* 74 (Fall/Winter): 181–90

Sciacchitano, Katherine. 1998. Finding the community in the union and the union in the community: The first-contract campaign at Steeltech. In *Organizing to win: New research on union strategies,* edited by K. Bronfenbrenner, 150–63. Ithaca, N.Y.: Cornell University Press

– 2000. Unions, organizing, and democracy: Living in one's time, building for the future. *Dissent,* Spring, 75–81

Stasiulis, Davia, and Abigail B. Bakan. 2002. Negotiating the citizenship divide: Foreign domestic worker policy and legal jurisprudence. In *Women's Legal Strategies in Canada,* edited by Radha Jhappan, 237–94. Toronto: University of Toronto Press

Tufts, Steven. 1998. Community unionism in Canada and labor's (re)organization of space. *Antipode* 30 (3): 227–50

Vosko, Leah. 2002. The pasts (and futures) of feminist political economy in Canada: Reviving the debate. *Studies in Political Economy* 68 (Summer): 55–84

Vosko, Leah, Nancy Zukewich, and Cynthia Cranford. 2003. Precarious jobs: A new typology of employment. In Statistics Canada, *Perspectives on Labour and Income.* Catalogue no. 75-001-X20031106642, 16–26 October

Warskett, Rosemary. 1987. Legitimate and illegitimate unions: The case of SORWUC and bank worker unionization. Paper presented to the Canadian Political Science Association (CPSA), Hamilton, June

– 1988. Bank worker unionization and the law. *Studies in Political Economy* 25:41–73

– 1996. The politics of difference and inclusiveness within the Canadian labour movement. *Economic and Industrial Democracy* 17 (4): 411–49

- 2002. Feminism's challenge to unions in the North: Possibilities and contradictions. In *Socialist Register 2001: Working Classes, Global Realities*, edited by Leo Panitch and Colin Leys, 329–42. Halifax: Fernwood Publishing

White, Julie. 1980. *Women in unions*. Ottawa: Canadian Advisory Council on the Status of Women

- 1993. *Sisters in solidarity: Women in unions in Canada*. Toronto: Thompson Educational Press

Yates, Charlotte. 1998. A unity and diversity: Challenges to an expanding Canadian Autoworkers' Union. *Canadian Review of Sociology and Anthropology* 35:93–118

- 2000. Staying the decline in union membership: Union organizing in Ontario, 1985–1999. *Relations Industrielles/Industrial Relations* 55 (4): 640–75

- 2002. Expanding labour's horizons: Union organizing and strategic change in Canada. *Just Labour* 1:31–40

- 2004. Rebuilding the labour movement by organizing the unorganized: Strategic considerations. Forum: Reorganizing unions. *Studies in Political Economy* 74 (Fall/Winter): 171–9

Index

gendered divisions and relations, 6; and techno-logical change, 7; and temporal order, 251
gendered labour market, 193–4, 204; insecurities, 14–15, 53, 55, 62, 67; and racialization, 17–18, 192, 197–8
gendered-racialization of hiring, 216
gendered temporalities, and class struggle over working time, 252
gender equity, 77, 83
gender gap: and contracting-out of health-care work, 337; employment, 47; in housework, 307
gendering and racialization, processes of, 209, 217
general educational devel-opment (GED) scores, 151
General Motors, and outsourcing, 173
General Social Survey (GSS): commuting to work, 305–6; computer skills, 141; time-use dia-ries, 340–1; working hours, 302
German Act on Part-Time Work and Fixed-Term Contracts, 89n47
Germany: employment gender gap, 46–7; pov-erty rates of single par-ents, 46; sectoral bargaining, 40; union density and coverage, 40–1
Gerson, Kathleen, 76
Ghent system, and Swed-ish unions, 40
Gibson-Graham, J.K., 372n14
Giles, Wenona, 204
Ginzberg, Effie, 210, 215

Glazer, Nona Y., 293
Glenday, Daniel, 13, 37
global capitalism, and the search for profit, 142
global commodification, of household labour, 306–13, 317
global economic restruc-turing, and temporal flexibility strategies, 18
global grain market, and Saskatchewan farmers, 276
globalization, 8, 10; of clothing and household furnishing production, 309; of food produc-tion, 309–10
globalized labour force, and cheap domestic labour, 307
globalized labour market, racialized and gendered, 312
Good Jobs, Bad Jobs (Eco-nomic Council of Can-ada), 39
Good Jobs, Bad Jobs, No Jobs (Duffy/Glenday/Pupo), 13, 37
greenfield sites, and dis-persion in manufactur-ing, 172
Guest, D., 352

Hall, P.A., 372n9
Hall, Ray, 318n1
Hamilton, Roberta, 195
Haryett, Kathy, 37
health and safety training, and temporary agency workers, 124
health and social services, work in, 326, 333, 334, 337
Health Canada: and deter-minants of health, 332; Health Policy Research Bulletin, 330, 331
health care: and allo-pathic medicine, 327;

and medical model, 21, 326–31; and re-engi-neering of work, 37; reforms in, 22, 335; ser-vice and clerical work in, 337–9; and social determinants of health model, 331–4
health-care labour force: counting the, 21–2, 326; gendered nature of, 337–8; occupational categories, 328–31; and union coverage, 337–8. See also ancillary work-ers; unpaid work
health-care providers, 21–2; ancillary, 334–40; and medical model, 327–31, 332, 344; and social determinants of health model, 21, 331–4; unpaid, 340–4; unregulated, 21, 326, 329, 330. See also ancil-lary workers; unpaid work
health status: and employ-ment strain, 101, 120–4; and precarious employment, 15, 101, 117–20; women com-pared to men, 118–20
hegemonic heterosexual masculinity, and men's traditional jobs, 194
Henry, Frances, 210, 215
heterosexual gender roles, and nation-building, 194
heterosexual nuclear fam-ily: consolidation of, 263; and sexual division of labour, 263–4
hidden knowledge, among workers, 144
Hiebert, Daniel, 202–3
hierarchical knowledge/ power structures, and learning, 135
high-tech sector, in Ottawa, 350–1, 362–3

tion of, 299–302; in manufacturing, 168, 176–8; nurses, 327–9; and part-time ongoing casual employment, 53, 58, 60–1; and part-time work, 37, 231–2; and precarious work, 339–40; and reduction in social services, 293; rural route drivers, 393; and service and clerical work, 339–40; and service sector jobs, 301; and sustainability of farms, 273, 275; and temporary employment, 105; and time-use diaries, 340–1; and unionization, 386–7; and union membership, 71–2; and unpaid work, 7, 19–21, 78, 176–7, 263–73, 283, 293, 301–2, 304–5, 314, 327, 340–4; and volunteer work, 342; wages of full-time permanent employees, 72–5. *See also* Aboriginal women; gender; immigrant women; visible minority women

women of colour, and labour market niches, 202. *See also* racialization; visible minorities; visible minority women; workers of colour

women's autonomy, and decommodification, 294

women's movement: demands for childcare programs, 253; and explanations of work transformation, 6; and studies on women's work, 176–7; and women's domestic work, 265, 267–9

women's status, and neoliberalism, 267

women's subordination: and feminism, 6; and neo-classical economics, 270

work arrangements, diversification and de-standardization of, 231

work change, 361; capacity to negotiate, 351; negotiation of, 365–9

Work Choices Act, 85n15, 85n17

work degradation thesis, 138–9

Worker Adjustment and Retraining Notification Act, 88n39

Workers' Action Centre (WAC) in Toronto, and unionism, 394

workers' compensation: early twentieth century, 99; legislation and protections, 124

workers' consent, to the conditions of production, 139

workers' knowledge: appropriation of, 142; exploitation of, 132; underutilization of, 133

workers of colour: discrimination against, 112; educational advantage of, 205–6; and workplace spatial segregation, 211; worsening position of, 205–7. *See also* immigrants of colour; racialization; visible minorities

Workers' Organizing and Resource Centre (WORC) in Winnipeg, and unionism, 394

workers with disabilities, discrimination against, 112

work-family balance, mushrooming of literature on, 233

work-family interface: gendered imbalance of, 252; and new temporal order, 234

work-family strategies, 307–8

working class: and control over work, 143, 145; and learning and education, 146; and technical skill, 144; and underemployment, 133

working-class families, in steel industry in Hamilton, 272–3

working-class positions, and underemployment, 16, 153–4

working poor, 351, 371; chronic problem of, 22, 360; and social citizenship claims, 361–5

working time(s), 18, 45, 76; in airline industry, 228, 250; atypical, 229; class struggle over, 230, 251–2; concessions, 248, 250; control over, 227, 230; distribution of, 252; diversification of, 231, 233; and forces of production, 230–1; of front-line service workers, 228; gendered patterns of, 19, 253; heterogeneity in, 229; hyperflexibility of, 233; lengthening of, 19, 228, 243; movement to reduce, 253; nonstandard, 229, 230; and pay-effort bargain, 227; polarization in, 230, 232; politics of, 18–19, 227; reduction and standardization of, 230; reduction for all, 81–2; and unpaid work, 294. *See also* temporalities